A Book of Prayers

A Prayer for Every Chapter of the Bible

By Rev. Stephen C. Magee

Pastor, Exeter Presbyterian Church
73 Winter Street
Exeter, NH 03833

www.exeterpca.org

Westminster Larger Catechism #186:
**What rule has God given for our direction
in the duty of prayer?**

Answer:
**The whole Word of God is of use to direct
us in the duty of prayer...**

A BOOK OF PRAYERS – Second Edition
Copyright © 2014 by Rev. Stephen C. Magee
Edited by Candyce D. Magee

Table of Contents

Genesis

Genesis 1

Creator God, You have made all things of nothing. You were in the beginning, and Your Spirit hovered over the face of the deep. In the person of Your Son, You have spoken the world into being. He is the Light of the World, and through Him Light was made. Your Spirit is a fountain of living water for our souls, and by Your Spirit You created the waters and defined their boundaries. You have given us the true Bread from heaven, our great Redeemer, and through Him You made all the vegetation that has covered the dry land. Father, You ordained that the sun, moon, and stars would have dominion over light and darkness. You have filled the waters above with the birds of the air and the waters below with the fish of the sea. You have given us all kinds of creatures, covering the dry land with such a variety of living things. O Marvelous Lord, You then created man, male and female, in Your image. You have granted to us all that we need for life, and have placed us in dominion over all things in the created order. Blessed be Your Name, O God, Father, Son, and Holy Spirit, for You alone created the heavens and the earth.

Genesis 2

O Lord of the Sabbath, You rested on the day of Your choosing. Grant that we might enter into Your holy rest through Jesus Christ. He is the second Adam, through whom we have new life. Our father, the first Adam, was granted life in a beautiful garden. You warned him about the tree of the knowledge of good and evil, that he should not eat of it, lest he die. You granted to him a helpmate from his own rib in the beautiful form of the very good gift of a woman. She was a companion suitable for him, for she was like him but not like him; opposite him but not opposite him. This great gift of women you have given us even now, together with all family blessings, for You know our every need and give wonderful gifts to Your children.

Genesis 3

Father of All Mercies, we mourn the beginning of sin through the action of one man. A deceitful enemy lied to the woman with half-truths and seduction. The woman ate and gave to her husband. Then the man ate, and sin entered the world. With sin came shame, guilt, fear, and misery. Yet it was Your holy will to bring not only curse, but also great blessing to Your children. On that day You announced Your plan of grace. The woman would have children, and One of her descendants would come to save us from the vile enemy who stands against us and our children even to this day. You have given us food and work, though we mourn the thorns and the sweat of our brow. You have clothed us with better clothing than we could make for ourselves in a holiness that is not our own. This best of all garments comes at the cost of one Man's blood. By Your plan of grace You have made a way for us to enjoy the tree of Life through the promised Seed of the Woman, the righteous Son of Man, our Lord Jesus Christ.

Genesis 4

Lord of the Generations, there is a blood that speaks a better Word for us than the blood of Abel. The blood of Abel speaks of murder, even the murder of a brother. We mourn our ugly sin that so destroys the tranquility of family life. O God, forgive us. What have we done? The ground cries out to You, O God! Our sin and punishment are much more than we can bear. Yet even in this despicable state, You have put a mark upon us, that there would be a measure of Your protection, even for evil men, that the generations might yet move forward, and Your holy plan be fulfilled in all of its great detail. Forgive us for the progress of sin, for man has not been satisfied with one woman, or with any reasonable justice among men. We call upon Your Name, O Lord, and we thank You for a new line of spiritual life for us in the coming of Your Son Jesus.

Genesis 5

God of Justice and Power, You have created us for long life, but sin has brought death, and death has yielded mourning and despair. This was our own doing, for our father Adam was an accurate representative of us, and we have added sin upon sin. Even to this day, though You provide secret comfort to Your weeping children, we cannot seem to make our peace with death. We cannot agree with the progress of this enemy from generation to generation. We desire to be in the society of holy men of old, like Enoch, who walked with You. The day came when He was not, and those who loved him mourned. We want to walk with Enoch in a better day, for we believe that Enoch yet lives and walks with You. Thank You for those who find grace in Your sight, like holy Noah, who became the beginning of a new world together with his family. We believe that we will be with him one day, and with all who yet live in Christ above.

Genesis 6

O Father, the details of our sin are so ugly that we cannot bear to hear of them. There is lust and murderous hatred everywhere, and we have grieved You with our transgressions. The thoughts of the hearts of human beings are only evil continually. Yet You make a way for the flock of Your choosing to walk with You. Like Noah, Your sheep hear Your voice, and they follow Your Word. Though Your instruction seems like folly to the world, You will surely vindicate the truth of Your commandments on the Day when judgment comes.

Genesis 7

Lord God, You make an ark of safety for us in Your church, the redeemed body of Your Son. May we enter into that ark today through faith, as those who determine to be in Him, for You have called us effectually by Your powerful Spirit and have spoken to us clearly through Your matchless Word. A Day of Judgment is coming. We cannot stand on that Day without the safety of an ark. Thus we go in. Shut us securely within the church of Your Son. Though life in that place might not always seem desirable during these days of waiting and working, keep us in the place of hope while the storm prevails outside. You will preserve Your new creation in Jesus Christ, Your Son.

Genesis 8

God of Our Salvation, You have remembered us over many years. You know our weakness. At just the right time, You bring an end to the flood of trouble. You give us solid land again for our feet upon the Rock of Christ our Redeemer.

You grant to Your people a new beginning, as You did in the days of Noah. Together with the whole family of faith, we are made alive in the land of the living by Your sure and powerful promise.

Genesis 9

Father of Blessings, we rejoice in the new beginning that You grant to Your children. We have a wonderful provision for life in all that You have created. You give us the gift of justice within human society. You give us a future, for surely we could not live if You determined to bring the floods of Your judgment upon us every day. We thank You for Your covenant promise for all creatures, granting to us a world with a measure of daily safety for fruitful life here below. Despite the great beauty of these gifts, we will not think of this world as our place of greatest hope. Sin comes quickly, and even Noah faced not only sin but death. We have a better and more lasting hope in Immanuel's land.

Genesis 10

Father of the Nations, You have a plan not only for Your covenant people of old. You have a plan for the world. Names of nations long forgotten among men are yet well-known to You. From fathers remembered no more come peoples of ancient centuries and cities that are still among us to this day. All these places, times, and human beings were a part of Your perfect plan that we live in now. Our hope is not in all the variety of people groups on this earth, however numerous or powerful. Our hope is in You, and in the descendant of Shem who has brought us life through His death on the cross.

Genesis 11

Sovereign Lord, we have sinned against You. If we were left without Your grace, we would seek only to make a name for ourselves and to resist Your glory. You have granted to us great abilities which could be used to build a city dedicated to our own small desires. Father, we are grateful that Your chief goal in all that You do is the glory of Your own Name. We have been helped by Your Spirit to see this as the most worthy goal. In pursuit of Your good plan, you brought about the generations leading to our father Abraham. You brought him and Sarah out of barrenness and idolatry, and made them to be believers in the promises that we also hold dear; promises which are all Yes and Amen in Jesus Christ our Lord.

Genesis 12

Holy Father, speak to us of the future. Speak to us of covenant blessings that are ours in Jesus Christ. Make us to be a blessing to the nations of the world. We count Your Word as precious. When You promise to give something to us and to our offspring, You will surely do what you have said. You watched over the lives of Abraham and Sarah as people of the promise. Through most unusual providences You protected them from great danger, and provided for their every need. You made them prosper in the land of their journeys. Your plan for them was great. Your plan for us is also completely trustworthy, for we are heirs of these same great promises through faith in Jesus Christ.

Genesis 13

God and Father of Abraham, Isaac, and Jacob, we call upon Your name. You hear us through our mediator Jesus Christ. We live in a world of strife, even within our families and in Your holy church. We should be people of peace, but others seem to insist on war. There is so much that is good and beautiful all around us, but we have not been satisfied with Your ample provision for us. What You give to us is Yours to give. We can have no claim against You, as if You owed us anything. You have been so generous in both the gifts of this world, and in the spiritual blessings of Your heavenly Kingdom. We thank You, O Lord.

Genesis 14

Father God, there is danger all around us. How will we survive? The kings of the earth with all their power and wrath desire to turn against Your people and Your Law. We are nothing to them except objects of scorn and derision. They would be happy to take what little we have and to bring it home as their own. They would seize the righteous if they could. The day will come when Your children will be separated forever from the wicked. Your enemies will no longer be able to harass the people of Your covenant promise. Lord, send forth Your Deliverer, the Man of Faith, who will rescue us today. Your Son is both King of Peace and King of Righteousness. We give You all praise through Him. Nothing we have comes from the generosity of the world. All that we have is a gift from You, O Lord Most High.

Genesis 15

O Author and Finisher of Our Faith, You were true to Abraham so long ago, for He believed You, and it was credited to Him as righteousness. His offspring is beyond our ability to number. You brought Him out of the land of pagan religion, and gave Him a place for His descendants. You have given to him and to us a great covenant sign. You assured us that Your Son would give His life, so that Your covenant with Abraham would be kept. You have promised to give us a great land, far beyond the land of Canaan. We believe You, O Lord, for Your promise is sure.

Genesis 16

Merciful Lord, why do we take matters into our own hands, as if Your great promises wait for us to fulfill them? The way of Hagar is not the solution to our barren lives. You must bless, Lord, for our own plans are troublesome. They lead only to death. You are so faithful. You know our weakness. You are aware of our scheming. We have been like wild animals, trying to impress others with a display of dominance. You are so different from us, providing us with the free gift of the water of life, that we might live forever.

Genesis 17

Lord of glory, You are God Almighty. We should always walk before You and be blameless. You made Abraham a father of a multitude of nations, You gave Him the covenant of circumcision. One day Your Son would be our circumcision through His death on the cross. He would be cut off from the covenant community for our sake. His obedience was perfect. There was no law by which He could be justly removed from the people of Your choosing. Nonetheless, He was cut off for our sake. Our sin was upon Him, and we have been greatly blessed beyond the expectations of men. When we might seem to have given up on Your Word, You continue to bring about all of Your holy will. You are God. We are the community of the faithful in Jesus Christ our Lord. We will walk before You. We will take upon our hearts and upon the lives of our children the sign of the covenant, for You will accomplish Your every Word.

Genesis 18

O Father, there is a day of destruction coming upon the world. We have received a taste of this day in the signs of Your judgment upon Sodom and Gomorrah. How will we stand? We have laughed at Your promises in unbelief, yet You have not abandoned us. You continue to look at us as the faithful. We don't even tell the truth about our unbelief. In our fear, we insist that we have not laughed at Your promises. Do not hide Your face from us. Show us what we need to know that we might be true to You. We are so weak, O Lord. Give us help from on high. You will not sweep away the righteous with the wicked. You will be just. The Day of Judgment has come upon Christ on the day of His suffering and death. This was done for our sake. You have heard His cries for us, and we have hope. Do not be angry with us O Lord, for Your Son has won for us a great salvation.

Genesis 19

Lord God, You know how to rescue the righteous from the hands of the wicked. Righteous Lot was surrounded by a wicked rabble. You sent Your angels to deliver him even though the men of the town had strength and zeal in evil. Such power is nothing for You to overthrow. You have the ministry of powerful heavenly beings, who are servants to the heirs of salvation. So many around us do not see imminent danger. So many look back at the world longingly, as if this current world would be the greatest prize for those who have been given the blessings of heaven. You have given us the hope of eternal life. Yet sin remains a problem within our families. We are impatient and unbelieving, and so we have brought trouble upon ourselves by our own depravity. Restrain our evil and that of our children. We must turn away from all that is wicked and unnatural. We must resist the devil, that He will flee from us. Keep us far from the foolishness that comes from drunkenness. Make us patient for both Your goals and Your ways, and fill us with Your Spirit, that we may be awake and full of life as we serve You.

Genesis 20

God of All Our Journeys, watch over us in the day of darkness, for we travel in the land of dead men who do not know you. Make us to be men of integrity. Help us to pray for the peace of those around us with great power and happy results. As we live among those who seem to have no fear of You, preserve our lives and keep us in the faith, lest we become like those who despise You. Your Word is always before us. May we abide in it. Keep us free in Christ through Your kind help day by day.

Genesis 21

Father, we believe that You will do what You have promised. Though we wait through many barren years, you will bring forth the day of Isaac. We laugh with joy as we consider the fulfillment of Your beautiful Word. In the day of resurrection, there will be a clear division between the righteous and the wicked. We

9

will see the revealing of the sons of God and will dwell in the land of the living. Until that day, Your care extends to all Your creatures. You have given food and water to the hungry. You have given skills and work to all kinds of people, but You are with Your beloved covenant people for our eternal salvation. There is much strife and deceit all around us. The world would leave us nothing if it were in their power, but You have provided for us a measure of peace and have satisfied our longings, that we might live. You are the everlasting God.

Genesis 22

Lord God, You tested Abraham. You gave him a child. That child was Yours, just as Abraham was Yours. You asked Him to sacrifice his only son, this child of the promise, Isaac. He reasoned that You would provide a substitute for his son, and that You could raise the dead. You held him back from slaughtering the boy, yet he proved that he feared You and loved You above all. May we also fear You, and entrust our children to You. For Your Son is the great provision for our salvation. He has taken our place and faced Your wrath, and He has surely risen from the dead. In Him the earth shall be blessed. In Him we have a perfect hope.

Genesis 23

Lord God Almighty, we live and die according to Your good plan. Even in the death of our loved ones we have a seed of victory and a proclamation of our faith. As we bury our dead, we believe that a day of resurrection is surely coming. When Abraham bought a burial place in the land of Canaan, he took possession of his first small piece of ground in the land of promise. Lord, we believe in the resurrection, and we proclaim that we are even now citizens of heaven through Jesus Christ our Lord.

Genesis 24

God of Hope, You are the giver of every good gift. You gave to Isaac his wife Rebekah. You have given to so many men of faith great women who have loved and served You. This gift of a wife is surely from You. Grant to Your church success today in family relationships. Many are lonely. So many others face challenges in marriages that should be full of love and service. Some are close to divorce. Others are recovering from some loss or disappointment that cannot be remedied by men. God, grant us the water of life in the day of disappointment, and lead us to the fulfillment of all good desires. Raise up a generation that will believe and be faithful. You have not forsaken Your steadfast love to Christ and His church. May we not be easily deceived by those who love the world more than You. Laban is always standing nearby at the door. Make us wise in our words and dealings. Some only long for the possessions of this world. We want You above anything else, O God. Send angels alongside us to prosper our ways, that we might stay in the path of godliness with contentment, which is great gain. If along the way of life You should choose to bless us as the world counts prosperity, help us to thank You, and to share what we have been given with those who are in need. We bless You Lord. Throughout our lives You have led us in a good way. All that we have has come from You. We bow before You. Send us forward on the pathway that leads to our Master, the Lord Jesus Christ. Make our marriages and families fruitful in every way, and may we have appropriate joy in our lives with one another. Through our relationship with Your Son, may Your church know the gift of the best love, and may we be granted comfort in this world of death and trial.

Genesis 25

God of Glory, You made a promise to Abraham that he would have many descendants, and You fulfilled this promise in part even before he died. When his time came to be buried, he was placed in the ground in the Land of Promise. Grant that each of Your servants would be buried in faith when the days of our lives are over and we breathe our last. We look for life beyond the grave. Bring Your plans to fulfillment as future generations are born. Distinguish between a Jacob and an Esau according to Your perfect decree. Help us to rightly estimate the great value of our relation to Christ, and the rights that we have as sons of God. May we never be so foolish as to despise this birthright, for we are people of a glorious resurrection.

Genesis 26

Lord God, You are our provision in the day of famine. Though we face scarcity, Your promises will never fail. May we keep Your commandments in all times and places. Protect Your people as we travel in this world full of danger and difficulty. Give us what You have planned for us in Your wonderful decree, and protect us from the murderous envy of cruel men. Give us the water of life as we travel through desert lands. Help us to be at peace with others, for You will surely make room for us, and we will be fruitful in the land where we live. Multiply our offspring, granting us children in our homes, and new children for Christ in His holy temple. May we live in peace here below. May many find the water of life and be counted as those who have been born in the house of the Lord.

Genesis 27

O Lord, Your servants grow old, and we do not know the day of our death. May we bless Your church before we die. Help us to share our table with the hungry and the lonely. Help us to speak words of hope in a world that is full of lies and deceit. May we believe Your Word, though all men be full of lying words, spoken by lying lips, and springing forth from deceitful hearts. Convince us that we do not inherit Your promises through trickery. Grant to us the courage to speak the message of Christ forthrightly. We are Your children, and You will surely bless us. You will bring glory to Your Name and preserve us, even when we forget Your truth, and walk far below the privileges that we have as members of Your family. May we take hold of Your promises now by faith. A day will come when men will not be able to claim Your covenant blessings, even if they seek them with many tears. The world will rail against You and against Your chosen sons, but You will protect us from the murderous hatred of those who despise You. May we forever enjoy the fullness of blessings that are at Your right hand. Move us through this life. Protect our bodies and souls from the wicked plots of Your adversaries. Thank You for the lives of blessing that You have granted to us now and forever.

Genesis 28

O God Who Sanctifies Us, You know the road that we must travel in order for Your holy plans to be fulfilled. We are not sanctified by that pathway so much as we are sanctified by You, as You lead along the way. Throughout our days grant us a true sight of the One who is the sure and only connection between heaven and earth. He is Your Son, and angels ascend and descend upon Him alone. Keep us close to Him, and be with us, providing for us everything that we need to love You. You are God, and where You are, that place is Your house, and we are Your servants.

Genesis 29

Father God, be our Shepherd through a world that is most perplexing. You are very capable of bringing us blessing in a place where people would lie and steal continually. Who has been more deceived than our Father Jacob, who served for one woman, and woke up with another? Yet You raised up the tribes of Israel not only from beautiful Rachel, but also from her older sister Leah. Even the servants of these two women were used for the building up of Your people. Grant us perseverance in our callings, trusting that You know how to overrule the oppressive plans of wicked men. You gave wonderful children to a woman through a husband who did not love her. Even Judah, the one from whom came our great Messiah Jesus, was born of Leah. In the day of cruel rejection and in every time of trouble and disappointment, we will yet praise You, O Lord.

Genesis 30

Lord of Hope, who can understand the wonder of Your holy providence? Through this one family of Jacob, and through four mothers, have come all the tribes of Israel. Your promises to Abraham and Sarah have found their fulfillment in a household where there was much strife and trouble. We envy others, and we play foolish tricks to get our way, and yet You still fulfill Your amazing promises. Surely all glory belongs to You. We look for the love and approval of men and are so frequently disappointed. The day will come when our Joseph will be born. Even in the day of our greatest celebrations on earth, our troubles will not be over. We still live in a world of deceit and sin. Through trials we are changed. You bless us despite all of our scheming. The gifts that You have given are from Your hands and will fulfill Your holy purposes.

Genesis 31

Great Protector of Your Children, You send us home at just the right time. The days of our pilgrimage must come to an end. Eventually, Jacob must be freed from the oppression of Laban. On that day, You will lead us home. We long for Your coming, O Lord. Though our mothers and fathers might sell us for nothing, You will not abandon us. You will move us along through dangerous places, and will overrule all our sin and folly. You can restrain the hand of an enemy. Though there is so much unrighteousness, both inside and outside the household of faith, our perseverance toward the day of our homecoming is sure. Even a Rachel in our midst may be secretly hiding idols as if they were something of value. Despite our deceit, we have been kept from disaster. We see grace everywhere in the stories of our lives. You have looked upon us in our affliction and rebuked our enemies. You carry us forward toward a day of perfect holiness. We will be made perfect by Your grace. By the Sacrifice appointed, You have secured for us a perfect peace.

Genesis 32

12

Lord of Hosts, You meet us along the way of life. You lead us in love. There is much about the future that we do not understand. Is the crowd of men coming toward us fixed upon our destruction? Like Jacob, we see an Esau and his company moving toward us in the distance, and we call upon Your Name. You have provided for us until this day. Please do not abandon us. Give us both faith and wisdom. We are Your servants, O Lord. Use us for Your glory. When evening comes, we wonder what awaits us in the morning, but You know all these things. You will protect us, even wrestling with us until the breaking of day. We now boldly beseech Your blessing in accord with Your greatness and love. Allow us to prevail in prayer. In Christ, we have seen You face to face. Though we wrestle with You in times of fear, we soon find out again that You love us and are working everything for our good.

Genesis 33

God of Our Fathers, we receive Your love. We humble ourselves before You and commit ourselves to the service of others for Your sake, for You have graciously given us every good gift. We thank You for Your protection and provision. Our fears melt before us on the day of Your mercy. Years of needless worry can be gone in a single moment of blessing. You have given us a new beginning as we meet with you in worship. We have found favor in Your sight through Christ our Lord. We gladly give our lives to others in need. Nonetheless, on the day of unusual blessing, help us to be grateful and wise, knowing that we yet live in a world of danger and difficulty.

Genesis 34

Father God, what can we do when our loved ones face assault and attack? What can we do when our daughters are seduced and enticed into the way of evil? The weight of wickedness all around us and even within us is too much for us to bear. There is great risk that we will lose all restraint in the grief and outrage of the moment. Our hearts quickly turn to war. We seek vengeance, and quickly try to take control in order to destroy our enemies. Your Son, the Lord Jesus Christ, is our righteousness. Will we abuse His Name and Your holy ordinances? Would we use even the great signs and seals of the covenant as part of our own plan for unbridled revenge? Lord, hold us back. Lord, have mercy on us.

Genesis 35

Lord God Almighty, You have directed our fathers in the faith, and have called us away from foreign gods. We turn to You, Lord God, for we would give up all our secret idols, that we might have power from on high that could only come from You. You are a God with supreme power over all things. Make us fruitful that we might multiply according to Your commandment. Pour out Your Spirit upon us again, and give us life. Help us in our time of distress, and even death, for we face trouble as we journey toward the place of Your promise. In these few days that You give to us here below, make us faithful to the very end, for You are a God of grace.

Genesis 36

God of All the Earth, You know all things. You have the generations of Jacob in Your mind, and are also perfectly aware of the generations of Esau. One is the chosen line, but the others are not forgotten by You. Year after year You granted to them chiefs and kings with authority to lead. You gave them a land in which they settled and prospered. Where are they today, O Lord? People and nations come and go according to Your secret will. We observe what You allow us to see and to know, but there is much that is forgotten among men, and is only known to You. We come and go on this earth, but You are from everlasting to everlasting. You have a plan for leaders and peoples. You know both Jacob and Esau, but Jacob You have loved.

Genesis 37

Father God, we so quickly resent Your Word that would place a Joseph above the rest of His brothers. That same Spirit that was in Cain has yet worked envy within our hearts. Our jealousy would lead us to murder. We repent, for we have not been content with Your providence for us. Lead us to see the great superiority of our brother Jesus Christ. Let us hear the Word about His excellence and be quick to worship and adore Him, for He is the superior brother. When Your Son came He faced profound disrespect and the hatred of men. Many would have been glad to sell Him into slavery or even to kill Him. In all this, Your Son willingly faced great humiliation. Yet we have been false before You, as if we were not guilty for the horror of the cross. Forgive us for our sins, since it was on account of these that Your Son shed His blood. As Jacob wept for His Son Joseph, surely You mourned the loss of Your Son Jesus. We mourn our sin, though we celebrate the glory of redemption through this same cross of Christ.

Genesis 38

O Holy Father, the twists and turns that we take in our wicked lives! And yet You are accomplishing all Your holy will. Is it through the strange story of Judah and Tamar that David and even Jesus come? You can use the most amazing episodes of unclean behavior as the beginning of some great act of sovereign redemption. Blessed be Your name. Through the hand of wicked Judas, Jesus was betrayed. Yet through the cross that came from that betrayal, now comes the amazing power of redeeming love. So many women and children have been caught in situations of strange immorality and abuse, and yet You have your purpose appointed for every child born, some even for great signs of Your merciful love.

Genesis 39

Sovereign Lord, You appoint the details of our lives for Your great purposes. Joseph ends up in Potiphar's house, since there he will be trapped by the immoral wife of the Egyptian. By her deceit, this son of Jacob will end up in the right prison. If he had not been sent to the right prison, he would have never been able to save his brothers as second-in-command next to Pharaoh. Help us to trust You through all the details of our lives; the anger of men, the lust of women, the despair of prison, and much more. Help us to remember that when we are completely confused, You surely understand all things. Make us faithful wherever we may be, knowing that You reign and rule in every fact that may seem contrary to Your holy purposes.

Genesis 40

God of Truth, You know all that is past, and the present and future are also known to You. You know every fact of every life including every dream that you ordain to be in the mind of man. You also grant to Your prophets the right interpretation of the dreams according to Your will. Your Word in the Scriptures is secure and true. It is the judge of every controversy, and the foundation for faith and life. Grant to Your servants a correct understanding of Your Word, and give us boldness to proclaim the truth among men.

Genesis 41

Father of Mercy, we are impatient in suffering. Please forgive us. We could so easily believe that You have forgotten us, but this is a lie. You kept Joseph in prison for at least two years after he should have been helped by the cupbearer of Pharaoh. At just the right time, Jacob's son was brought from that prison-house in order to interpret Pharaoh's dream. Your ways are right. Your servants know that You give the interpretation of Your Word to Your prophets. All glory to You, O God. Who but You would have the wisdom and power to bring life and health out of the miseries of Joseph? Who could have known that You were working abundant salvation through the death of Your holy Servant Jesus? Bring us through times of famine and testing in the current age, and lead us into the age to come where we will have blessings beyond anything we have ever experienced or known. Fill us now with Your Holy Spirit, that we might rightly serve you in this day when we are strangers in a strange land. Though we may have the respect of men and great wealth and honor, we know that we are not yet home. We long for the resurrection, O Lord. Help us to be competent and useful now until the trumpet blows, and the dead in Christ are raised. Help us in our day of hardship, that we might be fruitful in the land of our affliction. May we have bread to share with the hungry, and storehouses full of grain when the severity of trouble comes upon Your people. In all our service, we will remember You, O Lord, for You give us our daily bread.

Genesis 42

God of Comfort, You lead the poor and hungry to the place of Your provision. Your care for the world is extensive. Even the animal crying out for food in the wilderness is heard by Your powerful ear. Yet beyond Your care for all Your creatures, You perform amazing deeds of special providence for Your children. You preserve our lives according to Your plan. You grant us bread for food, and the bread of life for the health of our souls. You bring us to an awareness of our ugly sin. In the day of Your mercy, we are made to remember how we treated some young Joseph, selling the weak into the hands of the treacherous. You are willing to bountifully bless us. When we presume that we would have to pay for Your every provision for our lives, we look in our sacks and find our money returned to us. We have One of our relatives who is now the Lord in the land, for all authority in heaven and earth has been given to our righteous Brother Jesus Christ. There is no payment that we could ever give for our salvation. We surrender to You as dead men who have no rights, but we find ourselves granted an amazing resurrection as the free gift of Your excellent love.

Genesis 43

Great God and Provider, we hunger and thirst for You today. Satisfy our eager longings, and grant to us all things necessary for life and godliness. Thank you for our families, for the heritage that we enjoy, and for the future ahead of us. Make us to be gracious and righteous participants in the events of our day. May we live for You above all. You are such a generous Lord. We do not deserve this kindness that You grant to us every day, but we receive it with great thanksgiving. You will restore to us in the resurrection all that may seem lost today. This will be done in accord with Your decree and for the praise of Your glorious grace. How we thank you, even with tears, as we consider the kind love with which you have loved us. Surely we have received a bountiful portion from Your hand, in accord with our unusual and wonderful position as sons of the Most High God.

Genesis 44

Lord God, You have charge over Your house. Through Your Son, You reign as the Builder and Maker of the house. You are right to uncover every wickedness, that we might receive Your holy correction. Even the secret things are well-known to You. Your plan of discipline is most wise, though often quite mysterious to us. We are assured that You are with us through all of Your great acts of providence. We are Your servants. Though You have surely found out all our secret sins, we have been declared free through Your justice upon a Substitute, and through Your bountiful mercy. We look forward to the Day when we will see Your face, for everything is "Yes" and "Amen" for us in the face of the Lord Jesus Christ. Thank You for our Redeemer, in whom we place all our hope.

Genesis 45

Great Lover of our souls, You have sought us and have redeemed us. Your commitment to us is full and heart-warming. We know that though evil men have plans of wickedness against You and Your church, yet Your plans are above all other plans, and You are for us and not against us. The days ahead of us are difficult for us to know, but our times are in Your hands. You will certainly care for us in the day of trouble. We receive Your embrace today as an expression of Your full commitment toward Your people. Not only are Your intentions marvelous, You have all power and authority in order to work Your holy will. You care for us, both in body and soul. You give us food and clothing for our bodies, and the greatest provision for our spirits, feeding us regularly with Your Word and clothing us with the righteousness of Christ. It is enough for us to know that Your Son is alive and that we will see Him face to face.

Genesis 46

Lord God of Israel, Your people went down to Egypt and sojourned there for a time. You went with them, and You brought them back to the Promised Land. We can trust You during our time here on earth, for You will surely take us home to heaven. Your care is not only for us, but also for our families. You know us and our children. Have mercy on us. Please do not cast us away. Our sin seems to be always with us. The story of our rebellion and foolishness is twisted and frightening, but Your grace is greater than all our sin. You know our marriages and our descendants, and You care about those we love. Protect us and provide for our families day by day. Let us see a measure of joy again, even here below, that we might be encouraged throughout the difficulties that we face in this world of sin and death.

Genesis 47

O King of kings, protect us from the evil intentions of powerful and wicked men who from time to time have ruling authority upon the earth. Be pleased to put men of wisdom and decency in the seats of power, that the church might flourish in peace without assault from those who should protect the weak. Even in an evil day, help us to trust You. Our hope is not in the weapons of ruling parties or in the methods that men use to exercise their might upon others. We are hungry, needy people who come to You for daily mercy. Nothing that we have is our own. We have been bought with a price. Look upon Your servants with favor, for we are surely yours. Let us be to You a company of dedicated priests, believing in You, blessing Your name, and speaking forth Your blessing upon others. A tithe is not enough to speak of what You are due from us. We give You our lives, and seek the Day of resurrection, that our service of You would continue in a world of delight forever.

Genesis 48

Father, we live at Your pleasure, and on the day of Your choosing we die. Day by day we summon our strength, which is nothing more than a gift from You. You give and You take away as You see fit. When we sleep in the grave, the remaining generations live on according to Your plan. Please bless them together with us. You have given us the pleasure of seeing our loved ones face to face for many days. You have blessed us and them in ways that are difficult for us to understand and anticipate. How much more is the greatest blessing reserved for us in the land where Abraham, Isaac, and Jacob live forever. Grant us that sense of Your purposes that is necessary for us today, that we might also bless others as we should. You alone know the beginning from the end. Yet You use us as agents of blessing, though we are very weak. Blessed be Your Name forever.

Genesis 49

O God Our Father, we gather at Your holy Word, and hear of what will happen to us in days to come. The Word for us in this life is one of suffering with ample opportunity for faithfulness, but there is a day beyond the challenges of this age. A Great Ruler is coming again, the Lion of the tribe of Judah. Would we dare to challenge this great King, the Lord Jesus Christ? He shed His blood for us, and He is our undisputed Master. In Him now we have the hope of abiding in the most wonderful land. You, O Lord, shall judge the nations. We wait for Your salvation, O Lord. Though some within the church may prove unfaithful, and may be cut off from the people of Your choosing, our hope is in the Great Shepherd who keeps us. Your blessings are beyond our knowledge. Our life is secure in Your holy promises. Though our bodies may rest in the grave, we will live forever, and we will know Your fullest benediction.

Genesis 50

Father, our stories on this earth must one day come to an end. Even the longest life here reaches a final hour. Then we shall be mourned by those who remain. We show our respect and try to follow the directives of those we love, now departed. Even when we are able to lament with the greatest love and honor, we can do so very little for the one who has gone. Therefore our hearts are overcome with grief. There must be more for man. Surely Jacob yet lives, for our Father is the God of Jacob. He is not the God of the dead but of the living. Since we have received the incomparable gift of eternal life, we are happy to provide for those within the household of faith, even though they may have harmed us. We will surely forgive the brother who has mistreated us. When the day of our departure comes and our bodies are committed to the grave, our hope cannot be in the most peaceful plot of land in a quiet meadow bought with our own funds. Our hope is in Immanuel's land, and we expect our bones to live again, and to have the breath of life returned to them as Your eternal children, for we will worship You forever.

Exodus

Exodus 1

Glorious Redeemer, You rescued Israel out of Egypt. You gave them great fruitfulness even in the land of their captivity. Blessed be Your Name. You hear the cry of Your servants who pray to You in a time of bitter need. You know our poverty and trouble, and You care for us. The world may hate us, and exercise murderous plots against Your church. Yet You raise up men and women that fear You, and foil the plots of the wicked. Save us in our time of need today, O God. There is an enemy who seeks whom he may devour, but You are mighty, and will deliver us from all evil.

Exodus 2

Father God, You create us and bless us at a young age in the care of families. You appoint others to aid us when father or mother can no longer serve. You draw us out of the deep waters of danger and sin. You raise us up that we might one day deliver the weak out of the hand of the oppressor. The work before us is hard, since we face not only the power of mortal enemies, but also the hatred of those who should be friends. Our hope is in our Redeemer, the Lord Jesus Christ. He was faithful throughout every moment of His life. He was a sojourner in a foreign land for our sake. Because You heard our groaning and remembered Your covenant, You sent Your Son from heaven to earth, that we might be saved.

Exodus 3

Great God above all gods, You have sent Your angel to speak to Moses, yet Your voice came to Him out of a burning bush which was not consumed. He stood on holy ground and heard Your Word. You have surely seen the affliction of Your people. You Yourself are a strong deliverer. You bring us out of the land of sin, and lead us to our heavenly home. There is no man of power who can separate us from Your love. You are with us, and we shall serve You forever. O Great I Am, send us forth in the power of the everlasting Name. O God of Abraham, Isaac, and Jacob, gather Your people together to hear Your Word of salvation. We will obey You as You lead us forward out of the habits of slavish living. We are free men, who have been called to serve You in worship and love. You can give us favor in the sight of those who hate us, for Your love and power are enough for us.

Exodus 4

Mighty God, You have sent us signs of Your presence that are undeniable. In the day of Moses You changed a staff into a serpent, and water from the river into blood. In the day of Your Son Jesus, You opened the eyes of the blind. Even with the greatest signs before our very eyes, we feel our obvious inadequacy. But You are the Creator of those who are judged to be inadequate by men, and You can raise up a prophet from a man who is slow of speech. You call us forward in service, simply using what You have put in our hands. A staff of wood is a tool for miraculous deliverance, if You choose to show Your power to men. You have given us the signs of the covenant, that Your church might know the power of the blood of Your Son. Especially through the fact of Your Son's resurrection, we are convinced that Your Word is true, and that Jesus Christ, our Redeemer, is the same, yesterday, today, and forever.

Exodus 5

Father of Mercy and Comfort, we are Your people. All people everywhere should obey Your voice. We must worship You always. Thank You for the rest that You have given us through Christ our Lord. Powerful men would oppress Your people and forbid Your worship. Hear our cry, O Lord, and keep us in Your love. Thank You for the one sacrifice for sin in the cross of Jesus Christ. We offer up our lives as living sacrifices to You through our Redeemer. Father, help us in times of perplexing providences. Help us to remember that You alone are God, and that You will keep Your promises.

Exodus 6

Lord God, You are well able to stop all wicked oppressors. O Great I Am, remember Your covenant with Your people today. You have redeemed us from the burden of sin through Jesus our Lord. When our spirits are broken because of our enemies, have mercy on us. Raise up leaders in our midst who will help us to follow Your Son. Thank you for the families that You have given us. Help us to believe that You will be faithful from generation to generation because of Your eternal purpose. Make us courageous in leadership and true to You in service. You are the Lord. Grant us every spiritual gift and powerful help in times of trouble through the perfect righteousness of Jesus Christ.

Exodus 7

Lord Almighty, Your suffering people face great difficulties from the powers of this world. Defend Your children in the day of danger. Hear the bold challenges that Your enemies speak against You, and meet us now with power from heaven. We must obey Your word. We must worship You even when strong men would prohibit our devotion to You. Your ways are good and right. Thank you for the powerful blood of Your Son. Our atonement is not through the secret art of magicians, but through the death of Jesus Christ for sinners.

Exodus 8

Lord of Redemption, much trouble comes upon many lands because of disobedience and rebellion against You. You have sovereign authority over the land and the seas. Every creature lives and dies by Your command. How could men be so foolish as to persecute the godly? There is no one like You, O Lord our God. You do everything according to Your Word. Do not harden our hearts in our disobedience. We need You, O Lord. It is foolish for us to turn away from Your Word, and to walk in ways that are very unprofitable. You can change us. Send forth Your powerful angels. Subvert the schemes of wicked spirits who attack our life of worship with many distractions and disrupt our households. In the sight of all the nations, show that we are Your people. We will not take our orders in faith and worship from powerful governments and wicked oppressors. We will hear Your Word and follow You. Father, You know the treachery of evil men and angels. Hear us and deliver us.

Exodus 9

Lord of the Church, we will serve You. You made all things out of nothing. All creatures live and die at Your command. O the hardness of the rebellious hearts of men! Have mercy, O God! We are from the dust of the earth, but You have filled us with Your Spirit. Make us bold in proclaiming the truth of Your Word. You have been slow to anger, but Your name will be proclaimed throughout all the earth. You will not be stopped. You will show forth the holiness of Your justice and the blessedness of Your mercy. We fear You, O God. When we look up at the stormy skies, and consider Your sovereign power over thunder and hail, we are humbled for a moment. The earth is Yours, O Lord. When the sun is seen in the skies, when the rain stops, and the winds are calm, men harden their hearts again. O deliver us from the wicked who are too powerful for us!

Exodus 10

Glorious Lord, is there no end to the trouble that comes from the rebellion of men? Speak words of deliverance for us, O God. We need food to eat, but the wicked have destroyed our businesses and whole economies because of theft and oppression. Strong governing powers have attacked Your church. They hate You and imagine that our purposes are evil. You have commanded that we would be submissive citizens, but men are insisting on evil, and prohibiting that which is holy and good. Remove death and destruction from us. We long for the return of Your Son, and the fulfillment of all Your purposes of joy and life. Until that day dawns, feed us with bread from heaven, for the poor must eat. Will evil men never stop? We long to see Your face, O God.

Exodus 11

Lord of Your People, bring the plagues of Your judgment to an end, lest everyone everywhere die. Speak a great Word of mercy over all the earth in the message of Your gospel. Turn the hearts of many to love You. Your only-begotten Son has died for our sins. He has become the Firstborn of the Resurrection. All men everywhere should hear Your Word of justice and mercy, repent of sin, and turn toward You. Help us, O God! Deliver us from the foolishness of our rebellion.

Exodus 12

Redeemer King, You have heard the cry of Your people and have delivered us out of horrible bondage through Your Son. You have not only rescued us from the worst danger, You have given us a new life, defining our existence by the events of this deliverance. Your people were once defined by the rhythm of Passover and other Old Testament festivals year by year. We are now reminded of the death and resurrection of Jesus in our holy assemblies week by week in the celebration of our communion with Your Son. You have sent Him as the fulfillment of every festival from the time of preparation. He has bid us to turn away from the dangerous leaven of all sin. His blood has saved us from certain wrath. Our consciences have been sprinkled clean by this same blood. We bow our heads in reverence before You, and we worship You together as Your people. The reminder of death is all around us in this world of suffering and sorrow. The sound of mourning is everywhere. Yet You have given us joy and abundance in the new life that comes to us through Your Son. Be pleased to add to the multitudes of Your church, that many more may hear Your Word and believe. May we all depart from a land of sin, and be led to You by Your own marvelous light. May we worship You, remembering Your Son's death and growing in grace, knowledge, and love.

Exodus 13

Lord God, we belong to You. We are Yours. By a strong hand You brought us out of bondage. You have given to us a land full of blessings, for we are citizens of heaven. May Your Word be in our mouths forever. We turn away from sin. Help us to teach the truth to our children. Make the next generation know and believe what You have done for Your people. Help us all to follow Your instructions, for You will lead us in the right way. Though there be danger on every side, You are powerful to deliver us from any enemy that might pursue us. Be with us day and night as our Protector and our Hope.

Exodus 14

God of Power and Love, Your works of deliverance continue to this day. You demonstrate to people near and far that You are the Lord. If You were not close to us for protection, surely our enemies would destroy us. When we see the strength of many adversaries our hearts are full of fear. Our faith is so small. Help us Lord. Fight for us and help us. Give us the strength to move forward in the face of insurmountable obstacles. You are the Lord, and You will be glorious against every enemy. You give us special protection and make the sea into dry land, that Your people might pass through the waters of judgment and find safety forever. Destruction will surely come upon the heads of Your enemies, but we will pass through with the waters as a wall to us on the right and the left. We fear You, O God, for You have shown us Your amazing power in bringing about our salvation.

Exodus 15

Lord God, we rejoice in Your triumph over Your enemies. You are our strength and our song, and now You have become our salvation. Those that stand against us are proud and powerful. You can destroy them with a Word. We shall not be afraid. There is no one like You. If You stretch out Your hand against an adversary, he will be utterly destroyed. Terror and dread fall upon Your foes when they hear of Your mighty deeds, and Your people pass by in safety. We will come into Your sanctuary, where You will reign forever and ever. We will sing to You, for You have triumphed gloriously. You grant us fresh water in a desert land. We will listen to You, O Lord, and we will follow Your holy commandments.

Exodus 16

Help us, O God, for we are weary and hungry. How will we live if You will not provide? Forgive us for our faithless words in the day of testing. You are the Lord, and You have delivered us out of sin and bondage. You will not abandon us as You lead us into the Promised Land. You will not allow us to perish from lack of provision. You give us good food day by day. More than this, You have given to us the true Bread from Heaven, Your Son Jesus Christ. He is the best food for our souls. Why will we not believe You? Forgive us, O Lord, for we would disobey You even regarding Your generous provision for us. You give us daily bread, and make special provision for us in a day of Sabbath rest. Yet we refuse to keep Your commandments, and in faithlessness we rush out to gather on the day when You have commanded that we rest. Help us to enter into the perfect rest that is in Your holy Son Jesus Christ. We are eagerly longing for perfect rest.

Exodus 17

Redeemer King, we follow You. You supply us water for our bodies and the cleansing fountain of Your Spirit for our souls that we might live. That water from above comes from our Rock, the Lord Jesus Christ, for He has poured out His Spirit upon the church. The hand of our holy Savior is never weary, therefore we will not be destroyed by our enemies. You are the banner over Your church, and You will vindicate Your righteousness and goodness in the sight of all peoples.

Exodus 18

Lord of the Church, You have led us out of slavery. We are on our way to the Promised Land, the fulfillment of all Your Kingdom promises. You are our Help, though we are travelers in a foreign land. We greet You with joy. You have provided every good thing necessary for our existence and for our deliverance from sin and death. We rejoice in Your presence and enjoy sweet communion with Your Son and with each other. Help us in our service within Your church. In every task, we know that we are not able alone to do what we must do. Help us to see our place within the larger fabric of Your Kingdom. Bring others who will bear the burden of worship and service with us. Appoint people of prayer and wisdom to assist in the governance of Your house, under the perfect Lordship of Your Son.

Exodus 19

Lord God, You are near us. We have a Mediator who is forever in Your presence. You have brought us along on eagles' wings as a kingdom of priests. We hear Your Law, and commit ourselves to obey Your commandments. Why would we ever sin against You? Forgive us, O Lord. Though we know that our Mediator has accomplished our redemption, it is still very frightening to think that we as sinners might somehow face Your wrath. We are assured that our Rock, Jesus Christ, has faced the fullness of Your justice that we deserved. Surely a mountain of punishment has been broken into nothing through the holy blood of Jesus Christ, who died for us. Your Son has come down to us through the preaching of the truth, and has spoken to us of good news. We believe Him, and believing, we find life in His Name.

Exodus 20

Father, You have delivered us from the bondage of sin. We should love and serve You as the only true God. We will not worship idols. We honor Your holy Name, and rest in the work of Your Son, who is Himself our everlasting rest. We thank You for the privilege of loving others. Turn our hearts away from covetousness and hatred. We love Your Word, and we know that Your commandments are good. We repent of our sin; all murder and adultery, all stealing and lying, all rebellion against authorities that are established by Your command. Your Son has sacrificed Himself for us, and has made a way for us to have fellowship with You, for we have deeply violated Your law.

Exodus 21

Almighty Lord, You have rescued us from the most horrible bondage. We are Your servants, O Lord. Yet You have made us sons by adoption through Jesus Christ. We have done much that is wrong. Some things are the sorry yield of some mistake or irresponsibility, but many other sins involve intentional wrongdoing. How can there be hope for us? There is sorrow upon sorrow in this world, and even the best system of justice cannot overturn the trouble that is all around us. What can be the answer to this misery? There is guilt in us for all kinds of misconduct, foolishness, and even accidental faults. A ransom needs to be paid. The duty of restitution and the penalties of further just compensation suggest an overwhelming debt. Who can make things whole again? We thank You sincerely and joyfully for the full answer to sin that has come to us through Your Son. We rejoice in the cross, and we look with a confident expectation to the promised new heavens and earth which Your Son will surely bring.

Exodus 22

Heavenly Father, Your sheep hear Your Son's voice, and they know Him and follow Him. Thank You for rescuing us, for we were wandering from You in spiritual stupidity. You have sent ministers of the Word to call us back. Those who are themselves sheep of the only true Shepherd have become under-shepherds of our glorious King. We respect the gift of such servants. You are the owner of all things, and You will make all things right though the world is full of evil and disappointment. We have been betrothed to Your Son, and our hope in Him is strong and sure. We shall not be left without a future, and even now we possess a measure of present comfort. When we cry out to You, You hear us and You help us. We can trust You with our families and with all of our possessions. You are God, and Your Son loves us with an everlasting love.

Exodus 23

Great God, we must not sin against You. We so quickly use our tongues in works of deceit and injustice. Forgive us, O Lord. You love justice and hate all unrighteousness. Help us to have compassion upon the weak. We call out to You for the needs of the poor. How will they live without Your kind provision? In times of desperation will they turn to evil? Father, we want to be found among Your worshiping family whenever You call us into Your presence. There we find our hope and courage renewed. Lead us along the way to heaven. Speak through Your servants as they bring us Your message from the Scriptures. Make us strong in the spiritual warfare that we are facing. How can we survive, Lord, unless You grant us help in a difficult day? We need to take possession of the Kingdom by Your grace. Help us, O Lord!

Exodus 24

Great Lord and King, we worship You. We draw near to You through Jesus, Your Son. All that He has commanded we will do. We remember Your deliverance of Your people of old from the hand of the Egyptians, and we remember the blood of Christ, through which we have been delivered from sin and death. We long to see You as You are. We desire to be with You, for You have promised that we will have sweet fellowship with You, eating together at Your heavenly table. We glorify Your Name even now as we wait for our full redemption.

Exodus 25

Lord God, we pray that You will receive our lives today. We offer them up to You. We are a sanctuary for Your Holy Spirit. We thank You for this wonderful privilege. We long for Your presence and Your power. Father, You have granted to us a testimony of Your Kingdom. We will hear Your Word and believe. Meet with us as we gather in Your presence. Speak with us, and tell us everything that we must learn about You and about Your holy ways. Add Your Spirit to Your Word, that Your people might follow You. May Your church be a bright lampstand to many. Grant us oil from on high that we might be a shining light into a dark world. At just the right time, purify us, and we will be perfectly holy forever.

Exodus 26

Father, we are Your people. You have broadened Your tabernacle to include us within Your worshiping assembly. Why should we ignore the joy of worship as if it were nothing? There is a battle within us. Will we view Your holy assembly as the world views us, or will we look beyond our weakness to the coming Day of Glory? Your heavenly tabernacle is full of wonder. Thank you for Your instructions to Your people concerning the earthly tabernacle. It was made according to the pattern shown on the mountain. We long for something more than any earthly place of worship. We need something more than a temporary mercy seat. We long for the permanent place of the fullest security and holiness. Come soon, Lord Jesus!

Exodus 27

Almighty God, Your Son was offered up for us, as our one great Sacrifice. Everything in Your earthly sanctuary was holy. Every item was to be treated with the greatest reverence and respect, for these symbolic items spoke to us of You and Your grace. Help us to revere You as the One true living God. Grant us oil for our lamps, O Lord, for we shine forth for Your glory. Supply us with a Word from heaven, that we might live.

Exodus 28

Our Father, we have a great Mediator in Your Son Jesus Christ. We are called priests in Him as we worship You in the priesthood of all believers. The names of Your people are like precious stones upon Your Son's heart. Grant us genuine love for Your children. Give us faith, for we must trust You from the depths of our hearts. The holy clothing of Christ has been given to us. In Christ, we are remembered in Your presence forever. Speak to us words of peace, and give us life. The Name of our Savior, "The Lord our Righteousness," is upon us. In Him who is clothed with glory and beauty, we have the forgiveness of our sins.

Exodus 29

Father God, You have set apart Your Son to be a priest forever. He does not require a ceremonial cleansing or anointing. He has the power of an indestructible life. He has the full anointing of Your Holy Spirit. He is God over all, to be blessed and praised forever. To think that this Jesus intercedes for us! He offered Himself as a sacrifice to You through His death on the cross. We have been sprinkled with that precious blood. Now we are counted as holy. Blessed be Your Name, O God! Through Him we offer You our worship. We give our lives as a living sacrifice. We thank You for the great blessing of participation in Your church, for You have gathered Your people in Christ, and we are counted as holy. We are no longer outsiders, but members of Your household, and fellow-citizens in a heavenly land. We rejoice together with angels for the good things that You have accomplished for the glory of Your name. May we be a pleasing aroma of life before You this day. Sanctify us and consecrate us for Your service. Please dwell among us and be our God, for You are the Lord.

Exodus 30

O God of Our Fathers, we come to You through the merit and mediation of Your Son Jesus Christ. May our prayers be offered to You in heaven as a sweet incense. You are our God. We want to worship You in accord with Your will. May the blood of Christ speak a good word for us in Your dwelling place. Our lives belong to You. We have been bought with a price. Whether rich or poor, our atonement could only come from that precious blood. We have been washed and cleansed by this same blood, for the death of Your Son has tremendous power for good. You have sent Your Spirit upon Your church, and anointed Your children for Your service. Draw us near to You, that we might come to Your Son as servants of Him and of Your church. We would be Your holy people by Your merciful election and by Your kind providential care. We are so thankful that we are able to meet with You, together with all Your people.

Exodus 31

Great Giver of every good gift, fill us with Your Holy Spirit, that we might honor and serve You forever. There is a task ahead of us according to the gifts and calling that You have granted to us. You are building Your kingdom, and You have determined to use us for this wonderful work. Help us to keep Your Sabbaths, for Your Son has risen from the dead. Sanctify us through the gift of this good resurrection day, that we might grow in grace and knowledge. Thank You for Your Law. We will follow it as a rule of life. May we learn how to keep Your Law of love by the power of Your wonderful grace.

25

Exodus 32

Lord God, we have violated Your commandments. What can we do? We must repent. Like our fathers before us, we have found idolatry strangely attractive. Why would we believe our hearts when an unclean impulse draws us to created things? We hear the lying and enticing words of enemies: "These are your gods!" Is that message so sensible that we must follow it? No, the hearts of Your people are so weakened and foolish through habitual sin that we quickly believe ridiculous lies. Father, we thank You for the intercession of Your Son on our behalf. Surely Your justice would have destroyed us, were it not for Your eternal covenant faithfulness. Give us hope again today. We have security and deliverance from all sin and idolatry through the greatness of Your mercy to us in Christ. Even our leaders fail and fall. Yet our Captain is without fault, and is full of compassion for Your elect. Merciful God, we are on Your Son's side, whatever the cost may be. All idols underfoot be trod! You, O Lord, are God. There is no other. We have sinned a great sin, but Your Son has made a perfect offering for us. He took the curse that we deserved, so that we would not face Your wrath against our iniquity forever.

Exodus 33

Father God, You lead us through the wilderness by the means that You see fit. But Father, we earnestly request that You Yourself will surely be with us. You have chosen to work through means. You give us preachers and teachers of Your Word. You give us baptism and the supper Your Son instituted. You give us prayer together as Your people. Nonetheless Father, we need You. Please do not depart from Your church, or we are done. We will not be able to accomplish even one Kingdom purpose without you. We must have Your Son as our Leader. We need Your glorious Spirit as our Teacher. You are the Lord. Be gracious to us. Be merciful to us. We must have You. Hide us in Christ, our Rock, and use the means that You have provided. But we will not worship means. We will worship only You. You are God.

Exodus 34

Lord, after we have failed so badly, would You give Your people another opportunity to serve You? If You would not, there could be no hope for Your church. You are the Lord, a God merciful and gracious. You have forgiven us in such a way that the penalty of our iniquity was paid through Your Son's holy work on the cross. Pardon our iniquity and sin again we pray. Do wonders before us as Your work moves forward even through us. Drive out those who would only be a snare in our midst. Cause the pure truth of Your Word to be known and loved day by day. Is there yet hope for us after all our weakness and sin? Yes. Your promises are all "Yes" and "Amen" in Jesus Christ. We have been redeemed through the blood of that One Lamb. There is no other Name for us. There is no other Lamb for sinners. There is no other hope than what Christ has won for us. We turn away from all foolish idolatry and false worship. You are here among Your people. We hear Your Word, and follow Your Son, by the power of Your Spirit. Shine Your holy light in our midst, that we might be changed. If we are worldly in our ways, how can we be the light of the world? You will help us to know You and to follow You in truth and love. We will do Your holy will.

Exodus 35

Glorious God, we will rest in Your Son's resurrection and work for His glory with joy forever. Our one new Man has led the way for us into a new world. He is clothed in majesty, and anointed with Your Spirit in fullness. What shall we do, O Lord? Your people are covered with His righteousness. Our hearts are stirred. We have given of our substance for the work of Your Kingdom. We dedicate all to You. We seek first Your Kingdom. We commit our lives to You. What shall we do, O Lord? Our leaders seek Your face. We are united together in Your Son Jesus Christ. You have called us by name, and have given us gifts for such a time as this. Bring forward from our hands and hearts all that is beautiful, orderly, wonderful, helpful, and good. May Your kingdom come, and Your will be done, on earth as it is in heaven.

Exodus 36

Great God, You are building a holy sanctuary. Your Son is a Master Builder with the greatest skill. Your work is beautiful, O Lord. You have bountiful resources for all that You have planned. To think that we are a part of this glorious sanctuary! We thank You that the place of Your presence has not been limited to one nation. Your tabernacle has been expanded to include all Your elect. O Lord, how marvelous are Your holy plans. Even now we see the progress of Your work throughout the history of Your church. What a beautiful place You are building! Not only are there people in that land, but even angels. We long to see the finished work. We are eager for You, and for the revealing of the sons of God.

Exodus 37

Lord God, how wonderful is the Ark of the Covenant, the place of Your special presence! To think that it was a seat of mercy! You are holy, O God. You have determined to have mercy on us. How could we ever turn away from You? Please forgive us, for we have sinned against You. Grant us Your great mercy again through Jesus Christ. We are His body. Your glorious lampstand is shining in the world, for Your Son is the light of the world, and in Him we are to be a light in a dark place. Make us to be a unified mountain of the finest gold, taking away from us every defect and impurity. Father, one day we will have no remaining trace of sin among us. You will purify Your church. Fill us even now with the holy oil of Your Spirit, that we might worship and serve You forever.

Exodus 38

Father God, Your Son gave himself on Your holy altar, not the Old Testament altar in the old temple where bulls and goats were consumed, but a better altar, where our sins were atoned for. We come into Your heavenly courts through Him. We have been washed in the waters of baptism. We are clean because of the blood of Jesus Christ, and the purifying water of the Holy Spirit. We long for Your courts, O Lord. We are already with You in Christ, and yet we are not yet with You, and so we long for You. All Your Son's work is skillfully done. Our destiny is secure and sure because of His great resurrection. Blessed be Your Name, O Lord. You are God. Jesus is Lord. The Lord is the Spirit. The Spirit is God. There is only One God. Blessed be Your One Name, the Name of the Father, and of the Son, and of the Holy Spirit!

Exodus 39

Glorious Lord, Your Son is High Priest forever. He is perfect in holiness. Our names are written on His hands, and Your people are upon His heart, like stones of remembrance. Thank You for Your wonderful thoughts toward us. Though we are weak and sinful, You have not forgotten us. Your Son has won a great victory for Your elect. Thank You, Father, for the hope that we have, for we will see Your Son face to face. We long for that day. Help us to use our time well as we serve You here below. May we remember the beauty of Your Son, with whom You are well-pleased. May it be our glory to magnify the name of Your Son. He serves us even now in His special care for the church. Words of comfort and blessing come to us from this One Mediator, who is most holy to You. Finish Your perfect and holy work in building Your tabernacle, and assemble us finally and fully in Your presence, filling us with Your blessed Holy Spirit. We lift up our prayers to You with confidence, for You have done great things, and Your promises are sure. We believe You, O Lord God. Build Your church throughout the world. May we always do what You have commanded. Bless us from heaven even now.

Exodus 40

Lord God, the time is drawing near for the fullness of Your tabernacle to be revealed. No man knows the day or the hour, but we know that the time is drawing nearer every day. Anoint us with Your Holy Spirit. We want something much more than the Old Testament picture of holiness. We have the credited righteousness of Christ. Now grant to us relief from the power of sin, for You have certainly delivered us from the penalty of wickedness. Sanctify us, for this is Your will. Put everything in order in Your holy tabernacle according to Your perfect plan. We seek You now with joy. We know that You will not leave this job in disarray. As we have spots and blemishes in us and throughout Your church, purify Your people for Your use. Descend upon us in the cloud of Your presence that we might be with You forever and ever.

Leviticus

Leviticus 1

Great God, Your Son came as a whole burnt offering for us. What He gave to You was in every way full and complete. Our sins have been placed upon His sacred head. We mourn for our awful transgressions, but we thank You for the peace that we enjoy in Christ Jesus our Lord. There was nothing wrong in His offering to You. He had no thought, word, or deed of sin. In Him we have been credited with this perfect offering, and we are grateful for this abundant mercy.

Leviticus 2

O Lord our God, the fruitfulness of every field belongs to You. Day by day we labor in this world according to Your provision. Your Son came and labored for us in the days of His earthly ministry. His work lasts forever. He offered all of His efforts up to You, for Your glory. What a lovely gift! His every word, His every touch, His every prayer was perfect. All that He had, He gave to You, from beginning to end. His offering was well seasoned with the salt of covenant grace and was made rich with the oil of perfect holiness from on high. What He has done for us will last forever, and is wonderfully full of the presence and power of Your Holy Spirit.

Leviticus 3

Almighty Father, throughout our sorry lives of sin, we have made war against You. We are so ashamed of our foolish rebellion. Even before we were born, we were justly credited with Adam's wicked violation of Your commandments. Now a second Adam has come into this world of strife. He has made peace with You on our behalf. Your wrath against us has been turned away, and we enjoy the perfect tranquility of the satisfaction of Your just demands. Help us to be at peace with one another through Him who is our peace.

Leviticus 4

Lord God, our sin has brought guilt upon us and trouble upon many. Please forgive us. In former days, the priests and rulers of the people had special temptations. When they sinned, there was a duty according to Your Law to shed blood for the sins of those in positions of authority and service. We now have a perfectly pure High Priest. He needs no offering for His own sin, for He has none. He is also the King of Your church. What a great joy it is to have a Ruler over us who is spotless and without blemish. Though our Head is sinless, the body of Your worshipers is still marred by impurity, both in each member individually, and in the congregation as a whole. What an amazing mercy it is, that our King and Priest has willingly offered up Himself to You as our Substitute, and has become the spotless offering for our sin through His death on the cross. Through Him we are regarded as holy in Your sight. We praise You and thank You, O Lord!

Leviticus 5

Father God, what offering could we give to You for our unintentional sins? What could we give for our open rebellion? There is no remaining system of daily atonement. We thank You that we have a better solution to the problem of sin than the blood of bulls and goats. Christ shed His blood for us. Now we are called to enjoy a sacramental meal that reminds us that Jesus gave Himself for us. Our glorious Lord had no guilt. He was tempted in every way as we are, but He never violated Your holy commandments. His blood has purified Your sanctuary for us, and a new and sure way into Your presence has been won for us through His love. Sovereign Lord, You will never abandon Your demand for justice. Your holy Law must be satisfied. We admit our guilt before You. We cannot afford the penalty that is justly demanded from us. Even if we were to give our lives completely to You with the hope that our death might satisfy Your demands, this would not be enough for our offense against You. There is Another who has paid our debt in full. He has added yet more to His sacrifice, so that the stain of our transgression has been more than covered. Our guilt has been erased, and His goodness has become ours by Your great plan of grace. Blessed be Your Name, O God.

Leviticus 6

Almighty God, we have sinned in so many ways. We have taken what is not ours. We must restore it in full, but this cannot make up for our offense against You and others. Only the blood of Christ can take away our sin. Our transgressions bring trouble upon Your church. Our lives should be given entirely to You, yet we have reserved so much for ourselves. What offering can be given for our peace? What can we do to meet the demands of Your justice? Only the work of Christ, our High Priest can remove our ugliness, for we are unclean. He has consumed the abomination of our rebellion, and we have been healed. We thank You for His great righteousness and mercy.

Leviticus 7

Lord God, why were Your people of old not allowed to eat of the fat of the sacrifice? What is in the fat of the animal? Is every impurity stored there? It is not suitable for our consumption. We cannot live on that kind of diet. It must be burned before You. The death of Christ has truly removed the guilt and power of sin from among Your people. All that is impure in us and all our iniquity has been taken far away from Your church. Your Son was cut off from Your people, that Your people could be brought near to Him. The blood of His sacrifice was precious to You. You set the requirements of complete atonement. You told us what we could eat from the sacrificial meal, and what could not be eaten. We receive the sign and seal of communion with You in Your holy supper. Here we remember the death of Your Son for us, and we are partakers of wonderful blessings by faith.

Leviticus 8

Our Father, Your holy Son was set apart for the work that He came to do. Just as the Old Testament priests were washed with water and were clothed with special garments, and just as they were anointed with holy oil, Your Son has received the substance of these shadows. In His baptism, He identified with sinners and acknowledged our need for great cleansing. He was clothed with our sins so that we might be granted His robes of holy righteousness. He was filled with Your Spirit beyond measure. He was installed to all of His offices forever through His resurrection from the dead. Now He lives at Your right hand in the eternal sanctuary. He is our Prophet, Priest, and King. In Him, we are near You in Your holy presence forever. Even now we have been consecrated for Your service. We give ourselves to the work of Your Kingdom. All things necessary for Your Son's reign over us have been fully accomplished, and we stand ready to serve You in accord with Your holy will.

Leviticus 9

Lord God, any offering that we could have invented to satisfy the demands of Your righteousness would surely have been an offense against You. We could never have made atonement for ourselves or for Your church. Where would we be without the work of Your Son? Surely ceremonial animals cannot satisfy You. Our great High Priest has made full atonement for us. This was planned from before the foundation of the world. In the earthly days of Your Son, these eternal plans were accomplished. When He ascended in clouds of glory, He raised His hands in blessing over us. In Him we are truly blessed.

Leviticus 10

Almighty Father, what will we do in the day of grief? There is no health within us because of our sin. Our loved ones have behaved beyond the limits of propriety. Our children, who should be priests in the priesthood of all believers, have wandered into ways of unbelief. Where is our hope? We mourn with bitter tears. Help us, O God! Where else can we turn? If You will not help us, we will only bring trouble upon everything that we touch. We must do the things that You have commanded us, despite the grief of sin and misery that weighs so heavily upon us. We cannot eat, but we must commune with You. We cannot serve, but we must obey. Help us to keep on going when it feels like life is already over. Such things as these have happened to us. Have mercy on us, O Lord!

Leviticus 11

Great God and King, You set apart Your people Israel from all of the other nations of the earth. You governed even the things that they consumed. They were not allowed to eat according to their own private judgment. You told them what was to be detestable among them. You gave them a powerful experience of being different from the world. This ceremonial law had its purpose for the time of preparation, reminding your people that we are to be distinct from the world, not because of what goes into our bodies, but because of what comes out of us. When the time of the Old Covenant was near fulfillment, Your Son announced to us a new freedom to eat according to conscience. We ask that You would aid us in turning away from the way of death, which is truly unclean. The things of sin that come out of us still defile us. Out of our hearts and our mouths come filthy desires and words that are an attack on the way of life that we have been given. Your Son was perfectly holy for us. May we walk in holiness with joy, observing all things that He has commanded.

Leviticus 12

Our Father, You have given us the gift of children in Your church. We thank You for bringing the mothers among us through the challenge of pregnancy and childbirth. We thank You for the life that is a gift from You. We know that we have all been cleansed by the blood of Christ. His true and perfect sacrifice has made both us and our young ones clean.

Leviticus 13

O God, the horror of leprous diseases of various kinds was a powerful sign of the trouble that we have all around us. We are not awake to sensations of true spiritual danger as we should be. The damage upon our lives has been substantial, and we bear the marks of death on our bodies and in our minds. Thanks be to You, O God, for sending Your Son. He has touched the leper and has made him clean. The deep insensitivity within us that seemed incurable has been healed by the touch of Jesus Christ. Our consciences have been awakened again. Much of the damage in our lives from times of ugly darkness has already been powerfully addressed by Your Son. What remains as memorials of rebellion against You will surely be completely healed in the resurrection to come. Thank You for the pronouncement of our High Priest that assures us that we are clean in Him. He has taken away our shame. As we follow Your Son, it is safe now for us to be connected to Your people in the covenant community. May we move forward in devotion to You day by day with strong confidence in the perfect holiness of Jesus Christ. Grant to us powerful mercy and practical help for those who live in isolation because of disease or shame. May they know the joy of the love of Christ in the sadness and misery of their brokenness. May many others know relief from guilt and hopelessness through the word and mercy of Christ working through His church.

Leviticus 14

Lord God, we thank You for the great work of cleansing that we have received through the blood of Your Son. Our hearts have been sprinkled and we have been declared clean by Your grace. Our great High Priest has done everything necessary that we might have access to You. We have in Him the perfect offering for our salvation. Your Son Jesus has made full atonement for us. Look on us in our poverty, and help us to be grateful for Your mercy. All that we have is Yours, O God. We have been marked with the blood of Christ. The oil of Your Holy Spirit has been poured out on our heads. Please bless our families, and protect us from the disease of unrepentant sin. Help us to call upon Your name regularly, that we might know the fullest assurance of the most perfect cleansing. Make our homes and churches clean by Your grace, that we might know Your presence and Your power in our times of prayer and fellowship.

Leviticus 15

O God of Our Fathers, we have sin sickness in body and spirit, and our disease seems to be communicable. We spread our illnesses to others we love. Help us, O God. Our condition is desperate. Take away our despair and grant to us a fresh awareness of the atonement. We are restored to fellowship with You and with Your church through the death of Jesus Christ. Grant healing to Your people. Bless our mortal bodies. Heal our broken spirits. Take away those things that cause vexation in our minds and make us vulnerable to attacks of the evil one. Lord, we ask for Your full blessing upon the marriages within Your church and throughout the world. There is so much potential for good within this close union of husband and wife. There is also much danger of evil and sorrow. Heal us, O Lord, and make us clean from all of our iniquities.

Leviticus 16

Father God, a way into the holy place has been made for us through Jesus Christ. We have been clothed with His righteousness as a most holy garment. We have a perfect atonement for ourselves and for our houses because of the blood of Jesus Christ, our sin offering. The guilt of our sin has been sent away far from us so that we may live. We offer up to You our prayers now with boldness. We shall not die. Our bodies may rest in the grave, but we will live. In Christ we have gone beyond the veil. He has made atonement for the holy place. Our sin made this necessary. Now we have a great Friend who is in Your presence, and we have a wonderful union with Him. All of our sins were put on Him. All of our iniquities were carried by Him. We have been fully cleansed in the most wonderful baptism. You have granted us Your Spirit, and our guilt has been washed away. We have a new life now, and a great expectation of resurrection in Your holy city. We are clean before You. Your Son now lives forever to intercede for us. There is no need for

Him to repeat His work of atonement year by year, for He died the death that we deserved once for all time.

Leviticus 17
Lord God, we want to give our lives to You in worship every day. Help us when we gather together as a church to recognize our unity in Your Son. From the strength of that weekly assembly help us to offer up our bodies as living sacrifices every day. The blood of Christ has made atonement for us. We do not want to treat the blood of the covenant as a common thing by walking away from Your holy assembly. We cannot bear the guilt of our iniquity. Your Son has done this for us. We live for Him.

Leviticus 18
Lord God, You are holy. We must not walk in the ways of this world. We live by faith in Christ. Help us to follow Him. Father, we are surrounded by manifold temptations and snares. Keep us away from those who would lead us in paths of immorality. Protect Your children. Restrain the evil man who would abuse the weak and hurt their lives. Bring healing and hope to those who have been attacked ruthlessly by those who are perverse. Thank You for the hope that we have in Christ. We know that there will be forgiveness for all manner of sins. Purify our hearts and our lives through Your Word and Spirit.

Leviticus 19
Father God, we must be holy, for You are holy. Help us to turn away from all idolatry, and to love and serve You as a matter of first importance. Grant to us such an overflowing love for You that we will love our neighbors with generous hearts. Help us to love the weak and even our adversaries. Guard our hearts and our tongues. We should be honest in our communications and kind to others. Grant that we would be pure in all of our dealings with others. Help us to look to Christ moment by moment for the strength that we need to live disciplined and godly lives. Protect our families from a world full of depravity. We will turn away from all false religion and oppression. We will also pursue justice and truth in all our commerce with one another. Forgive our many sins through the mercy and love of Christ.

Leviticus 20
Almighty Father, the consequences for our sin against You are so very serious. Through our murderous affections and actions the land is full of blood and misery. Turn us away from our strange and dangerous fascination with spiritual evil. Free us from all unlawful inquiry into demonic pathways. Keep us from the sea of immorality that many would think of as normal. We have done depraved things that have brought great trouble upon Your people. Father, we thank You for the atoning blood of our Savior. Through Him the gross uncleanness of our sin has been fully dealt with. Our future is secure. Though we will not be perfected in holiness until this life is over, we have already been washed by the blood of Christ and cleansed through the renewing grace of the Holy Spirit. Grant that we would understand our current privileges in Christ our Lord, and at just the right time, bless us with a fuller experience of the glory of Your presence, and the victory over sin that Your Son has secured for us.

Leviticus 21

Great God, we thank You for the provision of the greatest Mediator, the Lord Jesus Christ, our High Priest. He is holy to You forever. We are His bride. Through Him we have been made holy, despite the obvious fact of our defiling sin. We were permanently stained by immorality and corruption. Yet Your Son has touched us and we are completely clean. If our skin were to show our record of disobedience, we would be full of every kind of defiling blemish. How would we be able to come into Your presence? Yet now we have been cleansed by the blood of Christ.

Leviticus 22

Merciful Lord, we are amazed that You have provided a way out of our defiling sin. Because of our uncleanness we deserved to be cut off from Your people forever. Not only have we been defiled because of our own sin, but we dwell among an unclean people, and have been made impure through our imitation of the sin of others. Yet we have been brought into Your family now through our great High Priest Jesus Christ. We are forgiven, and Your Son has added an abundant righteousness to our account, a holiness that is far beyond any demand of Your Law. He was the one perfect Lamb, and was offered up to You in the fullness of His righteousness. We now move forward with confidence because of Him. We know that the blood of bulls and goats could never have made eternal atonement for us. Christ has done this perfectly for us. You have brought us out of a world of darkness, that we might serve You in the land of light forever.

Leviticus 23

O Lord of Creation, You ordered the lives of Your people of Old according to the feasts that You appointed for them. We too have our lives ordered by the rest that we have in Christ together on the first day of every week. He is our Passover. Because of Him we shall live. He is our Unleavened Bread. There was no sin in Him at all. He is our Firstfruits, for He has risen to resurrection life. He is our Pentecost. We have been gathered into the harvest by His Word and Spirit. He looked out upon the fields and saw that they were white unto harvest. He sent workers in order to speak the Word to us. We have heard, and been gathered into Your church. He is our Festival of Trumpets. One day the trumpet shall sound, the dead in Christ shall rise, and we will be together with our Lord. He is our Day of Atonement. On that great Day of Judgment when Your Son separates the sheep from the goats, we shall be kept with Him, for He was cast out of the covenant community for a time, that we might be kept in Your assembly forever. He is our everlasting Feast of Tabernacles. In Him we shall live with perfect joy forever. He is our All in All. On that great day of His return, we shall see the perfect fulfillment of His Kingdom. We believe in this great Sabbath fulfillment that is yet to come. In hope, we even now continue to enter into that eternal Sabbath rest through Christ, who makes all things new.

Leviticus 24

O God, there is such misery among us as we wait for the return of Your Son. We are privileged to participate in Your church. It is a lampstand for the light of the world. We even eat the bread from heaven as we feast upon Christ in Word, sacrament, and prayer. Nonetheless, we sin, and our children sin, and we cannot be satisfied with our disobedience and blasphemy. We need to have sin removed far away from us forever. We need mercy, for we disobey You every day. Help us, O Lord. Grant us secret joys and peace, for there is much all around us that weighs us down in this world of sin and death. We need hope again this day.

Leviticus 25

Merciful Lord, You have granted Your people rest in Your Son Jesus Christ. We are so often running in one direction, and then running in another. Please forgive us. One day a week is not enough for us to understand the fullness of rest that You have granted to us. We long for the age to come, the time of eternal Sabbath. Help us to enter into that rest even now. Grant us the material blessings necessary for us to live as we celebrate the little day of rest that You have commanded us to observe. We rejoice in You. Lord God, we pray that You would grant to our hearts the joy of the fullest Jubilee in Your Son. We are priests who attend to You through Him. We also care for our brothers, for we have been redeemed from bondage. We are Your servants, and now we are Your sons. What shall we be in the age to come? We know that we shall be like Jesus, for we shall see Him as He is. Grant us great joy in our families even now. Especially grant to us a fuller sense of our family joy in Your church. Why should the redeemed mourn or celebrate alone? We are Your people. We are Your servants. We are Your family.

Leviticus 26

God of Glory, You who made the heavens and the earth, why would we make idols? Why would we hate the rest that You so kindly bestowed upon us? Why would we turn away from Your Law? You have granted to us great promises for all who will believe and obey. Your Son has won for us the fullness of every blessing. We thank You, O God. By our own hypocrisy and disobedience we deserved the fullness of discipline from Your hand. You have disciplined us in love, but not as much as we have deserved. We turn to You now. We will not walk contrary to You. Please do not send the curse of the covenant of works upon us. Please do not send Your fury against us. Your Son has fully atoned for our sins. Grant us a full mercy forever, Bring us rest in Jesus Christ. Take away our tears and our anxiety. We shall not perish forever. Please bring us resurrection lives. Do not leave our bodies in the grave forever. Come soon, Lord Jesus. We know that we have spurned Your rules, but we hate our sin. You know that we cannot take much trouble or we will be ruined. We have had high spiritual pretensions, but low spiritual attainments. We have been given so much, and much is rightly required of us. Please forgive us.

Leviticus 27

Lord God, Your Son has made a precious vow upon the cross. We are the payment of that vow. His vow was a vow of persons. We have been promised to You by our gracious Savior. We will be perfectly holy one day, and we shall be Yours forever. We are Your servants, but we are also Your sons, and the bride of Your only-begotten Son. You have made such great promises to us, and we have been redeemed. You certainly will not abandon us. We are not ashamed to ask You for those things that You have promised us in Your Word. You have said to us, "Never will I leave You. Never will I forsake You." Please keep us in Your love forever.

Numbers

Numbers 1

Lord God Almighty, You brought Your people out of the land of slavery, and brought them into the wilderness. You appointed leaders of the tribes, and numbered Your people for military service. We have been brought into the church by Your grace. We are numbered not according to our natural descent, since we are now Your adopted children through Jesus Christ. In Him, our heritage is in the tribe of Judah. We too have been delivered from the bondage of sin through the blood of Christ. Our home is not on this earth, since our names are written in the Lamb's book of life. This is a cause of the greatest rejoicing for us. We are the priesthood of all believers. We are part of the church militant. We are a force of loving service. Forgive us, for we regularly forget that there is a battle going on all around us. Thank you for preserving our lives to this day.

Numbers 2

Sovereign Lord, You set up Your people according to their tribes under the leadership of the men that You appointed. We too have leaders in spiritual battle in our churches today. Will we follow their lead in our service of You? We pray that we might be led forward in the strength of God-centered worship. Help us to do all things decently and reverently. We go forth in a mission of conquest, not bringing judgment and death to the nations, but the light and life of the Word of Your Son. Help us in this great endeavor, and forgive our sins.

Numbers 3

Father God, You ordained priests to serve before You in the days of Aaron. In our day, all Your children are called to be Your priests. May we offer up prayers to You on behalf of the people, and speak words of blessing from You upon our brothers and sisters. It is our duty and privilege to be dedicated to Your worship and to guard its purity and dignity. Make us to be faithful to You in all that we do. Help us to love the body of Your Son, the church. We thank You that we have a great High Priest over the house of the Lord. His priesthood is eternal, and He is perfectly faithful in His office. We have a great sanctuary in the heavens. We long for Your house above. What would it be like for us to be among Your people there? May we be filled with all the fullness of Your presence even now. May we rejoice in the redemption that we have in the blood of the Lamb, Jesus Christ. There is no price that we could have paid for our freedom. We receive our liberty even now as a precious gift from Your hand.

Numbers 4

Holy God, You have work in Your house that You have prepared for Your people. Your work today is not the work of the tabernacle and its furnishings. You desire that we would have hearts for the needy and for the weak all around us. Bless Your service in our midst day by day. Your people are on the move. We go as You direct Your church, and we stay according to Your command. We have gathered to do our duty. Help us to bear one another's burdens. Thank You for the deacons that You have granted for important work in the midst of Your church. May Your ministers be able to rightly focus their efforts on Word, sacrament, and prayer. Teach us to give honor to those who are worthy of honor. Help us to have a right regard for those who are in need among the brothers and sisters in the body of Christ. Thank You for those who serve in various duties of finance, facilities, and administration. Protect us from the evil one. Help us to love peace and to forsake unnecessary disagreement. May we pursue godliness and love together for Your glory.

Numbers 5
Sovereign Lord, You have the right to direct Your people according to Your will. Grant us wisdom by Your Word to rightly understand who should be received into Your church. You will preserve Your people through these challenging days. The church is Your Kingdom and not ours. May she be a faithful bride by Your grace, Your Son has faced the curse of the Law for us. He has taken our bitter pain. We are now free from iniquity through the sacrifice of one Man. In Him we have been given a new beginning.

Numbers 6
Father, there yet remains a way of holiness for Your people. We are all called to this life of righteousness in imitation of Jesus Christ. That way of life is not merely outward and symbolic. It begins in the depths of a cleansed heart, and is expressed in actions of justice, mercy, and humility. We long for the day of perfect holiness for Your people. You will bring us into Your heavenly sanctuary. There we will not have even the tiniest remaining blemish of sin in our offering of our lives to You. There will be nothing unclean in that place. Here below we live in churches that are a mixed multitude, but even now Your name has been put upon Your people, and You bless us. Yet O how we long for that Day!

Numbers 7
Almighty God, You have a perfect plan that You are bringing about in a wonderful way. In the days of the Law, symbolic ritual actions were performed in Your presence. These offerings hinted at the provision of lives that would be fully consecrated to You. These gifts were not only for the leader who brought them forward. They represented the offering of a whole tribe. We celebrate the return of Your Son to the heavenly sanctuary. He is our Head. He is the One perfect Worshiper, our representative before You. His offering was the fulfillment of every picture of the ceremonial Law. Now we are called to offer our lives to You day by day. We cannot do this in our own strength. We give ourselves to You in Him who had no sin, and who lives forever to intercede for us. We worship and serve You in humble reliance upon the grace of the Holy Spirit. We rejoice when we see Your people making wonderful progress in the way of sanctification. Nonetheless, no matter how great our service to You might ever be as a church, our full confidence is in the perfect offering of Your Son on our behalf. We have peace with You through

Him alone, and our lives are perfectly Yours in Him.

Numbers 8

Lord God, Your Son is the Light of the World, and we are the light of the world in Him. We are ashamed of our sin. Bring Your people a new repentance, that we might serve You more faithfully. We are to be separated from this world in some ways, and yet we live in it. We must keep on going through the pain and misery of this life. We must also lay hold of the joy of the age to come. As we taste of the goodness of Your Word and experience something of the power of heaven, we rejoice in Your Son Jesus Christ. He never grows too old to serve You. In Him we have eternal life. We will serve You forever and ever.

Numbers 9

Great God, You established the Passover as a powerful display of redemption through the blood of a Substitute. Our hope is in Jesus Christ. Not only was He perfectly clean before You in His holy obedience, He has also carried the horrible weight of our sin. We have been bought with a price. You are present with us now in a special way as we celebrate the Supper that Your Son instituted at the time of the final Passover. Now we walk in the Spirit as those who abide in Your Word. In the light of Your sacrament of communion we remember Your Son's death for sinners, and we know that we must be imitators of Him in the way of the greatest love ever known.

Numbers 10

O Father, we long for the sound of the great trumpet from heaven, signaling the return of Your Son. We long to be gathered together in perfect covenant assembly. Today we face exhausting spiritual warfare. May we not be weary in well-doing, but press on as You lead us in the way of joy. You have appointed elders among Your people, that we might journey with order and obedience. Surely there is an enemy who seeks those whom He may devour. May we move forward in holy assembly as Your Son speaks to us in Your Word. He knows the pathway to heaven, for He Himself is the Way.

Numbers 11

O God, we must not murmur against You. We will only bring trouble upon ourselves with our continuous complaining. Please forgive us, O Lord. You send Bread from heaven, and we still find fault with You. We deliberately ignore all of the blessings that You have granted to us, even seeking the day of our death. We should be thanking You for our salvation and serving You with a joy that is forever full and real. Forgive us, and restore us again to useful service. Father, we thank You for taking us out of the land of sin. We thank You that Your hand is not shortened. You are able to pour out Your Spirit upon our leaders. They point us forward in holiness, but it is not as if we are devoid of the Spirit throughout Your church. We are filled with the Holy Spirit, speaking to one another with psalms, hymns, and spiritual songs, making melody in our hearts to You, thanking You in Christ in all situations, and submitting to one another out of reverence for our Redeemer. The promise is for us and for our children, as many as You will call to Yourself.

Numbers 12

Lord God, we have not been afraid to speak against Your chosen leaders in ways that have been inappropriate and harmful. Forgive us, O Lord. As when Miriam and Aaron spoke against Moses, our sniping against Your servants is an offense against You. Worse than all of this, have we actually spoken against Your Son Jesus Christ? Forgive us, and restore us to life.

Numbers 13

O God, You send us forth in mission, and we need to move forward in faith. Our flesh would rebel against Your clear commandments. We would be filled with fear, forgetting Your power, Your love, and Your faithfulness to Your own holy Name. Teach us to follow Your will, and not to prefer ourselves to You. Where You want us to go, we will go. When You want us to stay, we will stay. Help us, O Lord. How are we to know Your will? Please direct us according to the means that You have appointed, moving us and restraining us according to Your sovereign plan. How quickly we would believe and promote lies when we do not want to do what You have told us to do. Please forgive us.

Numbers 14

Our Father, we have sinned against You. We have refused Your clear direction. We have a continuing need for further repentance. Will we now return to the world, spurning the gift of the kingdom? We will not rebel against You, O Lord. You will move us forward in holy obedience. You will glorify Your servants. How we long for that day! You have directed us and have given us strength from on high. We are on the path that You have granted to us. Please continue to pardon us according to the greatness of Your steadfast love. Please do even more than this. Be with us. Have mercy on our children, that our rebellion and sin will not be passed on to our young ones. Show us the way to go. Grant to us godly men and women that will be good examples for us of courage and faithfulness. Though You discipline us, grant us a measure of assurance that nothing can overturn Your eternal promises. We do not want to be presumptuous in our service of You. We do not want to make up challenges for ourselves, as if we knew the beginning from the end. You must lead us in the way to go.

Numbers 15

Holy Lord, You are giving us the Kingdom. We should offer up our lives to You together as a living sacrifice. This sacrifice is a pleasing aroma to You only because of the perfect sacrifice of Your Son for us. We are Your people. As Your Son's body here on earth, we have Christ as our Head. Gather into this one body of Christ both Jews and Gentiles who call upon Your Name. Thank You that we who were strangers to the covenants of promise have been brought near to You through the blood of the Lamb. Forgive us for our many sins. We have sinned unintentionally, but we have also sinned in ways that were not accidental. Is there any hope for the man who commits high-handed sin? Who can be saved if only unintentional sins have been atoned for? Thank you that all of our iniquity has been laid on Jesus. You have made clear that the wages of sin is death, but Christ has died for us, and we are forgiven. Speak to us, O Lord, from Your holy Word. Remind us of Your Law. Remind us of our sinful inclinations. Remind us also of the sacrifice appointed to cancel our sins, and assure us, through the resurrection of Jesus Christ, that we have been justified through His abounding righteousness.

Numbers 16

O Lord God, what will we do when a movement of ugly rebellion rises up within our hearts and within the covenant assembly? What will we do when the power of our envy seems stronger than any holy impulses? Surely if our security among Your people came from our own holiness and obedience we would be utterly lost. Forgive our disrespectful thoughts and words against those who serve You in righteousness. Forgive us for our arrogant presumption that we would somehow do better than others in the tests that You have brought before them. O God, have mercy on Your people. Help us to stay far away from those who would encourage us in rebellion and covetousness. Their way is the way of lies and destruction. We want to live and to serve You. Give us hope for those who are weak, for we and our children are very weak. Help us to hold firmly to the truth. We do not want to go down to the pit forever. May our hope be real and heavenly. Make us holy, O Lord, for You are holy. May we remember forever that You have called us to a life of peace, obedience, and joy. Will we join the congregation of the disobedient and cause great trouble for ourselves and others? Give us a strength that comes from outside ourselves, that the plague of rebellion all around us will be stopped.

Numbers 17

Our Father, You have given us many demonstrations that Your Son is to be High Priest forever. Your Word on this matter is clear. The resurrection and ascension of Your Son has set Him far above every pretender to heavenly authority. We should bow before Him forever. He died for our sins so that we would not have to perish in our unrighteousness. There is nothing lacking in His perfect leadership over Your church. There is nothing lacking in His love for us. May He rule His people forever by His Word and Spirit.

Numbers 18

Great God, Your Son has borne our iniquity in His death on the cross. He has made the way for us to worship You. Without His mediation we would surely face Your wrath for all our sins of false and foolish worship. Now we have bold access to You. What a great privilege it is for us to gather in Your name! Yet we forget the wonder of this privilege. We become weary in well-doing. Please forgive us for this foolishness. We have been redeemed by the perfect blood of Your Son. We do not want to profane that blood with a life of continuing sin. Move us in the direction of the perfect obedience of Jesus Christ. Throughout His days of service, You were His portion. He was no man-pleaser. He lived for You in perfect holiness. He fully gave of Himself to You. May we be true imitators of His devotion to You day by day. You already own us, but we freely give ourselves to You again. Move us in whatever direction You see fit. We only ask that You give us hearts that would obey You and love You forever.

Numbers 19

Glorious Lord, the days of Old Testament ceremonies are now long completed. We rejoice in the true answer to the massive problem of sin in the blood of Jesus Christ, our holy Substitute. We know that there is nothing from outside a man that can make him unclean, but the things that come out of our hearts, these things are defiling. Yet even in the case of gross and willful wickedness we are able to come to you through Christ, confess our sins, truly repent, and believe. It is as if the most amazing and cleansing water for impurity has been poured out upon us. By faith in Christ we are clean. Thank you for the assurance that we have of new life by the power of the Holy Spirit.

Numbers 20

Father God, You lead us in pathways of righteousness, but we wander into rough patches of rebellion. Our sin grows in our hearts and is expressed in words and actions of impatience and evil. You are solid and stable. Your Son is a great provision for Your people. Grant special grace to our leaders in the faith as they deal with the strain of loving sinners. Help them not to hate us or mock us, for You have granted to them the privilege of loving the weak. Our Father, we pray that You would protect Your church as we travel through this world. Help us to accept the limits of what You have ordained for our lives. Be with us as we mourn the loss of those who have completed their earthly journey. Surely there is a place of perfect righteousness where You dwell. Surely You have a purpose for the pain among us.

Numbers 21

O God, what shall we do when our enemies seem too strong for us? What will we do when our own sin becomes a more formidable adversary than any outside foe? You have caused Your Son to be the Man of Redemption. We look to Him and live. Throughout our journey You are our constant Protection and our holy Companion. Provide us water day by day for our travels through this dry land. Fill us with Your Spirit and grant us joy as we continue on, though others have already completed their earthly days. Again and again Your people face the frustrations of those who will not live at peace with us. Grant us grace for the day of strife. The hour will surely come when You will judge those who have troubled Your people. Until then, we pray that many will be rescued from the snare of sin that they might know Your grace and forgiveness. We trust You, O God, and we extend forgiveness and love to all.

Numbers 22

Great God, there is no adversary who can sneak up on You. Your enemies flatter themselves. They imagine that they can thwart Your eternal decrees. Their plans seem very serious to us. We become easily frightened. Help us to understand why You laugh from where You sit on high. Surely no weapon formed against You shall prosper. Your plan for Your people is a plan for the greatest blessing. Why do we resist You? Why do we worry? Why do we still imagine that everything that You have granted to us is more ours than it is Yours? It was Yours before You gave us the privilege of serving You in this stewardship. All our possessions are Yours. All our loved ones remain Yours from before the beginning of the world and beyond the end of this age. You can give speech to a donkey, and you can surely bless Your people and protect those we love in the day of evil. When a man falls, surely there must be some plan that is bigger than any moment of weakness and evil. Help us to honor You more than the most powerful men. Help us to remember Your sovereignty and Your wisdom, and to rest in the security and tenderness of Your love.

Numbers 23

Father God, men build their pagan altars and make their burnt offerings, yet their wicked purposes will not prevail. There is no room in heaven for two gods. You are the God who made the heavens and the earth. You sustain all things by Your Word. If You will bless Your church, who will be able to stop Your holy plan? If Your Son blesses Your church, we surely will be blessed. Why is man so evil? O how we long for the age to come when wickedness will be put far away from us! Scatter false prophets and wicked leaders even today. Do not allow them access to Your holy sanctuary. Surely the only way to You is through the one gate of Christ. If any man will not enter through that one Gate, He will never know the fullness of Your benediction. We have entered Your kingdom through Jesus Christ, and we shall be blessed forever.

Numbers 24

Great God and King, will proud enemies continue to come against us? We become weary in Your service, and we begin to yield our hearts to sinful fears. Rescue us, for You are the exalted King over Your people. Scatter Your enemies who hate us, for we are weak, and are ready to fall. Is there a new day of relief for all who call upon Your Name? Grant us some of tomorrow's food today. Feed us with bread from heaven. Grant us the water of the age to come, lest our spirits become spent and we give in to all kinds of sin. Help us to remember that our current troubles are temporary. Your people will be blessed forever and ever. Grant us a bountiful supply of faith and remove from our weary hearts the burden of unbelief.

Numbers 25

Merciful Lord, will we win a great spiritual battle by the strength of Your Word only to fall to obvious fleshly immorality? Father, put our sinful impulses to death within us. Help us to honor the marriage bed, and to flee all unclean desires and actions. You hate immorality. Would we dare to test You on these matters? Protect us even now from wrong thinking and evil speech. Fill our hearts and minds with good things from above, and make us to be true to You in the day of temptation.

Numbers 26

Lord God, we have suffered losses and yet we are here. You have kept us in Your love. We are reminded of the difficulties that we have been through. We still feel Your hand of discipline upon the covenant community, yet You continue to lead us through the wilderness, and prepare us for entrance into the Promised Land. You have granted life to the next generation. They move forward in amazing numbers despite the sins of their fathers. We ask that You would continue to grant us a hope and a future. The land that Your Son has won for Your church in the heavenly Jerusalem is yet before us. Bless us with strength and wisdom that we might continue to serve You over the course of the days that You give to us. We will not make proud boasts concerning our future in this age, for we can only do here what You have given us to do. Be pleased to show forth the greatness of Your love among Your people, and shine the love of Christ through us beyond the borders of Your church.

Numbers 27

Great God, thank You for the women of Your church. They are such great gifts among us, and we are very appreciative for the blessing of their lives. May they know that they are highly valued by Your Son. Cause them to have a deep understanding of the rich inheritance that we have in Christ. Lord God, our sin has brought much trouble upon our lives and has hurt our families and congregations. Please forgive us and heal us. Provide for us godly leaders who will follow You. Grant us ears to hear Your Word as it is preached to us through the Scriptures, so that we might serve You with one voice and one heart.

Numbers 28

Our Father, it is our privilege to bring to You the offering of our lives. We are acceptable to You because of the perfect offering of our Redeemer Jesus Christ. Bless us as we gather in Your presence. We remember His life, and lift up to You our lives together as we worship You. Week by week we continue in Your presence. We gather on the Day of Your Son's resurrection, the first day of the week. From the blessing of this covenant assembly, move us forward to serve You in the week ahead. Father, how can we live without Your presence? Please go with us and lead us day by day, reminding us always that the power of Your Son's perfect offering is with us and is effectual forever.

Numbers 29

Lord God, when will the trumpet sound and the dead in Christ be raised? We know that we cannot have a specific answer, but we ask You because our hearts long for the sound of heavenly rejoicing. Until that day, keep us waiting for You with all hope, and working for You with all diligence. Father, when that trumpet is heard, the Lord Jesus Christ shall return. Surely our every hope is in Your Son. Bring us through that Day of Judgment and let us dwell with You forever. Your Son tented among us in His earthly days. May the great festival of eternal salvation come to Your people at just the right time, that we might tabernacle with Him forever. Our hearts long for His appearing. He will bring with Him all who are resting in Jesus. Grant us Your peace now and forever.

Numbers 30

Father God, Your Son has vowed a vow before You, and He will surely keep His Word. You have delivered Him from death, and He will give You the praise of the nations. You know our weakness, O God. We say we will do things, but have we kept our promises? Have mercy upon us, O Lord. Thank you for the protection that You give to us within our homes and within Your church. May we see the foolishness of promises that are beyond our ability to keep. May we not be caught in sinful or unwise snares because of our impetuous words.

Numbers 31

Almighty God, there are those who have dedicated themselves to hating and killing Your people. Surely You know all of their evil plans. They would trap the righteous and murder the unsuspecting. What will the end of such men be? They have no pretense of faith. They have hated Your Word, and have caused great trouble for Your people. It is beyond us to celebrate today in the destruction of the wicked. Cleanse us from our horrible sin, and bring us into the age to come. Then the righteous will know how to rejoice with You in Your justice. How can we be happy about such things today, when we ourselves deserve death and hell? Thank You for the great mercy which is ours in Christ. Cause many people everywhere to see the wonder of the truth of Christ and be saved. Draw many men to Yourself even among our sworn enemies. Provide for all of the needs of Your church today, and grant to us the heavenly glory that You have prepared for Your people in the life to come.

Numbers 32

Sovereign Lord, You give us everything that we need for life and holiness. We know that there is much spiritual warfare ahead of Your church. We would not shrink from that battle. Yet we long for a place of safety and happiness now. If we are to be on the front lines of trouble in this age, grant us astounding resources of faith, hope, and love by Your Holy Spirit. If we cannot take that kind of strain, move us to safer territory according to Your plan. It is for You to decide whether we go forth in the most difficult mission fields, or serve Your church in the most pleasant place of service. You know us, and You know what the battle is like on every front in our war against sin. What you want to do with us is up to You. Only You have the wisdom to unfold before Your church Your special acts of providence. We will trust You and follow Your commands faithfully. There is so much ahead of us to do. We must not give up. Grant us new strength, and needed rest, that we might live to fight another day.

Numbers 33

Lord God, in Jesus Christ our Passover Lamb we have a new life and a new hope. We are moving toward a destination. Our way is secure in Your grace. Throughout this journey we need the provision of Your Spirit. Those going through the desert need water; we must have Your Spirit day by day. Please send forth this blessing continually for Your church. By Him Your Word is opened up to our hearts. Through the Spirit we rejoice in the life and death of Jesus, our High Priest. Help us to see the wonder of Your providence and the promise of our entrance into our heavenly home. Your Son has gone before us. He has provided a safe way for us through life, and a holy habitation for Your people. We long to be with Him even now, and we are assured that He will be with us forever.

Numbers 34

Father God, any inheritance that we have has surely come to us by Your Word and from Your hand. We long to explore the land that Christ has won for us. He has assured us that He went to prepare a place for us, that where He is we also shall be. We want to see this new land, where even now we somehow dwell in our Redeemer. Move us day by day further toward the rising of the sun in that great place. Our King will rule over us there forever, and He will divide for us the inheritance among His people. All that will be granted to us on that day shall come by grace alone through the merit and mediation of Your Son Jesus Christ.

Numbers 35

Our Father, we should be serving You continually as a priesthood of believers. One day we will be as holy Levites, fully dedicated to Your worship and service in the sanctuary above. We look forward to the work that You have for us. May we dwell in that great city of refuge even now. We know what we deserve. We have violated Your holy law. Not only have we been greatly disobedient as a result of weakness, or in some way that was unintended, we also have the stain of high-handed, intentional sin. Nonetheless, we have full forgiveness because of the death of Jesus Christ for us. The avenger of blood has been stopped that we might live, for Christ has faced the fullness of Your wrath so that we will live and serve You forever. A ransom has finally come for us. Full justice has been accomplished, and an atonement has been provided. This could never have happened according to the provisions of the Law of Moses. Such a full salvation could only come through Your promise, and by the work of our divine Substitute, the Lord Jesus Christ. The fullness of Your grace and truth is ours in Him.

Numbers 36

Lord God, we live for the day of the fullness of Your Kingdom, but we must continue here below until that new day dawns. You have made provision for us in this world in ways appropriate for the present age. You know all about the reality of misery and death that we face here now. You grant us much hope and many consolations during our time of trouble. You also provide us with everything that we need in order to serve You faithfully. You call us Your beloved children. We are grateful. Keep us working for You while we wait for that new day of the fulfillment of all Your great promises.

Deuteronomy

Deuteronomy 1

Great God and Father of our Lord Jesus Christ, You are a covenant-making and a covenant-keeping God. Through Moses You gave to Your people Your holy Law. You redeemed them out of bondage and gave to them the land that You promised to Abraham, Isaac, and Jacob. Father, even our most wise and experienced men have erred badly, for men lack spiritual discernment. Have mercy on us or we will lose heart and disobey Your Word again and again. You rescued Your people from the land of bondage and instructed them to take the new land that You were giving to them. But Your people would not believe You. Even their appointed rulers did not obey. They led Your people in unbelief. Many died because of this faithlessness. Will we be imitators of their sin and live even now in the fear of men? Will we act like those who dream that they can only win the blessings of Your provision by our own strength? Hear us, O God, for we need to serve You now with true faith.

Deuteronomy 2

Great God, You have a great purpose for Your people, but we do not understand Your ways. Nonetheless, why should we complain? The journey that You have determined is according to Your design. The provision for this journey is also from Your hand. Each day has enough trouble of its own, and we should do what our hand finds for us to do for You today. We must serve You as You strictly direct us. We will search Your Word carefully to see what You command. We will also flee from those things that You have forbidden. Be pleased to lead us step by step in ways that we could never discern from our own study, observation, and consideration. The secret things are Yours, but we can seek You, and we will trust You. You can frustrate the plans of those enemies seen and unseen who may secretly stand against us. All that we have been given today we receive from Your hand, and we trust You for tomorrow.

Deuteronomy 3

Great Lord of Providence, You grant us victory over enemies who come against us. Even when we seem to lose, surely we do not see things as we ought. You who have given Your Son for our salvation will surely give us all things for the fulfillment of Your perfect plan. There are frightening adversaries who threaten Your people. They are powerful and crafty, but they are no match for You. You know when to give us land and provisions, and when to move us forward with few possessions. Surely You will give us rest together with all our brothers at just the right time. Your Son came to do battle for us. During His earthly days, when He taught and healed, He had no place to call His own and nowhere to lay His head. Yet He knew something of the fullness of the land that You promise us, and He moved forward without sin according to Your perfect plan. He trusted You even through the cross. We will trust You now by Your grace.

Deuteronomy 4

Lord God Almighty, we will listen to Your commandments and follow them as a rule of life. We will not take anything away from Your commands or add anything to them. Idolatry is not the way of life for us. Christ has won for us the land of resurrection. This land is far superior to any of the nations of men. Your Son is the best of all rulers. Your statutes are better than those of any people, and Your Son has kept these for us. The people of the Old Testament lost the land of Israel and were sent into exile because of their sinful corruptions. Christ was born under the Law, and even became a curse for us. What Israel could not do, Jesus has done. Grant us strength in prayer and service that we might take possession of the Kingdom even now. Lord we seek You with all our heart and soul. You are a merciful God, and You will never abandon those for whom Christ shed His blood. There is no God like You. Who but You could ever have rescued us out of the bondage of sin and misery? Blessed be Your Name for Your marvelous works of redemption. There were strong enemies against us, but You are God in heaven above and on the earth below. You have brought us to the city of salvation, and we are safe in our Redeemer. We move forward even now to take possession of all that You are granting to us by Your grace.

Deuteronomy 5

Our Father, there is something so very right about Your Law. We receive even now the testimony of Your goodness that comes from this Word. You are the Lawgiver of this great Law. We will have no other gods but You. We will not worship idols. We will honor Your Name. We will rest in Your Son and remember the Day of Resurrection. We will obey all lawful authority. We will not murder. We will turn away from every unclean impulse. We will not steal. We will be honest in all things. We will not covet what belongs to another, for You have supplied for us so bountifully in the gift of Your Son. Forgive us for our many sins. Even now we turn away from every wicked thought, word, and action. Speak to us again of the abundant pardon that is ours in Christ, and grant us grace for holy living. May we have the mind of Christ in us so that we will keep Your Law as a way of life. Where we have failed, Your Son has kept every one of Your commandments in fullest measure. Through faith in Him we have been credited with all of His bountiful obedience. What a treasure is now in our account! We thank You for Your mercy.

Deuteronomy 6

Almighty God, we know that a true fear of You is the beginning of wisdom. We need that holy reverence, and we need to hear Your Word. Help us to love You fully with everything that we have. Grant us diligence in training up our children in the way that You have spoken. Help us to teach them of Your marvelous grace. What good thing do we have that has not come to us as a gift from Your hand? We will be diligent about the life of faith that You have given to Your people. There is no doubt that we were once slaves of sin, but You have won an amazing battle against sin and death on our behalf. Now we have been given the kingdom of heaven through faith in Your Son.

Deuteronomy 7

Father God, we belong to You. You have fought against many enemies for our sake. These adversaries were too strong for us, but You have been wonderfully victorious in the death and resurrection of Jesus Christ. We could never have won heaven by our obedience, for we have the stain of Adam's sin. Even more than this fatal wound, we have violated Your Law through our actions and our inaction, through our words and our silence, through our thoughts and our thoughtlessness. Where is the commandment that we have kept? Where is the law that we have not broken in the depths of our hearts? Your Son has accomplished all the obedience necessary for our salvation. We have in Him a new holy representative. In Him we are victorious. Yet there is a warfare that You have ordained for Your church. You have granted to us strength by Your Word and Spirit so that we may fight the good fight. Lead us in continued assaults of Christ-like love. We will not follow the way of the world, the flesh, and the devil. We will not hate You, O God. We will love You. You are the Source of our holy armor. We hate all idolatry and wickedness. We love Your grace and truth. Grant us wisdom to guard our homes and our lives. Cleanse us from all that is offensive to You. Strengthen us by Your Spirit, and teach us to walk in the way of love.

Deuteronomy 8

Great God, only You could have brought the descendants of Jacob into the Promised Land. We have been given an even better possession through faith in Your Son. This we have learned from Your Word, the necessary food for our souls. We were once dead in our sins, but we have been made alive in Your Son. Feed us with the Bread from heaven, that we might hear His voice and believe. You are able to take us through the wilderness of this age. You are bringing us into a very good land. We long to walk in that place. We bless You for Your wonderful promises. Help us to believe and to live. Grant to us a living hope through the resurrection of Jesus Christ. Send forth the Water of Your Holy Spirit from the great Rock of our Salvation. We will not perish with the nations of the world. We will live.

Deuteronomy 9

God of our Fathers, the enemies who were against us were too strong for us. We could not have defeated them. It is not because of our righteousness that we now have been granted the kingdom of heaven. It is because of the righteousness of Your Son that we are partakers of heavenly blessings. If we had to stand before You in our own strength, the testimony of our ugly life of sin would be strongly against us. Would we bring to You our proud idolatry and immorality and suppose that You would receive it as an acceptable offering? We are so far from the necessary obedience that would merit the gift of the kingdom! Yet Your Son has provided this merit for us, and He is our great Substitute. Even now He intercedes for us. Destroy any remaining sin that infects us. Send Your Son quickly with the final consummation of His great kingdom. But we must wait and be ready. Until that day comes, preserve us, for we are Your people.

Deuteronomy 10

Lord God, when we fall in grievous sin, pick us up again by Your power and grace. Please help us to rediscover the blessings of faith and repentance, and grant to us a hope and a future. Help us to know that our High Priest is perfectly holy and undefiled. Help us to remember that He is on our side. To You belong the heavens, even the highest heavens. You are great and mighty. We turn our hearts again toward You. We shall fear You and hold fast to You, for You have chosen us by Your grace.

Deuteronomy 11

Lord God, we love You, and we will follow You. We consider Your discipline, and the distinction that You made between Your people and their enemies. We consider the way that You judge with righteousness. Therefore we commit to a full obedience to Your holy ways. Help us, O God! We will love You and serve You. We know that You will always care for us, for we are Your people. Father, when You bless us so bountifully, will we forget the Source of every good gift? Will we wander from You, as if we were the fountain of our own happiness and prosperity? Please protect us from this foolishness and ingratitude. Your people of old were given the clarity of a blessing and a curse. They were promised a land if they obeyed You. We have the fullness of blessing granted to us through the grace of our Lord Jesus Christ. Surely we could never have won a secure blessing through the Law. Thank You for Your abundant mercy and for the glory of the gospel.

Deuteronomy 12

Our Father, we have become a chosen temple in Christ. We turn away from all false places of idolatrous worship. We will not worship You according to the dictates of our own hearts. We will hear Your commandments and worship You in the way that You direct us according to Your Word. We will not live as those who have no king, for Your Son is King over His church. We rejoice before You day by day. You have chosen Your Son as the Head of a holy body. We are the body that He has sanctified through His blood and righteousness. Grant that we will always love Your church as an expression of our love for our King. He poured out His life as a holy offering for our sake. Through His good work we will always be accepted in Your sight. Protect us from false systems of religion that would only move us away from You.

Deuteronomy 13

Lord God of Hosts, Your Son is the true and final Prophet for Your people. In every day there are false prophets and dreamers who would turn Your people from the way of true obedience. Even among Your church there are those who would suggest that the way of false worship and sin is the true path of life and happiness. Help us to take every thought captive so that we will not be led astray by our own sinful impulses. One day all wickedness will be put far away from us. Teach us how to live with love and righteousness in the present age, as we wait for the glorious appearing of Your holy Son.

Deuteronomy 14

Our Father, why would we ever find the way of strange worship attractive? Help us to remember that we have been made clean only through the blood of the Lamb, Jesus Christ. The day of clean and unclean food has come to an end in Him. You have even cleansed all the people of the world, that we might bring the message of Christ everywhere. Help us to see our holiness in Him alone. He is the fullness of our joy and our all in all. We give back to You a portion of what You have given to us, but surely You have purchased us fully. We are entirely Yours. Take us and use us for Your good purpose and pleasure, for You have redeemed us from sin and death, and have granted us eternal life.

Deuteronomy 15

Lord God, we look for the fulfillment of the day of release. We know that there is nothing lacking in the atonement that Your Son has accomplished for us. Nonetheless, we do not yet fully see and experience all of the benefits of that perfect sacrifice. We do have everything in Christ. We even enjoy all blessings by faith. Yet one day our faith shall be sight. The day of poverty and oppression will be gone. Our glorious freedom will be experienced like a wonderful breath of sweet heavenly air. Fill our hearts with the victory of holiness even now, for we are Your children.

Deuteronomy 16

Great God, You have removed from us all sin through Christ. Why should we keep on adding the bad leaven of wickedness into our thoughts, words, and actions? Cause us to reflect deeply upon the cross of Christ. Through His blood the danger of condemnation has been removed far from us. He is the firstfruits of the resurrection. We are His harvest through Your Word and Spirit. We are being gathered together as Your people. We long for the fullness of Your Kingdom, that we might dwell in Your presence forever in the glory of Your great provision for Your entire family. In that day, there will be no more sin among Your loved ones. We turn away from sin even now with an eager anticipation of the life to come.

Deuteronomy 17

Father God, there was absolutely no blemish in the offering of Christ for our sake. He had no abomination in His sinless heart. Yet He was put to death for us. Our evil was purged through the death of this perfect Substitute. He is our Priest forever. He has declared to us Your holy will. We should follow His commandments forever. Please continue to forgive us, for we have sinned against You. Your Son is also our great King. He is not a king like those of the nations. He does not need anything from us, for all things are His. Yet in His gracious love, He showers us with many royal blessings. His Kingdom is forever.

Deuteronomy 18

Father God, we praise You that we have a better Priest than all of the priests that descended from Aaron. We have a better system of access to You than the ways of old. As great as it was to serve You in Your tabernacle, we now have a Great High Priest who has gone beyond the veil into the true Holy of Holies. We thank You also for our great Prophet. He is superior to all the other servants who came in Your Name. Every Word that He has spoken has either already happened or will surely come to pass, for all of Your promises are Yes and Amen in Jesus Christ our Lord. Through this great Prophet and Priest we hear Your Word day by day, and bring You true worship forever.

Deuteronomy 19

Sovereign Lord, You have granted us a City of Refuge in Jesus Christ. Here we have an answer of true security and peace. Because of Him, we have been given an amazing inheritance. Father, is there a way that we can see this inheritance today? Is there a way to walk around that place even now? We live in a world of murder and strife. There are false witnesses and covetous trouble-makers even among Your church. We are tired of sin and misery, O Lord. Grant to us more life in Christ. There is something better in Him than even the most enlightened systems of justice that this world could ever offer, something better than even the most well-ordered church court. There is a place of abundant mercy secured by His blood.

Deuteronomy 20

Lord of Hosts, You were with Your people of old in their battles, and You are with us now. Take away our fear and panic. Grant us relief from entangling distractions. As much as it would depend upon us, we would be at peace with the world. You must lead us in this battle of love. There is a challenging war raging within our souls even now. Please grant to us the strength to take every thought captive, so that we might serve You with a greater purity of heart and life.

Deuteronomy 21

Father God, the curse of death is all around us. Even our best efforts at justice reveal a world that we cannot completely understand. When a life has been taken, who is the guilty murderer? We do not always know. Father, please give us hope and joy as we travel through this land of trouble. You have purchased us through the blood of Your Son. We are redeemed, yet we live now in a world of grief and pain. Some children are treated with very little love. Some parents are shown much rebellion and disrespect. What is the answer for us? Your Son was put upon the tree, and by His death, our guilt and shame have been removed, and we have a living hope.

Deuteronomy 22

Lord God, grant to us hearts that are willing to care for our brothers. Law cannot save us. The rules of former days have been fulfilled in Christ, Your holy Son. We still need law, but we need something much more. We wander and must be rescued. We must be carried home like injured children. There is yet evil in our midst. We need practical help from the leaders and teachers that You have given to us. What will we do when our teachers are themselves overwhelmed by evil or sorrow? We need something more than rules. We need Your Holy Spirit. He is the Guarantee of a day of the fullest righteousness and joy. All our disappointment and weariness will one day be lifted from our broken hearts, and we will be alive again.

Deuteronomy 23

Our Father, is there to be another generation? Is there hope on this earth for a future? We want peace. We want prosperity. We need help. There is trouble everywhere. Why has this evil come upon us? We thought that we were serving You. We knew that we were sinners, but our trust was in Your Son Jesus Christ. Forgive us, O Lord, we have forgotten that this age is not the end of Your plans for us. Grant us patience and perseverance beyond a time of trouble. Teach us how a man can consider it pure joy when He faces the most serious difficulties. Teach us how to move from self-centered disappointment to a more godly grief. Teach us the mystery of hope. Grant us a taste of eternity again, for we long for Your embrace.

Deuteronomy 24

Lord God, we need help in our marriages. You have given us a wonderful gift when one man and one woman are brought together forever as husband and wife. Forgive us when we bring trouble upon ourselves by our sin. We are weak, O Lord. We may lack food, shelter, and companionship. We are troubled by the sins of those we love. We are troubled by our own sins. Teach us the wisdom of living well in a world that is under Your wrath and curse. You have redeemed us from the bondage of iniquity. Teach us to walk in the freedom that is ours in Christ.

Deuteronomy 25

Lord God, You love justice and righteousness. You love the way of right discipline. Yet what is the justice that we deserve? We cannot stand the punishment that would rightly be ours, for our offense is against You. Will our names be removed from Your book of life? Thank You for the mercy that is ours in Christ. You love life, and You keep a people for yourself even in this age of destruction. What a fearful thing it is for the names of Your enemies to be blotted out from under heaven. This is not our destiny, for Your Son has suffered in our place, and has secured for us all the blessings of eternal life.

Deuteronomy 26

Father, You give us great gifts of food and shelter. You care for our every need. We confess our faith in You in the midst of Your assembly. We were in the greatest distress. We cried out to You and You delivered us. You Yourself are the best provision for us. It is our privilege to be generous to those who are in trouble and to provide for the building up of Your people. We promise to be faithful with the gifts that You have given to us. Please look down upon Your children from heaven and build up Your church in righteousness and peace. We will listen to Your voice. We will follow Jesus Christ. Teach us to be devoted to You forever.

Deuteronomy 27

Lord God, we could never bear to face the curse of the Covenant of Works. That covenant, made with Adam and His posterity, required perfect and perpetual obedience. Through that Covenant of Works we deserve death, both in body and soul. You have kindly made us aware of the truth that we could never have peace with You through law. Especially through the Law of Moses and through the exile of Israel, we see that we will only receive the curse of any covenantal arrangement based on obedience to law. We add our "Amen" to the plain facts of both the goodness of Your Law and the wretchedness of our disobedience, but we also joyfully celebrate the fact that Your Son has obeyed Your Law for us. He has taken the curse that we deserved.

Deuteronomy 28

Our God and Father, you set before Your people long ago such wonderful blessings in Israel if they would only obey Your Word. You would have given them all that they needed to eat. You would have blessed them with many descendants, and would have given them great fruitfulness and abundance. You would have caused their enemies to flee and would have granted them great security in the land of their inheritance. We know the facts of what happened. They did not obey, and they brought upon themselves a horrible and destructive curse. Who could bear such devastating judgments? Lord, why will we not respond to Your discipline? Why are we so committed to sin? Do we want to see horrible troubles come upon our families and Your church? Thank You for the life that You granted to Israel beyond the curse of the Law. Thank You that You kept a remnant even through exile. Thank You especially that You did not abandon Your plan to send a Redeemer who was the Seed of that remnant. He has taken horrible curses for us, though there was no sin in Him. Now we shall serve you in gladness forever. Now we have a secure hope beyond the sadness and misery of this world of sin. Father, help us by Your Spirit to trust You even in the worst tribulation. Make us faithful to the end, though much trouble may come upon us and our children. Surely You have a great plan beyond the day of the most intense trial. Gather us to Your heavenly temple where we will dwell with You forever. Cut short the sufferings of this current age, for You know that we could never endure the full burden of the trouble that we deserve.

Deuteronomy 29

Our Father, gather Your people together week by week for the celebration of covenant renewal. Help us to remember the grace of our Lord Jesus Christ. Help us to hear the word of promise. Help us to grasp the fact of our sin, but help us especially to grasp the fact of Your promise. We must not turn away from You in our hearts. We must not have a root of bitterness in our souls. We must not worship the idols of the world. There is no hope for us in those false gods. Be merciful to us forever because of the faithfulness of Jesus Christ. He never turned against You. He trusted You and obeyed You completely. He heard the Word that You revealed, and He did all the words of Your Law. Surely this was not for His own sake. He did not come to earth to save Himself. He is God forever, together with You and with the Holy Spirit. He came for us, and He has accomplished our redemption.

Deuteronomy 30

Lord God, is there a way back home when we have wandered so far from You? You are able to gather us back from the most distant land. Teach us to return to You. Teach us to yield our whole lives to You, and to obey You together with our children. You have placed Your Word in our hearts through the preaching of the gospel. We have been made alive. We believe You and follow Your Son. We see plainly before us both blessing and curse. We choose life through Christ, and we rejoice again in Him. Bring us home, O God! Bring us home!

Deuteronomy 31

O Lord of Hosts, You have given to us a perfect Mediator of the Covenant in our Joshua, Jesus Christ. He alone can bring us into the land of heavenly blessing. This One Mediator will never leave us nor forsake us. Please let us hear again the Word of the Scriptures as those who are destined to live with You forever. Your Son lives even now to intercede for us. He once lived and died, but now He lives forevermore. There could be no hope for us in ourselves, even in our best intentions and in our moments of highest and fullest obedience. There is a witness against us in Adam's sin. There is a witness against us in our days before we surrendered to You. Forgive us Lord, but worst of all, there is a witness against us even from our lives after we came to see Your Son as King, even after we had tasted of many heavenly blessings. Is there yet hope for a blasphemer and a persecutor of the church? Blessed be Your Name, for we have been kept by Your grace. We return to You again with great thanksgiving.

Deuteronomy 32

Lord God Almighty, the heavens and earth are witnesses of Your glory and Your greatness. Your justice is perfect, but we have sinned against You. There is a better way for us, the way of heartfelt shame in the face of such abounding blessing. There is a way that is wonderful in gratitude. We consider Your power and the greatness of Your gifts to our fathers. How could it be that we would forsake You and provoke You to anger? Thank You for Your Son's faithfulness and for the wonder of Your plan of grace, even for the Gentiles. Our Father, we pray that You would use this extravagant gift to make many jealous who were marked with the sign of Your covenant in earlier days. Call many back to Your mercy and goodness. Vindicate Your people. Even more, vindicate the glory of Your Name and the power of Your salvation. There is no other God but You. Who can survive if You come in judgment? Surely there is more cause for rejoicing still, for there are yet those who are being drawn near to You through Jesus Christ. May Your church hear Your Word, not as some empty sound with no meaning, but as the very Word of life and our only hope. Father God, even Your servant Moses sinned against You, but with You there is abundant forgiveness.

Deuteronomy 33

Father God, please speak powerful words of blessing upon Your church day by day. You know all things, and You have chosen to reveal many wonderful things to us. Teach us to hear Your great promises with faith. Surround us with Your love and grant to us many good gifts of the earth and its fullness. Give to us even the blessings of heaven, for we have been made alive by Your Spirit. Your Son, the greatest descendant of Judah, is our King. He will reign forever and ever. He has come to His people even beyond the borders of Israel. Your plan is good. Surely You will win the battle against any enemy who would dare to challenge You.

Deuteronomy 34

Glorious God Almighty, the day of each man's death approaches. Beyond this day is the coming of all of Your good decrees for life. Grant us a glimpse each day of the age to come. In light of that new vision, teach us to live in the sure hope of the coming age. Fill us with Your heavenly Spirit, and use us for Your good purposes even in the land where we now live. We thank You for Your holy Law that came through Moses. Even more than this, we thank You that grace and truth have come to us through Your Son Jesus Christ.

Joshua

Joshua 1

Father God, help us to see the greatness of our leader Jesus, our new Joshua. No man is able to stand before Him and resist Him. He will lead us into the Promised Land. He will speak to us through Your Word. He is with us wherever we go. We will take possession of the land that You are giving us to possess. Make us to be men of valor as we follow the Lord Jesus Christ. Here we have One who is better than Moses. We will obey Him in all that He has commanded us. Make us strong and courageous in the face of every obstacle by Your wonderful grace.

Joshua 2

Lord God, You are the Protector of Your people. By many a Rahab You are well able to hide those who have been sent out in Your Name. You placed surprising grace within her, and she became a woman of faith. She rightly considered the greatness of Your acts of redemption. You alone are the Lord God Almighty. Through Your Son Jesus, You have delivered our lives from death. Grant us hope again in Him. We will follow Your every instruction. You have given us signs of redemption through baptism and communion. May we believe You as You speak to us through Your Word. Dangerous enemies would want to stop You and Your church, but You will rescue us and accomplish all Your holy will.

Joshua 3

Sovereign Leader, You are God. We follow You and the ark of Your presence. You have appointed One great High Priest to lead us forward. We will listen to His Word, and will follow this King and Head of the Church. Your tribes crossed over the Jordan on dry land. This was a great miracle, and a sign that they were on a holy mission. You gave them a wonderful victory. Father, what is the mission ahead of us in our day? Please speak to us and lead us.

Joshua 4

Lord of the Nations, You have loved Your people with an everlasting love. When You brought the tribes of Israel across the Jordon, You instructed them to build a memorial of twelve stones from the midst of the Jordon, to be a sign for the people forever. Help us to remember Your holy works of powerful deliverance. We have no ark to carry, no holy garments, and no priests to offer sacrificial animals. Yet we have One great High Priest who has offered up Himself as a sacrifice, and in Him we are all priests by faith. We have together become Your ark, for we are the temple of Your Holy Spirit. May Your church throughout the nations be a living sacrifice and a holy reminder forever, with Your Son Jesus as our solid Cornerstone.

Joshua 5

Father God, when the world hears about Your power and Your love for Your people, there is something of a fear that passes over the hearts of many. We too need to fear You, but we also love You as our Father. We must obey Your voice. We want to live with You in the land flowing with milk and honey. Circumcise our hearts and roll away the reproach of sin far from us through the cross of our Redeemer. May we remember that Christ, our Passover lamb, is our righteousness. We follow this one great Commander of Your army, O Lord, and we move forward on holy ground.

Joshua 6

Great God, You gave Jericho into the hand of Joshua, and You have given all lands and all power and authority to our new Joshua, Your Son Jesus. The walls of Jericho seemed to be an insurmountable obstacle to Your conquest of the land. Yet those walls would fall at Your command and through the ministry of the people under the command of Your servant. May we move forward at the order of Your great Son Jesus. May we be an army of love and service. May no wall be able to hold back Your church, and may those who hear Your voice and turn to You be saved from the judgment that is coming upon the world. One day, the world will be handed over to Your righteous wrath, but there will be a new heavens and a new earth by Your command. We long to be in the number of Your Israel when Your Son returns for His bride, for there is no future left for us in the city of destruction.

Joshua 7

Strong Deliverer, You have brought down the walls of Jericho. Will You not also defeat the enemy within our hearts, that indwelling sin that so quickly besets us? We have brought great trouble upon ourselves by our transgression of Your commandments. We have coveted what was devoted to destruction. A wedge of gold and a Babylonian garment have been more precious to our depraved flesh than the incomparable glories of Your great promises. Restrain our wickedness, O Lord, lest more trouble come upon our homes. We cannot bear Your wrath. Remember the full atonement that we have through the blood of Jesus. We have sinned against You. Thank you for the forgiveness that is ours through our Redeemer. He has faced the verdict that was against us. Though we have surely brought trouble upon ourselves through our covetousness and evil, You have turned from Your burning anger because of the sacrifice of Jesus, our Lord.

Joshua 8

Mighty God, we serve You with gladness in our day, because You have given us a great victory over a powerful adversary. We are ready for battle, O Lord. Give us wisdom and love. Give us the city, O God. We will be satisfied with nothing less than a victory in the battle before us. Help us to estimate the struggle rightly. Let us turn to You in prayer. Grant to us holy desires worthy of Your Name. May many be drawn away from wicked affections, and may they be surprised by Your gospel of grace, and the beauty of our Leader, the Lord Jesus Christ. Overwhelm the arguments of wickedness with the truth of Your glory. Give us eyes to see Your decisive victory for us, and grant to us a great day of faith. We thank You for the offering of Your Son, through whom we have peace with You. We hear Your word, and we will follow You. Bless us and our families because of Christ, we pray.

Joshua 9

Father, You have given us a mission that is uncompromising, but we are easily deceived. Those who would come into Your church through some other way than through the gate which is Christ may speak with smooth and persuasive words, distracting us from the tasks before us. Even still, we trust Your wisdom and strength. You are able to overrule our weakness. We should always seek Your counsel in the mission You have given us, but what will we do on that day when we have followed our own understanding? Bring about some good result for the glory of Your Name despite our foolishness and the lies of our enemies. Cause even impure impulses and actions to somehow yield praise for You and deliverance for men because of Your powerful electing love.

Joshua 10

O Lord of Righteousness, You have a plan for Your Jerusalem which has been accomplished at the cost of a great battle. Your Son's blood was shed for us, and a victory was secured for Your eternal city of peace. Long ago the sun in the sky stood still at the word of Your servant Joshua. Through this sign You demonstrated Your favor upon Your servants in the day of their warfare. Yet greater than this, the cross of Your Son Jesus is a sign of victorious love. He has fought for us and has defeated dangerous enemies. The demonic host that would have ruled over us has been consigned to defeat. Your Son has put His feet on the neck of all of our foes, through His own death on the cross. By this great battle, we have strength for the contest ahead of us. Your victory, O Lord God, is complete and glorious.

Joshua 11

God of Our Fathers, the battle before us seems substantial, and we wonder whether we have the strength to keep on going. Take away our fear, and help us to believe Your Word that there is a great tomorrow coming. In that great tomorrow the enemy will be captured and devoted to destruction. That day will be better than any other moment of victory that we have enjoyed in this past. Take all that is Yours, Lord Jesus. Grant to us help, and strengthen us for the challenges that are before us. Cut off enemies that would be too strong for us. Secure our promised inheritance and give us rest from war soon, lest we faint with weariness in our hearts, and die.

Joshua 12

Our Lord and King, there are many kings in this world, and they all have their territories and their scope of authority. We have You as our King. There is none better than You. No king is wiser, more powerful, or more devoted to His people. We will not turn to these lesser kings. We will follow Your Son, the true King of Heaven, who together with You and Your Holy Spirit is one God forever. We see the riches and armies of other men, but no one can compare with You, O Lord.

Joshua 13

Eternal Father, there remains yet much for Your church to do. You have told us that the gospel must be preached throughout all the earth, and only then will Your Son return. We who seek Him and long for the fulfillment of all things have a duty before us. Together with Your church throughout the world, we must be diligent to do the work that You have assigned to us. We must preach and teach. We must worship You, and extend Your worship to places where Your Name is not clearly proclaimed. We long for Your strength in battle, for we face devious enemies, like Balaam, who would have destroyed Your people with the filthy deception of immorality. We need You now. Fight for us, O Lord. We are the inheritance of Your Son Jesus, and we call upon Your Name.

Joshua 14

God of Hope, we thank You for our promised inheritance in the ultimate land of the living. We would take possession of all that You have for us. Give us the courage of Caleb when he expressed His confidence in battle even as an older man. Grant us necessary resources of strength for spiritual warfare and for faithful Christian living. Give us a blessed expectation, so that we will follow You where You lead, O Lord God of Israel.

Joshua 15

God of Justice, You know the right allotment of gifts for Your people. Any good claim that we might make upon Your justice is centered entirely in Christ, our representative. If we were to stand before You without the excellence of His mediation, there could be no inheritance for us in the land. Because of His willing service and love, we now have the justice that was due Him for His great obedience, and He has taken the justice due to us for our ungodliness. Now we have a delightful future, and many good gifts, even in this land of sorrow. We have wives, children, water, food, and useful work. Give us joy for the mission You have for us day by day, knowing that we live and serve at Your holy pleasure. Well in advance of our lives, You have prepared for us good things to do that we should walk in them. You have made cities and villages for us where we may live, love, and serve. How happy is the man who trusts in You! Help us to figure out our lives and our missions. Send angels to keep the adversary at bay in the battlefield of our minds. Take full possession of us, for we are Yours.

Joshua 16

Lord of the Church, we have brothers and sisters everywhere. We are not all the same, but we are all one body in Christ. May we serve You together with joy. Help us to avoid unnecessary criticism and discouragement within this family. There is one battle before us, and You are granting us the strength together for the victory of love.

Joshua 17

Father God, the generations move forward. The day of fathers comes to an end, and sons and daughters move ahead with the strength that You supply. Make us diligent in the tasks that You have passed on to us from earlier generations of faithful men and women. Your Son forever lives to intercede for us. Even those whose bodies rest in the grave, if they are in Your Son, are yet alive in Him. Use all Your saints for the praise of Your glorious grace. The adversaries who stand against Your church may seem to be too strong for us with their chariots of iron, but we have the strength of men and angels in Your Son Jesus Christ, who rose from the dead.

Joshua 18

Lord, the work yet ahead of us is substantial. How long will we excuse ourselves from the tasks that we have been commanded to perform? We would settle into comfortable homes, and forget that we are to seek first Your Kingdom. So few of Your servants seem to be on pilgrimage to a better land. We have become satisfied in the comforts of the flesh and the things of the world. Have we utterly forgotten Your Son? Awake Your church, O God! There is a world that is still waiting for the gospel. There are children yet to be born. Will there be no new generation for Your people because of our unwillingness to serve?

Joshua 19

Father God, You have not abandoned Your plans. For this we are very grateful. You announce the mission that is ours to perform. It seems too large for us, so You invite us to ask You, that You might provide others to gather in the harvest, for the yield that You have planned is abundant. There is hope for the future because of Your covenant faithfulness. There should be no confusion concerning the boundaries of Your church today. No nations can claim the right to keep the message of the gospel of Jesus Christ out of their lands, for they exist at His pleasure. All power and authority has been given to Your Son. Every tribe and clan, every nation and people group must hear Your Word. Why do we set out on strange new missions, when we have not taken possession of the territory You have given to us? You will not let us forget Your Word and Your call upon our lives. You will raise up faithful workers and shepherds for the glory of Your name, and You will gather Your flock.

Joshua 20

God of Mercy, is there a place of refuge for the willful sinner? Father, we understand that in former days You had a city for the man guilty of manslaughter, but is there any place of hope for the murderer who repents? We thank You that Christ has become our place of refuge, for He gave His life for the ungodly.

Joshua 21

Lord God, You own all things, and everything that we have is a gift from Your hand. Your Son has given us those who would be devoted to the work of preaching and teaching, so that the worship of Your church would be undertaken with decency, order, passion, and excellence. Thank you for the gift of people who teach, as well as the gift of elders and deacons for the orderly care of Your Kingdom. It is a joy to see Your work move forward as we serve together. We thank you for the privilege of supporting those who are called to these positions of trust and service. You are the One who provides homes and lands for those who are devoted to Your church. All of Your good promises shall surely come to pass, and Your Kingdom shall be blessed.

Joshua 22

Sovereign Lord, make us careful to keep the charge that Your Son has given to us. May we love You, and be kind to one another. Help us to run the race that You have marked out for us to the end. Let us look not only to our own interests, but also to the interests of others. We have a family connection with one another. Give us wisdom to understand how we can rightly care for others in the body of Christ. Give us courage to speak when we should speak, and to hold our peace when there is nothing that we can say. You are the Mighty One. You are the Lord. Teach us to trust You and to love one another. Help us to remember what we have in common with all who proclaim the Name of Your Son. Our portion is in You. Far be it from us to rebel against You and to unjustly turn against our brothers in Christ. May all who love You with an undying love rejoice in the Word of truth.

Joshua 23

Father God, as the day of our fathers has come to an end, our day to leave this place will also come. Let us be able to honestly confess that we have run the race that You have given us to run. Make us cleave to Your Son, for our Savior fights for us in every good battle. Each of us will one day go the way of all the earth. Every good promise and solemn warning from Your mouth is true and worthy of our meditation and obedience.

Joshua 24

O Lord Our God, we are so very weak, though we may seem strong to others. How shall we stand in an age of spiritual weakness? Be our strength. Our father Abraham was taken from the world of idolatry beyond the river. The land of Canaan was also filled with false gods. How can we return to the gods of paganism? Teach us how to serve You with integrity. We have no realistic hope that we will fulfill Your Law. You are a holy god. It is right for us to serve You in truth. Our consciences bear witness against us. Nonetheless our acceptance in Your sight has come through the perfect righteousness of Jesus Christ. He is our only hope. When our days are over, we will yet find peace in Him, and we will hope in the promise of the resurrection, for our Lord is risen.

Judges

Judges 1
God of Our Fathers, from Judah You gave the best of all leaders. He has won the battle for us against an overwhelming foe. You repay Your enemies according to their evil, but You have made a way for us to live in the Promised Land. We have a place of blessing far better than Canaan. We have discovered streams of living water in Jesus Christ, and we have been refreshed. Fill us with Your Spirit, and lead us on in the work that You have for us. Your people of old did not finish their work. Many of the Canaanites were not driven out of the land. We too have much good work in accord with the gospel of grace. Have we become complacent about our labors in the gospel? Our job is not yet completed. Help us to have hope and strength in You, for each day has enough trouble of its own, and we quickly become very weary in well-doing. Our confidence is in You alone.

Judges 2
Father God, we have been delivered from the bondage of sin, yet we have not obeyed Your voice as we should. We thank You for the measure of sanctification that You have granted to us already, but we are ashamed of our sin. Help us to remember day by day what Your Son has accomplished for us. If we forget You, we will surely worship idols and turn down paths that will be both fruitless and dangerous. We thank You for our great Deliverer and Savior Jesus Christ. Send Him to us when we would be foolish and lazy, and turn us back to the way of Your Word. Father, in our current weakness and sin there is a test that is too difficult for us to pass. Fill us with Your Spirit that we might serve You as redeemed men, and not as foolish beasts.

Judges 3
Lord God, this is a time of war for Your church. We do not use the weapons of this world. Nor do we struggle against flesh and blood. Nonetheless, help us to be aware of the spiritual battle that is raging all around us. If You bring us into some difficulty or oppression, You surely have a purpose in this time of trouble. Teach us to turn away from worldliness. All the food that the earth has to offer can never bring us the happiness that our hearts desire. There is a Bread that comes from heaven that is of far greater worth than all the wealth and possessions of men. This Bread is Jesus, and He has brought us life. We eagerly take into our hearts the sustenance that comes only from Him. Help us to believe that we have victory even now through Jesus. Save Your people from the hands of those who seek to destroy us.

Judges 4
O God, our base impulses would destroy us. Sometimes the deadly yield of lust comes almost immediately. On other occasions the disease lurks deep in our

flesh and destroys us many years later. Either way, this sin is so dangerous to our spiritual and physical health. Teach us how to have a proper enjoyment of the good gifts that You have granted to us. Show us the way of love and submission between godly men and women. We see one pattern among the men of this world. They would abuse women and treat them as disposable objects and not as companions to be cherished and blessed. They do not understand that their ways lead only to death. They are so easily fooled. They leave the path of safety and are soon captured by someone who comes softly to them. They lie down in their weakness and are overcome by the hand of death. Thank you for the courageous women that You have granted to Your church. Teach the men of the church to lead in righteous ways, forsaking all evil and laziness.

Judges 5

Our Father, may godly men be willing to take the lead within Your church for the glory of Your Name. We thank You for our one great Leader, the Lord Jesus Christ. Our confidence is in Him. We are in the midst of a great spiritual battle. We need Your help. May we not be those who sit out the fight, or hide in a place that seems peaceful. You have granted to us Your Word, sacraments, and prayer as good weapons in this struggle. Gather us together in the use of these good gifts. Thank You for strong and courageous women who are willing to work with us in Your congregations. We do not struggle against flesh and blood. We pray for those who are being deceived by the evil one. We pray that many will be rescued from the one who comes to steal, to kill, and to destroy. May Satan and his demonic host perish at just the right time, O Lord. May Your friends be like the sun that rises in its might. Bring forward the great day of resurrection life for Your church. Grant that Your Son will reign as King over His church forever and ever.

Judges 6

Sovereign Lord, what will You do when we pursue evil ways in Your sight? Surely You love us enough to challenge us in our errors. You may even send an enemy against us to teach us lessons that cannot be learned in times of peace and prosperity. Train us to call out to You for a Savior. We are too fearful of men in times of difficulty. Make Your church a mighty congregation of valor. Grant us eyes to see the signs of Your presence all around us. Help us see the miracle of the resurrection of Jesus Christ with new eyes day by day. You are with us. Your Son is still alive. Grant us a new awareness of the peace that He has won for us. We have peace with You, and peace with our brothers and sisters in Christ, but we do not have peace with idolatry. Make us strong for the tearing down of unlawful altars within our hearts and lives. Clothe us with Your Spirit that we might find new courage that can only come from You. Purify our consciences from past sin, and grant us daily repentance and faith as a sign of Your abiding love.

Judges 7

Lord God Almighty, You are very capable of helping us through every challenge. You can win a great victory with even fewer men than Gideon's small army of 300. Have You not won the greatest battle of all time through the weakness of One Man? Did not the Son of Man slay a legion of adversaries through His death on the cross? You are the one who grants true spiritual courage to Your church.

You have shown us much evidence of Your greatness and faithfulness. Open our eyes and ears to Your glory and love. We worship You with confidence in Your promises. Come quickly, great Lord of Hosts. Win the battle against fear and disappointment that rages within our souls. If we will resist the devil, He will flee from us. Why are we slow to do this? Build up Your church even in our day. Help us to be faithful to Your call in every situation of trouble that we face. You are surely with us.

Judges 8

Our Lord, forgive us for our disputes and divisions that are unnecessary and fruitless. Have we brought trouble upon Your people without cause? We repent of our sins against the purity and peace of Your church. Thank You for our great Leader, the Lord Jesus Christ. May He always lead us forward in the spiritual battles that rage around us. To Him belongs all power and dominion. He is the Lord, and He is the true King over Your people. Protect us even in the day of victory, lest we become like great Gideon of old. He won a great victory over his enemies, but then fell in the snare of his own foolish idolatry. Protect us from our impulse to exalt ourselves to the hurt of Your covenant community.

Judges 9

Father God, even from within our own families it is sadly possible that an enemy may arise who causes great trouble within Your church. We do not want some false and brutal Abimelech to force Himself upon us after a great Gideon is gone. Help us to hold fast to this truth: that Your Son is forever King over Your people. We want no other king but Jesus Christ. When we insist on ruthless men ruling over us, men who lust for power, they will surely bring violence and misery upon Your family. Give us zeal, not for strong men who insist that they are in charge, but for humble leaders who are most bold in seeking You and in following the commandments of Your Son. What shall we do now if we have foolishly sought leaders who are not godly men? Deliver us from evil that is too strong for us. You have told us that we are to submit to You and to resist the devil. Your promise is that our adversary will then flee from us. We claim this promise with confidence. You will purify Your Kingdom. Our hope is in Your Son, no matter how intimidating wicked men may seem to be who have usurped positions of leadership in Your church. You are able to bring a millstone on the neck of the man who troubles Your household.

Judges 10

Sovereign Lord, the generations come and go, and Your kingdom moves forward. Even our depravity will not ultimately stop Your holy will. How much suffering do we bring upon ourselves by our continual sin? What have foreign gods ever done for us? They are only a snare to us. We have sinned against You. Please deliver us from the trap of false worship even now. We ask You for godly leaders who will seek You, find You, obey You, and lead us as we follow Jesus Christ together.

Judges 11

Lord God, You can raise up a child of no consequence to be a man of Christ-like spiritual leadership. Who is the mighty man? Give us men who trust Christ boldly and who know the history of Your dealings with Your people. Is it only for naïve young men to desire positions of leadership in Your church? Surely there must be a place for patient men who have learned of the power of Your Word through godly experience. Our enemies may seem overwhelming to us, but You can provide a Savior who is our Helper forever. He sends forth under-shepherds who fight the good fight for Your flock in holy prayer and consecrated living. Such men find that the fight may be very costly for them and for their loved ones. What will happen to the sons and daughters of those who serve You in accord with Your calling? May we carefully consider the cost of serving You, and then do so with joy. Surely we can trust You for our own lives and the lives of our children, for Your promise is not only to us, but also to the young ones in our charge. We believe Your Word, and we wait with all of creation for the unveiling of the sons of God in resurrection glory.

Judges 12

Sovereign Lord, will trouble await the man who serves You faithfully? We understand that the world will resist Your truth, but what can we do when those who name the Name of Christ act with even less faith than the children of the devil? Surely it will not go well with Your church if we are led by faithless and lazy leaders. Surely we cannot safely follow those who call evil good, and good evil, and who are always ready to strike down the godly.

Judges 13

Blessed Lord, You have given a Son; a child is born. Shall a kingdom be born in a day? When Your Son was born a kingdom came. When He returns to deliver us from the curse, we will see that kingdom in its fullness. The conception of Your Son was a great miracle. You have testified to His greatness in Your Word. You have prepared us for our holy Savior through the Word of the Old Testament. Your Son came as the fulfillment of every wonderful hint of a coming Redeemer. He is our great Samson, announced by an angel, and worshiped forever by the host of heaven. Surely it is not Your intention to kill Your people with eternal destruction. By Your powerful Spirit, stir us up in holy service for the glory of Your Name, and for the vindication of Your righteousness and Your mercy.

Judges 14

Glorious Lord, keep our eyes focused on Your Son. Your ways are mysterious to us. How could it be that a Samson seeks a wife from the Philistines, and this plan is somehow from You? The events of our lives are similarly puzzling to us. We might expect that Your ways would be above our ways. Yet we are surprised to find such amazing experiences in the lives of men of faith in the Bible. We marvel at You. Evil men have their plans. They pressure others to do things against the Lord, and against themselves and their loved ones. So many things seem to go wrong, and yet You still work Your holy judgments against the enemies of Your people. We stand in awe of Your wisdom and Your power.

Judges 15

Father God, there is a great battle that is raging. We have a Solo Warrior who has done amazing things to work Your holy will. He came as our mighty Leader. No man had the courage or ability to work alongside Him. Forgive us, Lord, for we are so easily overtaken by fear. Left to ourselves we would surely have given up the fight so long ago. You are the great unseen Strongman for Your church. You deliver her out of every trouble.

Judges 16

Great God, there is a sin that so easily besets us. Even the greatest leaders of Your people face the challenge of entangling depravity. You work out your mighty purposes despite our obvious failures. Why do we continually return to places of temptation as if we were invincible? Will our souls be vexed until our weakness becomes our downfall? Why are we so easily fooled by those who hate You? Yet You will not be utterly defeated. In Your Son's death, His enemies imagined that they had surely won the battle against their powerful foe. Yet this was the crowing achievement of His life of perfect obedience. His death on the cross was the greatest victory that He had ever accomplished. Throughout the days of His earthly ministry He brought life and healing to many, but the life that He won for us through His death was far beyond the life that He had given to His people through all of His earlier deeds of power. In this one decisive moment in the history of salvation, our strong Deliverer accomplished the redemption of His people.

Judges 17

Our Father, there is a way that seems right to a man, but it is full of presumptuous sin. No matter how holy we think that way is, and no matter how we decorate a false road with many beautiful idols, it is still so very wrong. It is not the way of our King. We must give careful attention to Your Word, and not merely do what is right in our own eyes. We have a Priest who is over Your house. The way that He leads according to Your Word is the only safe way for Your children.

Judges 18

Lord God Almighty, there are crowds of people who claim Your Name, but many are only committed to violence and sin. It will never be safe for us to be in league with such men. There are those who call themselves brothers, but their lives are only examples of disorderly living, and they will not listen to any correction. You have warned us that bad company will not lead us to health in Christ. We need the help of true spiritual companions. We especially need a safe and close relationship with You alongside others who are willing to hear Your Word. Please provide us with such a company of believers in Your church. As our children grow and move on to new avenues of opportunity and service, grant to them healthy spiritual companionship, and protect them from evil men who are committed to violence and idolatry. Grant that we will submit to You, and that we will have new strength to resist the devil, that He might flee from us. Build Your church, and bless us with wisdom, that we will be engaged forever in holy and obedient worship.

Judges 19

Lord God Almighty, when there was no king in Israel, the people seemed to forget that You were King. There is a King in Your church today, the Lord Jesus

Christ. Why do we act as if we have no king? Will we give ourselves over to immorality and to folly? There can be no health in Your church until we are willing to hear and obey Your Word. The truth of the Scriptures must direct us in our homes, in Your church, and in every sphere of our lives. There is a world of sin all around us, and it has found fertile soil for evil in our hearts and lives. We forget about the beauty of Your gift of marriage, and pursue strange and cruel behaviors that have no place among Your people. Is this a secret? Is it not a fact that should be obvious to all, that even in Your church we have given ourselves over to gross worldliness and immorality? Heal us, and save us, for evil is closing in all around us, and we are weak.

Judges 20

Our Father, the consequences of sin have been revealed to us from the beginning. We know that the wages of sin is death. We see much trouble because of the evil that has taken hold within Your church. We think of ways of fighting against this enemy, but we forget that the disease is also in us. Thank You for the perfect solution to evil around us and within us in the cross of Christ. His death was an atoning sacrifice. The solution for us is not in the destruction of men, but the renewal of our hearts and minds by the work of Your Holy Spirit. If we attack one another because of sin, there will be no end to the destruction all around us. If we remember that we have died to sin in the death of Christ, we will also be reminded that the free gift that we have from Your hand is true life in Jesus Christ, our Lord. Help us to walk in the way of life as those who know that we do not battle against flesh and blood, but against powers and principalities from angelic realms that seek an ugly victory for evil in our lives. The decisive battle has already been fought on the cross. Our Savior has defeated sin and death, and we have been claimed according to Your mercy and justice. You have determined that Christ's obedience and death would be counted as ours through faith in Him. Fill us with Your Spirit again today, and grant that we would pursue the mortification of our flesh as we seek the righteousness that can only come from You. Put to death the evil within us according to the power of Christ at work in our lives and in Your church.

Judges 21

Father God, after we have accused others of sin and taken vengeance against the wicked, who will be left alive? Surely we need a way of grace, for we have not made an end to the practice of sin in our lives. Keep us from making up our own solutions to the discipline with which You are graciously chastening us. Help us to see the way of faith and repentance again, so that we will not pursue our own wild plans to gain for ourselves a life and a future. Your Son has done everything necessary for us. In Him we have hope. Every detail that troubles us surely has a solution in the wisdom that comes from above. Even if we must suffer and die at the hands of our enemies, there must be some way that this suffering and death is part of Your perfect plan. Your determination to glorify Your Name and to bless Your children will never end until You have accomplished the fullness of Your holy will. There is a King over Your people. We will trust Him now and forever.

Ruth

Ruth 1

Glorious Lord, You are well acquainted with suffering and loss, for Your Son visited us on this earth and tasted our sadness. To lose a husband, to lose two sons, these are heavy burdens. The Naomi who once knew life as pleasant has become a Mara through such providences, for she tastes the bitterness of suffering. Bring us godly companions in our distress. Help us to be determined in our commitment to our brothers and sisters in the faith. Grant that we would see the fullness that we have in Christ, though we face the challenge of emptiness around the family table.

Ruth 2

Great God and King, is there a Boaz for every lonely and needy woman? Grant Your comforts in fuller measure to those who do not know the answer for their loneliness. Thank You that You have given Your church men like Boaz who have a heart for holiness. Thank You for Your good protection and provision for Your needy servants who cry out to You day and night. Surely we are safe to take refuge under Your wings. Give us joy when we see Your hand of provision in situations of desperation. Please care for the weak and feed the poor in our midst. Thank You for every good gift that You give through the hands of men, for You have made us safe, and have satisfied our hunger in a dangerous world of scarcity and loss.

Ruth 3

Lord God, before the foundation of the world, You sought out for us an answer to our deepest needs. Even though Your greatest gifts may seem to be shrouded in mystery, confusion, sadness, and shadow, one day we will see Your goodness in the glory of Your Holy Son. He is our Redeemer. We have come to Him with fear and joy, and we have not been turned away. Though we are only worthy in the righteousness of Christ, in Him we truly are counted as worthy, for You have come to us in grace. We love because You first loved us. We have fared extremely well in Your Son. We have more than we need for our entrance into Your Kingdom, and we have something of incomparable goodness to share with all those around us.

Ruth 4

Our Father, bring about the glory of Your promises as the generations move forward. Our Redeemer is at the gate of the city even now. He greets all who come to Him when they finish their days here below, for He went to prepare a place for them. Lesser men would have turned away from the cost of redeeming Your church as a bride. The sacrifice was so substantial! What a love our Boaz has for His Ruth. Thank You, O God, for the most wonderful Husband ever known among men. We have Christ, and He assures us that we are the love of His life. May His house be fruitful, and may many holy men and women come forward from death to life as we are faithful witnesses of Your great covenant love. Thank You for the wonder of faith. Bring us the end of Your holy story of redemption soon, that our bitterness might be removed far from us, and that the fullest benediction of heavenly joy might be ours forever. Come quickly, O Son of David! In You we remember what it is to be truly pleasant.

1 Samuel

1 Samuel 1

Lord God, You have granted to us many blessings. Though we grieve for what we cannot have, surely You hear the cries of Your loved ones. We know of nothing that can be given to us that would take away our pain, but You are God, and You will help Your people. We give our lives to You. Our children are surely gifts from You. Though love for others opens the door to loss and sorrow, You will help us when we are troubled in spirit. There is an assurance of Your love that can only come from You. Even when we cannot feel any joy, surely one day we will laugh, for You will give to us our heart's desire. In Your Son, we have everything we need for the greatest happiness. You are so kind to us. Though we live in this world of misery, You are with us. We give our lives to You again. As we are able, we also give You the lives of our children. As long as they live, they are Yours. Even when they die, they are in Your hands. Blessed be Your Name.

1 Samuel 2

Sovereign God, we praise Your Name in the presence of Your great congregation. There is no one like You. You are full of knowledge, power, and wisdom. In You the last shall be first, and the first shall be last. You give life, and You bring men down to the grave. You bring the rich to poverty, and You allow the destitute to sit with princes. You accomplish a salvation that we could never attain with our limited wisdom and strength. You bring new hope to a home of sin and sadness. Father, we mourn the foolishness and evil within our own families. You must bring us strong help from on high, or we will die in our sins. Grant to us hope and fruitfulness. We trust in You. Have mercy on us. Give us the wisdom to see things rightly, and the courage to bless and to discipline with Your love. What can we do if people will not listen to Your Word? Surely those who will not repent are headed toward trouble. Grant us hope again beyond the grave, and beyond the depth of the sin in our midst. Those who despise You are in great danger, but You will raise up for Yourself faithful priests who will believe in You and will humbly serve You forever.

1 Samuel 3

God of Truth, speak to Your servants through Your holy Word. Teach Your church to hear Your voice in the sacred Scriptures. Help us to listen and obey as You correct and encourage us. Though Your Word may warn us sternly, it is the truth, and we must hear what You are saying to us. We will listen to Your Word, O Lord. There is no other way of life for us but the one way that You have provided for us in Your Son Jesus. You have revealed Yourself to us in Him.

1 Samuel 4

O Lord God, be our help today in the face of enemies seen and unseen. Do not allow us to be defeated today by those who hate You. Be present with us, for You have said that Your church is the temple of the Holy Spirit. May Your foes flee and run in fear because of Your Almighty power. In the day of the sons of Eli, Your ark was captured and this sacred gift came into the hands of the Philistines. In this day of Christ, we have no sacred objects made by Your command. But we, Your people, are Your sacred possessions. Help us now Lord! Accomplish all of Your holy will. Preserve life in the day of disaster, lest the whole of Your people be an Ichabod, and Your glory depart from among us.

1 Samuel 5

Lord of our Salvation, even when the events around us seem to suggest Your defeat, help us to remember that this is only a temporary vision on a cloudy day of disaster. False idols will surely fall on their faces and be utterly destroyed, and Your enemies will face horrible panic and retribution. Give us confidence today that we are Your children, beloved by You, and that the day of vindication is surely coming soon.

1 Samuel 6

Lord of the Presence, Your power in the midst of Your enemies will only mean disaster for those who are determined to attack Your Name and Your people. Even though they might seem to respect You in some slavish fear, we know that their show of devotion is not the way of true faith. We not only fear You as our Lord, but we also love You as our Father. We need no sign to distinguish today between coincidence and divine purpose. The Word that You have given us assures us that You are working all things for our good and Your glory. We offer to You our lives like a whole burnt offering, for we are Yours, and the blood of Your Son has secured our redemption and bound us forever to Your most blessed Name. How fearful a thing it would be to face Your anger, but Christ has secured our freedom and our safety. Draw us near to You again today.

1 Samuel 7

We need You, O Lord. The day of trouble has been near to us in recent times. The memory of it afflicts our soul still today. If this is by Your design so that we will put away all foreign gods, we pray that You would give to us the strength to do this very thing immediately. We will not cease to cry out to You, O Lord. May our great Prophet, Priest, and King perfect our prayers that we offer to You today. Till now You have helped us, even through the horror of loss. Yet You are here with us, and we are Your humble servants.

1 Samuel 8

Father, one day we will be old, if it is Your will. What will our children be? Will they walk in Your ways? Lord, be our God and the God of our children. We need You. Do our young ones seem to go their own way for a season? Do they seem to follow the ways of the world more than is safe for their souls? We weep here before you, for we do not understand Your providence in Your church. Have we gone after a false King? We know that You are good – yes, very good. Be our only King, and fight all our battles for us. We will not trust in anyone but You.

1 Samuel 9

Lord God, will we be so foolish as to think that we know who should lead us by looking at the outward features of a man? By this way we would choose a Saul, and reject the Lord Jesus Christ, Your Son. What do we have today to give to You that You might show us the way to heaven? We have nothing to give but our sorry lives. These moments and days of both trouble and opportunity we offer up to You. We live for You. Father, You know that we love You. We have no confidence in ourselves that we will do any better than we have done, since our weakness is evident. In a moment we can fall. If we are to be more courageous and noble than we have been thus far, it must be from Your strength and not from our own desires or power. Therefore be glorified as we come to You in the Name of the great Messiah of Israel. Send us on our way in peace. You are God.

1 Samuel 10

Glorious Lord, You have anointed Your Son to be Prince over His heritage. We bow before this mighty King, the Lord Jesus Christ. You know all things. You could easily tell us the details of the days ahead of us, since these are all known to You. Fill us with Your Spirit and give us a heart to do the good that our hands find to do. Grant to us a fuller communion with our great Prophet, Priest, and King. Draw us near to Him again in solemn covenant assembly that we might know that we have been chosen by You. Remind us that our worth is in our Messiah. Send us forth day by day in peace and security, despite the opposition that may come to us from worthless men.

1 Samuel 11

O God our Protector, Your enemies would eagerly desire to hurt us and bring disgrace upon us. Even now our brothers and sisters suffer at the hands of brutal foes. Send forth the strongest Deliverer, Christ our Lord, that He might put violent men to flight. May even the most brutal enemies of Your church become Your friends through the only Way of peace. Work salvation throughout Your church as many people are drawn to Your Son. We rejoice greatly in Him.

1 Samuel 12

Father God, we hear the words of our Mediator calling us to a life of faith and obedience. We have no word of testimony against the Lord Jesus Christ. He has done all things well. He has not defrauded us or oppressed us. Far be it from Him to sin in any way. You are our witness today that we find no evil thing in our great Redeemer, and we have no excuse to withhold from Him our full devotion. He has rescued us from every adversary, defeating even sin and death, and making Satan flee from us whenever we would sincerely resist that father of lies. We will obey the voice of the Lord. May Your hand be with us because of our great Messiah King. Our wickedness has been great. We fear You. May Your Son pray for us that our souls will not return to empty things that cannot profit or deliver. We are a people who live for Your Name's sake. We will serve You faithfully with our whole heart. Do not utterly sweep us away in Your righteous wrath.

1 Samuel 13

Great Ruler over Your people, You have defeated our mortal foe, for Your Son has won a decisive battle on our behalf. We do not need to hide in secret caves, trembling from fear of man. Your Son has offered up His life as a whole burnt offering. He never did anything foolish. He never attempted to get that which was not rightly His. Therefore, You have blessed Him in every battle, and He has won for us both heaven and eternity. Powerful enemies will never rule over us in the land of our Messiah, for You will cleanse Your home completely from any disturbing adversary, and we will dwell in peace with You forever.

1 Samuel 14

God and Father of our Lord Jesus Christ, in ways that we may never fully understand, Your Son has won an astounding victory for us. As a solo warrior, with none to help Him, He waited for just the right time and place to answer the taunts of a deadly foe. Through the cross, Your Son has utterly defeated the devil, making a public spectacle of Him. In the ranks of the enemy there is great confusion to this day as a result of this mighty victory. You have brought us into a land that is dripping with the honey of Your presence. In Word, sacrament, and prayer, You have made our eyes bright with the gift of the sweetness of Your Spirit. Help us to enjoy You with the eager desire of hungry people who have been denied food for longer than is necessary. We ask you to grant us victory in the spiritual battle before us. Restrain our foolishness, for we would destroy one another for no good cause if we were left to our own devices. May we not die from self-righteous and empty deeds that come from our own wicked imaginations. Grant that we would serve You truly and valiantly according to Your Word, for we are Your people, and the Commander of our forces is our great Redeemer and Lord.

1 Samuel 15

Father, there have been so many kings who have refused to follow Your Word with a full heart. Yet Your Son, the Lord Jesus, has followed You to the very end. This complete devotion cost Him His life. He has performed the commandment that You gave Him to do. He has left nothing undone. You have raised Him now in great power, and granted to Him all authority. He could never be blamed for any deed left undone, for He has not shirked any duty. In Him we are now acceptable in Your sight, though we have sinned so obviously and grievously. Please accept us in Him. We cling to the hem of the robe of Jesus Christ. He is enough for us. You will not turn away from us, for Your Son has done all things well, and then died for our sake. We will live with Him forever.

1 Samuel 16

O God of all Comfort, how long will we grieve over our disappointments? You are the Sovereign Lord of All, and You do all things well. Consecrate us by Your Spirit in the depths of our souls. Teach us how to see with the eyes of faith. There is much that You have not revealed, but there is also so much that You have made known to us. Teach us to hear Your Word and to move ahead in love. Do not take Your Holy Spirit from us. Have we grieved You deeply and neglected the duty of repentance? We fear that this is the case. Show us our hidden sins again that we might turn from them in truth immediately. Play music for our hearts that will refresh us in Christ, for surely You will rejoice over us again with singing, for we are Your beloved children, and the bride of Your Son.

1 Samuel 17

Mighty God, You can use the faith of a boy to slay a man of the most powerful stature. Though our enemies may be superior in natural strength, though they may have better weapons and proud taunts, we have You, O Lord, and we fight in the strength of the resurrected Jesus Christ. Your foes defy You openly, and claim that Your church is nothing. Within our ranks, even strong men fear to use the means of grace that You have given to Your people. We imagine that if we speak the Word forthrightly that we will be unable to gather the lost. We have not used Your sacraments in accord with Your instruction, thinking that people would leave if we did things Your way. We do not pray because we see it as powerless and useless, so we retain the form of strong spiritual armor, but we deny the truth and power of Your love. We are afraid to obey You. The man that speaks in favor of Your Word and Your worship can expect criticism as so many would dismiss him as naive. Grant to us David's courage to use the simple tools of warfare that You have given to Your church. You have delivered us from sin and death. Place in our hands again the spiritual weapons that we need for the battle ahead. Take off our backs the heavy weight of the world's armor, for we will never win the battle with the unbearable burden of worldliness. Grant to us godliness, faith, hope, and love. Let us move ahead with truth and gospel peace. Send us forward in the Name of our Savior Jesus, and grant us victory in the fight that rages throughout the church and into the world. We need no Goliath for success. You can make a simple stone that comes from the hand of our Redeemer powerful. You can win any battle against any champion that the world may deem undefeatable. Make us bold, that we might see a great day of vindication for the cause of Christ now, and even beyond our mortal lives. Whose Son is our Redeemer? He is the Son of Man to be sure, but He has shown Himself to be Your Son, and He is mighty in battle.

1 Samuel 18

Father God, our souls are knit to the soul of Your Son. We cast our crowns before Jesus. He is our Leader, and we follow Him with songs and dancing. Your Son has won the greatest victory for Your people. Would we be jealous of the One who has loved us with an everlasting love, and has proven His commitment to You and to us with His own blood? Would we be the murderers of Him who willingly went to the cross for our sake? But we have been treacherous against this One good Man. He came in godliness and lowliness. He was not haughty or proud. He raised Lazarus from the dead, and more than this, was demonstrated to be the very Son of God through His own resurrection to an immortal body. This is the true Son of David, and yet we have sinned against Him. We plead with You now for forgiveness. Return to us the blessings that come from knowing Jesus as our Lord and friend, and grant to us a good inheritance again in the power and holiness of Christ.

1 Samuel 19

God of All the Earth, will You allow wicked men to destroy Your church? Even leaders among Your covenant people turn against us and against our holy Messiah, the Son of David. They are treacherous in their words and unstable in their hearts. Yet Your Son continues to win the victory in every battle. Why would men who claim to walk in His Name turn against Him and deny Your Word? Why are

71

there so many Sauls and so few courageous Davids in positions of authority in Your church? Why are so many determined to bring harm upon Your people? These traitors commit themselves to hatred and are full of lies. Have mercy on us. Send us the Spirit of truth, and true and godly men full of the Spirit of Christ to lead us. We will live in the strength and holiness that You provide. We willingly give our lives for Him who died for us.

1 Samuel 20

Father God, wicked men seek the lives of Your saints. Show us the truth. We long for the revealing of Your true Sons. Even now, let the wicked leader within Your church be exposed as faithless. Bring repentance to many as the truth is boldly preached. Godless men would consume Your people as thoughtlessly as they eat bread with their meals. They swear falsely about their affection for You and their love for Your people. They love the world only for the things that the world can give, for they only love themselves. They do not love the Son of David. Expose them for who they are. In the day of the greatest apostasy, when the man of lawlessness is shown to be who he really is, send forth Your Son again to rescue us in the fullness of resurrection power. Cast down the vile enemy from His seat of honor, where He claims to be god, and where he demands absolute obedience from slavish worshipers. This anti-Christ even now shows forth who he is in fits of anger against Your children. His end will soon come. Though He might seem to have full sway within Your church for a brief moment, Your Son will surely win the victory in the Day of His power. Until then, we swear before You that we belong to the true Son of David, and not to any servant of the father of lies.

1 Samuel 21

Lord of Hosts, the righteous flee from the wicked in a time of necessary retreat. The day is full of danger, and evil men lurk in shadows even within Your church to destroy her ministry. Grant us bread from heaven for our warfare on earth. Though we hide for a moment among the Philistines, we will never forget who we serve, for You are God. Though we seem mad in the eyes of the foolish, You will use every means to protect us and to preserve us, for the gates of hell will not prevail against Your church. We sound the retreat of necessity, but only for a moment, in a day of dire trouble, for we are always on the offense in our service of You.

1 Samuel 22

Lord have mercy on us. Evil men have slaughtered priests among the priesthood of all believers. How can murderers have such power? We know that Your purposes cannot be stopped. In the day of trouble, the wicked traitor speaks against Your saints. He finds favor from an envious king of Your own nation, and is willing to kill Your true servants to gain what He supposes he can get from those in power. Yet on that day of mourning, the holy priests of the Lord go to a place of eternal hope, but a vicious man outside of your covenantal protection, though he seems to have safety for the briefest moment, soon faces Your eternal wrath. O how we mourn the evil done by Your enemies. Yet we know that with Your anointed Son we are safe forever.

1 Samuel 23

O God in Heaven, though Your Son has saved a people, how can it be that those who are saved by Him, would yet turn against Him? We do thank You for Your extraordinary mercy, for if You had no saving grace for a wicked church, how could there be any hope for us? We confess today two remarkable truths: first, the great Son of David has saved us by His mighty power through the cross; but second, we have given up the precious gift of gospel joy when we have turned against Your Son in sin. We have feared men more than You. The battle continues to rage to this day, but by still more grace from You, we are coming to our senses. We hate our rebellion against our Savior, and we thank You for Your wonderful and full mercy for Your unworthy servants. Our hope has never been rightly in our own faithfulness, but only in the righteousness and blood of Your perfect Son, who redeems traitors.

1 Samuel 24

Father, could there be some hope of heaven for a man like King Saul? Was He so oppressed by demonic spirits, and so foolish in the stubbornness of sinful envy, that he damaged his soul to a point of utter weakness? David showed Him mercy. He cut off the corner of His robe, but would not take his life. This seemed to soften the heart of the wicked king. He called David his son and wept. This was a good day for him, Lord, though the assault of demons would quickly return. But on that good day of faith, Saul even professed the truth that David would surely be king, and David swore that he would do no harm to Saul. What powerful mercy! O Lord, is there eternal hope for King Saul? Then perhaps there is hope for us, for we have shown madness in our sin and rebellion against You. You will have mercy even on us.

1 Samuel 25

Lord God, we live in a world of death and folly. You are the source of all life and wisdom. You have provided everything necessary for us, and have protected us from many dangers. Would we then forget Your kindness to us, and decide that we have no obligation to You? You have provided the way of redemption from eternal destruction through the blood of Your Son. Will we have no gratitude? Will we return to You evil for good? Send forth messengers of wisdom. Give us repentance, so that we will not bring further guilt upon ourselves in our foolishness. Help us to see the only hope for us in the way of faith, lest we die in hopelessness and unbelief. Grant to us the security of the Perfect Husband, for we are Your servants, and You are the Lord.

1 Samuel 26

Father God, treacherous men would betray Your Son and His church. Deliver us from evil and danger. Even within the people of Your promise, leaders and armies would rail against the Lord's true Anointed. Grant us restraint and wisdom in our daily response to wicked men and dangerous situations. Watch over us and help us in times of great trouble and opportunity. May we be innocent of further evil today. Forgive our sins. We will not serve other gods. We will show due respect for those in authority according to Your Word. We will turn away from our foolish mistakes. The life of Your Son is precious in our sight. He lives. We will go forth in peace, and pursue all righteousness with confidence in Your grace.

1 Samuel 27

Lord Almighty, will we perish today at the hands of Your enemies? You are the hope of the redeemed. Protect us in one place or another, that we might live to serve You another day. Keep our lives even in the land of the wicked, and give us strength in body and soul, that we might serve You well wherever You lead us.

1 Samuel 28

O Lord of Hosts, You are the God of the Living. Though Your servants of former days have died, yet they still live. We are not to be those who wickedly inquire of them, yet we know that those who are in You are safe in Christ whether they live or die. Keep us far from evil inquiry, lest we follow the doctrines of demons, but make us strong in hope according to the Word of Christ. You have spoken clearly in Your Word. Will we not obey Your voice, O Lord? Give us courage and strength, especially as we face the day of danger and impending death. Bring us home to You in peace, and forgive all our wickedness and sin.

1 Samuel 29

Father God, the world knows that we are different. Though they cannot rightly find fault with You, they know that we have a different Lord than they have, and a different life than that of Your enemies. Make us blameless in the sight of the world as Your holy angels are blameless, lest the world rightly accuse us of sin and hypocrisy, and we bring disgrace upon the name of Your Son.

1 Samuel 30

Lord God, what will we do in the day of the worst news? Is there hope when the city has been burned with fire, and our families have been captured in battle? What will we do in the day when our own comrades in mission blame us for great evil that has come upon us? We will strengthen our souls in Your presence. We will inquire of You, O Lord. We will surely move forward again in Your service. We will have mercy on the weak, and You will grant us victory. Your Son has redeemed what was captured by an enemy. We have complete confidence in Him. Not one soul in Your family will be lost. Therefore we are safe, for we belong to Your Son. Grant to us a great victory in Your service. When You bring blessing into our hands, help us to be generous with all our brothers and sisters who are in need. Let us also honor the leaders of Your people out of reverence for Your Son.

1 Samuel 31

Eternal Father, when great men of consequence die, it is a day of mourning. Though they may have been afflicted by evil spirits, and moved in grossly unprofitable ways, yet we honor them for what they once were, and especially because You are their Maker, and even their Redeemer. The wicked would want to expose them, showing brutal disrespect, but we honor the departed, and care for their bodies. We believe in the resurrection, and we trust in Your mercy for Your people. We belong to You, even in the greatest weakness and sin.

2 Samuel

2 Samuel 1

O Father of the Redeemed, we mourn for the loss of men like Saul and his son Jonathan. Foolish men are only able to see the sin of others. They presume to ease the pain by hastening the death of a fallen leader. Some would kill a great man because of his unwise deeds. So many would be devoid of respect for the great and without mercy for the wounded. How the mighty have fallen! What was Saul? Was he a strong man or a weak man? He was lovely in life and in death, together with his good son, Jonathan. We mourn over the loss of such great leaders, though they are weak and sinful men. Demons shall no longer harass and oppress them, for even they may still be covered by the blood of the Lamb. Thus there is yet hope even for us.

2 Samuel 2

Lord God, the Day of Your Son swiftly approaches. He has been anointed as King of the Church through His resurrection. He will one day be acknowledged as King of heaven and earth. Every knee shall bow and every tongue confess that He is Lord, to the glory of Your holy name. But we do not see every knee bowing before Him this day. We see Jesus as the Husband of the Church. We also see many false Christs and many false teachers. The day of their destruction swiftly approaches. Brutal men do vicious things in a world of the devouring sword. May the Man of Peace cause the trumpet to blow, so that the great Son of David may soon be acknowledged as the only King of kings.

2 Samuel 3

Father God, You have raised up the descendants of David in great number, but there is One alone who is the eternal King. We thank You for this incomparable ruler of Your church, the King of kings, the Lord Jesus Christ. We mourn the fact that there are many imposters who would desire to take His place. Father, we pray that You would bless us in our close association with the true King, Jesus. We are His bride, for He has purchased us with His blood. Use Your church, that we might gather all Your people to this one Savior. Bring into the fold of Your church all who will humbly submit to His reign. Forgive us for our disrespect and intrigue against Your Son and against the pastors and elders that would truly serve Him in accord with His Word. Why would we rail against You? Our rebellion is neither wise nor safe. Grant to us a greater wisdom as we serve among Your people. Make us gentle in this world full of sin and folly. Thank You for the blood of the eternal sacrifice, which is our sure hope.

2 Samuel 4

Eternal Lord, the day will come when Your adversaries will be put away forever, and all challenges to the reign of Your Son will be gone. Thank you for the mercy of Christ to us in our weakness and need. Evil men would accomplish their plans with violence and lawlessness. Some even think that You will be pleased with their hateful ways. Yet you will bring all such pretended servants to the destruction that is ordained for them. You are merciful. We live by Your grace and power.

2 Samuel 5

Sovereign Lord, we long for the day when we will see Your Son face to face. Our great Messiah will reign forever and ever. We celebrate His victory in securing the heavenly Jerusalem for us. He has entered the holy city above with the purifying sacrifice of His own blood. You have ordained a time of holy warfare for Your church as we serve Him here below, until the final day of heavenly peace fully comes. We do not fight with the weapons of this world, but we seek to win the hearts and minds of men with the truth of the gospel. Make us faithful in this battle that we might rest in the perfect peace of Jerusalem through the merit and mediation of Our Redeemer.

2 Samuel 6

God of Glory, there are so many disappointments that we face in this age of difficulty, yet You also bring moments of glory to us at just the right time. Help those who are facing severe trials. Many are ready to give up. Teach us the importance of Your Word. We know that obedience to You is not simply a matter of good intentions. Have mercy on us, for we are very weak. We rejoice before You with all our might. Though we may be despised by others because of our devotion to You, we pray that our hearts will not be unduly moved by the insults of those who do not love You. Make us pure in heart, mind, and body. We have been chosen by You that we might rejoice before You always.

2 Samuel 7

Faithful Lord, grant us rest from all the enemies that surround us. Father we would serve You with full devotion. Our plans are not always Your plans. Lead us in the right paths of fruitful service. Build up Your house and glorify Your Name. Bring glory to Your Son Jesus. You have made a house for David, and have established the Kingdom of His Son. Your steadfast love will never depart from Him. His throne is established forever. Who are we that You would grant to us a place in Your house? What can we say to You? You are great, O Lord, God. There is none like You, and it is the greatest privilege to be included in Your kingdom. You have confirmed Your Word of blessing through the death and resurrection of Your Son. Your promises are true. The house of Your servant Jesus shall know the security of Your love forever.

2 Samuel 8

Lord God, will we sink into despair because of the challenges of the past and our fears about the future? There is work to be done today, yet we are not sufficiently engaged in doing the things that You have called us to do. Help us to take up the shield of faith and all of the armor for the spiritual battle that You have ordained. We cannot mourn forever because of the miseries that we face. Your church must rejoice in You. This is a day of victory, for Your Son reigns. Men who are strong in Your Spirit have been placed by You in important positions of trust in Your church. Shall we ignore our duties forever? Strengthen us in Your service.

2 Samuel 9

God of All Covenant Faithfulness, show us Your kindness today because of our relation to Your Son, Jesus Christ. We are obviously weak. Look upon our weary limbs, and search our broken spirits. We confess our sins before You. Thank You for Your abundant forgiveness, O God. You have lifted us up and promised us food from Your table. Remember our desperate need. Even if we will be given food by men, no one can provide good nourishment for our souls today but You. Feed us with Your truth, for we long to walk again in the glory of Your Name.

2 Samuel 10

Glorious Lord, though we would act with sincerity and care for the world, we cannot be certain that we will be treated kindly and respectfully by others. Remind us again of the gospel, particularly at times of special disappointment and danger. Protect us from the hatred and violence of men. We would be men of peace. Assist us in the proclamation of the truth to every creature under heaven. Grant us courage in this task. Our forthright word of faith and repentance may cause some to attack, yet we must be true to You, whatever the danger before us may be.

2 Samuel 11

God of Mercy, how can we have hope when we have fallen into such grievous sin? Lord, we could be quickly and wrongly captivated by some person, and led by our own evil hearts into a web of deceit and destruction. Sin leads to sin in our lives. Adulterous thoughts can beget murderous actions. Help us, Lord. Our sin would lead to trouble for many. We bring forth the poisonous fruit of death for others to eat, others who may have nothing to do with our evil desires and schemes. Surely there would be no hope for us if Your valiant Son had not come to do battle for us. He did not come with lies or with a depraved heart. He fulfilled Your commandments from the depths of His being. His ways were always deeply pleasing to you. He has faced death, and has won for us eternal life. Have mercy on us for His sake.

2 Samuel 12

Father God, You have sent to us servants of Your Word to speak the truth boldly. Our sin has been exposed. You have given us so many gifts, and You would have given more if we had only asked. Yet we have despised You, Your Word, and Your provision, for we have taken what was not ours. The consequences of our rebellion against You are serious. We rejoice in the fact that You have put away our guilt through the provision of a perfect substitute. Nonetheless, You discipline those You love. We face the seriousness of great loss, and we mourn. In our grief, You speak sweetly to us of a better day to come, and we believe. Though our loved ones may rest in the grave and they will not return to us, yet we are assured that we will go to them one day, together with all who are in Jesus. You are able to help us with comfort and assistance, even granting life in the face of tremendous loss. You send us forth again in useful service, that our lives might be well spent for the glory of Your Name. Thank you for Your faithful love, and for the forgiveness of sins.

2 Samuel 13

Sovereign Lord, our affections have become perverse in sin. We live in a world that has long been full of strange evil. We would pursue unholy desires and would uncover great troubles for ourselves and many others. Have we lost all sense? Will we do outrageous things that are obviously foolish and shameful? Will we use our strength for violent assaults, rather than to protect the weak and vulnerable? Will we use the power at our disposal to abuse others? In this world of sin, how can we escape the ugliness of wickedness? Father, we need Your powerful help to keep us from disaster. Keep our hearts strong in Your Son, in Your Word, and in Your Spirit. Help us to believe Your promises. May our affections rise up to You in the time of temptation, so that we will not be mired in the depravity of this world and of ugliness of our own sinful flesh.

2 Samuel 14

Lord Almighty, we mourn the depravity of our sons and daughters, and ask for Your help. We ask that the end result of Your grace in both our lives and theirs will be consistent with a great eternal heritage. We stand in the greatest need of Your help in our lives. Please assure us again that our children will live to serve You forever. We love our young ones, but we need more wisdom that we might raise them up with integrity. There are so many temptations and troubles ahead of them. Will they have the spiritual strength to resist the devil and the schemes of proud and vicious men? Give us the courage to do what is right according to Your Word, despite the pleas of those who would insist on foolish plans. May we have the discernment to distinguish between the good and the bad, and the courage of our convictions to follow Your Son in the pathway of true integrity. We would love peace, but we will not have any rest through evil pursuits. Will we murder and destroy the property of others and claim to be in the right? Will we follow evil, and still be followers of Your Son? Grant us wisdom.

2 Samuel 15

Omnipotent God, we seek Your help today, for conspiracy against Your church seems to be everywhere. False rulers captivate the gullible. They steal the hearts of Your people. They plot with evil schemes. We play our parts with no sense of the danger that is ahead of us. Whole churches are attacked from deceitful enemies, and the work of many years is destroyed in a matter of days. These are times of trouble in Your kingdom. Faithful leaders are made to look like weak men who cannot be safely loved. Ruthless men amass great power for themselves and foolish men and women consider the wicked to be the hope of the future. Has Your church lost all sense? Is Christ not among us? How can we listen to lies? People deny the most foundational truths of our faith, and show disrespect for men of holiness and proven sincerity. In such an evil day, grant to us clear thinking. When we hear the plans of deceivers, make us wise in both our speech and our silence. Let us love the truth with a faithful heart, and serve Your Son in the day of a great apostasy all around us.

2 Samuel 16

Our Father, even those who come with gifts in their hands are not always speaking the full truth. We do not know what is in the hearts of men as Your Son did. How can we be safe in the face of the curses of the wicked and the lies of supposed friends? Help us to trust You, for You are working Your sovereign will and accomplishing Your deep and holy purposes despite the troubles that surround us. Though men throw stones, fling dust in our faces, and speak insulting lies against us, You are God. You are able to defend Your Name and to protect Your sons and daughters. Our hope is in Your Word.

2 Samuel 17

Father God, it is so discouraging to Your people when trouble comes against us from within Your church. We are persuaded that in all things You are working for our good. Grant us courage to continue in Your ways, despite any disappointments. Give us godly counsel. We need You. Look on us in our weakness. Forgive our sins. Give us hope in the day when an Absalom seems to threaten the Kingdom. We thank You for Your glorious Son. He is pure in heart and action, and is safely followed in every holy pathway. Protect us from wicked men and demonic enemies who come to steal, kill, and destroy. Curb our foolish pride and entangling sin, that we might not despair of life in the day of testing.

2 Samuel 18

Glorious Lord, Your forces of Kingdom love move forward under the banner of Jesus Christ. Your Son, our Commander, is safe in the heavens. He is beyond the reach of evil foes. He is watching and ruling over all. Attacks upon us are considered to be a strike against Your Son, and though we seem to fall, no one can stop our King. He has a heart for those He knows to be sons of God by adoption. Help us to consider the end of the way of wickedness carefully and to turn from all evil. Father, what a sad day it is when a child is dead. There is no joy, even though the son be an Absalom who aimed to destroy the king and to seize the kingdom. Your heart for the most troubled of Your children longs to see each young one live. You are powerful to save. Answer the longing hearts of mothers and fathers who cry out to You for their sons and daughters. Bring them good news of hope in the darkest night.

2 Samuel 19

Father God, we mourn over the sin and misery that we face in this world. Help us to understand the limits of our grieving, for we do not want to add sin to sin. Grant to us a clear understanding of how we can move forward in Your service when it would appear that our former life is gone because of some challenging loss. Remind us of our identity in our Savior and King, the Lord Jesus Christ. Show us that Your Son is the same yesterday, today, and forever. In Him we have stability. There is no loss so great that it could take us away from Your great love. May we live in a day of life and joy in Christ. Make us agents of abundant mercy through Him. Restore those who have fallen. Grant to us repentance. Give us the right words to speak in Your presence, that we might remember the security and blessing that we have in Your promises. As we grow in age, help us to look for our hope in a city yet to come. Bring the young along in the tasks that You have for them in Your kingdom, and grant rest to Your servants who have served You for many years. You know how to build Your kingdom, how to use those who are vigorous and young, and how to give rest and joy to those who are weary.

2 Samuel 20

Lord Almighty, as we seek the growth and holiness of Your kingdom, worthless men would work for disruption and trouble in Your house. Protect us from evil and self-seeking enemies. Give us holiness and love that are in Christ. Keep us from the deeds of men of intrigue who would kill and destroy in order to get revenge or eliminate dissent. Should such things be allowed to stand in Your church? Use all of Your men and women, high and low, to bring true peace and faithfulness to Your people. Help us to turn away from leaders who would only be haters of Christ. We return to You, O God, for You will build Your kingdom. Thank you for the opportunities that You grant to us for humble service as Your disciples.

2 Samuel 21

Eternal God, when men have long forgotten about the bloodguilt of their fathers, You still remember. Is there some curse upon us because of the wickedness and lies of those who have gone before us? Father, we have no way to make things right. First, we must understand our offense. Even then, what can we do, since we are already Your possession through the death of Your Son? We are not our own. We have been bought with a price. We plead the blood of Christ, seeking Your mercy and forgiveness, for many men have been unfaithful. Unless You make a way for the restoration of our fortunes, we will surely fall. Give us aid from above, lest our lamps be quenched in a battle that is too difficult for us.

2 Samuel 22

O Lord our Rock, You have delivered us from all our enemies. We take refuge in You. You have saved us from the hands of the violent. The waves of death would have been too much for us. When we called to You, Your help was near. You are able to answer Your children in the day of trouble. There is no God but You. You who rule the elements will help Your children who cry out to You night and day. You can push back any enemy from on high, no matter how strong they may seem. Thank You for the perfect righteousness of Your Son. He has kept Your ways blamelessly. You have rewarded us according to His obedience, for You are merciful to the humble. We turn away from all known sin. Be a shield to us, for You are a strong refuge to those who fear You. Grant us energy for the tasks ahead. May we worship You forever, for You have already destroyed our greatest enemies. Give us Your strength for the remaining battle that we face day by day. You are the God of Your people. Your Son is our Head and King. We serve Him with gladness. You have loved us with an everlasting love. Our future is secure. We will sing praises to Your Name forever in the congregation of the redeemed.

2 Samuel 23

Glorious Lord, You have granted to us the Word of Your Anointed, the Lord Jesus Christ. He has given us good news and has filled us with Your Holy Spirit. He is our great Ruler and King. He is the Seed of the Woman, who has crushed the head of the serpent. In our Redeemer, we have been made as mighty men, for even the devil is to be crushed under our feet. You have granted to Your servants water from the well of eternal life. At the cost of Your Son's blood, You have given us a spring of water that gushes up forever, a refreshing help for weary sinners. O Father, we long for the fulfillment of Your Son's Kingdom. There remain enemies all around us, and we are weak and weary in our duties. Even when we read Your Word and worship You we feel the challenge of our flesh and our sin. Deliver us forever from this body of death, and bring us into a land of abiding strength.

2 Samuel 24

Father God, we are so weak, and we would easily fail and fall at any test. Surely we need Your strength if we are to resist evil. We are so full of pride. We do what we do because of our own desires. Transform our hearts into something better and purer, that we might have holier desires. Your heart is perfect. Make us to love what You love, and to pursue these better desires with all the power and faith that comes from You. We would bring great trouble upon our lives and upon others all around us through our lust for power, fame, or pleasure. We need an atoning sacrifice for our wickedness. Your hand came against a Son of David, the Lord Jesus Christ, who was the Lamb of God for us. Through His perfect desires and His astounding love, a plague of death has been taken away from us. Through His own life and death, He has accomplished what could never have come to us through the death of bulls or goats. Though we can pay nothing for our salvation, the cost to You has been measured out in the blood of Your Son. Thank You for Your mercy, for Your justice has been satisfied at a great cost, and we have been redeemed.

1 Kings

1 Kings 1

Glorious God, we live and die at Your command. You know us when we are young, and You know us when we are old. The day comes when we step aside from our duties of responsibility, and the next generation takes our place. We come and go, but Your Son is forever King over the church. Here below, an Adonijah may attempt to make himself something, and he may even seem to succeed for a time. Despite the proud plans of men, You make a man rise or fall. You promised that Solomon would be king instead of Adonijah. Your Word cannot be broken. As we live among ambitious and treacherous men, we feel the danger of ruthless arrogance all around us. Despite these fears, You surely reign, and You will accomplish Your great will. Grant to us faith in You every day. We put aside our needless anxiety, and trust in You. Comfort our hearts as You teach us to trust in Your Word. May we serve You without doubt and fear all the days of our lives. We have been found in Your Son. Why should we live as orphans when we have such a good heritage in Your Son Jesus Christ? His throne is great and His Name is glorious. Thank You for our secure relation to You in the life and death of Your Son. Though we die, yet we only sleep in Jesus Christ. He will call our bodies forth from the grave. We live now in this most excellent hope.

1 Kings 2

Lord, how is it that You work Your justice throughout the earth? One man rises and another falls. One man is given more life by Your mercy, yet the day comes when old transgressions catch up with him, and a taste of Your justice is felt at the day of his death. Bloodshed is all around us, and we cannot sort out all the misery and sin that we see across the years of our lives. There are those who will attempt to accomplish their own plans with intrigue and lies. They worm their way into the homes of the righteous and cause difficulties as they seek a weak ear and an unsuspecting ally. If you were not our help, how could we live? There is much trouble all around us. Please do not take away Your mercy from us. We hate our foolish past and we turn to You as those who know the hope that is securely ours in Your Son. We have heard the truth about the way of life that You have for Your children, and we acknowledge that it is good. Give us the strength to resist evil, lest we die in disgrace. You have fully established Your kingdom in the hands of Your Son. We thank You for the peace that we enjoy in His service.

1 Kings 3

Great God, You have granted to us so many blessings. Your Son is the husband of Your church. What more can we possibly ask of You? He is full of righteousness and wisdom, and He will be our King forever. Grant us the privilege of being like Him. We would desire to have the blessing of an understanding mind, that we might serve You well. We thank You for the measure of riches and honor that You have chosen to give to us, but Your gift of wisdom would be far better than these other kind provisions. Surely You will help us in the daily struggles that come before us. You will give us insight so that we will make wise choices. Make our hearts yearn for Your blessing upon the weak who come to us for help in a day of desperate need.

1 Kings 4

Lord God, You have provided a system of order for Your Kingdom. We are thankful for the kind provision of leaders who pursue the orderly and blessed functioning of Your church. Please make the men who serve in this way wise and courageous. May they be honest men who understand the times. Help them to shine as lights in a dark world. Provide everything that they need for the job that You have given to Your church. We are to make disciples of all nations, and to train up Your church in holiness and love. Please provide all the resources necessary in order that these good goals will be accomplished. Thank you for all the excellent knowledge, skill, beauty, and wisdom that comes to Your servants through Your Son.

1 Kings 5

Almighty Father, You are building Your great temple through Jesus Christ. You have made us living stones in Your house. He is the great Cornerstone, rejected by men, but precious in Your sight. With the greatest patience and wisdom He is building us up to be a dwelling place for Your Spirit. Grant us enthusiasm and faithfulness as we do our part in this great work, that Your Kingdom may be established according to Your glorious plan.

1 Kings 6

Lord God, the work of building Your house requires much vision, wisdom, and obedience. Your resurrected and ascended Son is leading us in this important mission. Help us to keep His statutes, that we might be effective in worship and service for You. We now have access to the Most Holy Place in heaven through the blood of Christ. Your dwelling place with men is more precious than gold. What a creation is man, made in Your image! How much more wonderful is Your work of redemption, for we are now new creatures in Christ! Thank You for Your holy angels, created to be servants to the heirs of salvation. We long to see the gates of heaven. We know that Christ is the foundation of Your great house. We hear His holy voice through the witness of apostles and prophets.

1 Kings 7

Great God, where do You dwell? Where is Your house? No one can contain You, yet You inhabit the praise of Your people. We long for heaven, for You are there, yet You are everywhere. We cannot see You, and we easily forget You. Forgive us. Fill us with wisdom and understanding. Grant to us spiritual skill for the beauty of Your Kingdom. Thank You for the gifts that You have given to Your people. There is much beauty, order, and goodness throughout the earth. What must heaven be like, since it is surely superior to what we know and understand? Yet, there is some great purpose to the current creation, and we marvel at the magnificence and order of what we are permitted to observe. We long for You. We seek the complete removal of all sin. We wait for a permanent end to all disappointment and misery. Grant us joy as we see the beauty of the earth, the skies, and the seas. Give to us a great appreciation for the achievements that You have brought through the work and wisdom of men. Above all of Your creatures, blessed be Your Name, O Lord.

1 Kings 8

Our Father in Heaven, we long to be with You, and to know that You are with us. We thank You that You have granted to us a way that we might know You and worship You. Your Son Jesus Christ is the Way. Fill us with Your presence. Fill Your temple with Your glory. We would be so easily distracted by foolish endeavors and meaningless entertainments. When we are taken away from considerations of You and Your will, how can we serve You? Your Son is building a great assembly of worshipers. He is forever upon the throne according to Your promise. We thank You for His great ascension work in the building of Your kingdom. May Your Name be held in high regard forever. Father, forgive us for our sins. Look upon us and have mercy. When we wander far away from You and discover our foolishness, forgive us and bring us home again. When we face danger from any trouble within us or outside us, hear us and help us. You know our weakness, O God. Please help us. Come swiftly to the aid of all those who would call upon Your name, and draw them to Your Son and to His church. Grant us the gift of repentance and bring us home again to You. Hear our prayer and our plea. We need You, O Lord. We have a sense of the imperfection of our entreaties. We do not know how to pray. Have mercy upon us. May Your Son perfect our prayers. In all our requests, we plead the blood of the perfect sacrifice, Jesus, the Lamb. We bless Your Name forever.

1 Kings 9

Sovereign Lord, You hear the prayers of Your Son. We thank You. He has walked in perfect integrity and righteousness. His throne is established forever. Surely we have sinned, and turned aside from the right way. Where would we be without Your grace? Do not turn Your church into a house of ruins. For the glory of Your Name, have great mercy upon all those who call upon You in covenant assembly. Grant that we will be able to live in peace among the people with whom we dwell here below. May Your church be a blessing to others in accord with Your will. May Your kingdom shine as a city on a hill. Grant that many who are enslaved in the chains of sin will find new freedom in Christ. Help us to speak the truth in love, to expose what is evil, and to show forth the way of divine mercy.

1 Kings 10

O Lord God, why do people not see the greatness of Your Son, our King? Why is our breath not taken away from us day by day as we hear of the wisdom and power of Jesus Christ? Surely it is because of Your great love that You have sent us Your Son. You own all things as the Creator and Provider. Grant us what we need for our daily sustenance that we might serve you well. Bless us with the beauty of true holiness. Your majesty is known in the glory of sanctification, for we are living stones in a great temple. Place into our minds a vision of the grandeur of Your kingdom, that we might ask for and receive great things. Your Son and His perfected church are far beyond the glory of the kingdom of Solomon. Will we not have eyes to see? We do believe. Help our unbelief.

1 Kings 11

Lord God, we are so quickly led into traps of sin. Please help us. O Lord, we know that sin will quickly turn our hearts away from You. Guard our lives and protect us. Grant to us holy companions who will encourage us along the way of faith and righteousness. You have given the Kingdom to Your Son Jesus Christ. We are a part of that Kingdom and we are united to this great Son of David. May we stay near Him through Your Word. There are grave dangers everywhere, adversaries who stand against You and Your Anointed Messiah. We need strength and wisdom that is well beyond our abilities. Use us, O God, for the building of Your Kingdom. We desire to do good things for the progress of our brothers and sisters in the faith. You have a perfect knowledge of Your holy will. You shall not be denied. The gods of the nations are less than nothing. To follow them is to travel along the way that leads to destruction. Make Your Son to reign over a glorious Kingdom forever. We are weary, Lord. How can we keep on going? Carry us through this life, and take us home at just the right time.

1 Kings 12

Father God, not every leader that You provide for Your people is a David or a Solomon. Some take the counsel of fools, ignoring the mature advice of those who bring true wisdom. How can Your kingdom prosper with shepherds who do not understand the way that is right? Such men cause unnecessary divisions within Your house. Yet we remember that Your plan is above the schemes of foolish men. We have a King over Your house who is very wise. Help us to see that Your provision for us is very good. Restrain our sin. Speak to us powerfully through Your Word. Use us in the building up of Your kingdom, even though we surely are unworthy servants. Keep us from wicked idolatry. Help us to see Christ and to follow Him, lest we be led further into sin, and cause others to wander far from You by our foolish instructions and loose way of life.

1 Kings 13

Great God, You have spoken to Your people for centuries. Your prophets even spoke about future days centuries into the future. How can this be? Surely You know all things. You have certainly planned all things. Father, it is a great privilege that You have given to some men the task of proclaiming Your Word. May Your teachers within Your church consider the fearful responsibility that they have to live in accord with the truth that they proclaim. Grant to these servants unusual discernment, that they might recognize the difference between what is right and the lying words spoken by those who claim to represent You. Father, we thank You for the completed Word that we have in the Scriptures of the Old and New Testaments. Help us to take it all to heart, and to test all things according to this completed Word. Build Your Kingdom, and grant faith to men by the hearing of Your Word.

1 Kings 14

Glorious God, we live in a world full of sickness and death. You have granted to us a special love for our children, and our hearts are broken when they face grave illness and trouble. What must Your love for us be that You have called us Your children? What an amazing love You have displayed through the cross of Christ! There are times and seasons that You have ordained for the people that You have created. Your determinations are true and right. Help us to receive Your truth with humility, for You are God, and there is no other. Men live out their days. We sin, even within Your church. Our sins are varied and offensive. Your discipline of Your people is all around us. We cannot understand Your providence, but we know that Your love for Your children is sure. Will we not follow the clear directives of Your moral law? Have mercy on us.

1 Kings 15

Lord God, You have given Your people kings, yet some of these rulers did not truly follow You. By Your kind provision, we have the greatest of all kings in Your Son Jesus Christ. He will reign in perfect holiness forever. As we consider His intentions and actions, there is no point that requires any correction or exception. He is pure in everything. Thank You for His wisdom and His great generosity toward us. Lord, You have made a covenant with Your Son that shall never be broken. We are greatly blessed through this eternal covenant, because we have been united to Jesus, our King. Through this covenant we have a sure eternal hope. In the world and even in the church we understand that there are many who would lead in an evil way. Carry us through this age as those who belong to the age to come. This age is full of intrigue and war, but in the age to come we will know the most wonderful peace forever.

1 Kings 16

Sovereign Lord, Your works of providence for Your people over many generations are hard for us to understand. You are not the author of sin, yet You ordain all things that come to pass. You work through the means that You see fit to use, wisely governing and limiting evil, and working out Your good purposes. In the history of Your people we see our own depravity. Take away from us every impulse to evil conspiracies and murderous hatred. Purify our hearts and minds with the Spirit of Christ, or we will surely be overtaken by our own sin. Protect us also from wickedness all around us. Guide us into helpful, loving relationships, for we have seen in Your Word the evil that can come through marriage to one who is not true to You. Have mercy on us, O Lord, and forgive us.

1 Kings 17

Great God and King, we thank You for the provision of prophets, men of God who spoke Your truth even in times of great danger. You supplied their needs and cared for them during times of suffering. You who rule over all Your creatures and all their actions, are still well able to help faithful servants of the truth. You who commanded the raven in the wilderness can use any means you should choose to answer the requests of Your servants. Through the Word of Your prophets You even withheld rain and provided food for your children, and even resurrection life. May we find new life through the preaching of Your Word by faithful men of God even today.

1 Kings 18

Father, You bring rain upon the earth at just the right time. In the days of Elijah, you worked through Your servant to confront evil rulers. It is a frightening thing to face the sword of the civil government when it is in the hand of a perverse man. Even today Your servants throughout the world face great dangers from corrupt and incompetent governments. They are quick to call Your true servants troublemakers, when their own sins have brought trouble upon so many people. Worse than this, even those who claim to follow You have been led astray into horrible idolatry. You are the God who hears. You do not sleep. You are not impressed with desperate and idolatrous acts of humiliation aimed at forcing Your hand. The gods of the nations are nothing. They have no voice. They do not answer. They can do nothing. Grant Your wandering children wisdom in the day of a holy contest. Send fire from heaven that would touch our hearts and call us back to clear spiritual thinking. May we see Your hand and fall on our faces, for You, O Lord, are God. Answer us when we pray to You. Turn the hearts of Your people back to You, and glorify Your holy Name. The day of Your vengeance is surely coming. Our only hope is in Your Son Jesus. He is the true Man of God. His prayers are completely effectual, and He has prayed for us. Grant us sweet rain from heaven, that we might be refreshed in Your service in a day of intense struggle.

1 Kings 19

Lord God, even after we win a great struggle by Your hand, when we awake in the morning we are still here in this wicked world. Dangerous enemies that face some setback regroup for yet another assault. Jezebels lose one day, and are thus enraged to perform greater works of evil the next. We must not live in fear of them. We are not alone. You are with us, and Your people are everywhere. You have reserved many thousands who have not bowed the knee to Baal. You have work for us to do even today. Lead Your servants in a good direction, lest we waste our time in foolish pursuits. Help us to die to self, that we might live to Christ in the fullness of Your Word and Spirit.

1 Kings 20

Father God, will men of evil continue to disregard the true Word that comes from You? Yet even dangerous men within Your church encounter a day of fear when they face an enemy who seems stronger than they are. Will they turn to You in that day? If they do, will it be only for a moment so that they can turn back to their sin when they feel safe again? Lord, You are so merciful, and we are so quickly enticed into foolish works of unrighteousness. Grant to us hearts that are very willing to hear Your Word, not for a brief moment only, but forever and ever. You are the God of the hills and of the plains. There is no place in all of creation that is free from Your sovereign power. Even our spirits are within Your sure control. How wonderful are Your great purposes, O Lord! The history of Your saving work is moving forward in our times. Nations are hearing the Word of Christ, and light is coming to dark places. Even when we begin to celebrate the new progress of Your Word, the contest has just begun in that place. We foolishly make a covenant with evil, and forget that our warfare is not over until Your Son returns. Our great King Jesus will make a full end of the wicked when He comes to rescue the righteous.

1 Kings 21

Lord, we need wisdom to fight against indwelling sin. Why is there a continuing evil impulse within the souls of the redeemed? Help us to put that lurking foe to the sword. Make us wise in the battle. Let us petition the King of kings to send all His powerful resources to hunt down this brutal adversary who is troubling us. Help us to see that any evil is not alone, but is part of an army of wickedness. If one foe is put to death, another one rises up. Will we give in to sin without a serious fight? Would anyone believe the resolves that we make against sin, when we still reserve for ourselves some secret place of evil? We will surely run there when we feel the tug of our depravity. Help us to hear of Your judgment against Ahab and Jezebel. It will only be by Your mercy that the judgment against us will be put away in the blood of the Lamb, Jesus Christ.

1 Kings 22

Lord God, the danger of our sin is all around us. Not only do we have iniquity within us and in our assemblies and cities, but we also feel the danger of sin in high places in Your church and in our nations. Teach us to inquire of You in every situation. We humbly ask You to lead us every day. Order all the events before us. Help us to be sensible of the warfare all around us. Shall we go forth into battle without the truth of Your Word? We have a great King in Jesus Christ, our Lord. He pleads for us above. Send forth Your Holy Spirit with the truth this day. Keep false prophets far away from us. Help us by granting to us an accurate and bold presentation of Your Word. We thank You for the Scriptures. Give us the courage to approach You in humble prayer. Teach us to seek Your will above all things. We ask that You would use our prayers to grant to us those things that You desire for Your children. Teach us to have godly affections and requests. The battle rages all around us. Make us faithful to Your Word. If we die today, may we die the death of those who have loved You, and have been faithful to the commission that Your Son has given to His church. Where we fail, appoint others who will listen more attentively to Your voice in the Scriptures. From generation to generation move us along according to Your Word. Where we have been sadly stubborn in our rejection of truth, we pray that future generations of Your church will be moved to see the truth that we have rejected in our folly.

2 Kings

2 Kings 1

Father God, we need You. It will do us no good to inquire of foreign gods. We need spiritual wisdom that can only come from You. You are the one God in heaven who rules over life and death. You have created all things, and You sustain everything by the Word of Your power. You are a consuming fire. We must worship You alone. Please have mercy on us, that we might live. Give us hope in the day of illness and trouble. Forgive our sins, draw us near to You in Christ, and turn us away from all idolatry.

2 Kings 2

Sovereign Lord, take us up to heaven at just the right time. Grant to us wise hearts that will not cling to things here below. Thank You for our eternal hope, secured for us in the life and death of Your Son. We mourn the loss of those who depart, men of insight, full of Your Spirit. Yet You are the one who makes a man to be a strong servant for You. In the day that an Elijah goes to a better home, You are able to raise up an Elisha for the good of Your church. Grant us faithful servants, men of God who will truly speak Your Word. Grant us hearts that look to our great prophet Jesus Christ. May we always look to Him and live. Give us new hope and the fresh water of Your presence. Heal Your church. Supply great resources of heavenly wisdom for those who are young, that they might humbly turn to You and live.

2 Kings 3

Glorious God, You work out Your holy will according to Your plan. You rule over the affairs of men and nations. You see Your church in our weak condition, and provide for us servants who will speak Your Word in truth. Help us to turn away from false spiritual paths. Grant us the blessing of Your presence. Be a stream of living water to Your people, for we thirst for You, the true God. We hate our sin. Please forgive us. We need You. The battle before us is fierce. Idolatrous men perform extreme acts of devotion to things that are not gods. Will Your people not live in accord with Your true commandments? Will we not offer up our lives to You?

2 Kings 4

Merciful Lord, many of Your servants are in the most desperate condition. We are poor, sick, alone, and fearful. Grant us faith. We can do all things through Your Son who strengthens us. You will surely provide for Your church in the day of trouble. You grant wonderful gifts to us. It is by Your power that life is given, and it is by Your power that life is taken away. Will there be help for us in a day of the saddest loss? Please remind us of the fact of resurrection. In this world, all is not well. Your people are in bitter distress. Come to us in this horrible moment, that we might believe. We long for that day when each one that You have given to us will live again. Surely such good gifts as we have received for a time have been given to us for some wonderful purpose. Surely there is hope with you. You will glorify Your Name. We trust You, O God. Have mercy upon us. Give food to the hungry this day, O Lord. Grant us Your Son, the great Bread of heaven, that we might live, though we grieve.

2 Kings 5

Father God, Your plans of mercy have gone far beyond the borders of Israel. Your people, scattered throughout the earth, cannot help but testify to the glory of Your Name. Those who do not know Your grace and power can only fear men, but we have come to know You. There is a great prophet in the heavenly Jerusalem. By His Word the leper was healed. We have hope in Him. You have washed us in the fresh water of the Holy Spirit. You have sprinkled us with the blood of Christ. We are clean. One day we shall be whole. Until that day, help us to worship You in Spirit and in truth. You see our secret deeds of fleshly greed. You know even the thoughts and intentions of our hearts. We bring such trouble upon ourselves because of our rebellion against You. Forgive us, Father. May our hope of eternal life be strong because of the perfect righteousness of Your Son.

2 Kings 6

Lord God, Your servants have followed You for generations. You have provided for their needs. Requests that may seem trivial to us are not beyond Your concern. We worry that we are troubling You with petitions that are too unimportant. Correct our foolish thinking. You are not limited as we are. Your attention to a small matter does not distract You from more important concerns. You command us to cast our cares upon You. We will obey You, O Lord. Help us to see something of Your power in the daily events of our lives. Help us also to bring our largest petitions to You. It seems too big a thing for us to be delivered from overwhelming trouble. Bring our restless spirits to Your holy place, that we might rejoice in Your presence. Relieve us of sinful and fruitless plans, and bring us safely home. Will You feed the hungry when it seems that there is no hope of food? What kind of unspeakable wickedness would we be part of in the day of our distress? We will wait for You, O Lord. We believe that You hear our prayers.

2 Kings 7

Our Father, You have helped us with the very biggest problems that we could ever have. You use the weak and the poor to show Your great strength. You send away the threatening foe, and leave behind a feast for Your people. We have learned where the greatest riches are. Help us to go to all who will hear, and to tell them about the blessings that we have in Jesus Christ. This is a day of good news. Grant to us the charity to speak. Send forth Your messengers for this great purpose. The news that we bring is of the very best blessing. You have sent forth Your goodness to us, like an open window from heaven. We receive You with joy.

2 Kings 8

Almighty God, there have been many times and places where people have faced great troubles. Nonetheless, You have the ability to bring life to those who have died. There is nothing too difficult for You. Your sovereign power is not limited to the church. You even give good gifts to many people who do not call upon Your Name. There is much brutality in this world, and forceful men oppress the weak. Above all earthly powers, You are God. Your promises are forever. You have granted that a great descendant of David will reign eternally. He is surely the Head of the church. He also rules over all nations. We do not see kings submitting to Him today, yet every knee shall bow to Him in the day of His power. We long for the gift of a new creation. We long for the day when oppressive rulers have been put far away, when we will see the Lord Jesus ruling over all.

2 Kings 9

Lord God Almighty, You rule over all nations and all people. Surely Your Son is especially the King and Head of Your church. That assembly is comprised not only of the descendants of Jacob. People of many nations have been anointed with Your Spirit. You have granted us life, in the midst of a world that is full of death. We have a hope that is far better than anything the world can offer us. We have heard the sure Word of the life to come, and we believe. We will not run to news of false religion that is neither good nor true. There is a day of reckoning for all evil. Will not the cross of Christ be enough for us on that day? Are we dissatisfied with that full atonement, so that we continue searching for what is obviously wrong? May the Jezebel impulse of sin and false prophesy be removed far from Your church. May we learn to flee from immorality and lies. The way of evil is an ugly road in the end. It leads only to destruction. Keep us in the Day of Judgment because of what Christ has done for us. We will soon be with You in the land of the living, rescued out of this sea of evil and death.

2 Kings 10

Merciful Lord, You have granted to us the great gift of families. Each of us had a father and mother by birth, though we may have not known them. Many have been granted brothers and sisters. Some have enjoyed the privilege of being husbands and wives. Some have been blessed to be parents for a season. As great as these gifts are, they are far surpassed by the blessing of our family relations within the household of faith. Though we may lose our loved ones in our birth families through the treachery of men and Your own sovereign purposes, nothing can separate us from our new family relationships within the body of Christ. In that household of faith, no one will worship false gods. Nothing that offends will be in that holy place. Thank You for Your eternal plan, O God. Use whatever means You see fit to bring about all of Your holy will. One day the places of false worship that litter the earth and defile even Your church will be utterly consumed by Your wrath. Your Kingdom of light will shine forever and ever, and we shall dwell securely in Your city with joy.

2 Kings 11

Father God, there is such brutality in evidence throughout this world of sin, and even in Your church there is much evil. Yet You have the power to hide Your servants in the place of safety until the day of their appointed service comes. Even Your Son, Jesus Christ, gave His life at the time of Your choice, and not according to the plans of wicked men who would have thrown Him from a cliff or stoned Him. At just the right time Jesus died on the cross, and at just the right time this perfect Son of David was anointed King through His resurrection. This was a most surprising development in the eyes of Your enemies, but it was well known to Him and to You. We trust You with our lives. We turn away from all false worship and heresy, and commit our hearts to You. Purify Your kingdom, and grant to us a season of peace as we seek Your glory and pursue Your righteousness.

2 Kings 12

Lord God, You grant us lives to be lived for Your glory. We have opportunities for faithfulness that You give to us. You also grant us resources of money and time for the use of Your kingdom. Will we use these things for ourselves, and miss the opportunity to serve You sacrificially? Help us to love Your house out of our deep regard for You. Give us others with whom we may serve. Build up Your kingdom for Your own glory. Protect us from vicious men who have no intention of truly serving You.

2 Kings 13

Great Lord, trouble has come upon Your people. Evil leaders turn them over to the hand of their enemies. These foes would lead us into false worship. We seem to have no strength left in us. We want to come back to the way of faithfulness, but we do not remember the path of righteousness any more. We fill our hearts with foolish things, and lose sense of the great battle before us. Grant to us a fresh sense of the victory that we have through the resurrection of Jesus Christ. Look upon us in our weariness and grant us new strength by the power of Your Spirit. You have not forgotten Your promises to our forefathers in the faith. Help us to remember You, that we might obey Your precepts.

2 Kings 14

Our Father, our lives are short. How will we use the strength that You have given to us? Will we serve our own immediate needs, or will we be engaged in the battle that is ours this day? Will we be so captivated by the wonders of this world that we forget the blessing of the world to come? The day comes when even the best men die. We need something more than money, possessions, and power. All these thing swiftly flee far away from us. We need eternal life. Watch over us as we serve You in strange places where Your Name is not held in high regard. Keep us from doing what is evil in Your sight, and make us faithful to the light that we have already received. There must be some victory for Your Name beyond that which can be won with the weapons of this world. Lead us in righteousness, O Lord.

2 Kings 15

Glorious Lord, what can Your people do in a time of great instability and trouble? Some face challenges of health that are very difficult to bear. Others face sins that so easily ensnare them, and they are useless as leaders among those they must help. Many face the attacks of evil men, who conspire against them. Still others have their families destroyed by wicked adversaries. There is trouble within us because of our sin, and there is trouble outside us because of our enemies. Where will we find the strength to remember Your Law and obey it? Your Son was born in an evil generation. He faced a grave challenge from the devil. Leaders stood against Him, and rulers of the Gentiles were willing to see Him suffer. Yet He secured our eternal hope. Thank You that we can rest in Him, though we are facing trouble from every direction.

2 Kings 16

Our Father, when we think that we cannot bear any more trouble, there may still be more testing before us. How will we survive? People that should be serving

You may utterly give themselves over to idolatry and murder. How can we keep on going? Give Your servants new strength by Your Spirit. You supply us with resources of divine aid when it would appear that all is lost. Why should our leaders fall in love with the worship of false gods? There is no sense in this sin. Help us to feel again the true movements of Your Holy Spirit in the faithful ministry of Your Word. Give us a renewed respect for Your worship. Grant us a great repentance, and make even the sons of our most deceived enemies turn away from the foolish wickedness of their fathers.

2 Kings 17

Sovereign Lord, how can Your people survive under wicked leaders? Our sin is all around us, and we face enemies that are too powerful for us. O God, we admit to You our fascination with the idolatries of this world. Like Your people of old, we have secretly served false gods. You have warned us through those who spoke Your Word. We despised the message of the truth and Your holy commandments. We have moved in directions that have been horribly unprofitable. What trouble we have brought upon our lives! Please forgive us, help us, and rescue us from evil. We thank You for our strong Deliverer, Jesus Christ. He is able to help us. He is powerful and holy. He made a promise to be with us, and to help us and our children. Please teach us how to live in a world full of false religious philosophies and immorality. We do not know how to do this. We need You to help us today and always. We need to remember how to fear You and to follow You. Deliver us out of the hand of our enemies. Teach us to be dedicated to You with all that we are and all that we have.

2 Kings 18

Father God, You are able to bring good news to Your people at just the right times. You also know the right discipline to give to Your children. We thank You for the relief that You grant by giving us leaders who will listen to You and obey Your commandments. Even the best of these will yet have weakness and sin. Enemies of great power and skill may come and speak to us words of hate and faithlessness. Teach us to trust in You, O Lord our God. Help us not to fall into dangerous lies and traps. The world around us is full of trouble, but You are far more powerful than any foe. We will listen to You. Thank You for Your Son. His holiness and power are so far above even the best rulers. He will fight for us in our day of desperate need.

2 Kings 19

O God, we have been humbled by our troubles. We were so proud of ourselves until a day of distress came to us. You must help us, or we will not be able to survive. You can send powers and principalities fleeing, despite all of their proud boasts. Grant us courage today. Fill us with a spirit of heartfelt prayer. Hear us when we cry out to You. You hear and see those who mock You. Save us from the hands of enemies that are too strong for us. You hear our prayers, and grant us the gift of hope. We will stand with You. You are able to humble the proudest foe. The years of our most powerful adversaries will come to an end. Your plans are from of old, and You will do all Your holy will. We will be amazed by Your wonderful deliverance. Surely You are God, and we are Your people. The end of the story will be different than the sorrow of the present moment.

2 Kings 20

Our Father, our lives are in Your hands. When we face our mortality, we cry out to You. You grant us life according to Your good pleasure. We thank You that our King Jesus reigns forever. The resurrection of our Messiah is the greatest sign to us of the truth of Your promises. On the day of blessing, help us to remain in watchfulness. Teach us to remember the humbling providences that we have suffered in the past, and to resist the danger of foolish pride.

2 Kings 21

O God, how can it be that a child will not follow in the way of a godly father? Does one generation tear down the idols of wickedness, only for the next generation to build up the same abominations again? How can those who are called by Your Name be so foolish and hard-hearted? O Lord, bring us the blessings of the new age even today. Innocent blood is shed all around us in every age, but some times are worse than others. Grant us relief. How many years of sadness can we survive? You will surely hear us and help us. We long for the day of victory when all of our disappointments and sins will be utterly swept away.

2 Kings 22

We thank You, O Lord, for a surprisingly wonderful day of relief. We thank You for righteous children that come from homes that seemed to be committed to idolatry and sin. Grant that Your church will rediscover Your Word even in our day. Grant that we will be grieved concerning our rebellion against You. Help us to have a godly response to the troubles that we face. Have mercy on us. You know that Your church has so often forsaken You. If You were not true to Your great promises, we surely would have been destroyed long ago.

2 Kings 23

Lord God, we need You. We have been made sick by our sin. We want to walk in Your ways again. Cleanse Your temple. Remove those leaders who will not turn away from idolatry and wickedness. Bring a powerful repentance to many. Do Your work in the midst of this evil age and show us hope for a new life. We need the courage of Your Son among us again. Send forth Your messengers to call Your people to worship again in truth. Is there some horrible unseen adversary who is against us? Surely You know what You are doing, even governing all things for Your glory. Teach us to turn to You in a fuller imitation of Your Son. Do not utterly abandon us, O God. Give us hope for the future, even on the day when the most godly leaders are suddenly destroyed. Have mercy on us, O God. We know that we should trust You today. We will obey You, even though many give themselves over to sin.

2 Kings 24

God in heaven, what can we do when good gifts are taken away from us? The godly way of a father may only be a memory. Sons and grandsons have lost all sense of Your truth. They are taken captive by enemies that are too strong for them. How will we find hope again? Surely You will send Your Son for us. Come quickly, Lord Jesus.

2 Kings 25

Father, we love You and cling to You. We have no one left but You. Our pride and our joy have been taken away. Yet through it all, You are God. We will trust You. You have the words of life. The cross is still the only atoning sacrifice for sin. The resurrection is still our only hope. Our words flee from us. What can we say in the depths of our grief? Where is Your glory, O God? Will we provoke You to wrath even now? How can there be more wrath when our sins have been atoned for? Surely our hope in Christ is still secure, and we will eat at Your table in glory forever.

1 Chronicles

1 Chronicles 1

Great God of Creation, we have been made in Your image. From one man, our father Adam, have come all men. Each nation is known by You, where they have come from, and where they are going. Some have been mighty in their own eyes, and in the opinion of their neighbors. Even the strongest have faced trouble and death. You have granted to us the great gift of faith. Abraham, chosen by You, and sent out by You, is also a father to us, a father in this most precious gift of faith. Help us to walk in the power of faith today. Our days and our people come and go, but You are eternal. Through faith in our Messiah Jesus Christ we have everlasting life. This world will pass away, and so many of the names and nations of this world will perish, but You will remain forever and ever. Our life is in You.

1 Chronicles 2

Father God, You have chosen us in Your Son, Jesus Christ, the greatest descendant of David, of the tribe of Judah, the son of Jacob, the son of Isaac, the son of Abraham. This great royal Messiah Jesus is our only hope. Our hope is not in religious objects or other great possessions. We do not trust in our land or in our descendants. We do not gain eternal life through the family of our first birth, no matter how great our privileges may have been, whether our name among men was high or low. You have given us a second birth in Jesus Christ. Our heritage in Him is the best heritage that we could ever have, and it is ours by adoption. Help us to understand that heritage more deeply for our spiritual good. Especially help us to understand the benefit of being Your sons in Jesus Christ our Redeemer.

1 Chronicles 3

Glorious Lord, Your Son Jesus is forever the chosen King over Your people. He came from a long line of famous sons. We now have this royal heritage. Our current status of blessing is due to our relation to You through this great descendant of David. As children who have been brought into the best of all families through Your kind rescue, we pray that You would give us a greater appreciation of our new history, that we might walk in faith securely in Your eternal Son.

1 Chronicles 4

Father God, how is it that Judah came to be the tribe of our Messiah King Jesus? Surely it was not through their moral or physical strength, but by Your electing purposes. The story of every land and people is full of pain. Much of it has been lost to us as part of a forgotten past. In pain we have come into this world, and we have caused much trouble for others through our sin. Please forgive us. Help us now in our difficulties. Bless Your holy Son Jesus, who for our sake, faced the greatest turmoil ever known. Enlarge His Kingdom. May Your hand always be with Him. Keep His descendants from harm. One day we shall be removed from all trouble. Grant us a taste of that even today. May the story of Your Son's church not be everlasting pain, but the greatest eternal delight. Today we face danger and trouble, for not all have faith, but You know what we can bear and what would be too much for us. Look on us in the day of present danger and deliver us from evil.

1 Chronicles 5

Sovereign Lord, what trouble we have brought upon ourselves and others by our sin. So many have fallen into the hands of powerful enemies. If You were not stronger than every foe, there would be no hope for Your people. We are so thankful to You for Your marvelous strength and protection. Trouble is very near to us. We cry out to You with this urgent plea, not only for us, but for our brothers and sisters throughout the world. We face the hatred of ruthless men and unseen powers and principalities. Our enemies would desire to sift us as wheat, but Your Son has prayed for us that our faith may not fail. Help us to strengthen one another by that same faith, and to comfort each other in days of trial. You have granted to us great comfort in the gospel. Surely our troubles will not last forever.

1 Chronicles 6

Lord God, one of Your tribes of old was given over to special duties of worship. They were in charge of Your temple, and in the tabernacle of old. Among their number were the descendants of Aaron, who had priestly duties before You on behalf of all the people. Some of Your servants in the tribe of Levi had special duties of singing in Your presence. Our High Priest, Jesus, is not descended from this tribe, yet He is a priest forever for us according to Your Word. Through Him, we also are priests to You. Together we enjoy the special duties of worshipers. Give us spiritual strength that we might sing to You with joy forever. We flee to Your Son for refuge day by day, for we have sinned against You. Thank You for Your grace. Thank You for our restoration to the special privileges of those who worship You in Christ. Grant us Your great provision day by day. Bring us to the heavenly Zion, where we will worship You forever, together with all the redeemed.

1 Chronicles 7

Our Father, it is such a privilege to be a part of Your church. Though our stories will largely be lost to history, it is enough for us that we are known by You. We rejoice that our names are written in heaven. Why should we fall into a snare of sin because of our desire for fame and for the praise of men? Surely You have warned us to seek first Your kingdom, and not to give ourselves over to worry. Isn't it enough for us that we are Your children? Lead us in the pursuit of righteousness according to the commandment of Jesus Christ. Help us to be faithful to You in our families. Establish a good heritage in our children and grandchildren for many generations, a heritage of faith and obedience. We know that this can only come by Your grace, but we want to be faithful to Your command. Give us hope, even in the day when it might appear that all is already lost.

1 Chronicles 8

Glorious God, there are those who were heads of father's houses among Your people of old. They were well known people of some position and importance. Some of them had moments of great military victory. They surely had many gifts and had achieved great things by the power that You supplied. Yet even they were humbled and carried away by enemies in the day of disaster. Among Your people were those who were the ancestors and descendants of King Saul. He was a King in Israel, yet not the father of the Messiah. His dynasty would end with himself. Help us, O Lord. If we and our children are not found in the great Son of David, Jesus Christ, there is no hope for us. Our wealth and achievements can never save us.

1 Chronicles 9

Father God, You know how to bring a day of blessing upon those who deserve only Your wrath and curse. You are able to meet the requirements of both Your justice and Your mercy. Through the wonder of substitution, there is a hope and a future for those who would call upon Your Name. You have appointed one Man as the representative of Your children in the place of judgment. Over the generations, in anticipation of the provision of Your Son, You have shown much patience and granted much provision to Your people. You gave men to serve You in an earthly sanctuary. You kept a remnant for Yourself in the times of even the deepest wickedness. When all would have seemed lost, when it appeared that Your work of grace had been utterly overturned by wicked men, You restored people from the place of discipline, and established a presence again in the land in accord with Your promises. Without this one Substitute for sinners there could have been no hope for us, no future, no return from captivity, no gifts of faith and repentance, and no reformation when we had wandered so far from Your Word. Thank You for Jesus Christ. He has taken away our wickedness and leads us even now into a better sanctuary than the one made with human hands. There is a great day coming. The repentant have been given a secure hope in a good land through the life and death of Your Son.

1 Chronicles 10

Almighty Father, we mourn the loss of leaders who in previous days led us in good pathways. The mysteries of Your providence are more than we can fathom. Help us to have the strength of silence when words will only add to our confusion. Help us to keep faith with You, to seek guidance from You, and to walk in the way of Your Word.

1 Chronicles 11

Father God, we thank You for moments when we experience a new beginning and a fresh hope. We especially thank You for Jesus Christ, the Son of David. He will lead us into victory. We want to live in the church, the city of this great Son of David. Give us the joy of being with men and women who are strong in faith, service, and humility. Save us by a great victory at just the right time, and use

Your people according to Your wise plans. May Your Son be our stronghold. Give brave men and women the new water of Your life-giving Spirit that they might pour out their lives as offerings before You. This is how we want to live our lives in the camp of Your people. Help us to rejoice in You when You appoint some among us who will be doers of great deeds. Keep envy far from us, since we remember that everything that any of us has is surely by Your grace. You give strength, intelligence, faithfulness, and love from Your storehouse of all that is good. You are to be praised for every good gift. One falls, and another is raised up to serve. We are weak. You are strong. May Your Name be praised forever.

1 Chronicles 12

Great God, we thank You that we are not alone. Above all, You are with us, but You have given us the gift of living within the society of Your people. In even the most desperate situation, You will bring helpers to us according to Your will. We ask that You would bring us good friends and co-laborers. Keep away from us those who will not bless Your people with the peace and wisdom that come from above. There are those who only bring fruitless division. We cannot bear the trouble that such false workers bring. Will we even become people like that? May it never be. May our allegiance to the house of the Son of David be strong by Your grace. Grant us the ability to work peacefully and joyfully with others. We know that most of the service in Your kingdom is not the work of a few, but is a common labor under the leadership of our one great King. Help us to see the others who are the gifts that You have already given to us, and grant us an uncommon love for one another. Give us more compatriots who are blessed brothers and sisters in the holy warfare that You have appointed for Your children in our place and time.

1 Chronicles 13

Lord God, what an amazing gift You gave for Your people to build, the ark of the covenant, where You were pleased to dwell above the cherubim! Nonetheless, how dangerous it was to touch that ark! One of Your holy men died by reaching out his hand to steady it. Lord, there is a sense in which it seems to us that it is a fearful thing to serve You, for we wonder about the consequences of coming near You wrongly. We wonder about the remaining pride and presumption in our hearts. We wonder about what our sin and weakness will mean for us and for those we love. Lord, how can we serve You without danger or great trouble? Yet we see Jesus crowned with glory and honor, and we are called by Him to follow in the way of cross. Grant us courage and secret joy alongside our very rational fear.

1 Chronicles 14

Great Lord and King, You will use whatever means You desire in order to build Your kingdom. Even beyond the community of faith, there are those that You appoint to bring resources and skills that You will use for our good and Your glory. Grant us wisdom as we move forward in the mission that is before us. May we be an army of love, proclaiming the truth of the love of Christ to every land.

1 Chronicles 15

Sovereign Lord, at just the right time You shine the light of Your Spirit upon Your holy Word, and in the depths of our hearts we see the error of our ways and the glory of Your Son. Thank You for this tremendous grace. Thank you for the gifts of faith and repentance that You give to us day by day. As we see the wonder of Your holy Word, we give ourselves again to You. We give ourselves again to the joy of Your appointed worship. We give ourselves to holy singing and rejoicing in Your presence. We marvel at this great provision. Where once there was ignorance, disobedience, and death, now You have given to us new knowledge and astounding celebration. Grant to us the gift of holy discernment that we would reject false worship, but let us not despise those who rejoice in You in accord with Your will. May we join in that appointed service with a fullness of joy that could only come from You.

1 Chronicles 16

Father God, You are here in Your city, Your church. You give us food for our souls, as You have also given us food for our bodies. You grant to each of us a part in the service of thanks that we offer up to You. There is much reason for us to draw near to You in Christ. You are great. You have made perfect promises. You have redeemed Your people and have brought us into Your land in Christ Jesus. You have blessed us with a wonderful mission. We will extend Your worship everywhere. May all the peoples of the earth worship You, for You are the one who is the Creator of the heavens and the earth. You keep us, and You save us. Gather us again to worship You, for You should be praised forever and ever. May our rejoicing in Your presence be new and fresh every day, as Your people bring to You the fruits of Your abundant blessings.

1 Chronicles 17

God of Grace and Glory, You have put it within our hearts that we should serve You. Will we build a house for You? No, we will be a house for You, a house that You will build. Your Son is the Cornerstone in this new house. Through His death and resurrection that great Cornerstone has been placed into perfect position. You have given us a sure foundation for Your house in His Word spoken through apostles and prophets. You have made us to be living stones in this great house. You have brought us into the family of Your servant David, even calling us Your sons through Jesus Christ. There is no one like You. You have rescued Your people and have helped us to this day. May Your Name be magnified forever. We will pray to You with confidence, and ask You for great things according to Your Word. You have already promised us great things and have already given us great things in Christ Jesus our Lord.

1 Chronicles 18

Father God, we thank You that Your Son is such a mighty warrior for us. Surely the enemies against us are formidable. They are too strong for us. Your Son is far superior to every enemy. You are able to make even the attacks of our foes work for Your purposes, since You make the wrath of Your enemies to praise You. Your Son rules over His church and He brings equity and goodness wherever He goes.

1 Chronicles 19

Lord God, though we would treat even our enemies with love, we cannot be sure that our actions will be rightly interpreted by others. What shall we do when people are intent upon disgracing us? We need You to fight our battles, and we need to entrust our image and even our very lives to You. Protect Your church when the world comes against us. We are fighting a different kind of battle than the armies of this world, and we need to pursue victory using different sorts of weapons. May we have godliness with contentment, holiness of life, and Christ-like love. May we resist every temptation to sin. Fight this great battle for us day by day. May we especially live at peace with You under the authority of our Messiah King.

1 Chronicles 20

Great God, we are the recipients of such a wonderful inheritance. All of our holy expectations are secure in Christ. He has waged war on our behalf. He won a great victory against sin, death, and Satan through His death on the cross. The adversary who came against us was too big an enemy for us. We could never fight against demonic hosts without our King. He has convincingly defeated our foes, and has demonstrated His great success through His resurrection.

1 Chronicles 21

Our Father, please forgive us for our presumption, pride, and sin. Why do we insist on knowing things that You do not want us to seek out? Why do we ignore the highest revealed truths that are most important for us to consider? Even in our strange rebellion, You have determined to work out Your good purposes. In Your discipline of Your church, You will not change the Word that You have spoken, that the gates of hell shall not prevail against Christ and His people. Your Son did not sin at all, yet He was willing to let Your fury for our sin come upon Him. He became for us a Sin Offering. He is now the Cornerstone of a costly new temple. On that one Rock, the site for Your Kingdom has been firmly established. We are being built up even now on the foundation of apostles and prophets, with Jesus Christ Himself as our one Rock of Help.

1 Chronicles 22

Father God, we thank You that Your Son is building His church. Though it may not seem magnificent in the eyes of the world, its great glories are seen through the eyes of faith. Our Leader is the King of Peace. He built this house for Your Name, and You have established Him as King forever. He has fully obeyed all of Your statutes and has taken away the enormous debt of our sin. He is the Head, and we are His body. Your church is moving forward everywhere as a living temple of the Holy Spirit.

1 Chronicles 23

Great God and King, You have provided leaders and servants in Your church, serving at the pleasure of Your Son. Each one has a special role to play. Each is known to You and has been equipped by You for this service. Help us to train up the next generation of church leaders and workers, that they might move ahead in the plans that You have for Your people after our days here have been completed. You have given us rest through the blood of Your Son. The matters of Your church are most important to us, for Your church is an earthly outpost of Your heavenly Kingdom. Make us faithful in our duties as an expression of our love for You.

1 Chronicles 24

Merciful God, we have a great High Priest over Your house forever, the Lord Jesus Christ. He is true man and yet also eternal God. He does not need to be replaced, for He will never be removed from His office. He performs amazing works of worship and blessing. Through Him our worship is offered perfectly to You. Through Him also sure words of blessing are spoken upon Your church, that we might live and prosper in Your service forever. We are a part of the priestly league of the faithful through Your Son. Help us to understand our right role as those who worship You, receive Your blessing, and extend Your benediction throughout the earth. May Your church bring the message of redemption through Your Son wherever men live and move and have their being.

1 Chronicles 25

Glorious Lord, we want to make a glad noise to You day by day. Is it pleasing to You when Your people sing to You from the heart? You need nothing, yet You inhabit the praises of Your people. May our families sing to You with great joy. Grant to Your church integrity, desire, and skill, all useful for our service of worship. Help us to focus on you, and not on ourselves or the gifts that You have given us. Help us to remember that it is Your most excellent goodness that is so worthy of our fullest worship and praise.

1 Chronicles 26

Father God, in days of old You provided gatekeepers for Your temple and Your holy city. From the time of Adam's fall You have acted upon the necessity of setting a guard to keep people out from Your immediate presence, and to protect all who are so perfectly safe in Your heavenly temple. Thank You for the work of Your holy angels, whom You have appointed as servants to the heirs of salvation. Thank You also for the ministry of Your deacons, who work hard for You and Your people. They watch over all the facilities and finances of Your assembly here on earth and care for the needs of the poor. They lead many in performing important tasks of mercy throughout Your Kingdom. We also thank You for those You have raised up for order, truth, justice, and beauty in the world all around us. Blessed be Your Name, for You are a God who provides for decency and goodness among the affairs of Your church and more generally throughout the world.

1 Chronicles 27

Glorious God, there has always been a need for leadership, order, and even for military protection since sin entered into the world. We appreciate those who put themselves in dangerous situations in order to help with the security of our families, Your church, and the nations where we now sojourn. Help us to place our trust in You alone, rather than in the strength of men. Armies serve us with courage and diligence, but they cannot lead us home to our heavenly habitation. Grant us those who will serve with integrity and maturity in these important positions. As our young men move to the age of adult duties, we pray that you will help them through this time of transition. Provide excellent advisors and leaders as Your church moves forward with her mission. Teach us to follow our King, the Lord Jesus Christ, and to attend to His Word with a ready heart.

1 Chronicles 28

Glorious God, You have assembled us together for worship and instruction. Your Son gave instructions to His disciples before His ascension on high. He spoke as our great King. It is ours to obey. Let us be about the work that He has graciously given us. We are to build up His holy temple, not a building of stone or wood, but a dwelling place for You made up of people who have been granted spiritual life. Help us day by day in our work together of making disciples for Your Son. You are with us. You will not leave us nor forsake us. Gather to Your church willing people who have skill for service that we might work together with joy.

1 Chronicles 29

Great God, You will build Your holy temple. We provide our efforts and gifts as we are able, but unless You build the house, we would surely labor in vain. We ask that You would use the works of our hands and the gifts of our hearts. Build up Your temple with the rich blessing of people created in Your image. You are great, O Lord. You rule over all, and You can bring us into Your house forever. Who are we? All things come from You. We turn away from all foolish pride. All that we have given You has first come to us through Your gracious hand. Grant that Your people would love and serve You with full hearts. May we bless Your name forever. Thank You for the perfect sacrifice of Your Son, through whom we serve You day by day. Blessed be Your Name forever, for You have provided for Your church the best King ever known among men. We worship You now through Him who is our Lord and is also Your beloved Son.

2 Chronicles

2 Chronicles 1

Great Lord of Creation and Providence, Your Son is not only the perfection of Your power, but also the fullness of Your wisdom. He is with us and He loves us. He has encouraged us in prayer. We should ask, that we might receive. We ask You now for wisdom and knowledge for the purpose of service. We want to love and serve You during this present life. We also want to serve people all around us in accord with Your holy will. Thank You for the many blessings that You bestow upon us. Make Your Name great throughout the earth.

2 Chronicles 2

Our Father, Your Son is at work even now building a house for Your Name. But what is the purpose of that house of redeemed people? You inhabit the praises of Your people. The house that He is building will be a great and wonderful living place of holy worship. Is there something in addition to that? Is it also a place where You will express the wonder of Your life, working through all the redeemed for Your glory? Make Your house glorious. Make Your temple fruitful in every good work. We thank You for the joy of our inclusion in Your majestic kingdom.

2 Chronicles 3

Lord God, where is Your heavenly temple? The old place of worship in Jerusalem had a wonderful heritage. What a joy it was for Your people to travel to the top of Mount Zion, a place not unknown to Abraham, our father in faith. On that land he was prepared to sacrifice Isaac, when You provided an acceptable substitute, and spared his son. When the time came for our redemption, You did not spare Your Son, but gave Him up for us all. Surely the heaven that He has won for us is a much more glorious place than any building that ever existed on earth. We should be full of joy as we travel to that holy land. We know that Your Son even now is our holy temple, and that He is the way to You. Help us to survey the dimensions of Your glorious Son through the Word that You have given us. Help us to love the greatness and security of the One who is our everlasting heavenly Temple.

2 Chronicles 4

Father God, You have given Your Son as our perfect sacrifice. You send forth Your Holy Spirit, that we might be fully cleansed, our consciences washed and purified. We shall be holy priests in Your temple forever, through Your Son Jesus Christ. Thank You for the access that we have been granted to You through Christ, who is the gate to heaven. We have been brought into Your house even now. The keys of the kingdom have been used for the declaration of our forgiveness and our inclusion within Your family. We are grateful for this honor. We look to see with our eyes what we know even now by faith, that the doors of heaven have been opened for us, for Christ has purified the way for us into Your heavenly sanctuary through His precious blood.

2 Chronicles 5

O Lord, we want to do the work that You have for us with excellence. Meet us in our weariness and sin. Remember the blood of Your Son, and provide for us the strength that we need for our journey to Your holy place. Surely You can make our burden light. Why are we carrying unnecessarily heavy baggage that will be of no use in the life to come? Why are we wearying ourselves with tasks that have not come from You? Your yoke is easy and Your burden is light. Help us to remember Your steadfast love. Fill Your church with Your glorious presence even now. More than that, raise us up to Your heavenly glory cloud in time of worship as You call us together with all who would hear Your voice.

2 Chronicles 6

Father God, You have built for us a great place of worship, much better than the greatest building ever built by men. David could not build the temple in Jerusalem, but his son Solomon was the appointed servant for that work. Even so, Solomon could never build the New Testament temple of the Holy Spirit. His greatest Descendant would do this work through His death and resurrection. This same Jesus is using us now as He builds up that temple through Your people. When we pray to You in the midst of that temple, please hear us. Help us when we turn to You for justice in the case of the oppressed. Answer us when we need victory in our warfare against powers and principalities. Heal us when we are sick. Fill us when we are hungry. Especially grant to us Your Son day by day. You know us. We need You. Please hear also the cry of those seeking admission to this heavenly assembly. As they humble themselves and sincerely turn toward Your Son, please hear them from heaven, and grant them a place in Your house through the one Gate that You have provided. When we call upon Your Name for forgiveness, please hear us and restore us. Thank You for Your mercy. Remember Your love for Your Son as we daily bring You the prayers and petitions of Your people.

2 Chronicles 7

Lord God, people speak, but what can we do? You filled Solomon's temple with Your own glory, even with fire from heaven. We marvel at Your works. You are such a great God, and You love us! Your steadfast love endures forever. Your Son's sacrifice is far beyond the thousands of animals sacrificed by any king of Israel. Christ has accomplished through His life and death what no other man could ever have done. The temple in Jerusalem was a holy place of sacrifice in its day. Today we are Your holy temple as the church of Jesus Christ. We claim all Your promises now as those who are in covenant with You in Christ our Lord. Therefore, we humble ourselves before You, we seek Your face, and turn from our wicked ways. Hear us now from heaven, forgive our sin, and heal Your covenant assembly as we worship You. We cannot bear Your wrath. Remember that Your Son died on the cross for us, and that our sins have been atoned for. We earnestly repent and claim the blood of Christ as our only hope.

2 Chronicles 8

Great God, as impressive as some of Your servants of old have been, there is no one who can compare with Your Son Jesus Christ. The greatest among those men of Israel and Judah built cities and conquered peoples. They had thousands of servants, amazing palaces, and great achievements of all kinds. Yet none of them could call forth people from the grave. We have a taste of the power of Your Son in the amazing deeds recorded for us in the Scriptures. One day a far greater work will be done by Him when He returns to call both the just and the unjust from the earth. On that Day of Judgment our safety and blessedness will only be found in our King and Substitute. He died where a King should not die. He was only there on the cross because it was where we deserved to be.

2 Chronicles 9

Father, Your fame is known all over the world. There is a powerful testimony for all to see in Your great works of creation. All men everywhere should be like the Queen of Sheba in the days of Solomon. Our breath should be taken away from us when we hear of Your wonderful deeds. We should seek to explore Your greatness with our own eyes. We should cry out to You for Your holy revelation, trusting that You have some plan of mercy that can make some sense of Your patience with the abundance of evil that is all around us. Make Your people like pure gold in Your holy house. Fill the earth with the glory of Your Name. Send to far off lands the message of Your wisdom and Your goodness. Grant to us the privilege of giving back to You a portion of what You have generously entrusted to us. Thank You again for the greatness of Your Kingdom, and for the glory of our eternal King.

2 Chronicles 10

Great God, what will we do when the next generation seems to quickly reject the wisdom of years? We are grateful that above any great new leaders is the Lord Jesus Christ, the one King over all of Your people. Your sovereign rule is governing everything in Your church. You also reign over every power in heaven or on earth. Help us to listen carefully to those who have served in former days. Teach us the wisdom that comes from reason and experience. Help us to have a generous heart toward those in our charge, lest we discourage them and incite some ugly rebellion against You and Your church.

2 Chronicles 11

Father, will we learn from our mistakes? Will we be humble enough to recognize when the trouble that we have is from You, and not merely from the schemes of wicked men? Thank You for Your work of sanctification in our lives. We are so grateful that we do not have to remain forever in the foolishness of youth. Help us also to recognize true wisdom and godliness in those whom You have granted to be our helpers in the important tasks before us. Thank you especially for the gifts of godly wives and gracious husbands, whereby You have greatly blessed so many of the men and women within Your church. Most of all, we thank You that all of us, men and women, young and old, are together the one bride of the most excellent Husband. He has proven His love for us through His atoning death. We offer ourselves to Him in humble submission.

2 Chronicles 12

Father God, how can we forget You after seeing Your grace and faithfulness for many years? Is there forgiveness for men who should know so much better? We are ashamed of our persistent sin in the face of Your abundant kindness to us. Yet You will hear Your people if they truly humble themselves before You. Thank You for this great mercy. Surely in the worst of times as well as in the best of times we should set our hearts to seeking You. We should remember that You have given us countless good gifts for our bodies and souls, even in the days of our worst rebellion against You. Thank You for Your great kindness and goodness to unworthy sinners.

2 Chronicles 13

Great Lord, You are the true King of Your people. Please intervene between brothers in the faith and prevent our warring madness. Show forth Your truth powerfully, so that all Your people will find it irresistible. Work by Your Spirit in our souls so that we will have a deeper thirst for godly submissiveness. Hear Your people when they cry out to You. Show Your power when our enemies seem far too strong for us. We mourn the animosity we see among those who should agree together that Your Son is our Lord and Savior.

2 Chronicles 14

Lord God Almighty, grant us rest in Christ as we serve You. We desire to stand firm against idolatry within Your church and within our own hearts. We seek You God, for You have given us peace through Christ. Despite that gift of eternal rest, it is a plain fact that multitudes of enemies come against Your people. Our hope is still entirely in You. Judge between the mighty and the weak. Help us! In Your name we face an angry multitude, seen and unseen. Let not men and angels prevail against You. Thank You for the great victory that is already ours in Christ. Rescue us now, and bring us home to the heavenly Jerusalem at just the right time.

2 Chronicles 15

Holy God, You will certainly be with us when we are with You. You have always heard Your people when they turn to You in distress. Help us to take courage now. We put away all our detestable idols, and attend again to the glory of Your kingdom. Gather Your people again for worship. Bring to our remembrance the sacrifice of Christ for sinners. In Him we have life even now. You have gathered us from age to age for covenant renewal. You have led Your people to destroy idolatrous images and to give to You great gifts as an expression of our thankful devotion to You. We wait in Your presence with holy expectation.

2 Chronicles 16

Our Father, You know the day of our birth and the day of our death. Our times are in Your hands. There are those that would block the way to Christ, refusing to enter the Kingdom themselves and preventing others from going into Your house. Such men must be removed from the way of the godly pilgrim. More difficult still is our own pride. Unless You remove this enemy from the pathway of our hearts and minds, we will not be open to the conviction of the truth that comes to us from Your Word. What will it take to break our foolish pride, that we might live and serve You? We shudder at the thought. Yet You know our weakness, and You will not give us more than we can bear. We need You more than any other gift. Father, we seek You now with our great troubles of body and soul, and we trust that You hear and answer prayer.

2 Chronicles 17

Merciful Lord, the generations come and go, but You are God forever and ever. You are always able to raise up a faithful man to serve courageously, doing great acts of obedience that former generations have left undone. Send forth faithful teachers throughout Your kingdom. May Your church be granted ears to hear and hearts willing to obey. We need mighty men of valor to strive together for the defense of the truth in the service of Your great kingdom. Send forth Your gifts from on high, and glorify Your holy Name.

2 Chronicles 18

Father God, bad company corrupts good morals. How can Your people be kept spiritually strong when they are unequally yoked in marriage with those who do not believe? Yet You are able to protect us even in such situations. Give us an ear to hear Your Word, even when our closest friends and family members may be hostile to the truth. Though there are false prophets everywhere, You are yet able to raise up a godly man who will speak the truth. Even the ungodly know in their hearts that lying men speak false words, yet they suppress the knowledge of the truth in unrighteousness. Will we in our sin-weary souls also agree to be easily deceived? Will we also somehow desire to hear a false report, and eagerly embrace such a message when it is spoken? May it never be! Keep lying spirits far away from us. Fill us with Your Holy Spirit so that we will always be eager for Your Word. May we resist the false reports of wicked men. You will surely protect Your chosen servants. Whether we live or we die, we want to be near You as faithful followers of Your holy Son.

2 Chronicles 19

God of Truth and Power, the deeds of our best men are a mix of courageous acts of goodness and foolish works of compromise. Give us the clarity of seeing the difference between the holy and the profane. Help us to choose the pathway of righteousness day by day, and to reject the way of the wicked, lest we be unduly moved by the applause of men.

2 Chronicles 20

Glorious Lord, You must have a purpose for the enemies that You send against Your servants. Surely You bring forth from us great moments of petition and faith. You are the Lord of the nations. You have granted to us a holy sanctuary in Christ. Through Him we offer up earnest prayer before Your face. You see our enemies who seem so powerful. They are bent upon the destruction of Your people. They would love to blot out Your name under the sun. We are so easily overwhelmed. We do not know what to do, but our eyes are on You. Your message to us is one of courage and divine strength. You give us a way out through Christ. We stand firm in Him, and we see Your victory on our behalf. We move forward into spiritual battle with a great hymn of praise on our lips. We are clothed in Your steadfast love, and in the righteousness of Christ for Your chosen servants. You surely win the victory for us, for we would never be able to win against the formidable hoard of enemies who would despise Your worship. You give us rest in Christ, despite the troubles that we face in this age. Every man has his sin, and every man has his end, but Jesus Christ lives forever in the beauty of perfect holiness. We find our safe haven in Him alone.

2 Chronicles 21

Great God, we are clearly not in charge of everything. We feel our limitations as we hear of wicked sons taking over from faithful fathers. We certainly cannot guarantee the future, but You have made precious promises, and You will not be denied. We are sickened by the actions of murderous kings, but we cannot even stop our own ungodliness. How can we stop others who murder men that are better than themselves? You must come with power. O the trouble that we bring upon ourselves and on others we love! Men die in agony, but You have the key to life. Free us from the grip of the wicked who seem to die with no one's regret.

2 Chronicles 22

Glorious Savior, You make one man reign for many years, and another to rule only for a few months. You ordain the rise and fall of men who serve in Your kingdom. Despite Your obvious sovereign power, we are responsible for the matters before us. We cannot charge You with sin. You are God. Will a wicked woman kill her own children and grandchildren just to serve like a queen over Your people? Yet You will reserve for Yourself a little child, that Christ might yet be a descendant of David. Your promises will never fail.

2 Chronicles 23

Father God, at just the right time You will reveal Your secret will. Though an evil woman may seem to have absolute power, when the time is right, the young king of Your choosing shall surely be revealed. Your Son's birth was announced by angels. A wicked ruler among men was intent upon the Baby's destruction, but the Child lived, and the evil ruler died. Even when Your Son was killed by the wicked, this was done according to Your perfect foreknowledge and in accord with Your sovereign will. What looks like treason to evil despots may well be Your powerful help for Your children in their most desperate hour. Protect the purity of Your holy temple, O Lord. Though someone may assert himself as the one to be worshiped in Your church, You will bring that antichrist to a swift end through the coming of Your Son.

2 Chronicles 24

O Holy God, we will do right if we listen to godly counsel. We will do good works for Your temple and bless Your kingdom. We will give of our substance joyfully. The work of the house of the Lord will move forward in beauty and strength. There will be many blessings upon Your people. But if we lose our love for good counsel, and begin to listen to evil men, surely we will break Your commandments. If true men of God speak the very words of the Scriptures in that day, will we have hearts to hear Your voice? How sad it is when a man who begins by hearing the Word of the Lord, ends His days by rebelling against that same Word. Have mercy on us, Lord. Protect Your Kingdom, and save Your troubled servants who are harassed and tempted by evil men and angels. Grant us grace in our moment of most profound weakness and sin.

2 Chronicles 25

Lord God, Your Son now reigns forever in the Jerusalem above. Every day He does what is right with a full heart. He never falls into the devil's trap. He will not show any desire for false worship. He never gives in to fear or greed. Even good leaders here below will show their weakness and their sin over the course of a long reign. Our King Jesus reigns forever in perfect holiness without even the smallest inclination toward idolatry or false pride. He lives as a resurrected man and will one day bring in the fullness of the age to come, granting to us the clarity and beauty of sinless resurrection life. Thank you for the strength of Your mercy toward Your children even today. Keep us by Your unfailing power and love.

2 Chronicles 26

Our Father, guide your children as we move from youth to old age. Lead those in positions of power and authority among Your people. Who can say when a man will come to his position of influence? Who can say when a man will die? Who can tell what the pathway of any one life will be? Will our young people become proud when they are strong? Will a leprosy of sin break out in their lives? Please have mercy upon us. Even a great man can easily face a horrible moment with awful consequences. Your sinless Son Jesus Christ has healed us of the leprosy of our sin and rebellion. Have mercy upon us for His sake.

2 Chronicles 27

Almighty God, send us each a helper to be with us in our day of weakness and misery. We need someone with us to comfort and assist us, for there is much that we cannot do. Beyond any help that could come from the sons of men, please grant to us the greatest Counselor, Your Holy Spirit, that we might order our ways rightly before You. May we find our final resting place in the heavenly City of David, with the greatest Son of David at our side.

2 Chronicles 28

Father, there is a son who only follows a godly man by being born after him. Help us to follow Christ better than this kind of Ahaz. We mourn our own sin and the rebellion of those who should follow us. Only Your grace and power can change this kind of problem. Will our children be granted true repentance soon? There is so much trouble that comes from the devil and the world. There is a day of difficulty that would be more than a man could take. Protect us and our children from such a day. Father, how does a covenant child like Ahaz wander so far from his true hope? How could he settle for filth when he has a place around the king's table as a son? Lord, we know this is not all about us, though we surely have sinned, and we do repent. We also know that this is not all about our children, though they surely have sinned, and they need to repent. This is finally about You, and Your good and mysterious plan, and that is the very best news for Your grieving servants in the day of a broken heart. Every faithless act will be of no use to us. It will only be our ruin. Grant us access to Your house again through the merit and mediation of Jesus Christ, and bring a better day for the glory of Your Name, even if it must come in the day of our descendants after we rest in the grave.

2 Chronicles 29

Thank You, O God, for the relief of a Hezekiah after the horror and disgrace of an Ahaz. Raise up strong men who will speak the truth about sin, and begin the necessary work of cleansing Your church. There is so much evil all around us, and it must be addressed, lest You remove Your lampstand from among us. We need You now. Our eyes are full of tears from the grief of former days. Give us joy as we do the work of Your kingdom. Grant us efficiency and diligence in this important mission. We must in some way make up for the negligence of those who have come before us, but we can never make our lives acceptable to You through our works. We thank You that Your Son has made atonement for all His people through His own life and death. We give our lives to You as one greater than Hezekiah leads us in covenant assembly. Thank You for Jesus Christ. We worship You with great rejoicing. The thank offering of our hearts is greater as a result of the suffering that we have faced in former days.

2 Chronicles 30

Lord God, thank You for our great Passover Lamb Jesus Christ. Gather Your elect far and wide. Call Your people to return to You, that we might worship You together. Help us to serve You in truth. Many may laugh at our heartfelt call to worship, but You will bring whoever You will according to Your plan for this time. Give us joy as we gather together in covenant assembly. We have a sense of shame concerning our lives and our lack of full preparation to worship You. Help us to remember that our devotion is only acceptable through Christ. In Him we are clean.

Lord, You hear Your Son when He prays for Your mercy upon us. Grant us an unusual thankfulness for Your grace, so that we would have a surprising desire to continue to rejoice in You. Thank You for the coming of such a day of joy, and for the relief that we feel when some measure of wickedness and disgrace is rolled back from Your people.

2 Chronicles 31

Father, You bring order into Your kingdom. You remove idolatry among Your people, and appoint leaders for service throughout Your church. You remind us continually of the offering of Your Son, for He Has given His life for us. Prosper us in peace, so that we might have great mountains of blessing to share with others in need. May the ministry of the Word throughout the world be well supported, and may the poor have hope for the future as they receive help from godly men and women who worship You. May all this be done with good order, that Your work would move forward with excellence, and the ministry of prayer and the Word would be attended to by those appointed to that task. Thank You for Christ our King. May every success within and through Your church be cause for thanksgiving and praise to You, for You have brought the increase.

2 Chronicles 32

God of our Fathers, even among the faithful, powerful trouble may soon arise. We do not struggle against flesh and blood. Since the fall, an enemy has plainly been at work against us. Grant us relief from minions of foes who hate us and who hate You. Proud men would arrogantly speak against You. They will face Your wrath in due season. You are able to deliver us from the hand of every evil accuser. Many would speak contemptuously against Your leaders. They would make You to be just another god among many powerless gods. You can send armies away in frightened flight, and the most wonderful commander can soon face the end of his days. Even Your good kings must face the fact of mortality. Help us to look to You for eternal life. Bless us not only with possessions, but also with godliness and humility. Grant us wisdom in the day of testing. Surely You know that we are weak. Nonetheless, You are very strong.

2 Chronicles 33

Father God, there is a dedication to evil that brings about the end of a holy way of life among Your people. Keep a Manasseh far away from us. When we are overcome with evil and distress, bring us the gift of true repentance. How amazing is Your grace! You can bring an end to Judah based on the wickedness of a Manasseh, and then bring true repentance to that very Manasseh so that there would be little doubt that He is with You now in Your heavenly sanctuary. Thank You for this wonderful love. Some never humble themselves at all before You. What a mystery is the hardened evil within our hearts! Surely You will work out all things for Your own glory and for the good of those who are called according to Your purpose.

2 Chronicles 34

Father God, when it seems that all is utterly lost, You raise up a great Josiah. Blessed be Your Name! More than this, centuries after even this great man had come and gone, when all hope was only a distant memory, You gave Your people a King of far greater worth than even Josiah. Our great King Jesus has crushed the power of evil around us and within us by His death on the cross. Through Him we have a sure and powerful eternal joy. Your Word has come to us in Him. We hear and repent. We believe and are justified. Your temple is being built up again, and we are a part of that great place of worship. Fill us with Your Word and Spirit, that we might serve You with full hearts. Grant to Your people true repentance. May this be a more lasting testimony to this dark world than all of our former acts of ugly sin. While we cannot stop the judgment that is coming upon Your church and the world, You are able to bless Your repentant children in ways that are refreshing and beautiful. We will walk after You, O God. We will confess our sins and follow You. We will receive Your gospel word of restoration, and we will rejoice in Your holy Name.

2 Chronicles 35

Lord God Almighty, we thank You that we are regularly able to be reminded of Your Son. In the days of the Law, Your people enjoyed the Passover only once every year. Now we remember Your Son's death whenever we eat the bread and drink the cup that Your Son established for Your people. The true offering that brought life to us has come, and we remember a better event than even the miracle of deliverance from bondage in Egypt. Without the shedding of Your Son's blood, there could never have been hope for us. Keep us from foolish and fruitless battles, lest Your judgment come upon Your church. We long for the arrival of Your Son in glory, though we know that this will not happen without many trials coming first. All this is too complicated for us. We do not know what to ask for. We want Your Son now, but we do not want the apostasy and trouble that must come before He returns. You will accomplish Your good purposes in Your perfect wisdom and love. Come soon Lord Jesus! Surely this is the cry of the godly. Come soon, even if it means that great trouble must come upon us now.

2 Chronicles 36

Father God, Your people suffered through the end of the days of the Davidic kingship after the death of Josiah. His sons and his grandson were nothing compared to him. There was much wickedness perpetrated by those who should have known Your Word. At just the right time, some centuries later, You brought a final end to the age of the Law. It had been a great era of Your revelation. Your people heard wonderful truths from Your prophets, but the old age had to end. It had to give way to a new age of the gospel of Jesus Christ. We thank You now that the age of the Law is gone. It was a yoke that neither we nor our fathers could bear. Now You have brought to us that greatest Son of David, the great Lord of the Sabbath. Be with us as we move further and further toward the end of this present age. This too has been a great age. The gospel shall be preached to all nations, and then the end will come. That end will not be easy, but we are looking for the glory of Your Son's great Day, and for the fullness of the new resurrection age.

Ezra

Ezra 1

Father God, You fulfilled Your Word that You gave to Your people through the prophets. You kept a remnant from among them during the years of exile and then restored them to the land of Judah. But You have done much more than this in the redemption that has come to us through the gift of Your Son. You are building Your church throughout the world. Your promises are entirely reliable. The matters of Your greatest interest should be our focus as well. We are so easily distracted by our own smaller thoughts and fascinations. Help us to seek first Your kingdom and Your righteousness day by day. We trust You with all things, great and small.

Ezra 2

Lord God, You know Your people. You sent many out of the land in the day of discipline. You brought them back according to Your prophetic Word. Thank You for Your particular care for Your people today. You know our names, but Your knowledge is much more extensive than that. You know our heritage. You know our extended families and the towns we came from. While this is true of all Your creatures, it is especially the case for Your chosen people. The particular care that You have shown for the sons of Abraham, Isaac, and Jacob is undeniable. Your actions of love and discipline for the people of the Old Covenant are recorded in the Scriptures. But there is a vast multitude of chosen men, women, and children who have become Israelites indeed through faith in Jesus Christ. In Him we have a safe place within the worship assembly of Your people. We are even part of the priesthood of all believers who shall serve You forever in a better land than Canaan. Blessed be Your Name, O God.

Ezra 3

O Lord of Hosts, we have a job to do, for You are using us to build a temple. Your Son has promised to build His church, yet He grants to men a part that we are to play in His great work. We certainly cannot do this holy work unless You lead us, and supply what is necessary. You have perfect plans for Your eternal temple on high. You have given Your Son as the Cornerstone of this greatest of all houses. Your apostles are the one foundation set in perfect order according to that one precious Stone laid in Zion. What a marvelous truth! We have a place in Your church, for we are living stones set upon a sure apostolic foundation given to us in Your Word.

Ezra 4

Our Father, the work of building Your kingdom goes forward in an environment that includes demonic enemies. There are subtle attacks of weariness and discouragement that come over us like waves of trouble. Help us to contemplate Your nature and Your work. Help us to meditate upon Your great promises, for we should not lose heart. We have been warned by Your Son that we will face trouble. Our King was despised by men. Why are we surprised when men lie about us and seek our destruction? See how Your adversaries try to use civil authorities to bring trouble upon Your church. We suffer strange setbacks for a season, though You are sovereign in Your power and bountiful in Your love. O the mysteries of Your providence! It is all too much for us to understand. Grant us faith when the facts that are against us seem insurmountable.

Ezra 5

O God of Grace and Glory, thank You for the encouragement of Your Word that comes through Your prophets. You are above all human authorities. There is no place that is closed to You. There is no good work that men will be able to stop if You say that it must proceed. Grant us diligence and wisdom. How can we keep on going with such opposition from enemies seen and unseen? Above all we seek Your leading and power. We need discernment to distinguish between useless projects that You have not commanded, and works of mercy, justice, and truth that You will surely bless. Grant us wisdom that we would spend our lives on those things most pleasing to You.

Ezra 6

Lord God, You are surely above all rulers. You will work out Your holy will. No adversary who sets himself against You will finally win. You make even the wrath of Your enemies to praise You. Providences that seemed an insurmountable hindrance turn out to be just what was necessary for Your work to be done with the greatest blessing and fruitfulness. Help us to trust You even in the day of great disappointment and confusion, and grant us eyes to see Your vindication in the day of Your power. We long for the completion of the building up of Your heavenly temple as You bring people to Yourself and turn us away from sin. We thank You for the one great offering of Your Son for us. We give ourselves entirely to You for Your good purposes. We turn away from the unclean lusts of the world, and we give our lives again this day to the building of Your holy city.

Ezra 7

Father, we shall not give up in our mission when You give us strength for the moment before us. You have prepared us for this work of prayer and service. You have trained us and have placed around us others who provide much help. You place Your hand upon Your ministers, and they are granted a heart to study Your Scriptures and to teach Your people. You provide the financial resources for Your Word to be taught and known. You bring to our minds the facts of our redemption by the sacrifice of Your Son, and we are suddenly helped by Your great power. Even the presence of enemies all around us can become the very thing that is necessary for Your good work to go forward. Grant us wisdom from Your Word, so that the greatest glory will come to Your holy Name. Fill the hearts of many men and women with godly impulses according to Your great plan.

Ezra 8

Great God and King, there is no power that will stand against You, for You will accomplish all Your holy purposes. There are many people that You have called into Your church throughout the world. Some are gathered together with a few others in modest surroundings. Others are attached to much larger assemblies. All of us are a part of one body. Grant us ministers, men of discretion, who will serve You by lovingly and truthfully presenting Your Word to Your children. Surely Your hand is open to us for our good, for we seek You. You will protect us from those who hate You. We have been given much aid for our needs and for the progress of Your work. Help us to be wise in Your service, for we have been trusted with gifts more precious than silver and gold. We have been blessed with the care of bodies and souls, and with the task of loving Your children and leading them in the ways of life.

Ezra 9

Glorious God, we feel the danger of the world all around us. There is so much false thinking and idolatrous worship everywhere. Even some of Your leaders have been quickly overtaken by temptation. We pray that You would hear our cry for help as we humble ourselves before You. We have been walking without sense in the midst of great sin and danger. We should know the truth by now. We cannot travel along the way of death in order to find life. How could we be so foolish! So many are enslaved by sin in what should be a day of great opportunity and hope. We have work to do. It is so close to us, and yet our hands will not move. It is right there for us to take and to do, but we are turned away by entangling distraction and iniquities. Would we test You by despising Your commandments again? See our weakness and hear us as we appeal to You for strength.

Ezra 10

Great God, when all the noise of our lives is silenced by trial and disappointment, we are brought to remember why You have placed us on this earth. We have been distracted from the work of Your kingdom by obligations that we have foolishly chosen. We have joined ourselves to projects that are not consistent with our faith and our calling. Give us wisdom to know what must be done, so that we will follow in Your ways. What will we do in the day when we discover that we have greatly transgressed Your Law? Give us the clarity of Your truth not only to see our sin, but to see the way out that You have provided. Grant us then the courage to follow You. Bless us with unusual clarity so that we will not again be enticed into cares and responsibilities that would lead us away from Your perfect purposes for Your people. Help us to take responsibility for our mistakes and to repent as those who know You and remember Your Word. Bring blessing upon us again, for we have rediscovered the road that leads to fruitful service in Your kingdom. May we never forget the lessons that You have taught us at such a significant cost to ourselves, our families, and Your church.

Nehemiah

Nehemiah 1

O God, Your church faces great difficulty. We need You. Deliver us from trouble and shame. You are the God of heaven. We confess our sins before You. Please hear us and help us. We return to You now according to Your Word. We cast off all sinful patterns of thinking and living, and seek the gift of Your Spirit in fuller measure. Hear our prayer, and grant us success in our desire to serve You.

Nehemiah 2

Lord God, teach us the appropriate boldness of Your servants as You call us to a great work. May we turn to You continually in prayer. Grant us success in the mission of Your choosing. Your good hand will be upon Your children for the sake of Your Son. Fill us with hope in the darkest of nights. Show us the brokenness of Your kingdom and give us a vision for the rebuilding of Your holy city. Grant to us allies in faith who will believe with us in the calling that You have placed upon our hearts. Teach us to take courage, even in the face of opposition.

Nehemiah 3

Our Father, we must take a first step when we are engaged in a great work. Should we be successful in that first step, give us energy and wisdom for the next task in front of us. If we would build the wall around the city, we have no choice but to go step by step. While there are those who may consider themselves above hard work, Your men and women who love Your Name will count it a privilege to work on the mission that You have given to Your people. While each of us is weak and lacking in many important attributes, You are in the midst of Your people and are capable of using us in exciting ways. The work that You have for us is a person-to-person mission. What will we do in Your kingdom if we will not love Your people? You must fill us with the love of Christ, so that the work will move ahead in accord with Your holy will.

Nehemiah 4

Father God, You must be with us when our enemies mock us and laugh at the mission that You have given to us. Hear us, O Lord, for we are despised. Could it be that some of those who hate us might be granted a true heart of repentance? Many will only be moved to anger if we seem to succeed. They will not be humbled. Even within our ranks people may arise who counsel that we must abandon the work. Teach us to be wise in our thinking and in our tasks. Protect us with help from on high. May we daily hear Your Word in the depths of our hearts. Grant us a godly plan and strength of heart. May Your enemies be put to shame when they see Your faithfulness, for You know how to use our weakness for Your glory.

Nehemiah 5

Our God, will we destroy our own people in Your church and ruin Your mission from within? Grant us godly leaders who will move forward in truth. We need to walk in Your fear. We need to use our resources in a godly way. We must not abuse the weak. Sanctify Your people and purify Your church. Teach us the blessing of not taking what may seem to be our right, so that we can care for those who need our help. May many people be fed at our tables and give glory to Your Name, for You are the Giver of every good gift.

Nehemiah 6

Father God, why must there be those who conspire against Your people? We are doing a great work, and it is a work that You have called us to do. Make us wise to know how and when to reply to the baseless accusations of those who seek to harm Your people. Help us not to run away because of the fear of men. We must do what You command, and not be unduly moved by the plots of those who seek to frighten us. You will make a good end to the work that You have called us to do.

Nehemiah 7

Lord of Hosts, there is a day of celebration coming. While we wait for that greatest of all Sabbaths, there is yet work to be done. Put it within the hearts of Your people to consider seriously and deeply that our names are recorded in the Book of Life. When our callings require steadfast perseverance, help us to remember that You have chosen us from before the foundation of the world. Bring about a most glorious celebration at just the right time. Send forth Your Son, together with the holy angels and all who rest in Christ above. May our King separate the righteous from the wicked in perfect wisdom, that we might live in Your grace and rejoice in Your mercy forever. We have a godly heritage in this Son of David. In Him we can prove that we are rightly in the land of promise, for He is Your eternal Son. He has given Himself for our salvation. Gather together the whole assembly of Your people that we might rejoice in Your presence forever. Even now we give You gifts out of the blessings that You have kindly bestowed upon us. May we dwell peacefully and joyfully in Your land forever.

Nehemiah 8

Father, we want to hear Your Word. Bring Your truth before Your assembly. Grant Your servants diligence in speaking and explaining Your Word, so that Your people may receive the sense of the Word that is spoken in their presence. May we rejoice in Your truth together. Teach us to love You with our minds and also with our hearts, our souls, and our strength. Teach us to hear and receive the joy of the Lord. Your grace is our sure salvation. When we understand Your words, there is hope, and cause for the greatest celebration. Teach us to love the truth that You are coming to dwell with us forever. May we hear Your Word day by day and rejoice in You without end.

Nehemiah 9

Lord God, when we truly repent, our hope shines forth in the brilliance of Your grace. Thank You for the day of conviction of sin. Thank You for the will and determination that You grant to Your servants to worship You. Teach us to remember Your great acts of redemption that You have done for Your people in previous days. You have given us a good rule of life and have provided for all the needs of our bodies and souls. Would we return to the slavery of sin? You will not let us go in the way of foolishness forever. You sustain us, and You lead us. All of Your promises are absolutely faithful. There can be no question about Your goodness. There is also no doubt concerning our sin. We have been hardhearted. We have hated both Your Law and Your prophets. You have sent us the greatest Savior, Your Son Jesus Christ. According to Your abundant mercy turn us again to the way of life in Him. Do not make an end of us. Do not forsake us. You who keep covenant for generations, look upon our hardships and have mercy. With true sorrow we acknowledge our sins. Look on us now. We must have You. We give ourselves over to You again. It is our solemn intention to follow You. Never forsake us. Bring us to a place where we will finally and fully give up our love of sinning.

Nehemiah 10

Father God, Your Son's Name is on the seal of the Covenant of Grace. In His faithfulness we have been granted life. We thank You for His Name, which is the Name above all names. He faced such trouble and pain for our sake. He set His heart upon doing what was right according to Your Law and He has accomplished this wonderful obedience. He did not need to do this for Himself. He had life through His divine nature forever. Yet He became man and obeyed You as our substitute. He came to build a new house for You, a temple made without hands. We are in that temple, for we are in Him.

Nehemiah 11

Glorious Lord, we long to live in Your holy city forever. Teach us to love Your church in all of her brokenness. We know that she is strongly connected to the glorious city to come. If we would be with You there where the streets are paved with gold, help us to be willing to associate our names with the place where Christ is preached now. We are united together in Your family of grace and truth. Must it yet be that Your church will still remain a place of failure and sin? Father, we are in this world in an age of waiting, but we are not of the world. We long for the age to come. Teach us the joy of hope so that we will love the weak and gladly receive that friendship from others which is a generous expression of Your care for each of us.

Nehemiah 12

Our Father, we are not alone. Thank You for the priesthood of all who believe. We have been given access to the Holy of Holies in Christ. We sing for joy as we worship You even now. You have not left us as orphans. You have given us a testimony, a hope, and a true presence. Thank You for our families and for this assembly of love that You have granted us together in Your church. You are with us now. You will be with us forever. Where You are, You are surely not alone. Hear our praise as we sing to You, joining our voices to those who praise You above. What great music there must be in Your presence day by day! What a wonderful celebration is coming when Your choir on earth will finally hear the voices of those who sing to You on high. We rejoice in You. We look for the appearing of the Jerusalem that is above. We give of our substance with the great hope of a new day, and we thank You most sincerely for all that You have promised to Your people.

Nehemiah 13

Glorious God, give us attentiveness to Your Word. Help us to interpret it rightly. Grant us the courage to obey You. There are those who would horribly misuse the resources of Your church. Will we confront leading men who weakly submit to evil enemies among Your beloved bride? We must follow You. Thank You, O Lord, that Gentiles have now found a place in Your Kingdom through faith in Christ. Thank You for the rest that we enjoy in Christ. He is our great Sabbath. He bids us even now to draw near and to come to Him. We were weary and heavy-laden, but we have heard Your Word and have found true rest for our souls. Teach us to speak the language of Your Kingdom with great joy. Your true Word is the language of grace, the language of faith, and the language of grateful obedience. Cleanse us by the blood of Jesus, and build up Your holy Kingdom. Because of our one great Leader, remember us for good.

Esther

Esther 1

Majestic King, You are greater than all the rulers of the earth. You have provided us with such riches from Your royal glory even in this current age. What wonders will there be when we go to be with Your Son? How great will the blessings be in the coming age of resurrection? Every command that You give to Your subjects is completely good. It is right for us to obey You immediately and with the greatest joy. Yet we have done great wrong against You and against all lawful authority. Please forgive us. We pray that we will not bring any more trouble upon those around us because of our former days of rebellion. We pray that You would break the chains of evil that may ensnare us from the wickedness of generations now in the grave. Please teach us to happily give honor to those who are due honor. Lawlessness can never be the answer for us, for we have committed our lives to You.

Esther 2

Father God, Your special care for Your church, Your royal bride, is most wonderful and gracious. Teach us the way to be pleasing to You through Christ. May we grow in the beauty of holiness. Lord God, the time of our remaining days here may be very brief. Show us how to live in wisdom and righteousness throughout our lives. We have heard from Your Word that You delight in us. May we always win favor in Your sight because of the work of Your Son on our behalf. You give us so many gifts through Your royal generosity. We want to serve You with diligence. We seek the honor of Your Name. We pray that all those who hate You would be stopped in their evil plans through Your perfect knowledge and power.

Esther 3

Lord God Almighty, within the courts of earthly power there are many who would stand against You and Your people. Despite their angry threats and commands, we will not bow down to them in worship. We trust You with our lives. Though there are some who would desire to see the destruction of Your people, we know that You have given a sure Word for our eternal life. Your promise to work all things together for our good is very secure. It will never be changed. Help us to rest deeply in Your Word. May we not be unduly moved by the confusion and intrigue all around us.

Esther 4

Father, what can we do to express our grief concerning the persecution of Your church throughout the world? We mourn in Your presence for the attacks against Your kingdom. The details of the plans of the wicked are deeply disturbing to us. We bring our plea for help to You. We know that we have a duty to pray for our brothers and sisters who are in distress. Help us to do this work with diligence. We will not keep silent. Perhaps we have come to the kingdom for such a time as this. If we perish at the hands of Your enemies, we perish. Our bodies and souls are always in Your hands, and we trust You.

Esther 5

Lord God, thank You for Your special providence in the history of Your church. Surely we have found great favor in Your sight because of the love and faithfulness of Jesus Christ. Give us wisdom as we face the challenges that seem to come upon us with such intensity in this current age. We know that we are to be as gentle as doves, but we must also be as wise as serpents. Father, we trust that You will not allow the plans of Your enemies to succeed, for they are committed to our destruction.

Esther 6

Sovereign Lord, You will never forget our acts of faithfulness, for they are gifts of Your own free grace. Even if we simply give a cup of cold water to a child in Your Name, this small work of mercy and decency will be remembered by You. What great things You have planned for Your servants! We do not yet see all the glories of the age to come, but we know that there is much good that is planned for Your elect. You will bring about our vindication at just the right time.

Esther 7

Lord of Glory, do You listen to our earnest requests even now? Grant us our lives and the lives of our people who are called by Your Name. Wicked men continually seek to bring distress and death upon Your children. You are a very powerful Father. You will not stand by forever when an enemy would seek the destruction of Your elect. You will deliver them at just the right time. The trouble that Your enemies have planned for us will fall on their own heads.

Esther 8

Father God, though the enemies of Your people may suppose that they own the world, the fact remains unchangeable that the meek shall inherit the earth. The calamities that wicked people plan against Your children are twisted and troubling. In our own strength and wisdom we could never deliver our souls from the hand of wicked men and angels. On that day when Your Son returns with His great and powerful host, He will take vengeance upon Your enemies. We will be rescued forever. In our hearts we shall be filled with perfect light, gladness, and joy. Grant us a taste of that victory by faith even now, lest we become weary in Your service.

Esther 9

O God, a great Day of the Lord is surely coming. A large and angry league of enemies would suppose that their victory is at hand. You will never allow this to be the final story for Your beloved bride. You will bring those who hate her to justice in a most surprising way. Your judgments against the wicked are not just for one or two days. Your justice is eternal. Because we know that Your day of complete victory is surely coming, even now we celebrate with gladness, for Your promises are very certain. It will not go well for the wicked, but we who are righteous in Christ will be kept in Him forever. Teach us to celebrate even now, though at the present moment an enemy would seem to be too close for our comfort.

Esther 10

Lord God, we thank You for the way that You bless a man like Mordecai, who was used by You to help preserve the life of Your people so many centuries ago. Far more glorious is our Redeemer Jesus Christ. He is forever great among Your covenant people. He has delivered us from the hand of a vicious adversary. He continues even now to speak peace to all those who have drawn near to You through the blood of the Lamb.

Job

Job 1

Glorious God, You show us the way of wisdom by Your Word. Throughout the centuries of Your dealings with us You raise up godly men who hear Your voice, who fear You, and who follow You. Thank You for the gift of men like Job who are upright and blameless among their generation. Even the best of the sons of Adam face horrible tests. Help us, O Lord, in the day when we lose our possessions and our livelihood. Help us when children die before their parents. How can we understand Your providence? Naked we came into this world, and naked we shall leave it. Blessed be Your Name. We worship You even as we mourn. You alone are God. Strengthen us in the truth.

Job 2

O God, we have faced such devastating trials, and we have been given grace sufficient for every need. We have feared You and have continued to turn away from evil. But what will we do if You stretch out Your hand against our flesh and our bones? What will we do when we face physical pain that is more than the worst grief? What is the limit that we can take? Surely every man has a limit. What suffering would be too much for us? Only You know the answer. There is no comparing trial with trial. When we are brought through one, the scar still remains. The next one adds to the grief. Are we stronger now or weaker? We cannot tell. Will we be finally overtaken by a small matter that was one test too much, or will we be given more grace from You to face the new stone thrown on the pile of rubble that was already on top of us? Will we rise above it all? Teach us, O Lord! Give us wisdom and a heavenly perspective, so that we will not curse You and die. You are God.

Job 3

Father, will You hear us when we have an unmeasured lament? Can it be possible that we would lament the day of our birth in our sorrow and that somehow those words would still be acceptable to Your ears? We do want to live today. Nonetheless we know that there is a pain and a turmoil that finally causes the strongest Sampson to tell his secret to some wicked Delilah. We know that You are sovereign. We absolutely refuse to believe that the trouble that comes upon us has some other first cause. Everything that happens must ultimately come back to You, for You are the Lord God Almighty, the God over all creation and providence. You can never be charged with wrong. You are love and goodness with absolutely no shadow of evil in You. Yet we will never reduce You to a mere spectator of this world or some sleeping giant. You know the beginning from the end, and You are working out Your holy will.

Job 4

O God, the righteous man has withstood the loss of his possessions and his children. He has even faced bodily pain and trials that seem too much to bear. Now must he bear the rebuke of smaller men who presume to correct him? Surely any man loved by You would need the patience of Job to take this additional trial. Thank You for Your Word, by which all other messages must be tested. Will the righteous man be accused of impatience in the day of suffering? Must he face subtle accusations that his suffering is a result of his own sin? Keep lying spirits away from us, O Lord, or strengthen us in Your Word so that we may resist the devil, that he would flee from us. Can mortal man be in the right before You? Yes, but only in the Righteous One Jesus Christ. Can a man be pure before his Maker? Yes, but only in the One who is the purity of God from on high. Is it true that You who charged angels with error have no regard for the sufferings of righteous men? No, precious in Your sight is the death of Your saints. You love the righteous, and You are with us in every affliction.

Job 5

Father God, in the midst of flawed and evil messages there may still be much truth. Grant us the discernment to see the difference between truth and error. Man is born to trouble after the fall of Adam. We should trust You. You are a marvelous Provider. We know these things and we believe them. Yet there is the overwhelming fact of suffering in the tent of the righteous. Who can understand Your ways, O God? You are in charge of everything. You are the Source of our hope. We hear the good Word from many voices. Why is it that we cannot bear that Word from some men? We could read it ourselves and embrace it. Perhaps we would hear it from someone we respect and readily receive it. Give us patience. Many would speak, and many more hearts presume to have a word of correction that is not spoken. We will hear Your voice, for we are Your sheep. You are able to keep us through the day of comforters who bring no comfort.

Job 6

Lord God, have mercy on those who suffer. Father, some who are exemplary for righteousness face terrible difficulty. How can Your servants keep on going? Grant to us a new patience and comfort when it seems as if all is lost. We know that You are here with us, but our friends and companions may not know what to believe in a day of grief. If we have gone astray, show us. We do not know what to say. Please Lord, be near us today.

Job 7

Our Father, our lives on this earth are portioned out for us by You. There is much that is unpleasant in even a normal stay of seventy years. In a day of unusual trouble and grief, normalcy seems far away from us. The trial is so deep for the man who is in anguish of soul. Father God, what are You doing? Where are You? We do not know. How can we stand this, O God? Even to see friends go through this kind of difficulty is so hard. What if we are the ones in the center of the storm? Lord, help us. The life of Your servant seems strangely empty. Remind us again of the cross. Grant us ears to hear the message of Your love.

Job 8

Merciful Lord, we have said more than we should. We have thought that we knew things that we do not know. Your providence is beyond our wisdom and understanding. Would we accuse a godly man of sin in the day of his greatest loss? He has been serving You in faithfulness in every way that we could ever see. We know that You do not owe him anything, but who are we to offer words of instruction? Forgive us, O Lord. Remember the prayers of Your Son for us, and help our brothers and sisters who seem to be swallowed up by astonishing and overwhelming trouble.

Job 9

Our Father, who can contend against You? You stretched out the heavens and formed the constellations. We see the works of Your hands everywhere, but we cannot see You. Who are we to say to You, "What are You doing?" We appeal to You for Your everlasting mercies. Teach us to have gentle hearts in the day of trial. We are not blameless, O Lord. You surely love Your servants. The testimony of the cross is the greatest story of love. We shall not be condemned, for Your Son has faced a pit of judgment for us. Thank You that we have a Mediator in Your holy Son. We will worship You forever in Him.

Job 10

Great God, what can a righteous man do when he hates his life? Keep us from guilt in our thoughts and our words. Father, You have made us. You are the Friend of those who truly serve You. What are You doing to us? Could it be that You are fighting against Your friends? Lord, we cannot win a contest against You. Is a relationship with You too dangerous for us to survive? Surely You know how to shorten the days of a trial that we cannot bear. Give us a glimpse of a better day. Help us to trust You again, and to live.

Job 11

God of Hosts, how can we stand the speeches of men in a day of deep trouble? We know that You are the Almighty God. Will righteous men be called stupid and wicked when they are facing crippling misery? The encouragement of lesser men who presume to correct their superiors is a dreadful burden. They have little of any worth to say to a troubled soul. Bring us through a season of dreadful trial by Your saving love.

Job 12

Our Father, give us a listening ear, a reasoning mind, and healing speech. You are almighty. You are stronger than any man. You are wiser than all Your creatures. You raise up and You tear down according to Your decrees. The pathway of nations is in Your hand. This we know very well. This we believe. Yet we face Your discipline. We do not know why, and we do not know what to say. Settle our restless hearts as we consider Your nature and Your works.

Job 13

Lord God Almighty, we would speak to You. We would argue our case with You in the day of trial. We know that judgment begins with Your household. How much more can we take? Though You slay us, our hope remains in You. Though You discipline us, Your Son has the words of life. O God, we do not understand what You are doing. Yet we consider the cross and we have hope. Surely there is a better day coming. Surely there is something more in Your hand beyond correction.

Job 14

Father God, our lives on this earth are brief. You have appointed our limits. The fact of death is all around us. What will come of us when we are laid low? Thank You for the great fact of resurrection. Thank You for the clarity of the age to come that has been displayed for us in Jesus Christ, risen from the grave. Despite our suffering, we cling to this hope, that as He is, so shall we be. There is life beyond mourning. Help us to see this in our darkest hour.

Job 15

Merciful Lord, in a day of trouble suffering people say things that they should not. When we hear such words, teach us to let love cover a multitude of sin. Keep self-righteous corrections far from our lips. Send us away from those in trouble if we will only be miserable comforters. We cannot fix everything today. The sum of justice is not here on this earth and in this age. There is another day ahead. You will speak at just the right time.

Job 16

God Almighty, send forth Your Spirit as the best of all comforters. Give us a heart that is willing to receive Him. Surely You are not a foolish teacher like so many men. Father, we do not understand the providences that we face. Lead us into more helpful thinking. Teach us with words that heal. We know that the answer for us is with You, but we cannot always see that good way.

Job 17

Father, there are times when our suffering is so difficult that we assume that our life must be over already. Teach us to persevere even in such a day. Train us to see some glimpse of light when all appears so very dim. Even when we are covered by deep clouds of trouble, Your Son is still the light of the world. Help us to see Him in Your Word, and to remember the cross.

Job 18

Lord God, will we be miserable comforters who can only think and speak of ourselves? Will we keep on correcting those who seem to have no light of life left in their eyes? What can we say about death? Is it time to speak about sin and misery? Is there a word of hope that will be useful, or should we say nothing? Is it time to smile? Is it time to cry? Restrain us from making brash accusations against those that You have blessed in former days. You can make a man recover from a difficult time of loss. Teach us the blessedness of waiting. Teach us the wisdom that comes from loving.

Job 19

Glorious Lord, in the day of our greatest trial there is no helpful answer that comes to us from foolish men. Our suffering is real and we do not understand what has happened to us. We seem to have no help from anyone. There is no mercy. You have touched us in discipline, and we do not understand. Yet we know that our Redeemer lives. We know that we will see Him in a great day of resurrection. We cling to this hope, for our best days are clearly not in this life.

Job 20

Father God, despite every trial and even every suggestion of Satan, You are with us. You bless us in so many different ways. Every gift that we have is surely from Your grace. Every kindness comes to us not by our merit, but because of the wonderful righteousness of Jesus Christ. All of us face the trouble of a death that seems to be approaching us. Yet we have hope because of Jesus Christ, for He has conquered sin and death for us.

Job 21

Lord God, not every event that happens in Your providence is easily understood by us. Some men who are very wicked live unusually long lives. They may have many descendants, and people mourn their loss when they die. A righteous man may die in the prime of His youth and no one knows what to say. Who can fathom the loss of the unborn child? There is so much that we do not understand. One man dies with such a wonderful life story of achievement and joy. Another has been witness to so many horrors. They both go to the grave. We are given no answer to these facts. They cause us to wonder about You. Yet You are the everlasting God, and You are worthy of our full and everlasting trust. We believe in You. We know that You are in control. Help us, O Lord.

Job 22

Great God, we know that You do not need us. Yet You have created us for Your purposes and You will be glorified through our lives. Even the wrath of our enemies will praise You. You are in charge of birth and death. All of the years in between these two events are also within Your sovereign power. We commit ourselves to the care of the weak, for You save the lowly. You who provide for the poor, please have abundant mercy upon us through Your Son Jesus Christ.

Job 23

Our Father, we want to talk with You. The troubles in our lives seem to overwhelm us. We cannot see behind the veil of this creation. We sincerely desire to keep Your ways. We know that You do what You desire. We have questions for You, O Lord, and we do not know where we will find answers. Thank You for the answer of Your Word. Thank You for the answer of Your Son. Thank You for the answer of the cross.

Job 24

Gracious God, grant to us insight from Your Word and from the experience of living in this world. How are we to understand the lives of the wicked? There are so many perplexing facts that fill this fallen world. We see such evil deeds over many decades and we wonder how a person can be allowed to live for even a moment. The wicked are able to live like all others, and then they die like everyone else. There must be something here that we do not see, because what we see does not seem to make sense. There must be a future that our hearts have not yet embraced. Bring about the great fulfillment of Your plans of justice and mercy. We long to see Your glory and goodness with our eyes in the land of the living. Teach us to believe Your promise of a future age of perfect righteousness as a certain fact even now.

Job 25

Father, stop the mouth of the fool who would say wicked things in the face of Your righteous servant. Silence the voice of the one who accuses with no knowledge and who adds insult to injury. We know that we are loved by You. We rest in the embrace of our Redeemer despite the troubles that assail us.

Job 26

Our God and King, we need the voice of truth. Please speak to us through the Scriptures today. You are the God of creation. What You accomplish in the skies and the seas are wonders to behold. Even these great things are but a whisper of Your greatness. If we were to see You in all of Your heavenly glory we could not survive for a moment. Help us to hear the Word of Your steadfast love and to worship You even when there is so much that we do not understand.

Job 27

Lord of Glory, we thank You for the perseverance of Your Son. He was continually being charged with impropriety when there was no sin in Him. He kept on walking toward His atoning death for us as lesser men accused Him in their arrogance and ignorance. His end came in His work on the cross. In the eyes of men this seemed to be the worst disgrace, but it was His greatest act of obedience. Now we have found our glory in that cross, for we have been reconciled to You through the suffering of our faithful Mediator.

Job 28

Great God, reveal to us Your wisdom according to Your plan. You know how to do many great things that cannot be seen by men. Gems are formed in the secrets of the deep. You are doing wonderful things in the hidden place of our souls through the suffering that may be evident to all. Bless us with the great blessing of wisdom according to Your decree for us, for this great gift can only come from Your hand. You have established great wisdom that no one can know, and You have searched it out. You who control the wind and the waves have appointed that some would fear You and turn away from evil. For us, this is true wisdom and understanding, for we could never search out all the hidden resources of Your greatness.

Job 29

Father, we do not know how to return to an earlier day of joy and honor. Now we have been brought to a time of such loss and disgrace, and we do not understand why. What can we do with our new life? The old life is forever gone, for we are different now because of the suffering that we have faced. Help us to receive trials as gifts from Your hand, and to move ahead to the day that You have prepared for us. Surely You are doing some good thing.

Job 30

Lord, we thought that we had the insight that we needed to keep on going, and then in just a moment we were struck again by thoughts of trouble and accusation. We have been humbled again, and the wicked scoff. Your Son was mocked by rude soldiers who knew nothing of Your covenant. Why, O Lord? What was the purpose of the crown of thorns? Was that necessary for our salvation? Did every detail of His suffering for us have a purpose? Surely all of this was ordained. You love Your Son, and You love us. We have been united with Him in His sufferings. We will also be united with Him in His resurrection.

Job 31

Glorious Lord, we will not give in to sin. We will fight against the impulses of evil that may rise up within us. Despite every false accusation, and regardless of every pain and temptation that may fill our lives, we will believe You, we will love You, and we will serve You. Give us grace for the day of the most severe trial. Please cut short the day of testing, lest we be swept away by our own sin and our thoughts of revenge. Teach us the way of the cross. Forgive our enemies. Hear us, O God! Help us now!

Job 32

Father God, we must not justify ourselves and accuse You. Help us to humbly receive the true correction of one who rightly speaks in Your Name. Though Your servant be young, and though his credentials may not seem impressive to us, help us to discern rightly the truth of the Word preached and the power of the Spirit at work in the life and ministry of Your ambassador.

Job 33

Lord God, may the servants who bring Your Word to Your people do so with boldness. May they rightly listen to Your suffering servants and may they be made to know our needs. Above all we need You. You are greater than our problems and greater than us. May Your servants continually point to You. Even in the worst pain or trouble, we need to think about Your character and Your works. May our Mediator plead for us, and may He be our eternal Ransom before You. Use Your teachers to show us the wonders of Jesus Christ. Help us to hear true wisdom by the power of One who is the very Spirit of Truth.

Job 34

Father, there is so much about You that is so very right and very good. What a joy it is to contemplate Your greatness. There is no wickedness in You. You will repay man according to his ways at just the right time. You love justice. You are righteous in everything that You think and do. Your knowledge is perfect, and Your ways are always right. You do not need to hear the testimony of any man, for You already know all things, and all of Your judgments are perfect. You do not need to repay anything to man as if You owed anything to anyone. We humble

ourselves before You. We hate every rebellious thought that we once cherished.
You alone are God and we worship You.

Job 35

Almighty God, we look up to the heavens. Though we would rail against You in our discontent, we cannot actually force You to give us an answer for what we deem to be unfair behavior on Your part. We have been so wrong in our thoughts and in our unrighteous anger. You are the Provider of every blessing. You give us songs in the night. Have mercy on us now. Forgive us, for we have multiplied words without knowledge.

Job 36

God of Wisdom and Glory, You are both righteous and mighty. The most powerful men of the earth must answer to You. Their days come and go. The arrogant man thinks great thoughts about himself but he cannot add one day to his life. If You speak he must listen. You will surely remove him from his place of authority whenever You please. You are exalted in Your power. Your works of creation are all around us. You rule over all Your creatures and all their actions in a way that should inspire the greatest fear among men. We should worship You. We certainly cannot charge You with evil.

Job 37

Sovereign Lord, You thunder wondrously with Your voice. You do great things that we cannot comprehend. We see Your grandeur in the heavens over many days as the seasons change. We know Your majesty in a different way when You roar from above with a sudden storm. You rule over the changing landscape of the hearts and minds of men. We have seasons of life that come upon us slowly. We also face unexpected troubles that seize us in a moment. There is nothing in all of the events of men and angels that is beyond Your authority. We bow before You in the day of gentle showers. We must think of You as well when the skies suddenly burst forth with violent thunder. You reign over us. You call Your weary children home at a time that is in accord with Your holy decree. You give and You take away. We live and we die. Blessed be Your Name.

Job 38

Father God, You speak. We must listen. There is no one like You. You have created all things out of nothing. The sun rises and sets. The seas have come over the land and they have been pushed back to their appointed limits. You know the wonders of snow, hail, ice, rain, heat, light, stars, and every living thing under the heavens. O God of glory, if we have any wisdom, it is a gift from You, for You are the source of all wisdom.

Job 39

Great Lord of Glory, we cannot run our own lives. We certainly could not rule over the wide array of living creatures as You do. There is such an amazing variety of animals everywhere. Each species has special abilities and limitations. You reign over all of this amazing display of Your creative power. Who are we to question You?

Job 40

Glorious God, we are cut to the heart. Have we been faultfinders who have spoken against You? Would we dare to charge You with evil and condemn You as if we were right? Our own right hand could never save us. There are large and powerful creatures, seen and unseen, that are stronger than us. Would we imagine that we could contend against You? Have mercy on us.

Job 41

Mighty God, Your Word is wonderful. When You speak of Your creatures, we know that You are greater than them all. Give us the sense to bow before You. Thank You for the holiness of Your Son for us. We have sinned against You first in Adam, and then in our own lives. Yet You have redeemed us with all Your great power and love. We remember again who You are, and we worship You. We cannot fight against You as if You were our inferior. We have been proud and rebellious. Please forgive us. We remember the love of the cross and have hope.

Job 42

Lord, You can do all things. No purpose of Yours can be thwarted. We have heard of You, but one day we will see You. Teach us to speak of You what is right. Thank You for our Mediator. He is far above us in righteousness. Bless our latter days more than our beginning. What may seem to be lacking in the present age will surely be given to Your servants in the age to come. Precious in Your sight is the death of Your saints. We believe Your promises and we worship You.

Psalms

Psalm 1

Blessed Father, You grant to us many good gifts and a sure hope through the One Man who was perfectly holy and fruitful. We would have been chaff blown away by Your fury in the Day of Judgment. But now we are known by You in Him, and are called righteous. Move us forward by Your grace in the pathway of truth and life.

Psalm 2

Glorious Creator, this world is full of powerful enemies who oppress Your people and reject the Messiah. Your power is far above all that You have created. You have secured the position of Your Son as King of kings. All the world should kiss Your Son, lest they perish.

Psalm 3

Lord, Your Son faced enemies who were all around Him. He cried out to You, and You helped Him in a day when thousands of traitors were against Him. Salvation belongs to You. Bless Your people who come to You through Jesus Christ.

Psalm 4

God of our Righteousness, You have helped us in the past. Give us relief again today. Our godliness is in Christ alone. We trust You, O God. You will show us goodness, and You will put joy in our hearts again. We will dwell in safety.

Psalm 5

Please hear us, O God. We pray to You morning by morning. We are Your humble servants in Jesus Christ, perfected through Your grace and Your steadfast love. Lead us in Your righteousness, O God. May the wicked fall by their own plots, but let the man who takes refuge in You and loves Your Name rejoice in You forever.

Psalm 6

Father God, we know that You are with us despite our troubled bodies and souls. You will help us at just the right time. You will take away our grief that seems to swallow us up in tears and clouds. You hear us, O God. Our enemies will suddenly be put to shame.

Psalm 7

O Lord, help us and save us from the hand of those who pursue us without cause. Grant deliverance to the oppressed who love You with an everlasting love. Thank You for the vindication of Your Son, even through the horror of the cross. We rejoice in His resurrection. Deliver Your church from all injustice and falsehood. We will give You thanks and sing praise to Your Name forever.

Psalm 8

Creator God, we see all Your marvelous works and extol You. You have a special place for man in Your holy plan. We bow before You and Your Son Jesus Christ. All things are Yours, and everything everywhere should rightly give You praise.

Psalm 9

Glorious God, we give You thanks for all Your wonderful deeds. We praise You for Your justice and Your mercy. In the day of trouble, You have been our strong Help. You are a righteous judge. It is good for us to trust in You. We come to You in the Name of Jesus Christ. You heard Him when He called out to You. We also rejoice in Your great works of salvation. We have been found in Christ and have been credited with His perfect righteousness. We live in the secure hope of Your mercy, for Your Son has rescued us.

Psalm 10

O Lord God, please continue to draw near to us in every time of trouble. We thank You for the righteousness and goodness of Christ. He was moved by our desperate condition and He came to save us. He did what no one else could ever do. He rescued us in the saving protection of the good news and brought us home by the power of Your Holy Spirit. Purify our hearts, moving us closer and closer to Your Son, and then send us forth in works of love and service for the glory of Your Name. Thank You for Your great mercy, eternal King. You hear our cry, and You help us.

Psalm 11

Lord God, You are the refuge of Your people. Will we be forced to run from men and angels who pursue us? You are safe in heaven and we are secure in You. We know that the day of rescue will come. We will see Your Son. We will behold His face.

Psalm 12

God of Our Salvation, there are troubles and dangers all around us. Please help us. The needy cry out to You every day. In Your purity and love, You will keep us and rescue us.

Psalm 13

Lord, You will not forget Your righteous Servant who made satisfaction for our sins. Our foes will not win the day, for in Your steadfast love You help us.

Psalm 14

Father, Your holy Son knows You and understands us. There is no corruption or hypocrisy in Him. He called upon Your Name and was heard. Therefore You are with the generation who takes refuge in Christ. Bring great salvation out of Zion for Your Israel throughout the world.

Psalm 15

Lord God, may we live with You forever in Jesus? He was without sin and has called us friends. He shall never be moved, and so we have peace.

Psalm 16

O God, You are our strong hope. We thank You for Your church. We are together in Christ. We will not follow other gods. You are our portion. Our inheritance is beautiful. You are with us and our hearts are glad. You have heard the prayer of Your Holy Son. We have eternal pleasures at Your right hand forevermore.

Psalm 17

Great God of Justice, Hear our prayers. You know us. We have committed our lives to You and turned away from all evil. Please hear us now, for we seek refuge in You. There is an adversary who stands against us as a deadly enemy. He has no pity, but is full of arrogance. Please defend us by the Word of Your mouth. Help us, O Lord, for evil men would pursue us to destroy us. We will awake in Your presence.

Psalm 18

God of Our Salvation, we sing to You with love and joy. You are our Rock. We call upon Your Name. Though death drew near to us, You heard our voices, and attended to the cry of our hearts. Like a father who runs to the defense of His children, You came to us and rescued us. You are able to scatter our strongest enemies. They were too mighty for us, but You have loved us and rescued us. Deal with us according to the righteousness of Your faithful Servant Jesus Christ. We have received Your abundant mercy. Grant to us the light of Your presence every day, that we might live for the glory of Your Name. Your way is perfect and true. We take refuge in You. We go forth in battle for Your holy purposes. Crafty men make hidden plans, but they will be defeated, for You have equipped us for the day of battle. You know Your own people, O God, and You have appointed Your Son to be the Head over the nations. You have subdued so many lands under Jesus Christ. We will sing with joy to You forever, O mighty God.

Psalm 19

Creator God, we hear of You from every mountaintop and from the vastness of the oceans that exist according to Your will. In the skies we see who You are from all that You have made. But now You have spoken to us so clearly and wonderfully in Your written word. Help us to love Your speech, and keep us from the foolishness of willful rebellion against You. Change us that we might love Your Law more and more with a pure heart.

Psalm 20

O Divine Helper, You deliver us from evil in the day of trouble. Lord, we ask that You would purify our desires, and grant to us all our holy petitions. We trust in Your Son, O Lord. He is the King over Your people, and He will answer us when we call.

Psalm 21

Mighty God, we rejoice in Your strength and in the glory of Your Son, the King over Your people. He is full of splendor and majesty, for He has trusted perfectly in You, O God. Your day of wrath is coming, and You will separate the wicked from the righteous. Be exalted, in the greatness of Your perfect power.

Psalm 22

Merciful God, Your Son was cut off for our transgressions. We trust in You. We will not be put to shame. Your Son suffered greatly from the hatred of men. They railed against Him without cause. They nailed Him to a cross. He faced death for our salvation. Yet He trusted in You to the end. You rescued Him. Now He has won for You the praise of the church. We cry out to Him for powerful help. We are not only saved; we are also satisfied. People from many nations shall serve You, even those who are long gone from the earth. All generations shall proclaim Your righteousness, even people not yet born. You have done everything for our salvation, and we will praise You forever.

Psalm 23

Shepherd of Israel, You lead us and provide for us. Though death is near, You are nearer still. We trust You, for You fill us with Your Spirit. You have secured for us an eternal home in Your great house.

Psalm 24

Great God of Our Salvation, You created the earth. You have loved righteousness. The Man You have chosen has made the way for us to be with You in heaven. The Lord Jesus is the King of Glory. He has entered the heavenly sanctuary, and we are united with Him forever.

Psalm 25

O Lord God, do not let us be put to shame. Lead us in the way of Your Word. We wait for You. We love Your mercy and Your covenant faithfulness. We humble ourselves before You, because of our sin and because of Your greatness. Teach us Your truth. We follow the Man of Righteousness. He has obeyed You perfectly, and has delivered us from the worst trouble. We take refuge in You, O Lord. You will redeem the church from all her troubles.

Psalm 26

Lord God of Righteousness, help us today. Your Son lived in perfect innocence. Make us true followers of Him. May we walk in His integrity. We worship You as Your chosen assembly, for we have been covered by the atoning blood of our holy Savior.

Psalm 27

God of Our Salvation, there is no one like You. No matter how great the danger, our hope and confidence is in You. Please bring us to Your heavenly temple. We are with You even now in Christ. We long to be close to You and to see You. Be near us now. You are the God of our salvation. Lead us on a level path. We wait for You, O Lord.

Psalm 28

Hear us, O Lord! We cry to You for mercy and help. In this evil world, men speak peace to us, but they plot our speedy destruction. Your Son faced trouble in the days of His earthly ministry. He suffered greatly for us. You will surely save Your people and bless our future. You will carry us forever.

Psalm 29

Lord of Hosts, all worship of men and angels is due to You, for You alone are God. Your voice is fearful and wonderful, like glorious thunder from the heavens. Blessed be Your Name, O great King. We hear Your Word of peace, and are greatly blessed.

Psalm 30

Father God, we know the day of difficulty, and the day of Your great deliverance. We have been foolish in sin, but You have granted us repentance. When You hid Your face, we cried out to You. You have heard us and helped us. We will rejoice in Your presence forevermore.

Psalm 31

God of Providence, You are the only hope of the righteous. Be our Rock and our Fortress. We trust our souls and bodies to You. You know the depth of the affliction of Your servants. You see our tears, and You hear our sighs. Though our neighbors may hate or forget us, our times are in Your powerful hand. Save us in Your steadfast love. Your justice will come against Your enemies in the day of Your glory. When all hope seems lost, You remain the sure hope of Your people.

Psalm 32

Father, You have counted the righteousness of Christ as our righteousness. His death was ours, and His life above is also for us. Our sin has been forgiven, for You have delivered our lives from Your wrath. You make us messengers of faith in Your Son. We will trust in Him forever, together with all who have been counted as upright in heart by Your grace.

Psalm 33

O Lord God, We come to You in joyful praise. Your Word is true and good. Your great works of creation are amazing and lovely. You have power beyond the force of mighty men and armies. You know everything about men, even their secret deeds and the silent intentions of every heart. We hope in Your steadfast love. We wait for You. We trust You.

Psalm 34

Father God, We praise You in gladness and humility today. When we cry out to You, You hear us. We take refuge in You and lack no good thing. Grant us effectiveness as we would teach our children about Your ways. You will deliver us out of the many afflictions that are a normal part of the righteous life. We have tasted of Your goodness and have seen the wonder of Your glory.

Psalm 35

Protector God, powerful foes are pursuing Your people. Let them be disappointed in their wicked goals. Foil them through the ministry of holy angels. Stop the progress of the man who seeks an evil conquest over the weak. Help us to be safely innocent regarding the ways of evil. May we feed the hungry, and help the poor in their time of need. Bring us one day into the great congregation of perfected men and angels in Your heavenly sanctuary. You see all things. Help us now in a true and holy cause. Bring about a wonderful victory for the glory of Your matchless name. Great are You, O Lord! We will praise You forever!

Psalm 36

Holy God, we hate the way of wicked men. Take us far away from the evil path. You are perfect in righteousness and steadfast love. We would follow You forever. Grant us Your love, that we might always see Your light in the land of the living.

Psalm 37

Lord of Justice and Mercy, why do we worry about evil men? You are with all those who trust in Your power and goodness. We wait for You, O Lord. We shall inherit the land according to Your great promise. We are happy in the assurance that comes from Your Word even today. The wicked have no solid hope, but You will help us in an evil day. Our hope is everlasting and secure. You have ordained our every step, and will take us into Your glorious presence. You love justice. You are a God of mercy to those who trust in You. We love You, O Lord. We know You will never abandon us. There is a great day coming for us in the land of Your perfect glory. We look to You for the future of every good hope.

Psalm 38

Father God, You know the truth about our iniquities. We have violated Your commandments. We have brought great trouble upon ourselves. Our bodies are weak from sin. We have been full of worry and shame. Forgive us and heal us. We confess our iniquity with a true and godly sorrow, and we hope in Your kind mercy.

Psalm 39

Merciful Lord, the wicked are in our presence all day long. Though we would try not to speak foolishly, we may end up saying things when we should be silent. Help us to remember our days. We know that we are but a breath. We are here for a moment and then we are gone. You are everlasting. Give us hope again today.

Psalm 40

Almighty God, You have helped us and have given us joy. We were mired down in trouble. Then we remembered that Your Son came and delivered us. He obeyed Your law from the heart. He testified to His great success through His resurrection. Help us again today. Help us to remember Him. He will deliver us in our daily struggle, and we will rejoice and be glad in Him. Be near to Your people, O Lord.

Psalm 41

Lord God, You care for the weak and the poor, and You call us to follow You in this love for the needy. We see ourselves as desperate recipients of Your merciful condescension. Ruthless men seem to be everywhere, even among those who claim to be the friends of Your church. May Your name be blessed forever, as the weak of the earth are made mighty in Your strength.

Psalm 42

Father God, in the day of depression and sadness, You are still God. Though we seem to forget You, You have never forgotten us. We will hope in You. We will remember You even in the worst time of trouble. You will surely deliver us. You are powerful. You love us. You are present everywhere, and You will save. We hope in You now.

Psalm 43

Almighty King, You are not intimidated by strong men with evil intentions. Well-armed nations with thousands of soldiers do not impress You, no matter how powerful and wicked they may be. You are above them all. We will praise You forever. Our hope is in You alone.

Psalm 44

Lord God, so many of Your great deeds are recorded for us in Your Word. You have won the victory for Your people through centuries of trouble and deliverance. We do not trust in ourselves. We boast in You. But where are You today, Father? We do not understand our current situation. While we do not doubt Your power and Your love, we are ashamed of our present condition. Your Son is still the King and Head of the church and our perfect Substitute. Yet we are in great need. Our affliction and oppression are obvious. We need You. Help us today, in accord with Your steadfast love.

Psalm 45

Great King, we thank You for the joy that we have in knowing You, for You are marvelous in all Your attributes and deeds. We are so greatly blessed to have such a wonderful Messiah. Your throne is forever. You are full of the Spirit of God beyond measure. We bow to You Lord, for we are Your holy bride. Though we are scattered throughout the world, we belong to You. You will gather us in Christ. You will make us fruitful, and we will praise You forever.

Psalm 46

Strong Deliverer, You are the Help of Your people every day and through every time of trouble. There is a great river of Your Spirit coming to us out of Your heavenly sanctuary. You have made us glad. You have defended us in times of trouble. You will glorify Your Name in us, for You are the mighty fortress of Your church, and we are Your people.

Psalm 47

Sovereign Lord, You are the Most High God. You have ordered all the events of human history in accord with Your glorious plan. You rule over every lesser power. You will be exalted forever.

Psalm 48

Lord of heaven and earth, we look to Your great sanctuary in glory and we are astonished. Your Word teaches us about the place of our citizenship in that heavenly Jerusalem. We are deeply impressed. Our expectation of the life to come is a matter of great joy for our souls. We will pass on this good news to the coming generation, and will speak of You throughout all the nations of men.

Psalm 49

Holy God, You are over all, forever to be praised. We have some awareness of the sins of men and we confess our own transgressions. How can we be saved? Yet One has come for us as a Redeemer, that we might have a hope that extends beyond the grave. Our mortal bodies will die, and our achievements under the sun will swiftly be forgotten. Grant to us understanding of Your eternal glory, that we might live in Your presence forever.

Psalm 50

Almighty God, You are perfect. You come to us. You speak. Your righteousness is declared in the heavens. We hate our hypocrisy. We would pretend perfect devotion, but You know the truth. Help us now, that we might glorify You. We turn away from all wickedness. Help us to love the truth from the heart. You are perfectly holy, and You care for us. We give You our thanksgiving as a pleasant sacrifice, for we offer You our lives.

Psalm 51

O Lord, our Redeemer, You know the truth about our sin, and have uncovered transgression before our hearts at just the right time. You bring Your Word to bear upon the very points of our obvious faults. How could we have pretended that everything was alright when we continued in sin? Fill our souls with Your Holy Spirit. Change us, O God. We will lead others in the right way, for You have forgiven us. You have received us again through Christ. We give You all glory and praise through Him.

Psalm 52

Almighty God, men of evil turn against You. Surely a day of reckoning will come. We have made You our only refuge for that coming day. Your Son has trusted in You perfectly, and has won salvation for the congregation who fear You and are called by His name.

Psalm 53

Lord God, You are real. We come to You today in faith. We need You for help in every situation of trouble and terror. Bring salvation to us. Restore our fortunes, and make us glad in Your Son.

Psalm 54

Savior God, we need You now. There is danger and trouble on every side. We ask for Your deliverance, that we might look with triumph over every adversary.

Psalm 55

Hear us, O Lord! We feel the danger of trouble and wickedness everywhere, and we are greatly concerned. We would like to run away from all our anxieties, but we do not know where we can go. Even familiar friends seem to be against us. We call out to You. Surely You will save us. There is a dangerous battle going on here. Please help us, and deliver us from those who make false promises of love and loyalty. We cast our cares upon You, for You care for us.

Psalm 56

Father God, You are gracious. We trust You. There is much danger everywhere, but You will protect us. You know about every enemy who stands against us, and every difficulty that will come before us. You are powerful to save in every situation, and You are with us.

Psalm 57

Creator God, we take refuge in You. Troubles are many, but Your steadfast love is above them all. People come against us, but You are stronger than men. We will worship You early in the morning. We will worship You when our situation seems hopeless, for You are God.

Psalm 58

Righteous Lord, there are many who rule with injustice. They justify themselves and insist on their own way. They use the power they have been given for immoral purposes. Our trust is in You. The wicked will not win forever, for You are God, and You will judge.

Psalm 59

Glorious Lord, though our enemies are making plans to destroy Your people, You will see and help. You are awake to the needs of Your people, and to their cry for aid. The day will come when every foe will be trapped and destroyed. Everyone will see that You love Your people with unwavering faithfulness, and we will worship You forever.

Psalm 60

Lord God, help us now. As we look around our lives we see trouble and destruction everywhere. Send Your salvation and help Your church. Claim Your people again with Your strong Word. You will bring us home in triumph. You will have the victory over all of those who oppose You.

Psalm 61

Great Lord and Helper, give us strength. We want to be with You now and always. Grant to us eternal life and love in Your Son, our King. We live in the security and power of His holy promises to You.

Psalm 62

Our God, we rest in You. The dangers around us are real. In silence we wait for You. When we cry out to You, You hear us and help us. Forgive us when we would put our hope in evil schemes. Your Son is our Redeemer. What more do we need? We have You, O God.

Psalm 63

Lord God, You have put something within us that longs for You. You have made our souls alive to Your goodness. We praise You when we are together, and we praise You in secret communion. No matter how dangerous the enemies against us may be, You are our refuge and our help forever.

Psalm 64

Father, why do we fear powerful enemies? They have an evil purpose and seem to be invincible, but they will not be able to stand against You. They have not adequately considered Your love for Your children, and Your power to save. You shall surely deliver the upright in heart from the grasp of even the strongest foes.

Psalm 65

Glorious God, You should receive our praise all day long. We come to You now, for You have drawn us into Your house, and we see Your goodness and Your righteousness. You have created the land and the seas. You govern even the spheres in the sky. You bless us with great fruitfulness. There is a joy everywhere that can be seen and heard throughout the world. We will magnify Your Name forever, O Lord.

Psalm 66

Father God, we call everyone everywhere to submit to Your glory and to shout for joy. We know that our Redeemer lives. He has heard us in the day of impending doom. We live, O God, for You have rescued us. We have known Your discipline in a time of fatherly chastisement. Our training is swiftly coming to a close. You have heard our prayers, and You will take us to a place of perfect righteousness and safety.

Psalm 67

Gracious Lord, be kind to us. Show forth Your grace to all the peoples of the earth. Draw them to Your worship. Move all nations to yield themselves to the celebration of Your eternal goodness.

Psalm 68

Our Father, there are enemies who would threaten the safety of Your family. What will You do, Father? You are the Protector and Defender of Your people. No matter how desperate our condition may seem, You will bring us the exact help that we need. Speak, Lord, for Your servants listen. Send forth Your men and women to speak of Your glory. There is no one like You, for You are a towering mountain over everything that You have created. Make us to dwell with men and angels who will praise You forever. You have brought us back from the depths of disaster. You will surely judge the wicked. We have a hope of the greatest eternal celebration because of our Messiah, Your Son. We bring our gifts to You. We have been freed from the chains of men, and we sing with joy as we walk in Your Spirit. Grant us power today for the praise of Your glory.

Psalm 69

God of Our Salvation, we are in a sea of enemies who seek our destruction. Though we have sinned, we hope in You. We are in great need, for we love Your house, and Your enemies hate us. Even our own families do not understand our zeal for Your Kingdom. Help us, O God, for we would be swallowed up by the earth in death. Come quickly, O God. Speak the word of our redemption again through the blood of the Lamb. He was entrapped by faithless men, but He has won His battle through the victory of the cross. Hear the prayers of Your Son, who surely lives forever to intercede for us. We are weak and close to death. We are weary, O Lord. You will give us life, for we are in Him.

Psalm 70

Mighty God, it seems that we cannot wait much longer. Trouble is very near to us. Our confidence remains in You, for You are great. Be nearer than any danger, O Lord.

Psalm 71

Lord God, we take refuge in You, and we come to You every day. The wicked man would fight against us continually. We will praise You forever. We know that You will not cast us off when we are weak. Evil men would accuse and destroy the righteous. They actively seek our hurt, but You will come with mighty deeds and with a powerful love that will never end. You have done great things for us. You are bringing us up again from the dead, and we will shout with joy forever.

Psalm 72

Great God, bless the Name of Your Son. Bring about the fullness of His reign. May He provide for His people forever, and may His dominion be both complete and eternal. Lord, we long for the day of the return of our perfect Savior. He will bring the greatest prosperity and peace. Thank you for this great hope. He is our King, our Lord, and our God.

Psalm 73

Glorious Lord, forgive us for our foolish envy. We forget what You have done for us. We treat eternity as nothing. We look at someone in their momentary dishonest or crass gain, and think that such a man is better off then we are. Bring us back to You in worship together with all of Your people. Help us to contemplate our existence in a real world of blessing which You have secured for us through the blood of Your Son. It is good to be near You, O God.

Psalm 74

O Lord of Hosts, we are in great need. Is there any hope for us on this earth? Your church is in trouble. Enemies have come upon us and have overtaken us. From within our own number foes have arisen. They use Your Name and claim that they are with You, and yet they deny the truth of Your Word. They ignore Your great works of creation. They rail against Your Law, and would accuse You while claiming to be Your friends. Do not forget Your church, O Lord. Come quickly and deliver us.

Psalm 75

Our Father, we thank You because of who You are and what You have done. We humble ourselves before You, Almighty God. You will judge the wicked. You will vindicate Your people forever.

Psalm 76

Lord God, You bring peace through great strength. You have overturned powerful foes. Through Your judgment, the humble are saved. We give You our lives with great thanksgiving, for You have rescued us.

Psalm 77

Merciful Lord, hear our prayer. We turn to You night and day. Why is there so much trouble in our hearts? Where is our faith? Have You given up on Your covenant faithfulness? Never, O Lord! We meditate upon the history of our redemption throughout many centuries. We also consider the strength of Your promises. You will hear us and help us. We believe in You. We have faith in Your Son Jesus, who leads us through a dangerous wilderness.

Psalm 78

Almighty God, we are ready to hear Your voice in the reading and preaching of Your Word. Speak to us, Lord, that we might remember Your works, and that the next generation might grow in their faith. Centuries of wickedness have been overturned through the great redemptive work of Your Son on the cross. Look at the provision You have granted to us. You have gathered Your church. You have brought us the fulfillment of every good purpose in Your eternal decrees. You provide for us everything that we need day by day. What a kind and mighty Lord You are. In the day of Your gifts, we still sinned against You. You have surely disciplined us, for You love us. We repent of our lies and our iniquity. You have kept us according to Your loving purposes. You will continue to love us even now. What have we done, O Lord? How could we rail against You in our hearts, forgetting that Your purposes are always good? Have we forgotten what You have done in the case of Your Son? His death was for us. Surely You will give us all things. How magnificent is Your Name. We turn away from all sin and treachery. You have kept Your remnant through every trouble and misery. You have defeated the world, the flesh, and the devil. Because of Your commitment to Your Name, because of Your covenant with Your Son, You have granted us everything necessary that we might live with You in perfect blessedness forever. We thank You, O Lord.

Psalm 79

God Almighty, our situation is critical. We need your help soon, or we die. We do not see how we can be rescued, but we count on Your compassion and Your great wisdom. There is surely a way of deliverance that we cannot see. We are Your people. We love Your Name. Help us, O Lord.

Psalm 80

Lord God, You are mighty. Look upon Your church in our day of great need. You have done so much for us already. Surely You will keep all of Your great promises. Have regard for us. You have chosen Your Son to be our King. This great Son of Man is our sure hope.

Psalm 81

Great God, we should praise You with fullness of joy and expectation. You have redeemed us out of the greatest distress. We should listen to You completely. Why should there be strange gods among us? Why do we not follow Your commandments? You have great blessings planned for us, even through times of trouble. Will we still continue to deny You?

Psalm 82

Father God, what must it be like to be in the divine counsel above? You have an instruction for us here below. We must care for those in our charge. Come soon, O Lord. Rescue the weak from their foes.

Psalm 83

Lord Almighty, where are You? Please speak to us through Your Word. Help us to survive when enemies attack Your covenant people. You will surely come in the Day of Judgment. What shall we do until that day? We will trust You, and we will remember that You are at work even now. You are the Most High God, over all the earth.

Psalm 84

Our Father, we long to be with You. We rejoice in the opportunity to be together in worship even in this age, but we especially look forward to the age to come. We long for a day in Your courts above. Help us, O Lord. You have blessed us, and we trust in You.

Psalm 85

Sovereign Lord, You have been so kind to us. We have the fullness of forgiveness in Christ. Please revive us again. Speak peace to us through Your Word. May we have growth in holiness that could only come from You. Your Son is the King of Righteousness. We trust in Him.

Psalm 86

Glorious God, we come to You in great need. Day by day You move us along in a most holy faith. We call upon You and ask for Your grace. You are the only true God. Your works are amazing. Teach us Your way. Unite us together in Christ. There is danger in this age. It comes so close to us. Help us, O Lord, for You know all things, and have promised to be our God.

Psalm 87

Merciful Lord, You have built up Your holy Zion in the praises of Your people. Even those who were far off have been drawn near to You in Christ. We joyfully confess a new birth, for in Him we were born in Zion. We will rejoice in You forever.

Psalm 88

Great God of Our Salvation, You hear Your children when they call upon Your Name. We cannot trust in our strength, for it is almost gone. We cannot trust in our companions, for they have rejected us. Make us to praise You in resurrection life. Those that lie in the grave cannot sing praises to You. We are helpless unless You speak life again into our mortal bodies.

Psalm 89

Lord God, Your love is steadfast forever. Help us to believe Your Word today. We feel alone in misery and trouble, but You are surely a mighty God. Father, the waves of grief and danger are too much for us. Come and save us. Come in all Your righteousness and love. Encourage us now with Your glorious Spirit. When we come to You in weakness and anxiety, let us be sent forth again in peace. Our life is in Him who is the perfect Son of David. He is the answer to the removal of all our fears. He is King of kings, and there has never been anything lacking in His obedience. You chastise us out of love, but we are safe in our great Messiah King. Lord, You know our secret tears and our many faults. Your people are in great trouble now, but Your wrath came upon Your Son for us. He has delivered our souls from hell. We are mocked by men, but You are surely faithful. Blessed be Your holy Name forever.

Psalm 90

Eternal Father, in You we live and move and have our being. We are here for a season and then return to dust, but from the dust You call us back to life. Who can stand before You? You know all our secret sins. We live for our seventy or eighty years, and then we are gone. Have pity on us. Help us to rejoice in You forever, so that we will consider our current troubles a light affliction when

140

compared with the glory that will soon be our life and portion without end.

Psalm 91

Strong Deliverer, You are our refuge and our fortress in the most horrible danger. You are so faithful, O God. Even if we die, we shall live. We will see Your great deliverance with our own eyes. We will see angels, who help us in a day of trouble. You have spoken great promises to us in Christ. What a blessing it is to live in the light of His glorious resurrection!

Psalm 92

Our Father, what a joy it is to praise You! You have done great things. Your thoughts are deep and wonderful. You are far above all idols. You have blessed us in great ways. You have planted us in Your kingdom and we are growing in Your righteous love.

Psalm 93

Lord God, You rule over all. You are the Creator and Sustainer of the world. There are so many people on this earth, but You are far above the most powerful and numerous mobs of Your enemies. Your holiness will endure forever.

Psalm 94

Almighty Lord, You will judge the proud and the wicked. You will help us as we face great difficulties from foolish people who move in powerful malice against us. They have forgotten You. They have not remembered that You will defend us in the great day of trouble. You will rise up for us against the wicked. You will be with us in steadfast love. You will help us against strong foes. We take refuge in You day by day.

Psalm 95

Great God, we sing praises to You. We thank You for the many blessings You bestow upon us. Your works of creation are deeply impressive. We are Your people. What a blessing it is to belong to You, O Lord! We repent of all our sin. We will not put You to the test. We will follow You in the way of faith and obedience.

Psalm 96

Father God, we sing to You in worship day by day. You are great. The idols of the world are nothing. You made the heavens and the earth. People everywhere should praise You. The true worshiper should bring You perfect holiness. Is this not what Your Son has done for us? He has rescued us through His righteousness and His atoning death. He will come again to judge the earth.

Psalm 97

Almighty Father, You rule over the earth. You are a mighty God. You should be feared by all men. All the earth should worship You. There is no god that men can make with their own hands. We have been made by You. We love You, O Lord. We turn away from evil. We rejoice in You.

Psalm 98

Lord God, we sing You songs of glory and rejoice in Your presence. You have saved Your church. All the world will bring You worship. We rejoice before You with our voices and with instruments of celebration. You will surely come to judge the earth.

Psalm 99

Lord Almighty, You are High and lifted up. You love justice. We should worship You always. You have raised up men to worship You in days gone by. You are alive today, and You are holy forever.

Psalm 100

Father, the duty of worship is not only for Israel. All Your people throughout the earth should love and serve You. We thank You for Your steadfast love, secured for us in the life and death of Your Son.

Psalm 101

Great God and King, we sing to You with joy. You are a God full of integrity and holiness. We will follow You. We will love what You love. Surround us with the righteous forever. You will surely bring us into Your land, the place of utmost purity and love.

Psalm 102

Father God, hear us today. We need You. We live in this age of misery and confusion. We cry out to You all day long. There is trouble all around us. When will You wipe away every tear? You are God. You are sovereign forever. Please come quickly, O Lord. You will build up Your church. Bring forward future generations of those who will serve You. Grant Your people life from on high. Let us live forever in Your presence. You are from everlasting to everlasting. We are safe in You alone.

Psalm 103

Glorious God, thank You for Your abundant mercies. We glorify Your name. You have given us true love that will never end. You have blessed Your people of old. They are alive now in Your presence. Thank you for the forgiveness of sins. Take away from us all the evil that remains in us. You are full of compassion and You will help us forever. Our lives seem so small and so temporary. In You we will rejoice throughout all eternity. We will bless Your Name in the company of angels and resurrected saints. We bless You from the depths of our hearts, O Lord, forever and ever.

Psalm 104

Great God of Providence, we bless Your Name. Your wonderful nature is displayed before us in all of Your great works. You have created all things. You also rule and reign over everything You have made. You formed the mountains and the valleys, and have filled the earth with intriguing creatures. You make the land beautiful to look at, and You give us so many blessings to investigate and to experience. Thank You for these daily gifts that are such a wonderful part of our lives. Thank You for attending to the multitude of details that regularly escape our notice. No matter how intelligent any man may be, You will always be far above all the creatures that You have made. We will sing praise to You, and we will think about You with great joy. Surely You are not surprised by the wickedness of men. You rule over all. Blessed be Your Name, O God.

Psalm 105

Glorious Lord of All, we worship You and give You thanks. It is wonderful to sing to You. We seek You and we remember what You have done. Your judgments are wise. You keep all Your promises. You made a covenant with us in Christ, and You are fulfilling that good plan in great ways. You have announced news of a future age through Your prophets. So much has already come to pass, and yet much more is still ahead of us. We marvel at Your works in gathering a people for the glory of Your Name. Even today You continue to rescue us from the sin that distracts and ensnares us. You bring us out of danger and cause us to trust again in Your Son. Be with us as we go through this life. We are looking forward to the coming age of glory. May we keep Your Son's commandments as we wait for the day of His return.

Psalm 106

O Lord our God, You are good. You show favor to Your people We rejoice in You together with all of Your children. You met us with salvation when we had nowhere left to turn. You made a way for us through the tumultuous sea of Your righteous judgments. You have seen us when we were trapped in the snare of our sins and have provided a way out through the life and death of Your Son. If You were to charge us for our sins, there would never be any hope of life for us. Your Son stood up on our behalf at just the right time. His righteousness has covered over our rebellion. We have been cleansed by His blood. We are assured of Your love for us through Him. You see us even now in our distress and help us through every situation of despair and disaster. Please save us again and again, until we are with You, body and soul, in our heavenly habitation.

Psalm 107

Our Father, You have steadfast love for us through Jesus Christ, our Lord. Are we hungry and in physical need? You have given us food and shelter. Are we trapped in dark prisons of evil men, or bound up in the chains of sin? You have brought the strong man Jesus to break open the prison house and to deliver us into the fresh air of freedom. Are we stuck in sickness and pain? You have granted us help. Are we overwhelmed with fear in the midst of some horrible storm? You have heard our cry. You have calmed the wind and the waves, and we live. Surely You can do all things. You will move heaven and earth for the sake of Your elect. You have given us blessing upon blessing. In love, You discipline us, but You will fill our hearts with hope again. We are persuaded that Your steadfast love will continue forever.

Psalm 108

Great God, Your special commitment to Your people passes all our understanding. Your promises are absolutely sure. Your very being is everlasting and beyond all measure. You will not treat the world in the same way as You do Your church. Help us now, for dangerous enemies are near. You will give us victory over even the most powerful adversaries. You will give us deliverance and peace.

Psalm 109

Our God, please speak to us powerfully through Your holy Scriptures. Save us in Your infinite strength. There is one who comes to make accusations against us. We know that our battle is not against flesh and blood, but there are those who have fallen under the foul sway of a wicked adversary. Surely You will make a final end of Satan, together with all His allies among men and angels. They have despised You, and have hated Your mercy. We trust in You. Please continue Your great faithfulness to us for the glory of Your holy Name. Continue in Your everlasting love for Your people.

Psalm 110

Great Redeemer, You are Lord, and Your Son is also the Lord at Your right hand. Together with Your Son and Your Spirit, You are one God. May Jesus Christ rule as the King of Your kingdom forever. May we be willing servants of our royal High Priest every day. Surely no one can stand against Him, for He reigns eternally in the fullness of Your Holy Spirit.

Psalm 111

Merciful God, we give You thanks. As we meditate upon Your works, we see the greatness of Your character. Our future is secure because of Your trustworthy Word. We bow before You with reverence, and we receive Your many gifts with grateful hearts.

Psalm 112

O Lord Our God, we praise You. Make our young ones mighty in Your service. Bring Your light into our homes and show forth Your glory in Your church. Give us courage in the spiritual battle that we have before us. Grant us hope and security in Your everlasting love.

Psalm 113

Lord God, You have blessed us in so many ways. We thank You sincerely. You are above all nations. There is no god like You. You saw us in our poverty and need. You met us in our barrenness. You have granted us godliness with contentment. You have promised us a future forever in Your Kingdom. We praise You.

Psalm 114

God of the Nations, You know how to save Your people from dangerous adversaries. You are the God of providence, and You move heaven and earth in order to preserve and protect Your children. Blessed be Your Name forever.

Psalm 115

Great God, we give You glory. There is no one like You. You do all that You please. The idols of the nations can do nothing. They are a dreadful snare to all who trust in them. Grant that we would trust You and follow You forever. We will fear You and serve You every day through Jesus Christ. Forgive our sins, and cause us to walk with a confident expectation of the coming resurrection.

Psalm 116

Merciful Lord, we love You. You have heard us when we cried out to You. We faced distressing thoughts and agonizing fears. You heard our cry, and have caused us to rest again in Jesus Christ. Your promises are very secure. We will not be moved. The age of resurrection is surely coming. We are the payment of Your Son's holy vow. We will praise You in the land of the living. We long for the coming of the perfect Jerusalem. We are there even now in Christ.

Psalm 117

God of all the earth, everyone everywhere should worship You. Use us as Your servants to extend the glory of Your Name to lands that have never heard of You. Bring the power of redemption through the blood of Your Son to every nation.

Psalm 118

O Lord, You are so very good. You are a God of covenant faithfulness. When we cry out to You, You hear us. Your servants need You every day. When our situation is desperate, You are able to help us, and You do help us. You discipline Your children, but You do not give us over to everlasting destruction. Your Son took the death and hell that we deserved. He was rejected by men. More than that He faced the full weight of our just penalty upon the cross. The death that He died Has brought life to us. His sacrifice was completely acceptable to You. He has won for us an everlasting salvation.

Psalm 119

Our Father, we should follow You in everything that we do. We should pay very close attention to Your Word. Your Son has followed You perfectly. We admire His perfect love of Your Word. He spoke the truth in everything. He also had perfect wisdom. He knew when to say nothing and when to speak up. We marvel at the story of Jesus Christ. He grew in wisdom and stature. He learned Your Law, and He eagerly walked in the way of Your statutes. He kept Your testimonies to the end. Through Him we have life. We do not speak of Him as merely a man from the past. Jesus is alive forever. The One who faced such difficulties for our sake was perfectly victorious in His mission. Therefore, He lives forever. He will always love Your instructions. There were many who stood against Him. Despite the challenge of the test that was before Him, He remembered Your Law, and He walked in the way of Your precepts. He loved You and loved us. This was perfectly displayed in His death on the cross. Your Word is so very valuable. It is worth much more than gold. Even the afflictions with which You test us are surely for our good. Forgive us when we would turn away from Your Word. There is no good reason for us to do this. Lord, we pray that You would give us life in the midst of great difficulties. Will we fall from the delight of knowing You? Will we be among the foolish who reject Your commandments? May it never be, O God.

Your grace is so very necessary for us. Give us understanding. Help us to turn away from every temptation. Teach us Your rules. There is no hope for the one who would reject Your Word forever. Your Son never deviated from Your Law for even a moment. Lord, why would we consider the world more reliable than Your Word? Why are we drawn toward foolishness and sin? Father, we do love You. When we are in trouble, we do not always know what to say. Please help us to remember Your Word, and give us the right words to speak, that we might humbly express our reasons for the hope that lies within us. You are righteous, and Your Law is righteous. We are willing to be despised by the world. We do not want to wander from You again. Please help us in every test. Enemies would try to destroy us. You are near to help us in our affliction, for Your Word is in our hearts. No matter how many are faithless, we will stay in the way of life. Is there still hope for us? Surely You have forgiven our sins. You will bring us into the land of the living. We do love Your Law. Look beyond the foolishness of our murmuring. Surely You will let our souls live. If we go astray, please seek us, O great Shepherd of the sheep. We will not forget Your commandments.

Psalm 120

Lord God, please help us in our distress. There is much trouble all around us. It is a great challenge to live in this world. Our confidence is in Christ. For His sake You will hear us and help us.

Psalm 121

Father God, our help comes from You. You have created us, and You keep us through all kinds of difficulties. You will help us as we move along in our journey to the heavenly Jerusalem. You will keep us forever.

Psalm 122

Sovereign Lord, we long for Your presence. We thank You for the blessing of worship in Your temple even now. Your Son is full of the Holy Spirit. In Him there is full peace. We are united to Him, and we are the temple of Your Spirit.

Psalm 123

O God, we look to You. We need You day by day. There is no other place that we can go to for the mercy that we need. We need relief, O Lord. A proud foe is hard against us. We resist the devil and look to You for deliverance.

Psalm 124

Our Father, You have been our help. We are very thankful. Without You we surely would have fallen and been destroyed. You have helped us, Creator God. We will glorify Your Name forever.

Psalm 125

Lord God, we do trust in You. Make us to stand firm in Jesus Christ. Surround us and protect us. Cause us to live in obedience in the strength that comes from Your grace. By Your mercy bring Your church peace forever.

Psalm 126

Great God, You have given us laughter and joy in the day of our deliverance. You have done great things for us. Now we have tears, but we will come home to You with shouts of joy. Our labor in Your Name is not in vain.

Psalm 127
Father God, You build the house. You watch over us. You guard us. We can sleep at night because of You. You will bring the next generation of faithful people forward. Surely Your Son Jesus Christ has a multitude of children who will glorify You forever.

Psalm 128
Our God, we will walk in Your ways. The day is coming when all things will be right. You have granted us a glorious family in Zion. You will bring perfect peace upon Your church, and we will dwell securely with You forever.

Psalm 129
Merciful God, Your people have faced much persecution for many generations. Surely those who hate You and who kill Your loved ones will face Your wrath. Our only hope is in Your Name. In Christ we have great blessing forever.

Psalm 130
Lord God, we cry to You again today. You have forgiven our many sins. Because of the mercies of Christ, we now wait for Him with hope. Your Son is our plentiful redemption. A day of the fullest joy is surely near.

Psalm 131
Our Father, we rest in You. Like a child we rest in the security of Your embrace. We rest in You and trust in You even now. Your people will not be put to shame, for Your love will endure forever and ever.

Psalm 132
God in Heaven, be with Your people who trust in the greatest Son of David. We are Your priests forever. We are counted as Your holy ones in Him. A Messiah has come for us, and He reigns. His crown will shine forever. We will rest in Zion according to Your promise.

Psalm 133
Great Lord, it is a joy to be together with our brothers as we serve You in peace. We are Your people. You have given us the oil of gladness. Our security in Christ will never be taken away.

Psalm 134
Great God, we have come to our destination. We look to You with the fullest happiness. Your Son's hands are lifted up in benediction upon us even now. We are receiving a divine blessing from the heavenly Jerusalem. What a wonderful gift!

Psalm 135

O Lord God, it is so wonderful to praise You. You are good. We are Your chosen people. How great is Your mercy! You are far above all powers and principalities. You have wonderful decrees. You will accomplish all of Your good purposes. You are working out all the great events of the story of salvation. The idols of the world are nothing. How foolish we are when we make a god. May all of Your people praise You forever in the holy city of Your heavenly church.

Psalm 136

Merciful God, Your steadfast love endures forever. We give thanks to You. You do great wonders. You made the heavens. You also created the earth and You keep it going. You put the sun up in the skies. You gave us the moon and the stars for signs and seasons. You have performed great works of redemption. You rescued Israel out of Egypt. More than that, You have rescued all of Your people from horrible bondage to sin and Satan. You have granted to us a great hope. The rescue that we have experienced to this day is small when compared with the future age of glory that is coming. Surely Your steadfast love will endure forever.

Psalm 137

Our Father, You know our deep sadness in the day of our captivity and distress. Evil men would like to use Your songs for their own entertainment. They do not love You. They do not believe the truth of Your Word. O Father, surely the day of their destruction approaches. Give us grace to keep on going in times of trouble.

Psalm 138

Father God, we give You thanks. Thank You for Your faithfulness. When we called out to You, You heard Your servants and helped us. Surely You heard Your Son when He cried out to You in the garden of Gethsemane. You heard His cry from the cross. Now He is risen and even ascended. He is at Your right hand, and He intercedes for us. You will fulfill all of Your purposes for Your Son. We are the work of His hands. Please do not forsake the people of Your Son's possession.

Psalm 139

Great Lord, You know us. You created us. Our days were planned by You before we began any of them. You are everywhere and You know everything. What a wonderful love You have for Your people! You have helped us in countless ways, even when we have been utterly unaware of Your presence and goodness. May we bless Your Name forever. Please protect us day by day and deliver us from this evil age at the appointed hour. When we have accomplished the purposes that You have for Your servants here, lead us home again to You.

Psalm 140

Great God, help us in times of danger. We know that there are many wicked and violent men who create snares of trouble and distraction for us. None of them is a match for You. You will help us in the worst situation. Deal with our enemies according to Your ways. You know what to do for the humble who trust in You, and You know how to repay proud men and angels who seek the destruction of

Your servants.

Psalm 141
Father God, there is great help for us when we remember to call upon Your Name. You can tame our tongues and calm our restless hearts. You can turn away our foolish gluttony and covetousness. You can give us words of wisdom that are appropriate for every occasion. Our sin would be our downfall, but You protect Your people from the traps of the evil one, and bring us to a place of perfect safety.

Psalm 142
Lord God, hear our cry in the time of trouble. You see our weakness. Our help is not among the sons of men. You alone can rescue us. Pick us up in the day of our despondent condition. Cause the righteous to surround us with peace, that we may know Your bountiful love.

Psalm 143
Father God, is there yet a powerful help for us today? You know our sin, and You know the vigor of the enemy who has come against us. We want You. We remember Your word and study it with diligence, seeking a way out of our great trouble. You are God, even our God, and You will bring our souls out of danger at just the right time. You will turn our enemies away from Your humble servants in the day of their hot pursuit, for You care for Your beloved children. Even if we die, we shall surely live in Your presence forever.

Psalm 144
Glorious Lord, You use us in the thick of battle. You have trained our souls for a very significant spiritual war. You are here with us. You have given us the Word, that we might live by Your grace. We will be careful to follow Your anointed King. What will we do in the day when the blessings we long for the most seem so far from us? We will still turn to You and trust You. You are the Lord God, and You will help us.

Psalm 145
O Lord Our God, we praise you now, and we will never stop praising You. We will speak of Your greatness from generation to generation. There is so much to sing about in Your presence. Your goodness and mercy should never be ignored. Your might and Your truth are displayed in Your care for Your children. You are building a wonderful Kingdom. You are near to us, and we call upon You with great delight. We love You, O God. May all the earth magnify Your Name forever.

Psalm 146
Father God, we praise You throughout our days on earth and even beyond this present age. Our hope is in You, Our Creator God, the Sustainer of all things. Your heart, O God, is perfect. Your will for Your people is wonderful. We need not fear man, or give in to foolish fears. You are the God of Your children forever and ever.

Psalm 147

O Lord, You know how sad we are in the day of death and loss, but You will bind up the deep wounds in our hearts. You lift us up to Your heavenly sanctuary even now in Christ our King. You continue to feed and to care for us, even though we cannot stop crying. You bless us and help our children, even when we do not understand what You are doing. You accomplish Your will in the heavens above and over all the lands and seas. You give us Your holy Word from heaven, and provide a Redeemer in the person of Your Son. Thank You for Your greatness and Your glory, and for the Comforter who has come to help us.

Psalm 148

O God in Heaven, we worship You together with all the heavenly beings and all of Your creation in earthly realms. Your decrees are perfect and shall be perfectly accomplished. All that You have made will serve Your wise and holy purposes. You will display the greatness of Your glory at just the right time. We shall be near You forever in the majesty of Your Son.

Psalm 149

Father, fill our hearts with a melody of joy and grant our tongues holy words according to Your richest and fullest benediction upon Your people. We will sing of Your great nature and Your wonderful works. We will sing to You a new song. Even now in the day of pain and discipline we will honor You. You have granted to us the miracle of rejoicing, though our hearts are sad in the loss of some good gift. Surely everything You take away will be granted again to our longing eyes in new and better ways one day. The blessing that we seem to have lost, or something even more wonderful, will be our destiny in Christ, for You will be our all in all. Thank You for Your love and Your perfect promises.

Psalm 150

Lord God, there is no one like You. We will praise You for who You are and for what You have done. We will praise You with all that we are and all that we have. We will praise You with energy and excellence, for You have granted to us every good gift for the praise of Your glory. We will praise You, O Lord, forever and ever.

Proverbs

Proverbs 1

Great God of Light, we want to know Your wisdom. We want to receive Your instruction. We want Your Word to make a difference in our lives, that we might not only hear but also obey You. Your teaching is the very best gift for our ears and our hearts. May we take in Your Word deeply. Cause us to walk in holy society, rather than joining in the company of wicked fools. We turn away from greed, and we run with joy to hear Your Word of truth. We open our hearts to the full river of wisdom that comes from Your throne. We will be safe because of Your strength and mercy. We choose to fear You, and we hear Your holy reproof and encouragement. We will dwell securely forever, for You have given us ears to hear Your holy Word.

Proverbs 2

Father God, we call out to You for insight and understanding. You are the Source of all wisdom. Help us to walk in true integrity as followers of Jesus Christ. He served in the way of righteousness continually. Deliver us from adulterous affections, and from men who rejoice in doing evil. Help us to remember the way of wisdom and to live a life of holiness and fruitfulness. Give us a fuller expectation that we will be with You in the land that You have prepared for those who fear You.

Proverbs 3

Sovereign Lord, we have taught our children the way to go. Forgive us where we have failed in our duties. Will the next generation remember that way of righteousness and follow it? Father, we admit to You that we have been wise in our own eyes. This is not the way of hope. Thank You for the discipline that You have given us. We see that You have moved us in the way of the cross through Your hand of correction. May we walk securely in faith and love. Give us diligence and prosperity that we might have something to share with those in need. We want You, O Lord. Give us wisdom so that we will know how to live in humility and peace.

Proverbs 4

Lord God, there is no doubt that You give us good precepts. Help us to see the connection between true wisdom and obedience. As a matter of first importance, may we seek the way of wisdom with real earnestness. Protect us and our children from dangerous company. The way of the wicked would be very destructive for us. We must not think that we are safe associating with those of crooked speech and devious talk. Keep us on a straight path of what we clearly know to be right.

Proverbs 5

Great God, we need to hear You. We must have discretion. We cannot live in the pursuit of base pleasures. There are much better delights that You have for those who are willing to love Your Word and Your presence among us. We think back to former days. We hated discipline. But You rescued us from that dangerous life. You have shown to many the gift of the love of one woman. We thank You for the blessing of marriage, and we ask that You would keep us from seductive thoughts, words, and actions that would destroy our lives.

Proverbs 6

Our Father, please protect us from the foolish snare of inappropriate financial commitments. Help us to live in an orderly way, diligent in our duties, and seeking good in all situations. Thank you for the hope that we have of a coming day of perfect deliverance from all sin. Even now we turn away from those things that You hate. We thank You for the gift of those who have taught us the right way to go. Help us not to forsake their good counsel. Keep us from an adulterous woman. She destroys her lovers. We are so grateful for Your perfect faithfulness and holiness, credited to us through faith in Jesus Christ our Redeemer.

Proverbs 7

Lord God, what is our twisted confusion that we find wickedness so attractive? How many times do we need to hear warnings against adultery? Isn't the danger of sexual relationships outside of the protection of marriage a very obvious thing? Yet the young are exceedingly foolish on these matters, and even adults are slow to grow up. They still cling to the stupidity of unclean sexual behavior and look so foolish in their aging lusts. Protect us all from this way of sin long before it finds a dangerous resting place in our hearts. Surely we are not yet beyond this kind of evil. It could so easily infect our souls and destroy our lives. Protect us from this kind of deadly behavior.

Proverbs 8

Great God and King, You are the Source of all wisdom. Your Son is wisdom incarnate. He has spoken noble things. He has hated wickedness and lawlessness. He has perfectly attended to Your holy instruction. All knowledge and discretion are in Him. If we will seek wisdom with all our hearts, we will be able to lead well in the spheres where You have placed us. Grant to us the inheritance of those who have truly embraced Your wisdom. We marvel at what You have accomplished in all Your perfect wisdom. Through wisdom You have made the heavens and the earth. Through this same wisdom You maintain all of Your works according to Your plan. Through Your wisdom we have been delivered from the way that leads to death. Wisdom has always been Your delight. We will listen to the One who is Your wisdom, and we will find life and peace in Him.

Proverbs 9

O God of Wisdom, You have invited us to have communion with You. Grant us help from on high, that we may increase in wisdom. Help us to resist folly. Folly moves foolish people on a pathway of deceit, crime, and death. We need You. We need Your strength. It is not enough for us to know the way of wisdom. We must walk in it. We must come into Your home. We must sit down at Your table. We must rise up day by day and embrace You. Make us wise, O God.

Proverbs 10

Our Father, we want to rejoice in You as we walk in the way of wisdom. By that path make us diligent and true. Prosper us in plans of integrity and goodness. Make us careful and gracious in our words. Help us to have real love in our hearts. Help us to see the goal of true life, and to continue on the path toward that good destination. Show us how to restrain our desires and our mouths. Grant us Your wise Spirit that we might have the mind of Christ. We want to dwell in the land of the righteous. Keep us from all that is perverse.

Proverbs 11

O Lord, greed will destroy us so quickly. Deliver us from death, or we will fall by our own folly. We need help from You in the depths of our souls. If we can truly be righteous we will be of benefit to many people, but if we travel on the road of wickedness, we will be the source of much trouble for ourselves and others. We know that the way to true prosperity now and forever can only be by the way of wisdom. Make us generous and pure. What great character Your Son had in His earthly days! He never sinned. We have become His inheritance. He has captured our souls, and we are glad. His wisdom and godliness endures forever.

Proverbs 12

Lord God, we want to know things, but do we really love true wisdom? Grant to Your people wisdom in friendships as we move toward maturity. We need to have good sense in the choice of a companion for life. Please protect us from evil and foolish impulses. Teach us to listen to good advice, and to test all things rightly according to Your Word. Help us to make good plans that will lead to true peace. The way of laziness and sin seems so close to us at all times. Help us to be up and about our duties, and to grow in close communion with You.

Proverbs 13

Heavenly Father, is there some way that we could have the power to guard our hearts and our tongues? Sin that proceeds from our hearts seems to overthrow us. Please change us in our inner being, and renew us according to the purest and best desires that could only come from You. Point us toward the way of life according to Your Word. Help us to receive that Word through faithful ambassadors. May our inheritance that we leave for future generations be full of Your wisdom. Make us diligent in the love and discipline of our children. Raise up the next generation according to Your holy will.

Proverbs 14

Glorious God, You are building a holy house. You provide for us ministers and parents to move us in the way of understanding. Your Son grants us great spiritual wisdom by the power of Your Holy Spirit. Help us to flourish in Your presence forever. Keep us from pathways that lead only to death. Make us cautious enough to turn away from evil. Help us not to pass on folly to future generations. You make us generous to the poor, and diligent in all our duties. Thank You for the truthful witness of Your Word. The fear of You, O Lord, is a fountain of life. May we drink deeply of these good waters. May wisdom take root in our hearts, and bring forward glorious fruits in our own lives and in the lives of those who hear us and follow us.

Proverbs 15

Lord God, keep us from words that are unnecessarily harsh. Grant us gentle speech and ears that heed reproof. Our Father, how is it that wickedness so easily finds a resting place in our lives and in our homes? Give us glad hearts as we contemplate the many blessings that You have given to us. May we feast on the fullness of Your grace and wisdom day by day. Move us along on the good highway of righteousness, and grant us a healthy glimpse of our destination, lest we become discouraged and despondent, and turn away from the way of the cross either to the right or to the left.

Proverbs 16

Father God, bring Your help now to those who call upon Your Name. Grant us steadfast love and faithfulness, and lead us in turning away from evil. Enticing greed is so dangerous for us. We must not go down that road. Keep us far away from those things that are dangerous for our souls. We trust in You, for You have granted us eternal life. Your words are gracious, and Your way is the way of life. Teach us not to listen to words that will not be good for our lives. Teach us the wisdom of common endeavor with godly companions.

Proverbs 17

Lord God, Your Son became a servant for our sake. Help us to be willing to serve. We remember that You are the Maker of the poor. Teach us to cover an offense, for we are grateful for Your eternal love. What sense is there in returning evil for good? You have been so good to us. Should we be evil toward You? We should not even return evil back to those who have truly wronged us. How much more should we honor You, who sent us salvation at great cost to Yourself and to Your Son. Grant to us a fuller contemplation of Your goodness, and bring us a more joyful heart day by day. Keep us from foolish speech, that we might not unnecessarily parade our stubborn unrighteousness as if it were a badge of honor.

Proverbs 18

Master, we need to listen to Your wisdom. Forgive us for our wickedness, and for the foolishness of our speech. We desire both purity and peace. Grant to us wise restraint in our thoughts and our words. Rather than rushing into every situation with careless lips, we should rush to You in a time of trouble. We should seek knowledge from You, and listen to others first before we speak. Keep us from unnecessary quarrels. Why should we feed off of our own impulsive words? We would do much better to listen carefully to others and to consider all matters clearly in Your presence.

Proverbs 19

Our Father, grant us integrity and knowledge more than raw intelligence and wit. Grant to us a true generosity of heart that comes by Your grace. Make us to be people of good sense who know the glory of overlooking an offense. Grant us peace within our homes, and diligence throughout our lives. Your Son has come from a heavenly home of perfect integrity, and has given us the incomparable gift of a most wise and generous salvation. Thank You for the blessings of life that have come from Your hand. Even now You speak to us from Your Word, and You give us instruction and knowledge.

Proverbs 20

Great God, please keep us from drunkenness and addiction. Restrain us from all movements toward wickedness and sin. These things lead to death. Keep us working at our appointed posts where we serve You day by day. Thank You for the diligence, righteousness, and faithfulness of Jesus Christ. He had no stain of sin. He made Himself known by His conduct. His lips brought forth knowledge. He did nothing by deceit, but always served You by the wisest counsel of His own pure heart. He did not repay evil with evil, but came to die for our rebellion. He has given Himself to You in complete holiness. In His Spirit is the most complete purity of holiness. Grant us this Spirit even now.

Proverbs 21

Lord God, we have a powerful and holy King. He knows the truth of every heart. We have sin in the depths of our being, but Your Son was perfectly pure in the wonder of His holy life. He has sent forth the most abundant mercy to us. In His knowledge is life for our souls. Grant us the integrity of an obedient heart, willing to hear Your Word and follow. Keep us from the foolishness of drunkenness and gluttony. We will never be able to provide for those in need if we eat and drink everything that we earn. Place within us a new and powerful resolve to follow Your counsel, and to love the way of wisdom.

Proverbs 22

Father, how do we continue to make poor choices when the way of life is so clear? Help us to remember again the lessons that we learned in our youth. For what good reason have we abandoned the counsel of the godly? There is no hope for us in adultery and indolence. We will only be the joke of those who scoff at those who fall. Train us up again in righteousness from Your holy Word, for the way of Your Word is perfect. The way of our own foolishness will not be better for us and for others than the life of truth and grace in Jesus Christ. Grant us fresh resources from Your abundant wisdom.

Proverbs 23

Lord of Glory, forgive us for our many follies. Whether we eat or drink or whatever we do, we should do it all for Your glory. We must hear Your instruction and apply our hearts to the truth. What do we say? How do we bring up our children? How do we work, and what is our way of having fun? In all of these things we need Your wisdom. We long for the health, safety, and fruitfulness of future generations. Drowning ourselves in wine will never solve our problems. It will do us no good to pretend that we are stronger than we really are. You are God, and we are not. Our lives and the lives of our descendants are surely in Your hands.

Proverbs 24

Father God, there is a way of evil and a way of wisdom. Teach us to run from one, and to follow the other. We need Your strength to live wisely in our daily lives. Encourage our hearts in wonderful ways. Teach us to move along in righteousness and truth. Worry will never solve our problems. Grant to us a respect for governing authorities. We need to turn away from wickedness, and to pursue truth, diligence, humility, and even love. Thank You for Your grace. Train us to see the obvious lessons that You have provided all around us that we might live a life of true wisdom.

Proverbs 25

Glorious Lord, You know so many things that seem beyond us. What joy there is in seeking out knowledge in the right way! Thank You for the life of order and character that You have decreed for Your servants. Teach us to discover the way of goodness as we grow in years. May we remember the lessons that we have already learned. Make these to be good habits in a life that is well-ordered. How should we treat our enemies? How can we deal with the contentious? What is the right way to care for the poor? Lord, we will surely travel down fruitless pathways if we ignore Your wisdom. What great benefits You have given to us in a right

155

consideration of the lives of those who have gone before us.

Proverbs 26

Our Father, we need great wisdom to know when to speak and what to say. Give us caution and patience, so that we will turn to You and consider. Teach us when to be still, and when to say or do something that might be useful. Grant to us diligence in our duties. Keep us mindful of what You have given us to do, and aware of true opportunities for love and service. Cleanse us from the depths of our being. Take away all scheming and deceitfulness, for these impurities will only work toward our own destruction.

Proverbs 27

Lord God, You know the beginning from the end. We trust You. We marvel at the perfect wisdom of Your Son. Every impulse and detail of His heart and life was perfect. He related perfectly in all family relationships. He discerned every right opportunity for friendship and service. The heart of our Savior was perfect, just as the Man Himself was perfect. His glory will last forever. His righteousness is eternal. In Him we have a secure hope and a future of grace and truth. Grant to us the mind of Christ even now, so that we might serve You rightly.

Proverbs 28

O God, what will we do when the wicked come against us? Grant us powerful aid from heaven when the strong would oppress the poor. We will be generous to those in need. We will not lead the simple astray. Help us to guide Your people home to You through our words and actions. Keep us tender in our sympathies and our understanding. Teach us to walk in integrity. Make us faithful in every test by the grace of our Lord Jesus Christ. We thank You for those who have gone before us. We honor the memory of the godly, and thank You for Your grace in their lives and in ours.

Proverbs 29

Father God, we must not stiffen our necks against You. There are dangers all around us. Only by Your wisdom will we escape the traps that seem to be on every side. When we fall, Your Son is still near, and He will rescue us. Teach us to remember the day of discipline and to learn from our trials. Your Son has kept the Law. We are blessed in Him. We should be the most gentle people, for we have been saved by Your grace. We trust You, O Lord, and we find abundant safety in You.

Proverbs 30

Great God of Life, grant us energy and wisdom for living. You are the great Author of Creation, and Your Son is the Word of truth. Teach us the blessing of Your provision of daily bread. Train us to know that we are creatures. We turn to You and humbly submit to Your decrees. There is much that we do not understand, yet we know in our hearts when we have done wrong. Grant us the grace of repentance. May we learn the lessons You have for all men from observation of Your works of providence among the vast array of Your creatures.

Proverbs 31

Lord God, we must be men and women of character. Teach us to love integrity more than wine. Give us new hearts, that we might serve the poor and the needy. Grant that the young women within Your kingdom would have a true desire for diligence, wisdom, and generosity. Give them great skill and dignity. Grant to them excellence of thought and speech. May our young men desire women of character, women who fear You, and who are committed to serving You. May Your church rejoice in this great truth: that we together are the one bride of Christ, the greatest of all husbands, and that we are being sanctified to serve Him well now and forever.

Ecclesiastes

Ecclesiastes 1

Glorious Lord, You are above all the earth, and You rule over everything under the sun. There is a limit to our understanding. We see the weariness of the passage of time. In a way, there is nothing new here. Though it may seem new to us, it has been before in some way. We see so much that comes and go. We mourn over many things that are broken and cannot be fixed. In our work and our wisdom there is much reason for sorrow. Our Father, these obvious facts puzzle us. Surely there must be an answer. Give us settled hearts, and a ready ear to hear Your Word.

Ecclesiastes 2

Father God, even a Solomon cannot be finally satisfied with wine and laughter, with gardens and buildings, with treasures and servants. Whatever pleasure we have, it is yet fleeting. Even if we were the wisest people on earth, our wisdom could not satisfy the longings of our hearts. The stubborn fact of death is always there to consider. Is there an answer to this great problem? Is there a way out of despair as we consider the fleeting pleasures of life under the sun? We thank You for all the gifts that You give us, though they come and go. We genuinely enjoy all these wonderful things. Nonetheless, our peace of heart is restrained, for we long for something more. Thank You for revealing the answer to us through Your Son. He came from heaven into this world of loss and trouble. We thank You for the redemption that He has secured for us by His blood, and for the truth of resurrection life that is Your wonderful answer to our deepest longings.

Ecclesiastes 3

Lord of Hosts, You are sovereign over all things. You have given a time for ever purpose under heaven. You are gathering us as living stones for Your eternal temple. You are embracing Your bride in a love that will never end. Thank You for placing eternity in our hearts. Thank You especially for providing the very best answer to our longings. Your Son Jesus Christ is our provision, and we rejoice in Him. Help us to enjoy the many blessings of this life, yet with some measure of restraint, as there is a time for every matter and every work. Like the beasts of the earth, we will face the end of our lives one day. We too have the grave ahead of us. Yet You are the most satisfying answer to the question that You have placed within our souls.

Ecclesiastes 4

O Father, the troubles of this world are not small. Some face oppression every day. Even strong men and women may despair of life. Help us to enjoy a handful of quietness whenever we are able. Thank You for the blessing of fellowship in Your church. A three-fold cord is not easily broken. We are not alone. Grant us unity in the Spirit as we walk through these days under the sun. All the kings of the earth and their impressive kingdoms reach their appointed limits. Great leaders may have wisdom, but they also have some folly and arrogance, and even the best of them make some measure of trouble for themselves and others. Our King is in the heavens, and He does whatever pleases Him. Yes, our Lord does all things well.

Ecclesiastes 5

Lord God Almighty, we draw near to You now. What will You say to us through Your Word? We wait for Your truth and Your grace. We thank You for Your Son. He made the ultimate vow. He promised to give You a kingdom, even a people that You would then present to Him as a bride. We are the payment of that vow. He will surely bring You the praise of the nations. The work of men will fail, but the great labor of Your Son will have eternal fruit that shall never perish. He is the answer for us, and our toil and prayer have meaning in Him. Our labor in Christ is not in vain. His work continues beyond the grave. He is building a resurrection Kingdom. Abundant and sure blessings have come to us through Him.

Ecclesiastes 6

Glorious Lord, a man may gather much wealth, and then not be able to enjoy what he has worked for. Who can make sense of this? It seems without purpose, and surely You are a God not only of power and beauty, but of purpose. We see this in what You have created and in how You sustain and rule all things. Yet of what worth is life when a man is dishonored at His death? Is this the end of the story of men under the sun? Will the answer for poverty and disgrace come from beyond this creation? Will You send us a new heavens and a new earth? You have spoken to us through the prophets, and through Your Son Jesus, and have told us wonderful things that we now hear clearly through Your Word. We thank You for the coming fulfillment of the work and wisdom of Jesus Christ. He is the One who is more impressive than the temple in Jerusalem! He is the One who is wiser than Solomon! It is through Him that we have lasting fellowship with You.

Ecclesiastes 7

Our Father, teach us how to live in this age. Grant us the wisdom of a right assessment of times of mourning, and those difficult lessons in our lives that yield patience and hope. Keep us from foolish words, for we would wrongly imagine the past as better than it really was. We cannot return to a day that is long gone. The better life must come in some future time. Surely You have made many things in this age to be crooked and broken according to Your providence. Do we really think that we can fix them with our work and wisdom? How can we, since we are broken and troubled? Help us to have a balanced life, not showy in our righteousness, but humble in our thoughts and behavior, for there is no one who does not sin. What a wonder that Your Son was without sin! He has come to save us. He has taken away the final sting of death. Now we have something beyond the bitterness of loss. The fact of our transgression remains a glaring truth for anyone who has eyes to see, for You created man to be upright, but we have sought out many schemes. This ugly problem demands a true solution. We thank You that the answer has come. Your Son has defeated both sin and death through His perfect life and through the cross.

Ecclesiastes 8

Father of All Wisdom, teach us how to live submissively according to the powers that You have established in this age. Even the best rulers have evil within them, but it will not go well with the wicked. You are a God of justice. You rule over kings, though we find it hard to understand Your ways. Here is wisdom: that man cannot find out Your secrets. There is much that You have revealed through nature, providence, and Your Word. Yet there is much about who You are and what You have done that we cannot understand. We bow before You.

Ecclesiastes 9

Lord God, what can we search out and find through observation and reason? We examine the world that You have created. We consider the ways that You rule over the affairs of all Your creatures. We continually run into the wall of death. What a stubborn fact death is in this age! Yet we will enjoy the life that You have given to us even now. This is our portion today, though our present bodies are mortal. Teach us to love wisdom. There is something beyond the power of a man's hands and the strength of his voice. There is the heart and the mind. There is the life of the soul. Though our wisdom may be forgotten under the sun, it is a beautiful gift from You to be used for the benefit of a city. Your Son has used His perfect wisdom to secure for us a city beyond this age of death. What a blessing has come to us! What a great God we serve!

Ecclesiastes 10

Father God, our lives here are brief and there is so much to learn. Teach us to be wise. There is much that does not seem to make sense, yet You have a way of working out Your purposes even in this world of confusion. Teach us to hear the Word of true wisdom that You have spoken through Your prophets. There is much trouble in many lands. We have forgotten the appropriate appreciation of those who have been blessed with great gifts. We do not know how to bend the knee in order to show deference. How will we ever worship You? How will we ever move ahead? You are above us. We are below You. If we do not know this most obvious fact, how can we live wisely at all? Teach us the way of wisdom, though we are slow to understand many things. Surely You are God. You know the beginning from the end.

Ecclesiastes 11

Almighty God, we see the wisdom of generosity. You will help us in our day of need. Keep us working and thinking, but help us especially to trust You and to be kind. Thank You for the light that You give us day by day, for a time of darkness or confusion may be coming. Father, if we explored wisdom here for millennia we would not find the way to fix our own problems of evil and the curse that has come upon this world through sin. Will we solve the decay that we see all around us? We will not live forever through the most brilliant medicine. We will not create heaven on earth through the most enlightened politics or philosophy. The more we study and consider, the more we see our own ignorance, folly, and wickedness. There has to be an end to our days here. There has to come some silence for our over-exercised tongues. We long for You, and we wait for Your deliverance.

Ecclesiastes 12
Sovereign Lord, if only we could convince young men and women to be wise! There is a process or an event coming to all men of trouble and decay until the day that Your Son returns. The body is proceeding to the grave. There comes an injury that finally breaks the link between the body and the soul. Yet from generation to generation Your Word lives on. There is One Shepherd. He speaks. We hear You, O God. We fear You, O Lord. You are different from us. You are the Judge, and You are the Answer. It is profound wisdom to remember You and to live for You. Grant us that wisdom now and forever.

Song of Solomon

Song 1
Glorious Lord, You love us. Grant to us a glimpse of the passion of Your love day by day. Our souls love You as well. Show us how to follow You as those who know that there is One worth staying very close to. Come near to us even now, O God. Are we beautiful to You? Surely Your Son is beautiful to us.

Song 2
Father God, You have a wonderful plan for Your Son and His bride. There is a great celebration coming soon. There are moments of intimacy in the days ahead. Our Husband comes bounding across the mountains for us. Is there a Lover who truly loves us with such wonderful holiness and with perfect power? Are we truly the beautiful one of Your Son? Is it His voice that we hear in Your Word calling to us? Suddenly a new and glorious world has been born in us and all around us, and there is hope. We belong to Your Son, O God. We are His and He is ours.

Song 3
Lord Almighty, we are seeking the One whom our soul loves. Where is Jesus today? If we could find Him, we would hold Him and not let Him go. Now He comes to us in Word and sacrament, for we worship Him in covenant assembly. We bow before Him. Will we one day look upon our glorious Savior, crowned in majesty, and seated at Your right hand?

Song 4
Lord God, Your Son calls His glorious church beautiful. He admires our every detail. He seems to see beyond our current blemishes. He sees what we cannot yet see. He claims that there is no flaw within us. He calls us His bride, and insists that we have captivated Him. Father, how we long for the day of the fullness

of this love. We long for the beauty and wonder of the age to come. Come, Lord Jesus! Love us with an everlasting love!

Song 5

Great God, we have heard of our Husband and our Redeemer. We dream of Him, yet we walk in a world of danger. We long to wake in Your presence on a glorious day. Where is Jesus now? We need to hear His voice. Why are Your ministers hurting Your church? Will they beat us because we are lovesick for Jesus Christ? Can they not celebrate the love of Christ with us? Please teach them to speak to us of His greatness. Show them the One that we must have, for we only want to know the glories of our Husband.

Song 6

Holy Father, Your Son has gone to be with You, yet He is with us even now somehow. We hear His voice of love in Your Word, and feel our communion with Him in the supper of love that He gave to us. We are greatly blessed. Your Son calls us back to Himself moment by moment. Why would we ever wander from Him? We anticipate the great day of our love even now. Our Husband is somehow with us, though our soul yet longs for Him as if He were gone. We will wait for our great Husband. No other lover will do. No crowd of admirers could every satisfy us.

Song 7

Lord of Glory, the marriage of Christ and His church is approaching. The time of waiting will soon be over. We hear His voice saying wonderful things about us. He knows perfectly what we will be one day, and He truly loves us even now. We will not resist Him, for He seeks communion with us. We give ourselves to Him, for He is our glorious King. He is a Husband who has proven His love for us at the greatest cost.

Song 8

Great God, is today the day when we will meet our Husband more fully than every before? We hear His word of pledge. We receive the fire of His earnest love. The time has come for us to know that love more and more. No one can keep us from our Savior any more. He has purchased us by His blood. He finds His joy in us. Be near us forever Lord Jesus! You will never die again.

Isaiah

Isaiah 1

Lord God, help us to know You and to know the truth. Teach us to turn away from rebellion. Your Law is good and right, but we have sinned against You. We have brought great trouble upon ourselves in our disobedience. Yet You have a plan of grace that goes beyond our disobedience. You have provided a Substitute who did more than offer ceremonial righteousness to You. He heard Your Word and loved You. He listened to Your voice and obeyed Your commandments. There was no evil in Him. He cared for the weak with true sincerity. He has taken away the deep stain of our sin and has granted to us the perfectly glorious robes of His unfailing goodness. We seek You now for a season of true faithfulness among Your worshipers. We long for the age to come, when all of our sinful thoughts, words, and actions will be taken far away from us forever. The way of idolatry leads only to destruction. Teach us to be earnest followers of Your Son.

Isaiah 2

Glorious Lord, according to Your promise establish Your church as the highest mountain of truth and righteousness throughout the earth. Teach us to walk in Your light, O Lord. There is great danger for us in all that is proud and lifted up against You. We long for the day when You alone will be exalted. Even now, we yield ourselves to You as the only God. Loosen our grip on every idol and cause us to worship You in Spirit and in truth.

Isaiah 3

Lord God of Hosts, what will Your church do when You come to purify us? There is much weakness around us and within us. We want to trust You, even in the day of worst tribulation. Give us grace to be faithful in every time of trouble, and cut short the days of testing, for You know the limits of our strength. Father, Your people have been crushed by their leaders. Men and women have become haughty and complacent, but how will we be proud when powerful enemies come to destroy us? Unite together those who belong to You, and show us mercy because of the wonderful righteousness of Your Son, who shed His blood for our sins.

Isaiah 4

Almighty God, we come to You now. Grant that we may be called by Your Name and connected to the One Branch, Jesus Christ, who is our hope. Cleanse us from all sin. Move us in the pathway of Your glorious presence, and dwell with us forever.

Isaiah 5

Father, we are Your vineyard. You have provided everything necessary for us that we might be a fruitful harvest for You. Yet we have yielded wild grapes in our rebellion against You. Like Your people of old, we have violated Your Law, and we are in danger of being swept away. Despite our sin, You will surely keep a remnant according to grace. You will build Your church, and the gates of hell will not prevail against it. Sanctify us for Your purposes. Teach us to understand the time and place in which we serve You. We long to live as Your beloved sheep, grazing peacefully in Your pasture. Bring about the day of lasting peace. Only You can accomplish such a great blessing. Help us to endure through this time of trouble. You will not be angry with us forever, for You will not turn away from Your promise of grace. We need You now, for enemies come against us, and they are too strong for us. You can scatter them with one word.

Isaiah 6

Holy and Majestic God, You are the Lord. You reign from the heavenly sanctuary, and You are holy. Our sin is made more obvious in the light of Your presence. We thank You for the full atonement which is ours in Jesus Christ. We have been set apart for Your purposes and are willing to be sent out for Your glory.

Grant us strength from on high for the service to which we have been called. May we be faithful in speaking the truth by the power of Your love for Your chosen flock.

Isaiah 7

O Lord God, the King that You have provided for Your church is faithful and true. You know the wickedness of those who seek to overwhelm us, but You have the power to stop the hand of every adversary. Make us firm in faith. Help us to rejoice in the sign that You have chosen for us. A virgin has conceived. Immanuel has been given to us. Through Him, sin and death have been overthrown. We thank You for the wonder of His mighty love. The very thought that You are with us through the person of Your Son is a comfort in the present day of trouble. Though all of our problems have not yet been removed from us, the sign of Immanuel speaks to us of a powerful victory that can never be reversed. The Christ has come for our atonement. He will return again to rescue us from this evil age.

Isaiah 8

Almighty Father, You have spoken through the prophets. Your words were faithful in the mouths of Your holy servants, but they longed for a better fulfillment, one that is ours now in Your church. We still desire the best of all answers to our holiest longings. Come soon, Lord Jesus! Until that final day, there is some measure of difficulty among us. Yet You have given Your church the privilege of being a sign to the world. You have planted the seed of Your true Word in our hearts, and we believe. Why will men turn to deceiving demons, when You have clearly spoken to Your people? We trust in You and we cling to Your Word and Your testimony.

Isaiah 9

Lord God, we have been so greatly blessed. Your Light shines upon the nations. You have broken the rod of our oppressors through the birth and death of Your Son. He is our King forever and our mighty God. Forgive our arrogance when we think that we could have a victory over evil without Your grace. Christ and His cross is our great power. His death has given us life. Why do we think of the grace of our Lord as so weak, when it is clearly strong? Grace insists that we cannot save ourselves. We imagine that our weakness must mean that the plan of grace is somehow weak. Yet Your holiness and love made grace mighty for the tearing down of every stronghold, and for the building up of the kingdom that bears the Name of Your Son. All glory to You, O God.

Isaiah 10

Our Father, there is a way that is right and there is a way that is wrong. To abuse the weak is against Your Law. We dare not tempt You by despising the powerless. You can bring a very powerful empire against Your people to discipline us in our sin. When You have used that empire for Your purposes, You can correct their arrogant presumption. We should never trust in the strength of any nation or people. We must lean on You. You will make a full end of wickedness. You are the Creator. You will be the Judge. You have shown Your abilities so many times. There can be no question of Your strength. You are the Lord God of Hosts. You will be exalted forever.

Isaiah 11

Lord God, we long to see the Branch who has come from the root of Jesse. The greatest Son of David has proven Himself by His atoning love. Now we wait for His return, for His judgment will mean peace and vindication for the people You love. On that day, the earth shall be filled with the knowledge of You. We shall see the perfect peace that Your Son won for us through the cross. Father, we are the remnant of Your people from all the nations. We are the Jews and Gentiles who believe in Your Name. We are the ones that You spoke of so long ago. We wait for You and serve You with both joy and expectation even now.

Isaiah 12

O Lord, we give thanks to You. You were angry with us, but Your anger has been turned away from us through the life and death of Your Son. We rejoice in Your mercy, O God, for You are with us. Your presence is our life. You are great in the midst of Your people.

Isaiah 13

Father God, You are right to be angry with men in their arrogance. In Your people of old and in Your church at the present hour there is much surprising haughtiness. What will we do with our pride in the day of Your fierce anger? Where will we flee in that day? If judgment begins among the people who claim to know You, what will become of those who refuse to acknowledge Your Name in any good way? We grieve for those who suppress the knowledge of Your truth in unrighteousness. You have used powerful armies for Your purposes, but weapons and strategies will never save the world when You come to judge. Kings and kingdoms will not be able to stand when You determine that the end of their days has come.

Isaiah 14

Lord of Hosts, have compassion upon Your people, and give us rest from our pain. Men and angels have struck Your people with unrelenting persecution. You will bring the pompous low. Even that angel who made a plan to ascend upon the clouds shall be cast down. Judge the way of antichrists who have tried to deceive multitudes. If they had their way, we would have been utterly swept away from the land of the living. Your Hand is much stronger than any adversary. You will bring us safety and rest at just the right time. We take refuge even now in Your Son.

Isaiah 15

God of the Nations, You can destroy a powerful city in one night. We should repent of all sin. Every people in every land should flee from the wrath to come, Everyone should run to Jesus Christ. Our only safety is in Him. The sign of guilt is upon the hands of men. Only the blood of the Lamb of God can cleanse us.

Isaiah 16

Lord God, the trouble that will come upon men one day will quickly overwhelm them. We taste that even now in the many trials that are a part of this age. One day there will come One who will be swift to do justice. Surely the nations of the earth have provoked You for centuries. You have provided so many good gifts to the sons and daughters of Adam, but we have worshiped false gods, and deliberately ignored You, the Creator and Sustainer of all Your creatures. We confess our sins before You, and we plead for those who have not yet called upon Your Name. Rescue many by Your kind provision of mercy through Jesus Christ.

Isaiah 17

God of Glory, Your works of redemption are marvelous. We would not see the wonder of salvation if You had no wrath against sin. There will be a powerful display of Your righteous judgment when Your Son returns. This would have been our portion had You not rescued us from great trouble. How can we thank You enough for Your kindness to us? We do not know what to say or do. Lead us forward as Your children. Show us how to follow You.

Isaiah 18

Lord of the Nations, use Your ambassadors to bring the most excellent message to people who are presently far away from You. The final word for distant lands will not be wrath, though we surely all deserve to die for our rebellion. Even now people who were once so far off have been drawn near to You through Christ. They bring tribute as they worship You in Spirit and in truth. Bring Your Word to all the nations of the earth for the glory of Your holy Name.

Isaiah 19

Lord God, the idols of the nations are nothing. You are the God who preserves the world and all that is in it. Men could not live without You for even a moment. Yet we love idols that should be thrown away, and we ignore You who should be worshiped. Please forgive us. We long for the day when You will save many who live in the most unexpected places. May all nations worship You together. May we know our unity in Christ, and celebrate our communion with one another in Him.

Isaiah 20

Father God, You will accomplish all of Your holy will. You have used Your prophets to bring us signs of Your judgment against the sins of the world. You have used these same men to speak boldly of the hope that is to be found in Christ alone. We will not trust in the power of men. Thank You for the deliverance that is ours in Your Son.

Isaiah 21

Our Father, help us to embrace the truth of trial and tribulation. We live in an era that You speak of as labor pains. How are we to rejoice in tribulation? Help us to see the bigger picture of Your plan. We are like those who have been troubled from difficulty in every direction. Teach us to embrace suffering as a gift, and to be willing to be remade during a time when the flesh has become weak.

Isaiah 22

Sovereign Lord, You are full of love and mercy for Your children. Help us to see Your discipline in light of Your great plan of grace. Help us to know You in the deepest valley of trial. Make our time of devastation and destruction to be a valley of vision. Teach us to see Your hand in any day of trouble, that we might rightly profit from every difficulty. You can surely throw off the oppressor in a moment. You love Your elect. You must be working out some great purpose of grace. We long for the fullest expression of Your Son's reign over all His people.

Isaiah 23

God of Grace, in every season of life we should turn away from evil and turn toward You. The world does not understand what to do in the time of trouble. Will we who acknowledge Your glorious Name be just as foolish as the world when we face overwhelming difficulties? Teach us to turn away from everything unclean. We do not want to be enslaved in spiritual immorality. We long to be Your pure bride forever.

Isaiah 24

Our Father, Judgment Day will finally come upon all the earth. You have spoken. You have promised Your perfect justice for centuries. You have given numerous powerful signs of great destruction. Though many people ignore You, this should not be our story. May we give glory to Your Name everywhere. Though terror may come against us on every side, You are still God over all of creation. Your judgment does not come upon the world without reason. You reign from heaven, and You will judge men and angels with perfect justice. Your Son is our everlasting refuge. We call upon Your name through Him.

Isaiah 25

Father God, we praise Your Name. You have done wonderful things. You hear the prayers of the needy, and You provide a place of rescue in Your Son. Beyond the Day of Judgment there is a wonderful eternity of peace. Death will be swallowed up forever. You are God. We have waited for You. You are faithful to Your Word. Though You lay us low, we will find our greatest joy as those who are blessed by Your grace.

Isaiah 26

God of Heaven and Earth, we trust in You. You are an everlasting Rock for Your people in Jesus Christ. We wait for You. We look for You now and forever. Those who seek You will surely find You, though You may seem to be hidden for a moment. You have granted to us a hope of resurrection, and not only to us, but to all who have come to You through Your Son. The great birth that is coming for Your kingdom in the age of resurrection will be wonderful forever.

Isaiah 27

Lord God, You rule over all men and angels. You will judge our oppressors, and You will keep us as Your people forever. We will be Your pleasant vineyard. Your church is filling the whole world with the message of Your Son. We believe, and thus we rejoice, even in the day of great persecution and affliction. We know that the troubles that we face now are temporary, but the rejoicing of Your worshiping people from throughout the earth will be eternal.

Isaiah 28

Glorious God, You will purify Your church in the days that are coming. How large is Your mercy, O Lord? What will You do with those who have been oppressed by the devil and who have fallen into enslaving sin? We know that we are guilty sinners. None of us could stand before You in our own goodness. Our only hope is in the righteousness of Christ. We pray for Your mercy upon our sons and daughters who have been caught in foolish lies and worldliness. Surely You know the sincerity of the faith that You gave to them in the days of their youth. Annul their covenant with death that they make when they seem to forget Your ways. They have not utterly forsaken Your Name. You must have held them through the raging storm of deception and immorality. They have faced the destruction of this creation, will they face a second destruction in the age to come? Our hope is for something better than this. You will not discipline Your people forever. Though the body be dead because of sin, the Spirit will be alive because of righteousness. We thank You for the abundance of Your grace. Our God and the God of our children, have mercy on us, for we are weak.

Isaiah 29

Lord God Almighty, we should not be surprised when distress comes upon Your church. You will not be content with our destructive disobedience. You will visit us with discipline. Many of Your true servants will yet be caught up in difficulties that come upon Your people. Nonetheless You are able to preserve our souls for the coming day of resurrection. Even when Your righteous judgment comes upon Your church, we continue to look for a day of tremendous joy. This will be a day when the blind will see and the deaf will hear. We have been granted a wonderful taste of that coming day in the visitation of Your Son. We look for the fullness of His mercy when He returns for us.

Isaiah 30

Lord God, when we face problems that are far beyond us, we should turn to You with persistence and faith. Why do we run out of energy almost before we have asked You for help? Why do we turn to the world and long for the word of false prophets? Father, our sin is deep. We need You. Teach us to run to You day by day. We are sorry for our continued rebellion against You. We know that You will hear us when we cry out to You. We trust that You will answer us and will lead us in the way of help. We turn away from idolatry and calmly rest in Your embrace. We look for Your glorious light. You will bind up our wounds. Grant us a song in the night that we might be true to You throughout the pilgrimage of this life. Help us to put one foot in front of another that we might continue on the pathway that leads to You.

Isaiah 31

Father God, we look to You today in the midst of our troubles. We see now that the praise and aid of men will never be the ultimate answer for us. We cast away the idols of our hearts, and we remember You. Thank You for the great gift of Your Son, for His cross, and for His resurrection. Thank You for Your abiding love, and even for the trials that point us homeward again to You.

Isaiah 32

Great God, we praise You for Your Son, our King who reigns in righteousness. He has displayed His power. He opened the eyes of the blind. He provided food for the hungry. He planned and accomplished noble things. This Jesus is the same yesterday, today, and forever, Now He is at Your right hand. He is powerful to save. Pour out Your Spirit from on high. Bring fruitfulness, righteousness, and love to us in our misery and sadness. We long to dwell in Your eternal peace. Conquer our fears even now and bless us with the security of a more solid faith.

Isaiah 33

Father God, we were wandering and we did not even know it. There was a destroyer who was troubling us, and we thought for a moment that he was a friend. We fear You, and we remember You. We look around Your church and we see that the land is mourning. Rise up and be exalted. Take away our godlessness, and help us to remember the perfect righteousness of Jesus Christ who gave His life for us. He dwells on High. We will behold Him in His beauty. The day of the hateful adversary will be gone, and there will be perfect peace and provision in Your holy Jerusalem. You are the Lord, and You will keep us. We will have glorious health and the fullest restoration in Your presence.

Isaiah 34

Perfect Lord, You are wonderful in Your mercy and glorious in Your justice. Your Day is coming. You will not be stopped. You have a sword. You will bring this age to an end in the Day of Your vengeance. You have not forgotten the church for whom Your Son gave His obedience and blood. The power and fear of the world will suddenly be nothing in that day. There will be a wonderful peace for Your servants. We read about this in Your Word and we believe. There is a place for Your people that can never be taken away. From generation to generation we will dwell in Immanuel's land.

Isaiah 35

Father God, we had wandered so far from You, but You have strengthened us and You have saved us by Your strong hand. We have been given new life, and streams have suddenly appeared in the desert. There is a road for us that leads to Zion, for we are Your ransomed people. Cause sorrow and sighing to flee far from us, for we are Your beloved children, and You will never forsake us.

Isaiah 36

Lord God, Your adversary comes against us making accusations. He would entice us away from the path of faith with deceptive words. He would sift us as wheat for our destruction. Father, You are so different from him. You bring trials to Your people for a good purpose. Your discipline of us is a part of Your merciful plan of grace. Our enemy seeks only evil. He works for our destruction. You are the Lord, and You will deliver Your Jerusalem out of His hand.

Isaiah 37

Our Father, in the day of His earthly ministry, Your Son Jesus Christ turned to You in faith continually. You heard His cries. He was not afraid of the words of men. He trusted You. By His life and death, our deliverance was accomplished. We thank You for the mercy of the cross. We will not believe the lies of the adversary who came against Your Son so long ago. He was defeated through the same cross that became our salvation. We will not listen to the words of men who would mock You. Hear from on high and help us. Your Son takes our prayers and perfects them. He intercedes for us. You will surely glorify Your own Name. The proud boasts of Your adversaries will be utterly overthrown. You are able to capture every enemy. We shall be a band of survivors, though men succeed at taking our lives. What can they do to us? We will surely be in Your blessed presence forever.

Isaiah 38

Glorious Lord, You know the struggles that we face. You know our fears and our desires. You know our hearts and our deeds. Your mercy is wonderful. You are able to give us more time here below. You hear us when we cry out to You. You send away sickness according to Your plan. You enable us to live. You restore us to health. If You decree disease or trouble, surely You do even this for our welfare. We shall go up to Your house with the multitude of Your holy ones at just the right time. We shall worship You forever.

Isaiah 39

Father, do we know an enemy when he visits us with smooth words? Are we so foolish that we say much more than we should? Our bragging will bring us great trouble. Teach us how to be quiet about our accomplishments. There is a day when it is best for us to say nothing. Teach us that the way of pride will not be good for us. If we boast, let us boast in You and not in ourselves.

Isaiah 40

Lord God, bring to us ministers who comfort Your people with words of good news from on high. Speak forth Your glory so that all flesh shall hear of Your greatness. We are like grass that withers and fades. Your Word will stand forever. In that Word we behold You, Your Son, and Your Holy Spirit. There is no one like You. You are before all things and You reign over all that You have created. All the nations are as nothing before You. How could we display You with some image that we have created? You are the everlasting God. You bring the greatest powers of the earth low and they die like men. You rule over the stars in the heavens, and You know Your children. You do not faint or grow weary. Give us power and strength as we wait for You. Teach us to fly, to run, to walk, to stand, and to wait.

Isaiah 41

Sovereign Lord, You will judge all the nations of the earth. You are the First and the Last, and it is right for You to bring about all of Your holy decrees. We are Your servants in Jesus Christ. We will not be afraid, for You will strengthen and help us. You are the Redeemer. You are the Holy One. We will rejoice in You in the day of our deliverance. You bring springs of water in the desert. It is Your Hand that has brought us a time of refreshing in these days. By Your power there shall come an age of resurrection. We call upon Your Name, O Lord, and You hear us.

169

Our strength is in Jesus Christ.

Isaiah 42

Father God, there is no one like Your Servant Jesus Christ. He brings forth justice upon the earth. Look upon us, O God. We are bruised reeds. Do not break us. We have no real flame left in us. Do not utterly snuff us out. Breathe new life into us again by Your Spirit. Thank You for Your mercy. Your Son will establish justice throughout the earth. We long for His day. Come, Lord Jesus! Even now open the eyes of the blind through the preaching of Your Word. Teach us to praise You everywhere and at all times. You are powerful to save. Speak, O Lord, and rescue us. Your church is like a woman in labor. There is suffering here, but You are surely leading us. You will not forsake us. Your Son has taken upon Himself all our infirmities. Restore our fortunes, O Lord. Help us as we cry out to You.

Isaiah 43

O Lord, You have redeemed us. Through water and flame, through every fiery trial, You are still with us. You call us Your sons and Your daughters. You love us and protect us. We are Your witnesses throughout the earth in Your Son Jesus Christ. There is no other Savior. There is no other Judge. You are the Holy One, and You are the King. You are doing a new thing, and You will not be stopped. Forgive us our sins, O Lord. We sinned against You in Adam, and we have sinned against You in our own days. You forgive us. You discipline us. You love us.

Isaiah 44

Father God, You made us, and You call us to believe. We trust You. You will have wonderful mercy upon Your people. Your promises are so big and so true. You speak of things yet to come, and Your words are completely reliable. The lover of idols will be put to shame. You are God. There is nothing wise in the worship of objects. We will not fall down before the work of our own hands. We will not pray to something that was carved out of a block of wood. We cast off every lie that we once believed. We will sing to You, O Lord. You stretched out the heavens. You confirm the words of Your prophets. You raise up a Cyrus for Your purposes. You are building Your temple.

Isaiah 45

Lord God, You have a Messiah King who is better than any emperor of old. Every other great king pointed forward to this one King and Lord. This Redeemer is the Son of God. He is also the Son of Man. He is the Potter. Has He now become the clay for our sake? Your Son shall build up Your city. He shall set the exiles free. Even now it can be said that freedom Christ has set us free. Yet we wait for Him. We long for the fullness of salvation that is ours in Him. We seek You and we find You. You have gathered us from the nations. You declared this long ago, and have vindicated Your holy Word. Every knee shall bow, every tongue shall confess that Jesus Christ is Lord, to the glory of Your holy Name.

Isaiah 46

Father, now that You have revealed Yourself to us so fully in Your Son, will we turn to the foolish idols of the nations? Surely when Christ has been preached to all the nations, if Your people would turn back to some false messiah it would be an abomination. We trust You. Your plan is perfect. Your righteousness has come near to us in Christ. We shall not be moved.

Isaiah 47

Lord God, men may exalt themselves now with all their wealth and glory. Yet they will be brought low in the Day of Judgment. The ones who have had no mercy on Your church, what will they receive from You when You come in vengeance? You can bring a sudden ruin upon those who counted on sorceries. How could the nations turn back to false gods and rituals when Your Son has been so clearly proclaimed as Lord? We will hope in Jesus Christ. We turn away from all false gods.

Isaiah 48

Father, should we be shocked when we face persecution and trial? You have warned us of the troubles that would come. You know our pride and our reckless wandering. You know the temptations all around us. You have seen our treachery and have heard our presumptuous boasting. You will not give Your glory to another. You have called us, and You will save us. You will use strong measures to keep Your chosen ones. You have not spoken about this in secret. We should pay attention to Your commandments. Then our peace would have been like a river, even when Your enemies abused us. Yet Your promises shall still stand. You have redeemed us from an adversary that was far too strong for us. We shall praise You together with all Your holy ones and we shall glorify Your Name forever.

Isaiah 49

Great God, Your Son is the One! He is the Savior. He is the Suffering King. You have called Him from the womb. He has saved Jacob. He has even saved Your beloved elect from every tribe and tongue and nation. You have made Him to be a Covenant to Your people. A day of the greatest provision is surely coming. None of this could every have happened without our Messiah. You have comforted us in Him. Even if our mothers and fathers have forgotten us, You will never forget us. Your plans for us are glorious. We are to be a holy bride. The children of our bereavement will yet speak in our ears. There will be many for the ones who thought that they were left all alone. This will be the day of resurrection glory. We will know that You are the Lord. We wait for You, and we shall not be put to shame. You will save our children who have been taken captive by a foul adversary. You are the mighty one of Jacob.

Isaiah 50

O Lord, the church is suffering in the filth of her own foolishness, weakness, poverty, and rebellion. How can we come to You as a pure bride if not in the righteousness of a Substitute? We have only one Man who was not rebellious. He suffered for us. He set His heart toward the perfect obedience that you require, and He was not put to shame. You have been His strength, and He is now our hope. We will fear You and obey You. We will walk by the light that You have provided us in Him.

Isaiah 51

Lord our Rock, we have come from You. You have called men before us to be people of faith. Surely we must follow in this way. We are in One who was the hope of Abraham. He is a light to the peoples. We wait for His strong arm even today. The day of our salvation is approaching. You have put your Law in our hearts, and Your righteousness and salvation rise up within Your holy people. You will not be stopped by the most evil foe. You can make us glad again today. You are the Comforter who lives in us. You alone made the world, and You have brought about the new creation. Blessed be Your Name, O Lord of Hosts. Speak to Zion today in Your Word. Take away the cup of Your wrath, since this has already been consumed to the very dregs by our Helper who died on the cross for our sins. Yet today there remains an adversary against us. Help us, O Lord.

Isaiah 52

Come in strength, O God, in the garments of Your power. We were sold for nothing, but we have been redeemed through the precious blood of the Lamb. Speak in the voice of Your gospel herald soon. Let the weary come again to Zion, that we might sing to our God. Your arm is strong. Show us Your salvation. Release us from the filthy chains of wickedness and be our God. Thank You for Your amazing Servant. He is our strength.

Isaiah 53

O Lord, so many have ignored the truth of Your grace. So many were offended by the lowliness of our holy King. How is it that men would dare to despise Jesus, who was wounded for our transgressions? Thank You for this great truth: that the Shepherd died for the sheep. The One who was oppressed and afflicted in silence, now lives forever in the strength of resurrection power. When He is seen again, every knee shall bow before Him who was an offering for sin. He has justified many by His knowledge. He has carried our guilt. Through the strength of His death, and through His intercession for us, we have been saved.

Isaiah 54

Lord of the Harvest, You are bringing forth children for the desolate woman. We are the descendants that You have made for the glory of Your Holy Servant, Jesus. He is the Lord of Hosts and our Husband. Your people were cast off in their sin, but now they are being brought back home in Your divine compassion. Your steadfast promise is fulfilled in the One who is both just and justifier. Therefore we rejoice in You and in the covenant of peace with which You have made us glad. We are precious stones now in Your holy temple. The day without fear will soon come in all perfection, and we will be changed from glory to glory. Even today, no weapon fashioned against us will prosper.

Isaiah 55

O Father, we are thirsty and hungry, and we come to You. You will satisfy us with abundance that can only be found in the Bread of Life and the Cup of our Salvation. You have redeemed us, and we seek You now. We turn away from all sin and turn toward You, O Lord. Your ways are high, and Your thoughts are pure. We are yours, O God. Your Word has accomplished what You have purposed by Your holy decree. Bring about the fullness of a renewed creation.

Isaiah 56

Lord of our Salvation, we will keep justice, and consider Your Law to do it. Though we are weak, You are capable of taking a fruitless servant and granting him an everlasting name. We will hold fast Your covenant and come streaming to Your holy mountain for the fullness of Sabbath rest. All the nations shall find rest in Your Son. The dogs who tear and kill will be shut out from harming Your sheep. You will grant to us the wine of holy rejoicing.

Isaiah 57

Lord, our Lord, will the righteous man perish while the wicked man rests in his soft bed? You have given us hope in Your justice, and we call upon Your Name, knowing that Your Word will not be powerless. You know the secrets of every idol worshiper. They are spiritual prostitutes. They seduce false gods, and find themselves slaves to demons. Lord, rescue us from evil men and angels. Idols cannot deliver us from trouble. We take refuge in You alone. We will rest on Your holy mountain. You inhabit eternity, and You will revive the spirit of the lowly. Blessed be Your Name. Your Spirit heals the mourning soul. Bring us settled hearts.

Isaiah 58

Lord of the Sabbath, we have done foolish things. We pretend to seek You and to serve You, we have even fasted and prayed, and yet we have sought our own way and boasted in our own Names. We yell at those we should be gentle with, and we have turned away from Your goodness and Your life. We should share our bread with the hungry and clothe the naked. We should love our families near and far. But we have looked on the poor and done nothing to help. We have ignored Your good promises. We want close communion with You. We want the bright joy of Your holiness and the fruitfulness of a watered garden. We must follow Your Word again, that we might be repairers of the breach all around us. We will take our delight in You, and You will rescue us.

Isaiah 59

Lord of Strength, You hear us and You save us. Turn us now from all our filthy iniquity. We turn away from all lies and deceit. We come to You for our strength, for we are very weak. We will no longer run to evil, but will cry out to You in the day of temptation. Make a road for us that leads to Light. Shine upon Your pilgrim children who are weak and needy. So much sin! How can we live? We confess and come for mercy. Pretty words will not save us. The Truth that is alive and dwells in men will be our only hope. Come, Lord Jesus, in the full armor of battle and help us. We are Your beloved children, for whom You gave Your blood. Come, Redeemer Lord. We turn from transgression this day. Do not depart from us and from our children and their offspring forever.

Isaiah 60

O Glorious Light, come to Your children this day that we might come to You. Let us rejoice in the sight of Your face. We bring gifts from far off, things that you have given to us. We bring You our children and our lives. We will fear You above every King, and love You more than any other lover. You are God. You are building a glorious sanctuary out of the living stones that You have gathered in Zion. We will feed upon Your good gifts, and be strengthened by Your Son. You make us to be a temple that lasts forever. None can destroy Your good Work. You are the glory of Your people, O God. We shall possess the land forever. You will bring Your Day of victory at just the right time.

Isaiah 61

O Spirit of the Living God who so filled our great Messiah, we ask that You would fill us, that we might follow this great Man of Blessing. You have fed us and healed us. You use us to rebuild what sin has destroyed. We are priests to You, O God, and we rejoice in You, for You are our portion. You hate injustice, and will keep it far from us on the day of our deliverance, for we are Your blessed offspring. We have been covered with the righteous robes of Your Son. We live and grow in You, O God.

Isaiah 62

In You, O God, we live and move, and have our being. We have heard that we are a crown on Your head, and Your delight. What a blessed condition, that our God should rejoice over us! We thank You, O Lord. For You will establish Your Jerusalem above, and we shall praise You in the courts of Your sanctuary. We who were once not Your people have now been called the daughter of Zion, a city not forsaken.

Isaiah 63

God of Vengeance and Justice, You will come to judge, but for our sake You have been willing to sully Your garments with Your own precious blood. You protect us from all our enemies. You have been good to us in the abundance of Your steadfast love. You have saved us through the Messenger of Your presence. You have disciplined us in Your love and righteousness, but You have turned again toward us with a powerful salvation. You have made for Yourself a glorious Name throughout the whole earth. Father, never abandon us. Do not harden our hearts, but change us and overrule our foolishness.

Isaiah 64

Come down now, O God. We need You here today. There is much to be done, but there are enemies within and without the gates who are against Your Kingdom. We are fading like a leaf. We need to be a strong tree of righteousness in Your Son. You are the Father, even our Father. You are the Potter. Shape us to be vessels of Your mercy for Your own good pleasure.

Isaiah 65

Great God, Your patience is beyond our understanding. We know that You will repay iniquity. Our hope is in Christ and the cross, since Your justice has come upon Him there for us. Thank you for Your unchanging love for Your elect children.

We will not forsake You. We will answer when You call and turn away from those things in which You do not delight. Feed us this day. Grant to us refreshing waters from above. Bless us, we pray. Call us by the name of Your Son. O God of Truth, make us glad in You today. May Your Jerusalem above be a cause of rejoicing forever. Bring about the fulfillment of all Your holy purposes. Give us hope for this eternal city as we face the sufferings of this world of death. Answer us in peace. We come to You in faith.

Isaiah 66

O Lord, it is amazing that You would care for us. Your Son came in humility and trembled at Your Word. His perfect heart of worship moved toward You continually in sincere devotion and obedience. This He did for our sake. We shall not be put to shame. We look for the sound in the heavens of Your Son's return in glory. Bring forth Your holy nation. May Your Kingdom come, O God. We rejoice with the Jerusalem that is above. Bring peace to her like a river. Bring joy that we have almost forgotten in the day of trouble. Show forth Your mercy to us. Grant to us a taste of Your perfect peace even today. You know the works and thoughts of Christ which have been credited to our account. Use us today to declare Your glory among the nations. Draw all Your people to Your holy mountain, that we might gather together in Your house in the new heavens and the new earth. We worship You, O sovereign Lord.

Jeremiah

Jeremiah 1

Lord God, You sent Your prophets with Your Word to speak to Your people. You care for us, for You knit us together in the womb, and have accomplished great things for us at a very high cost to our Redeemer. You have put Your words in the mouths of prophets for our sake. You watch over Your Word to perform it. You have spoken words of disaster in warning, words of judgment against our evil, and words of comfort for the day of deliverance. You have been with Your holy prophet Jesus, for the fulfillment of every prophetic word.

Jeremiah 2

Father, we have a job to perform for You today. You have been faithful from the beginning. You raised up Your people, and they have gone far from You. There is no fault in You. There can be no justification for our rebellion. We have made Your church an abomination to many because of our disobedience and pride. How could we turn to idols? How could we exchange Your glory for that which does not profit? You are a fountain of godliness and life for Your people. Why have we forsaken You as You led us in the way, only to choose broken vessels of bitter and polluted waters? We turn to You again in repentance. We turn away from wild ways of defiling sin. Cleanse us now by Your pure and powerful Spirit. Restrain our spiritual lust when we would move in the direction of strange gods. A tree is not our father. A stone cannot rise up and save us. You are the only true Source of life for us, and Your Son is the Rock of our salvation. Gather us again from the wilderness of foolishness, for we have forgotten You for many days. We are only innocent in the blood of the Lamb. Our shame is obvious, but our holiness is also real through the cross of Christ.

Jeremiah 3

Husband of Your Church, we have been an unfaithful bride, and have polluted the land. Your people of old claimed You as their God even as they had done all the evil that they could. Will we follow in this treacherous way, and not return to You in truth? Please restrain our sin. We are not interested in the way of pretended religion. We want You and not some worthless foreign idol. You are the Master of Your people. Take us back, so that we will know Your love again. We will not stubbornly follow our evil hearts. You have brought us into a pleasant land. We turn from every perverted way. You are the Lord our God, and in You alone is the salvation of Your church. We honestly admit that we have sinned against You from our youth, even until this day, for we have not obeyed Your voice.

Jeremiah 4

O God of Jacob, we return to You. We remove our detestable things from Your presence. We look to You alone with a heart that is able to mourn for our sin by Your grace. We will take up the tasks that You have for us today with confidence in You. When You call us to lament for our sin and fruitlessness, we take up that true cry and turn our hearts to You. Do not speak in judgment against us, for Your Son has saved us. There is trouble among us, O God, and we need You. Our ways and our deeds have brought this upon us. We come to You in anguish as those who love You and love Your people. Much of Your church seems to be a wasteland. Where is that wisdom that is from above? We need One Man to come and rescue us. Come Lord Jesus! We mourn for our sin. Will You utterly forsake us, O Lord? We turn away from our prostitution and murderous hate. We trust in You again.

Jeremiah 5

Righteous Lord, we have filled Your church with sin. Even when we have been disciplined by You, we have refused to repent. This is not merely the record of the ignorant, but leaders in Your house have forsaken You. We are full of adulteries. Where is the church that remains clean? Like the house of Israel and Judah, we have been treacherous against You. Is there a way of mercy for us? Please do not utterly consume us and destroy us. For the glory of Your Name, purify Your church, but leave a remnant through the grace of our Lord Jesus Christ. As we have served foreign Gods and strange religious ideas, we have brought trouble upon Your people. We have turned away from You over and over again. Wicked men are easily found among Your people, even among those in important positions of trust and authority. Preachers preach falsely, and those who lead move us along in projects of sin. What will we do when the end comes? Please forgive us and help us.

Jeremiah 6

Father God, the Day of Your Wrath is coming. Before that final day, there are many days of trouble for Your church, for You discipline those whom You love. We thank You for Your care that claims and restrains us. Our ears are not listening to Your Word as we ought to. We are not blushing at Your correction. We ignore the warnings of Your watchmen. We love the things of this world. When trouble comes, we are sometimes made more willing to consider Your Law. Will we be doomed to fall over the stumbling-blocks that have come into our path? This is no one's fault but our own. We have had hearts of iron and have been unwilling to hear. Have mercy on us.

Jeremiah 7

Lord God Almighty, there is much evil in the land. We imagine that we will be safe in Your church because of our dedication to a sacrament or some show of religious worship or act of dedication. Yet we go on doing all these abominations that are against Your Law. You have spoken persistently, but we have not listened. Father, we need the intercession of Your Son, the Lord Jesus Christ. Please forgive us, O God, and hear the perfect prayer of the One who atoned for our sins. Though we violate Your commandments, we continue to cling to the hem of His holy garment. What else can we do? We resolve to obey you, but we keep on sinning. You know the truth about us. Our only hope is in Christ. We will listen to Your Word, and we will be attentive to Your discipline. What will you do to us when we forget our promises and false asleep when we should be hearing Your voice? Surely we deserve to be food for the birds of the air, as our fathers were in the days of the prophets. Yet You are a God who will keep Your covenant, and You will magnify Your holy name. Save us, O Lord.

Jeremiah 8

Eternal Lord, we live for a time on this earth, and then all that remains of us are dry bones. Is there hope for resurrection? Surely Your Son has risen from the dead. He has assured us that we have resurrection hope in Him. He said that He went to prepare a place for us, that where He is, we also shall be. Though we have sinned badly, He is the hope of our weak souls. We have been greedy in our hearts for unjust gain. We have joined a loud chorus of those who claim to know You, and yet who keep on sinning. Is there a way of peace for people like us? We thank You for the way of life through faith in Jesus Christ. He has defeated that serpent of old. Though our joy on earth may be gone, we have yet a spark of hope and a weak flame of new life. Hear our prayer and heal us. Restore us once again to a more vigorous spiritual health.

Jeremiah 9

Lord God, we mourn for our loved ones in Your church. They are Your people, but they are adulterers, slanderers, and workers of iniquity who refuse to know You. Refine them, O Lord. Is there some other way besides suffering? Father, we pray not merely about some unknown creatures, but about our own friends, even our sons and daughters, who have not obeyed Your voice. We raise a wailing because of Zion. Lord, we lament concerning Your people everywhere. Young men and women who should have more sense and maturity are in love with foolishness. How can we reach their hearts, O Lord? You must touch them, O Lord, and draw us all back to You.

Jeremiah 10

God of Truth and Beauty, we will not be fooled by the idolatry of the nations. Their gods are objects made by men. You alone are the Lord, full of wisdom, and speaking words of the most valuable instruction. You are clothed in majesty. You have wrath that we could never endure. You made the earth by Your power and understanding. You control the motions of the clouds, and the lives of human beings. You are the portion of Your people and the Lord of angels. You bring distress upon us when we need Your fatherly discipline. Take away our stupidity. Give us sense. Show us the way of life. Do not correct us in Your anger, or we will be brought to nothing.

Jeremiah 11

Lord of the Prophets, You have spoken to us in the words of Your covenant. Your people have known the truth of Your provision and Your Law. Yet they have not been willing to truly hear Your Word. You brought upon them words of trouble in the sanctions that came against them. We thank You for the sacrifice appointed for us in Christ, our Lord. We confess to You that we have not had hearts ready to obey You. How could this be? Surely our prayers are hindered and our usefulness in Your Kingdom is limited when we have not humbled ourselves before Your Word. Our deeds testify against us. We have devised schemes against You and Your servants, even though we are a part of Your church. How we wander, O Lord! Have mercy on us, on our towns, and on our families.

Jeremiah 12

Righteous God, the way of the wicked seems to prosper all around us. Stop their progress in sin and rebellion, lest we die. Even within Your church, though men speak friendly words, there is danger everywhere. Have You rejected Your heritage forever? Many shepherds have brought great harm upon Your people. Destroyers have come from within and without. Surely we deserve Your fierce anger. Purify Your Kingdom in mercy, O Lord. We commit ourselves to You again. Do not forsake us forever, O God.

Jeremiah 13

Lord of History and Redemption, You have sent forth Your prophets to show clearly the uselessness of a worldly church. We have become a spoiled piece of despised clothing, for You will destroy the pride of Your people. We should cling to You, but we have not listened. Fill us with Your Spirit, and take away our foolish drunkenness. Make us to be men, O God, holy saints who are dedicated to You. Take away our stumbling. Free Your flock from the captivity of sin. Remove those who lead us toward the devil and are hardened in their rebellion. Do not cast us all away, like chaff in the desert. You have seen the moral filth of our sins, but Your Son has become a sin offering for us. He took our wretchedness upon Himself for the glory of Your name, to the praise of Your wonderful mercy.

Jeremiah 14

Father God, hear our cry to You, for we are still Your children. We have been marked with the waters of baptism, and named with Your holy Triune Name. We know that our iniquities testify against us. Act on our behalf for the glory of Your own Name. You are in the midst of us. Do not leave us. We confess that we have loved to wander, yet surely nothing can separate us from Your love that has come to us in Christ Jesus our Lord. The prophets have spoken to us of a real peace

– not the lying peace of false prophets that You have not sent, but the full peace spoken of by true prophets who saw in shadows Your glorious plan of redemption. They wondered how You could every justify the ungodly and retain Your own righteousness. We now see in Christ what they longed to see. Your Son has come as our Substitute. You have kept Your covenant, vindicated Your righteousness, and poured forth Your abundant mercy to sinners who are called by Your Name. We repent of our sins, and we pray for Your church.

Jeremiah 15

Lord God, we have a better Mediator than even Moses or Samuel. There is One who pleads for transgressors, in accord with the words of the prophets. Surely there is no peace for Your people through the Law, but in Christ there is abundant and eternal peace. We have great trouble among us, O Lord. We acknowledge our shameful behavior. We deserve every frightening discipline that could come upon us now. Though we serve as slaves for our enemies, Your Son came from above not to be served, but to serve, and to give His life as a ransom for many. We are part of the many that He has saved from worthlessness and destruction. Do not let the wicked prevail over us forever, O Lord.

Jeremiah 16

Lord of the Scriptures, Your Word is completely true and reliable. Help us to understand it rightly. Your holiness is far beyond us, yet this same holiness of Your Son has been credited to us. We know what we have deserved. There could be no gladness among us if we were to stand before You in our own righteousness. We have gone after other gods, and have not kept Your Law. Yet we will be warmly embraced by You as members of Your household and citizens of heaven. You shall restore us again as those who have been shown Your glorious favor. We long for the new heavens and the new earth. We think of the joy of seeing Your Son, face to face. Though we have polluted Your church with idols, will we see Your saving power in person? Blessed be Your Name. We hate our sin. You are the Lord.

Jeremiah 17

Father God, our sin has brought great trouble upon us. How can we be effective and fruitful for Your purposes if we will not turn away from iniquity? Yet we will trust in You. Grant to us a new repentance based upon the power of the cross. You search hearts, and You bring life. Father, we desire that we might be sustained by You, our fountain of living water. We turn away from death. Heal us and save us. You are our refuge in the day of disaster. Sin and death have come against us, but Your Son has won a great victory for us. You are our strong and eternal Sabbath rest. We have come to the Holy Redeemer who has accomplished our Salvation. Therefore, we humbly confess our sin before You, and bring our lives as a thank offering to You. We shall live, for in Your life, we have life.

Jeremiah 18

Creator God, we have been formed by You and fashioned for Your holy purposes. We live for a time here below. The day of our birth is known to You as is the coming day of death. We will serve You as long as we live. We will abandon our evil plans and deeds. We will return to You. How could we have wandered so far away? We have left the good pathway on so many occasions, yet You grant to us eternal hope through Jesus Christ. Show us the truth of Your Word in the day when enemies dig a pit for our lives. Grant us deliverance and hope, and may mortal foes be made friends through faith in Your Son and the power of the cross. Overthrow the old man of sin within us, and bring the new man of resurrection life into the eternal fullness of joy in Your presence forevermore.

Jeremiah 19

Lord God, the end of the wicked is a shocking reality that requires our serious consideration. This is what we deserved because of our sin, and this is what Your Son has suffered for us through His death on the cross. Father, among the people of this world over the course of centuries we have learned of times of devastating destruction. In the pages of Your Word we have read about the things that took place in Israel and Judah, times of suffering and exile that were severely troubling. Thank You for rescuing us from the greatest calamity. Grant to us ears to hear Your Word faithfully today, that we might worship You in Spirit and in truth.

Jeremiah 20

Father God, Your servants the prophets have felt the violent blows of false men who claimed to serve You. Especially Your only-begotten Son faced the hatred and brutality of those who were Your priests and the elders of the people. His Name was a word of derision in the mouth of fools who wanted to be something. Many watched for His fall with cruel envy. Though they seemed to succeed in the day of His sacrifice, His life was delivered from the grave through the marvel of resurrection. Though His days were filled with such great frustration and seeming futility, through His life and death our salvation has been securely accomplished.

Jeremiah 21

O Lord of Hosts, what shall we do when Your enemies persecute and kill the righteous? Many think of themselves as vastly superior to the humble. Yet who will heal them of the pride that destroys their lives? Pity us. Spare us. Have compassion upon us. We will follow Your Son throughout our days among the city of men unto everlasting life. We will execute justice and mercy for the weak, as much as it is in our power to do what is good. Look beyond our sin, and gaze at the perfect righteousness of Your holy Son, Jesus, for He has destroyed death for us on the cross, and won eternal life for all who call upon His Name.

Jeremiah 22

Lord God, we should use whatever power that we have to do justice and to care for the weak in accord with Your Word. One King of the Jews has done this perfectly. We have a Savior who has seen us in our great need and who has accomplished both justice and mercy through His death for us. The justice that we owed, He paid. The mercy that we longed for, He has granted. This Jesus is so different than other men of power. He looked upon our poverty and helped us. He had no oppression or violence in Him. Though He endured the unjust hatred of those who should have been His subjects, by His death He has redeemed many. We now hear His voice in every Word of the Scriptures, for all of the Law and the prophets testify of Him. Even wicked kings who are cursed by You today speak a Word of

Christ, as the Scriptures are rightly preached, for our King shines in holiness by contrast with these evil rulers. He has become the source of fruitful blessing, though He was an object of Your wrath for our sake, taking upon Himself the curse that we deserved.

Jeremiah 23

Sovereign Lord, Your shepherds should have cared for Your people. They all fell short of Your holy command. Then One came whose name was "The Lord is our Righteousness." He became the only Shepherd of the sheep. We hear His voice in the Scriptures and follow Him. He leads us now in pathways of righteousness for Your Name's sake. How different He is from the adulterous kings and prophets of ancient days. So many were false men. They spoke deceptive words of peace upon Your people, words that minimized the evil of their deeds. Christ has given to us true words of secure hope. He has exposed the deceits of our hearts, but has given us the light of the gospel of the kingdom. He gave forth Your Word like a fire, but then took the flames of Your wrath upon Himself for our sake. Your Son has delivered us from a burden that we could never bear. You have answered us in our great need through this one Prophet, Priest, and King, our Lord Jesus Christ. He has taken away our everlasting shame.

Jeremiah 24

King of kings, have mercy on us in the day of our greatest disappointment. Your plan is sure, good, and full. We have violated your holy commandments and deserve your wrath. Nonetheless, You have set Your eye on us for good. We will return to You with a whole heart. If you treated us as our sins deserve, we would be utterly destroyed from the land, but because of Your Son we have a confident expectation of the fullest blessing.

Jeremiah 25

Lord God Almighty, You are able to deliver us from situations that seem hopeless. You have spoken to us consistently through the Scriptures, showing us the way to go. We have not listened to You. We have not obeyed You. Please forgive us and help us. Take us through days of discipline. Hold us and keep us. Bring us beyond the time of desolation. We long for the life that can only come from You. We long for the resurrection of the dead. Bring us a taste of life even now when we face great difficulty and even disaster. Help us to have faith that You are bringing about a very good plan. Though You roar against Your church, yet we know that You love us and will save us. We remember the cross, by which Christ has taken away the horrible wrath that was coming against us. He has faced Your fierce anger for us, and we have a secure and full hope in Him.

Jeremiah 26

Father, we need You. Your church has been given a most important task. We are to speak forth Your Word, which we love. Yet there are many who do not love the message that we bring, and we are tempted to turn back from the truth and to either speak the lies that people want to hear or to speak no word at all. Help us Lord, for there is an enemy against us. Disaster seems very near, and we need You. Protect us from those who do not love You. Give us energy for each day, lest we sleep and do nothing.

Jeremiah 27

Lord Almighty, You have called us to bear the yoke of Christ. His yoke is easy and His burden is light. Our fathers could not bear the yoke of the Law. You have brought us a Word of grace, and have filled us with Your Spirit. In Your providence You may bring us under the yoke of powerful men and nations for a time, but this is for our good. Help us to trust You today. The words of false prophets are lies. They sound smooth and appealing. They promise us an easy and speedy victory, but they do not speak the truth. Can we trust You in the suffering that is our portion this day? Be with us now, for Your Son suffered and died for us.

Jeremiah 28

Lord God, You spoke to Your children through prophets, yet not every man who claimed to speak for You was true. In Old Testament days there were many false prophets, as there are even to this day. Many seem to speak only what people wish to hear. The Word that You have for us is wonderful. Why would we ever reject Your blessings and insist on answers that are not good? Your plan of eternal salvation is far better than the instant gifts that we would demand from You or the man-centered answers to our questions that we would invent. Give us patient ears and submissive hearts. Stay near us, O Lord.

Jeremiah 29

Father God, there is so much that we cannot comprehend. There is much trouble all around us. Who can understand the glory of Your plan? You have sent us into a particular place, and we are to seek the welfare of the place where we live. There will be an end to every act of divine discipline. Your plans for us are good. We will seek You and we will find You, for You have sought us first and have found us. Have mercy on us, O God. We have not paid attention to Your Word as we ought to. Help us to distinguish lies from the truth. Grant this discernment not only to the elders of Your church, but to all who have the joy of hearing Your Word. False shepherds would lead the sheep away, but we will do what You have commanded. Help us to reject all lies, despite the strange appeal of the false claims of men.

Jeremiah 30

O Lord, God of Israel, when will You restore the fortunes of Your church? We live in fear and distress, yet You will save us out of every trouble. If we are far away, You will draw us back. If we are near in body, but far away in spirit, You are able to bring us home. If we face the strongest enemies, You will still restore us to the place of Your compassion. There is no enemy who can destroy us. We thank You for the Ruler of the Church, for He is our strength. He will accomplish all the intentions of His heart.

Jeremiah 31

Sovereign Lord, Your plan shall surely be accomplished. Your church shall be perfectly adorned with the righteousness of Christ. You bring forth shouts of joy from the voices of Your people. You will bring us to the place of Your presence.

You will gather Your flock and give to Your people a New Covenant. Built on the Rock, which is Christ, Your church will be blessed according to Your promise. Restore us again, O God. Let us not be put to shame. We will return to You from the land of unbelief. We will follow our great Redeemer. The answer for us has come in the child of a woman. He watches over us for our good. Build and plant, O Lord, for Your ways are marvelous. We have broken Your Law, but Your Son has obeyed every commandment. We look with joyful expectation to the coming day when we shall no longer disobey Your commandments. Your love for us is both strong and sure. Your Kingdom will be built up, and Your Son shall reign forever.

Jeremiah 32

Father God, Your plan for Your people is sure and wonderful. Despite the troubles that come upon us, You give us news of a great future. We are citizens of a better land, and we long for the day when we can take full possession of the good things that You have for Your children. Give us strength to persevere through the current age until the promise comes to us in full. O Lord God, we trust You. You can bring about that great day. Even now You can help us as we cry out to You. You see our weakness, but nothing is too difficult for You. We would not have anything had You not determined long ago to give good gifts to Your children. Show us today Your power and Your love. Preserve us through whatever means You see fit. Though the city be burned with fire, and though You would come in anger against Your unfaithful people, You are still fully able to carry us through the worst trials. We turn away from our sins, O Lord. We will worship You according to Your Word with a full heart of obedience. Sanctify us, Lord God, that we might dwell in safety in Your presence. Remember Your own covenant love, and help us in the time of trouble that is too much for us to bear. Do Your great work within the troubled souls of those who call upon Your Name.

Jeremiah 33

God of Peace and Truth, You have made the earth. We worship You. You work out Your plans for Your church. There will be health and security for Your people. There will be full forgiveness for us through Jesus Christ our Lord. You have a plan that includes great joy and prosperity for us. We will have peace as we worship You forever. In the power of Your steadfast love, the fortunes of Your people will be restored. O bring forth that great day, O God. You will fulfill Your promises through the Righteous Branch, and we will be called by His great name. Thank You that Your Son has ascended into heaven and has given great gifts to Your church. Fill us with Your Spirit, and multiply the offspring of Your Servant, the Son of David. As the sun rises every morning, and as night follows day, so Your promises of mercy and restoration for Your people are absolutely secure.

Jeremiah 34

Lord God, there is a tremendous need in Your church today. We need spiritual resources for the battle that is near us and even within us. We would give in to worldliness without even seeming to know what is happening. We would be caught in enslaving sins and encourage others in that slavery, and think that all that we were doing is just normal living. Even when we make some small progress, the attack against us may be fierce, and we would quickly turn to some evil way. Have mercy on us, and send us the spiritual power that we need for the challenge of this day. Your Son has confirmed Your covenant love for us through His own blood. Bring us back home again to You, for You are faithful in Your kindness to us.

Jeremiah 35

Our Father, the disobedience of Your people is so unusual. We have been given a very good and holy law. We would do well to follow it carefully. Yet we find obedience to Your commandments to be a great spiritual struggle. Others may be able to do what their ancestors have handed down to them. They follow old customs and do not hate the ways that their fathers have given them. Your people have treated You with such a dishonorable rebellion, despite the fact that Your moral law is so far superior to the traditions of men. Forgive us for this deep treachery, and remember the full obedience of Your Son on our behalf. Your ways are so very good. We will obey Your commandments. Have mercy on us.

Jeremiah 36

Almighty God, we thank You for the gift of Your Word, spoken to us through the prophets. We are very grateful that You have provided for us a written record of Your voice in the Scriptures of the Old and New Testaments. Grant to us Your Spirit that we might hear Your Word with deep reverence and with a willingness to worship and obey You. Use the ministers of Your Word to accurately explain to us the meaning. Show us the great themes that are so clearly put forth in the Bible. Some would have the most profound disrespect for Your Word. They would not tremble at Your warnings, but would gladly destroy any record of Your message to us. They will not succeed in their wicked plots. Though they would seem to be the most powerful people on the earth, they will not be able to take away the power of Your promises to us. We hear Your voice through the Scriptures, and we bow before You.

Jeremiah 37

Lord God, will we utterly ignore Your warnings to Your church? You have told us to repent, lest You remove Your lampstand from among us. Would we put You to the test? Lying messengers assure us that everything is alright, though Your church would be dedicated to false teaching and wicked living. We have spoken against loyal ministers of Your Word, treating them as traitors. We willfully forget that false prophets who we once eagerly listened to have been proven wrong through events that we have seen with our own eyes. Save Your church, O Lord! Fill us with a true and right Spirit we pray. We need Your power and love.

Jeremiah 38

Merciful God, the servants of Your Word are in great need. Some are being threatened by those around them. Others are already in prison or have had their property confiscated from them. Appoint someone to help them today, that they might have food to eat, healing for their illnesses, aid for their financial distress, friendship for their loneliness, and especially Your strong presence in their lives. Make them to be men of great courage. Though the wicked seek their lives, You are able to preserve Your servants again this day. Through all this distress, help those who are true messengers of Your Son to continue with the fullness of Your holy counsel. Though their homes and even their families be destroyed, preserve Your servants through every trial.

Jeremiah 39

Lord God Almighty, when an agent of destruction and discipline from Your hand comes, will we see him rightly? How will we patiently receive the challenges that are a part of Your decree for Your church here below? Will we strike Your hand and run from You, or will we faithfully bear the affliction that You have sent for our good? Do we really believe that You know how to deliver us out of all harm? Do we truly know that You are working all things for our good? We believe Your Word. Strengthen us as servants of Your Son in a day of trouble.

Jeremiah 40

Father God, we are a part of a larger whole. We are closely associated with one another in the body of Christ. We care for each other in days of difficulty and distress. We are willing to associate with the poor and lowly in their need. Provide us with faithful leaders in a day of trouble. Bring us food day by day, though we are captives of men. We know that You are the one true God. Help us to hear the Word of warning that comes to us, that we might be informed concerning the dangers all around us. Preserve our lives forever that we might love and serve You always.

Jeremiah 41

O God our Help, wicked men would murder those in authority and bring horror and trouble upon many people and lands. We do not know the secrets of men's hearts as You do. We are unable to see the dangers all around us. You must protect us. Defend us against secret foes who insist on their own ways. Provide for us those resources that are necessary for life and godliness in this world. We know that our labor in Your Kingdom is not in vain. We want You first, above ever other pleasure. Keep us from self-seeking short-sightedness, and the ruin that comes from worldly living.

Jeremiah 42

Great God, there is danger around us on all sides in a time of great trouble. Still we know that Your ways are right. You are working out Your holy will. We will obey Your voice. This is our promise, but do we know what we are saying? What if Your Word goes against the strong intentions of our own thoughts and feelings? Will we really follow You? Please forgive us, O Lord. The dangers of our day are too serious for us to rely on our own understanding. We cannot safely follow the customs of the world. Even the church may be very weak in her commitment to the Scriptures. Father, protect us from foolishness. We do not want to go back to the place of worldly wisdom. We must be kept by You through Your strong Word.

Jeremiah 43

O Lord of Hosts, against our holiest impulses and the plain teaching of Your Word, some have been forced to walk a dangerous path that is against Your revealed will. Please help us and be with us. As You know us Lord, there is some evil that is not our choice. Powerful men who usurp authority among Your people have forced our hands in ways that are wrong. How are we to submit to such foolish and unspiritual men? Yet we may have no choice today. Surely there are brothers and sisters who have been led away in chains into wicked situations and places. Meet us in our place of despair, and have mercy upon us. We would not willingly choose this slavery. Help us and deliver us.

Jeremiah 44

Great Provider, You know how to save the righteous who are forced to live among the wicked. You can never be charged with wrong. We do not understand the events swirling all around us, but we do know You, and we love Your Word. Lying men have claimed to follow You, but they continue in idolatry with impunity. We fear You, O God, and we will walk in Your statutes. How could we be back in the land of slavery again? Surely Your people will only die here. Have mercy on the weak. O Father, our situation is very dangerous, and our hope is failing. Yet You are God. Those who claim Your Name are brazen and hardened in their rebellion against Your Word. The issues are not complex. You say, "Yes!" Your people insist on "No!" The people who bear Your Name have lied about their troubles. They cling to idols and pretend that all was well when they were scrupulously dedicated to evil. Go then, evil men! Do your wickedness! But do not let them use Your Name, Father, for they are not for You. They are against Your Word, and would destroy Your people who truly love You, and who would follow Your Truth. Deliver us from evil, O God, and have mercy on us, that we might be strong in a day of overwhelming temptation and sorrow.

Jeremiah 45

Great God, You have grieved deeply over the trouble of Israel and the sins of Your church. Help us to see our own trials in light of Your greater grief. Grant us faith in Your Word, for You have given us our lives now and forever.

Jeremiah 46

Lord God Almighty, all nations are known to You. Lands devoted to idolatry cannot pretend that they do not know of Your great works of creation. Yet people everywhere are full of confidence in themselves. You are in charge of the affairs of every land. The warrior considers his own strength invincible, but a greater foe can come in a moment. Your people must not put their trust in the powers of this world. We trust in You. One nation may seem to have the strength to last forever, but that country will not stand forever against you. You, O Lord of hosts, will judge the rulers and idols of all nations. Give us hope in a better day, a hope that is secure not through the weapons of this world, but through Your divine power and love.

Jeremiah 47

Father God, for generations people of power have feigned a great confidence in their strength, yet at heart men know that they are dust. Who can pretend that the day of our death is so very far away? Make us sensible to the fact of Your existence. Help us to worship You in the beauty of holiness.

Jeremiah 48

Sovereign Lord, ancient cities have been planted and plucked up in accord with Your great plan. Many names of peoples and places mean nothing to anyone today. They have had their great moment, and are now gone from all memory. Will we not be humble before You? How foolish we are when we demand only comfort in our lives. We need to be brought to You, at times through great suffering. In a time of trouble we may finally turn away from false gods. They are an abomination in Your sight. What is the might that we are counting on today? Do we have muscles or weapons beyond our neighbors? Are we people of the highest wit and wisdom? Will we defend ourselves against the Lord through our clever responses or our great military tactics? Father, we have been foolish in our lofty pride. Our boasts have been false. Our deeds and achievements will amount to nothing. Our labors will be utterly vain unless they are in Your Son. We hear Your Word today calling us to a better hope than man can provide. We have turned away from the love of money, and the pleasure that seems to come from the applause of men. There is a better foundation for life in the greatness of Your Son. We will no longer magnify ourselves against You, for You are God, even our God. We are pleased to be Your children, and we submit ourselves to Your will and Your holy commandments.

Jeremiah 49

Glorious God of the Nations, what a variety of false gods the peoples of the world have invented. You are the Creator of the heavens and the earth. Where are the Ammonites and the Edomites today? What has become of ancient Damascus and Kedar and Hazor? Where are the many cities and peoples that men have utterly forgotten? They once had mighty powers to give them a great defense against powerful foes, but could they stand against You, O Lord God Almighty? Father, You are a sure foundation and a mighty fortress in the day of trouble. Any challenge that men face in this world is nothing compared to the coming wrath that will be a true terror on every side. You are right to be angry with men because of our sin. You are the Maker of the world and of all that is in it. Surely You have the right to determine our destiny and to punish us for our iniquities. Nonetheless, You have not been content to show only Your righteous wrath. You have a plan for latter days that involves an amazing restoration of fortunes for all who trust in Your Son.

Jeremiah 50

Lord God, in every age there would seem to be a superpower. Each one imagines itself to be invincible. Can we see nothing from history? Will we not believe Your Word? You make a people of power to be an instrument of Your plan for a brief time. When their pride reaches a summit, they will be brought low, like all the superpowers that have come before. Your wrath, O Lord, is far too much for the mightiest Babylon. How strong is Your Son, and how invincible in His Kingdom! We marvel at Your ways, O God. Your Son came in weakness. When He died on the cross, it would have appeared to every observer that His days were gone forever. How could this one man be anything compared to mighty empires like the Assyrians or the Romans? Yet He has established a kingdom that shall not perish. Through His death and resurrection a temple is being built up that will never be torn down. All those who have proudly defied Your Son will find an enemy in Him that is glorious in mighty power. The God-Man who died on a cross will come again to judge the living and the dead. We rest in Him. Whatever strength or wisdom other kingdoms may seem to have, it is only for a moment. Our Jesus lives, and His Kingdom is forever. The Stone which the builders rejected has become the chief cornerstone. How we long for the fulfillment of all Your promises! We dream about the peaceful valleys of Your great Land! There we will live in security and joy forever. Every brutal enemy will be harmless against us in that great day.

Jeremiah 51

Father God, who can stand when You bring judgment upon a nation? Who will stand when You bring judgment against the world? What a Babylon we live in. The world is against You and Your people. You have stirred up the Spirit of one nation to bring down another land. Those who trust in their treasures will not stand when foreign enemies come by Your Hand. You bring forth the rain and the snow. You control the wind and the waves. You formed all things. You use armies for Your purposes. Idols are formed by men. These false gods are nothing and they can form nothing. You are God. If You are against the world, against men, against idols, You can bring about a complete destruction of a whole nation, breaking that land in pieces. Your purposes against any nation shall stand. Did we really imagine that any nation would be able to remain by her own power? You will repay the nations of the world for the way they have expressed their hatred against Your church. With a Word You create, and with a Word You will destroy. If we are able to even live through such an ordeal, it is a matter of great mercy. Why are we so amazed by the trials that we face when we live amongst a world that will surely face judgment? Did not the prophets face great difficulties and the violence of men? Why are our expectations so different from their earthly destiny, when You will surely judge men and nations? Lord, there is no safety in any place where we live. There is no land on this earth where we can think that we will have peace and prosperity. It is not by the wisdom or power of worldly empires that the new heavens and the new earth will be established. When You say the word, every Babylon shall sink and rise no more. Our safety is in You. Our citizenship is in heaven. Our home is in the body of Christ. We are eternally grateful for Your many mercies.

Jeremiah 52

Father God, what will Your people do when Your church is led by worldly men who will not listen to Your holy Word? Powerful enemies come against us from the nations of the world. Grant us leaders who will follow You, even if we must die. Though our bodies may soon rest in the grave, we know that we will yet live in Christ. Lord, help us to fulfill the purposes that You have for Your people. The nations come and take from Your people their gold, silver, and bronze, but nothing can separate us from Your love. If we suffer for Your sake at the hands of men, we are greatly blessed. Grant us faith, that we might have eyes to see things as they are. Fill us with Your Spirit. Help us to follow our King Jesus, who died for us. Build up Your true temple through the preaching of the gospel. Gather Your Israel from every nation, as people are granted eternal life in Your Son.

Lamentations

Lamentations 1

Great God, we are in need. We cry out to You. Send forth Your Comforter, the powerful Spirit of Holiness. We suffer bitterly in this great battle. We have faced horrible defeat in warfare all around us. We have spirits, but we also have bodies. We are fearfully and wonderfully made. What has happened to our homes and our places of worship? Where are our children? How have we come to this sad place? Father, we have felt something of Your discipline. You are in the right. Yet, look upon us in our suffering. Our young men and women are gone. Many have died. Others are far from Your sanctuary. We do not pretend to be strong. Our groans are many. Our hearts are faint. Send forth Your Comforter, and rescue us.

Lamentations 2

Glorious Father, have You utterly forgotten us? In Your just wrath, You send Your devastating judgments. What must the cross have been like for Your Son? You came upon Him with the fullness of punishment. He was the spotless temple of Your presence. He had no sin. Yet He took all our filth and rebellion upon Himself on that awful day of atoning death. Your wrath came upon Him for us. Lord, we are in horrible trouble now. We are in need of basic things so that we can stay alive here and now. Feed us from heaven. Though false prophets may have been removed from our midst, our enemies are still all around us. They think that they have complete victory over us. What can we say to You? Our cries are too deep for words. We are in distress. We have had such trouble beyond anything we ever expected. There is terror on every side.

Lamentations 3

Sovereign Lord, we have faced great tribulation. We cry for help. Do You not hear us? Where is Your help? O God, we hate our sin. Father, we feel no hope in our hearts. Yet we remember Your steadfast covenant love, Your mercy, Your great faithfulness. We should wait patiently for You when it seems like we have no future. Help us to take this affliction now. This will not last forever. You are not vicious toward us, O God. You must have a purpose in this day of testing. Help us to turn now from all sin. Grant us a very large repentance. Surely there is something good that will come from all these tears. There must be some good in this horrible loss. Do not close Your ear to our cries for help. Through Christ, You have surely redeemed our lives from complete destruction.

Lamentations 4

Lord God, what has happened to Your church? We were precious stones in Your holy temple. Where are our children? Where have our companions gone? Where are those who once professed faith in You? How is it that they have gone out from us? Were they never part of us? Have mercy on us, O God. Your people are deeply bruised by an enemy that we cannot see. Brutal men and angels must be all around us. How could we have become a people that seem to be cursed by You? We look for help from far off. Where is our help, O Lord? The enemy seeks the ones He may devour. Yet His day of punishment will surely come. Help us, O Lord.

Lamentations 5

Father, we face the truth of our affliction with brutal honesty. Food, shelter, safety, life… these are things we need. Celebration is only a bitter memory. Yet You are still the Lord. You will reign forever. Restore us, O God. Our confidence is in Your Son, for He was utterly condemned for our transgressions, and rose again for our justification.

Ezekiel

Ezekiel 1

Glorious Lord, You are with Your people in the place of exile and suffering. Your Word comes to us even there. You grant to us messages from Your heavenly courts to encourage us even in a land of imprisonment. Thank You for the work of Your angels, who are before Your holy presence continually. There is so much that we do not understand. We ask that You would help us to know what we should know, and to have peace regarding those things that we cannot know at present. You go where You will, O God. We are confined to a place. We face limitations. You are different. You are a fiery presence of purity. We are afraid as we hear Your Word, and are comforted by our remembrance of Your Son's death for sinners.

Ezekiel 2

Father God, You have a purpose for the Son of Man. You have sent Your own Son as a true man to Your people of the Old Covenant. When He spoke, surely the greatest prophet was among them. He faced great suffering, for they were a rebellious house. Forgive our many sins, O Lord. Your Son had no rebellion in Him. He was a faithful spokesman of Your everlasting truth; both a true Servant and Your eternal Son.

Ezekiel 3

Sovereign Lord, we love Your Word. Help us to follow it. Thank You for Your prophets and apostles who have spoken this Word of truth. Thank You especially for the work of Your Holy Spirit. Without Him we would never have the will to hear and obey You. Restrain our sin, and not only our sin, but the sin of Your church throughout the world. Father, constrain Your ministers to speak Your Word in truth. They must warn Your people not to sin, or the guilt of many rebellious souls will be on the heads of Your ambassadors. They must not speak to us whatever our itching ears demand to hear. They must be true to You.

Ezekiel 4

Lord God, great trouble came against Your holy city of old. This was well known to Your prophets, and they warned Your people. Yet those who were called by Your Name still would not hear Your Word. Will we be so foolish? Having the completed Word of truth in the Old and New Testaments, will we consider Your holy Scriptures as nothing? We are defiled by the filth of our wickedness. Our uncleanness is not merely outward and ceremonial. We are unclean within. Grant us ears to hear and hearts to obey by the gift of Your Spirit.

Ezekiel 5

O Father, how can we dwell in Your presence? You demand righteousness, and there is much testimony that confirms that You are uncompromising concerning Your holy Law. Your people of old rejected Your statutes. They did not even act as well as the nations all around them who did not know You. The depth of the sin of Your people was obvious, and You withdrew from them. So many died. Your anger came upon them. Are we any better in Your church? Do we imagine that You now have no call to us, no claim upon our lives? Thank You for the cross and resurrection of Your Son, which is our hope. May we not forget the life we have been called to live.

Ezekiel 6

Father God, You will not tolerate false worship in Your sanctuary. Your people must give up our foolish evil. Loosen the grip of our sinful minds on idolatrous thoughts and affections. Help us to feel the wretchedness of spiritual adultery. It is enough. We must repent now. We must not excuse ourselves anymore. Must more people die because we are so unwilling to devote ourselves truly to You? Our blood cannot make atonement for our own sins, or for the sins of our children. Your Son's blood is more than sufficient for our greatest assurance of Your steadfast love.

Ezekiel 7

Great King of Heaven, Your wrath against sin is justified and completely righteous. Any trouble that could ever come against us is more than deserved because of our sins. All of this righteous punishment came upon Your beloved Son on the cross. He took this great wrath and has worked out the demands of Your holy justice for Your servants. Thank You, O Lord. We will not be ungrateful for such a wonderful love. Take away from us the love of sinning, so that we will worship You from the heart. We long for our complete sanctification, not only for us, but for all Your elect. Today the church is full of bloody crimes and envious rebellion. Only You can change us, O Lord. We plead the blood of Christ. Our hope is only in You, O God.

Ezekiel 8

Father God, there is much trouble and filth within Your church. Please forgive us. We have idols in our hearts and in our lives that must be destroyed and removed from Your sanctuary. You know the truth of what is in us. Though we may have a white-washed exterior, we cannot fool You. Inside there are dead men's bones. We have even become brazen in our worship of created things. Our lives are also obvious evidence against us, for we do what is evil. Please change us and forgive us.

Ezekiel 9

Lord God, the Day of Judgment will surely come. Even before that Day, we see signs of Your judgment against all that is evil. Father, we sigh and groan over all the abominations that are committed in Your church. We long for the purity of Your Kingdom. Yet we also have sin within us. Please pardon. The guilt of

Your church is exceedingly great. We know that You have not forgotten us. You see us and You know Your children. Please have mercy on us, according to Your righteousness and grace.

Ezekiel 10

Great God, please do not take Your Holy Spirit from us. Protect us from all evil. We need You. Speak to us clearly through Your servants. Grant us hope for the future because of Your great promises. At just the right time, send forth Your angels to gather Your elect from throughout the earth. Until that Day when the trumpet will sound, keep us in Your love and grace. Our brothers in places of danger cry out to You night and day. Hear and save. Send forth Your ministering angels like flames of fire. Protect us, and use us to proclaim Your glory.

Ezekiel 11

Glorious Lord, You have appointed leaders among Your people, yet many do not obey You. Forgive us, O Lord. Grant to us a heavenly-mindedness that would be true to Your Word. What shall we do when those who are charged with bringing Your Word to Your people give their own message, and turn away from You? Do not make a full end of Your church. Assemble us together again as Your covenant people. Fill us with Your Spirit. We will be Your people, and You will be our God. Speak to us words of truth that we may live.

Ezekiel 12

Lord God, take away our rebellion. We would claim to have ears and eyes, but we do not hear and see. You have spoken to us in ways that are unmistakably clear, yet Your people have followed their own ways. We repent, O Lord. Speak to us again through Your messengers. Do not cast us away from Your presence. Scatter the enemies who would come against Your church. Gather us together in Your presence. You are the Lord. We thank You for the union that we have with Jesus Christ, the Son of Man and Son of God. Bring to an end the preaching of false doctrines among us. Speak a true Word to us and perform it at just the right time. Glorify Your great Name.

Ezekiel 13

Father, what shall become of foolish messengers who follow their own spirits? They claim to speak for You, but they do not bring forth the truth of Your Word. We thank You for the Scriptures. Help us to expound these truly. Grant that Your ministers would teach the full breadth of Your whole counsel. There is a Day of Judgment coming. We know that judgment begins with Your church. Take down the whitewashed walls that we have built, prophesying out of our own minds. Take away from us all our idolatrous and foolish magic charms that are of no use to us for any real spiritual growth. Turn us from every evil way, for You are the Lord.

Ezekiel 14

Lord God, we ask that You would give elders to Your church who would truly follow Christ. What will we do if our leaders are worshiping only idols? This is not the way of Your Son. Rid our hearts of false gods. Raise up faithful men to speak the Word of truth to Your people. Be our God. We are Your people. Forgive our sins. We have wandered so far from the pathway of truth. Is there any hope for us? We ask that Your Son would plead again for us today; for us and for our sons and our daughters. Restore Your church, that we might grow in the grace and knowledge of Jesus Christ.

Ezekiel 15

O God, will Your church be a useless vine? Are we so set on our own pride that we will not be useful for anything? Make us to be a strong tree, planted by the waterside, full of the Holy Spirit. Look upon us again, not in wrath, but in the faithfulness of Your covenant love.

Ezekiel 16

Our Father in Heaven, we have sinned against You. Your people have wandered into filth and lawlessness. We have done what is both foolish and unnatural. You have spoken life into us, and yet we have been loud and filthy in our own ugly ways. You have done for us everything necessary for peace and growth, yet we have loved other gods. We have insisted on our own desires for false worship. Please help us, O Lord. Grant to us again the spiritual wisdom that we so desperately need. Have we utterly forgotten Your kindness to us? Are we beyond rescue? We confess to You that we have looked to the world for our strength. We have looked for what the world could give to us with enthusiasm, but we have had no energy for seeking You. We have taken the tithes and offerings of Your people and have spent them on the world. We have not honored You according to Your Word. Please do not discipline us forever. Grant to us a new repentance. Why are we so foolish as to follow in the ways of those who are bound for eternal judgment? Will we follow in the way of the world forever? Grant that we would resist the devil. Restore our fortunes, O Lord, that we might find again a godliness with contentment, which is great gain. We cast our cares before You. Remember Your everlasting covenant with Your children. You have surely atoned for our sin through the blood of Your Son, Jesus Christ.

Ezekiel 17

O Lord, there is much that we do not understand. Speak to us clearly through Your Word, and fill us with a Spirit of wisdom and revelation in the knowledge of Your Son. You have blessed us with so many wonderful gifts. Cause Your church to be a fruitful plant with deep roots. You know the secrets of our hearts. You know of the foolish schemes of wicked leaders among Your church. Thank You for the perfection of our One Head, the Lord Jesus Christ. He surely is a new tree of righteousness for Your people. We find protection under His branches. In Him, You have fully accomplished our rescue from sin and death.

Ezekiel 18

Father God, we have such foolish sayings that pass among us as if they were from Your Word. Please forgive us for our lack of careful attention to the Scriptures of the Old and New Testaments. You demand righteousness from Your people. The righteous man will truly be righteous and will live righteously. Such a man will live. Father, what will become of us, for we have sinned against You? Where is our perfect righteousness? We have heard of the good news that Your Son lived and died for us. Our Savior has suffered for our iniquity. Since we have received so great a salvation, will we now be fools and commit horrible sin? Will we tempt You in this? Take away the foolishness of Your children. The injustice that we do, will it now lead to death? The right course for us is very clear. We will confess our sins to You. We will repent and turn from all of our transgressions. Do not let our iniquity destroy us. Grant to Your people a new heart for You, that we might attend to Your good Word.

Ezekiel 19

Lord God, we cry for the leaders of Your church. They should be under-shepherds for the Lord Jesus Christ. Will they devour men and seize their widows? Is this the way of love? Is this the pathway for a people who know the salvation of the cross? Draw us back again to Yourself in love. Please grant to us faithful shepherds who will love You and will feed Your flock according to the directives of that one great Shepherd of the sheep.

Ezekiel 20

Sovereign Lord, Your Word is true and good. We want to hear the truth. What is wrong with our hearts that we would ever resist You? You have given us so many good things, and have warned us concerning the detestable nature of idolatry. Nonetheless we have been attracted to what is wrong and foolish. Lord, we would rest in Your Son, for He is our great Sabbath. He has accomplished our redemption through His death. We are the ones who have violated Your commandments, but He has paid the great debt that we incurred. He never rebelled against You, but we have profaned Your Name and Your Law throughout all the nations where we live. You are the Lord. Speak to us now in great power and love. Draw us near again by Your Spirit. We hate all our false worship, and we turn away from all this defiling spiritual adultery. We repent. We hate our sin. We hate our desire to be imitators of the world, rather than imitators of Your Son. If You enter into judgment with us face to face we will never stand. You have seen Your beloved Son face to face in judgment for our sake. We were scattered, but now we have been gathered. We were rejected, but now in Him we have been accepted forever. You have not dealt with us according to our evil hearts and our arrogant ways. You have granted us mercy, according to the righteousness of Your Son, our atoning sacrifice.

Ezekiel 21

Merciful Lord, we cannot face Your sword of judgment. Will all Your people be destroyed? We groan because of Your wrath and because of the sin of Your church. The nations are full of iniquity. This we could stand. But how can it be that Your people are so full of sin? They will not respond to discipline. Trouble is coming against us. Pagan armies do what they think to be the directives of their gods. Yet You work out every detail of Your will. There is a deep weariness among Your people. How can we continue, O Lord? We need Your Son. He is in us, and His love is in us. Surely You will help us. We are weak, and we need You even now.

Ezekiel 22

Lord God, how are we to judge? There are abominations all around us, and trouble is very near. You must cast out the filth that is in us, so that we can speak for you with boldness. Surely we will always need the mercy that you have shown us. We have pursued all kinds of uncleanness. We are at the forefront of a great company of sinners. If we have any strength left, it must be from You. You are the Lord. Purify us, O God. Your Son went through the furnace of Your judgment for us. Teach us to love Your true Word, and to stop our ears against false prophets. Is extortion and robbery acceptable within Your covenant community? We are in danger because of our evil ways.

Ezekiel 23

O God, we have heard the Word that You have spoken. For generations Your people have ignored the true call to holiness. We lust after the world, and display no spiritual sense. We have touched things that should be far from us, and have followed enticing adulteries. What possible reason could we rightly have for our defiling ways? Do we really love the gods of the Assyrians and Babylonians? Will we only do as Israel and Judah did of old? We are so impressed with the ways of the world. We want what they seem to offer, and we have no sense of the way of the cross. Do we love soldiers and chariots more than the Savior who speaks to us in word and sacrament? There is only one way for us. Your Son will surely lead us out of our current disgrace. The power of the cross is everything to us. We turn away from the worldliness that is attacking Your church. Your temple is holy, and we are that temple. We will not waste our hearts on false spiritual ways. Move us in the way of Christ. Help us to eagerly embrace the way of the cross by Your grace. The judgment against us would come speedily were it not for Your steadfast love and Your Son's amazing grace.

Ezekiel 24

Almighty God, You are the Lord of the church and the Lord of our lives. Your Word has come to us. Each day has a special purpose according to Your eternal plan. Nothing is without some good cause, and some holy intention. You will purify Your church. This is what we seek, but who can bear the trials that are so near to us? You will cleanse us from our uncleanness. You are utterly committed to what is right. O Lord, thank You for the delight of our eyes. You have given us wives and husbands, You have blessed Your church with children. Will these be taken away in a moment? Even so, You are the everlasting God. Father, there must be a better day coming. This grief cannot be the final story of our lives. The news for us must somehow again be good. We cling to Your promises, though we do mourn in the depths of our hearts. There is surely a better day coming.

Ezekiel 25

Lord of the nations, even our enemies can have no other God but You. Though the world rails against You and brings much trouble upon Your church, is there any other hope but You? There is no other god. If they worship demons, can fallen angels save them? Would a demon have love for men? Is there any good that comes from hateful spirits? Surely even our enemies should turn to You now! Why should anyone be satisfied with idols that are not gods? Why should Your enemies add to the weight of sin? It is already an overwhelming burden, but there is a way out of the weight of Your judgment in the wonder of Your love.

Ezekiel 26

Father God, help us to have mercy for those who suffer affliction, while continuing in Your Word. We cannot pretend that falsehood is truth. We cannot forget Your standards of righteousness. That would not be kindness. We know that we need to mourn over the bad condition of Your church and still do for others as we would desire them to do for us. Thank You for the love of the cross. Grant us wisdom to know how to love others with whom we disagree, to know that vengeance is Yours, and to wait for the day of Your deliverance.

Ezekiel 27

O Lord, teach us to raise a lamentation when even our foes suffer. The day will come when we will rejoice in Your perfect justice and will judge even angels. Today we do not know how to do this without hypocrisy and sin. The world has been engaged in all kinds of dedication to money that is the root of much evil. Surely we cannot pretend that greed and covetousness are just another lifestyle choice? There is a dangerous love for wealth that leads so many astray. We cannot go this way and still pretend that You are Lord. We cannot serve both You and unrighteous gain. We are happy to see prosperity around us, but not the love of riches. Teach us how to relate to the world with kindness, and to proclaim Your truth with integrity.

Ezekiel 28

Lord God, keep us from self-destructive pride. We have wealth and intelligence. You have given us many other good gifts. Yet are we so foolish as to think that we are superior gods? Our lives are in Your hands. We were created by You. You have cared for us throughout our lives. You brought us to faith in Your Son. You have rescued us out of many dangers. You have watched over us and helped us in every trouble. You have even selected trials for our good. Will we then act as if we are somehow above You? Do we really want to contend with You? Surely Your church must not be full of pride like some rich nation. Though Your Son was equal with You in essence, He willingly humbled Himself before You. Is it too much for us to be lowly? Please restore us again to the sweetness of fellowship with You. Forgive our sins, and grant to us a more righteous frame of mind.

Ezekiel 29

Great God of Heaven and Earth, there is much trouble all around us. Proud enemies have confidence in their strength. They are frightening in their power and hate. How will we survive? Surely we will be rescued by You. If You were not watching over us even now, we would not last for a moment. Our enemies come against us, but You can stop them as they seek to do us harm. We marvel at the extent of Your great decrees. You know where nations come from and where they are going. At just the right time, You sent Your Son to be an atoning sacrifice for Your people. If You gave Your Son for us, will You not freely give us all things? Will You not protect us from every danger? We trust You.

Ezekiel 30

O Lord God Almighty, when will the Day of the Lord come? We know that we are to consider it near. We have been told that we shall not know the day or the hour. Help us to be ready for that Day. Our only hope is in Your Son. When anguish comes upon all the people of the earth, we shall rejoice in Jesus Christ forever. Desolation is coming against the earth, but we will be rescued. What will it be like when there is no more sin in us or among us? What will it feel like when we are with You and with each other in resurrection life forever? You will put every foe far away from us. No longer will we be harassed by an unseen enemy bringing turmoil upon our souls. On that great Day, we will surely know that You are the Lord.

Ezekiel 31

Our Father, there is an adversary who is spiritual and powerful. As we consider the great kings of evil empires from days gone by, we know that the most powerful man returns to dust. Like a great tree of the field, though he seems to rule forever, the day of his death will come. More frightening still is the angelic foe. Yet we are told that if we resist Him, He will flee. How could we have that kind of power except by Your decree? One day the worst of our foes will be cast into a place of punishment forever. We flee to You again for safety. We remember Your Son, His cross, and His resurrection.

Ezekiel 32

Great King of the Nations, You do not fear the powers of the great men. Though they rail against You and persecute Your children, You can capture them and destroy them in a moment. You have a plan for every nation, and You have a great blessing for Your church. We do not need to search for a King for Your people, for the Lord Jesus Christ is the King and Head of Your church, and He is alive forever. When everything seems to be lost, when we do not know the way out, You are still God, and You will certainly accomplish all of Your holy will. What will it be like when the Day of Judgment comes? What will happen to those who have spread their terror everywhere? Father, we pray for the salvation of people from every nation. We pray for abundant mercy for all kinds of people. Bring the message of hope to the remotest ends of the earth. The trouble ahead for those who will go down to the pit will be beyond anything that we can imagine. Grant many people ears to hear the truth of Christ.

Ezekiel 33

Our Father, we know that we have a special responsibility to those all around us. Particularly our ministers of the Word have an important job as watchmen. They have heard the Word from Your mouth. They must warn the wicked to turn from their evil ways. You have no pleasure in the death of the wicked. There is hope for any man today in Christ. We do not trust in our righteousness. Day by day we turn away from the path of sin and flee to Your Son again for life. You are just in Your punishment of the wicked. You have also satisfied the demands of Your justice even in Your mercy for Your people. Was there anything lacking in the cross of Christ? Have not the demands of Your justice for us been fully satisfied in His atoning death? There is evil all around us. There is yet evil in us and among us. Grant to us a Word from heaven through Your servants. Teach us to hear You and to live.

Ezekiel 34

Lord of the Harvest, You sent Jesus Christ to be both Son of Man and Son of God. He is the Good Shepherd of the sheep. False teachers and greedy men have scattered Your sheep. They are imposters. They have fed themselves and not the sheep. Your Son has come as the Shepherd of Your flock. He is gathering many through His Word. His sheep hear His voice and they know Him and they follow Him. He is the One who seeks the lost. He brings back the wandering ones. Those who came before did not really care for the sheep. They have created many troubles for Your people. Send Your servant, the Son of David, to be our Prince forever. Send down showers of blessing upon us, and provide everything that we need that we may live, Take away the reproach of Your people, and keep us as Your sheep forever.

Ezekiel 35

Our Father, Your love for Your people is a special love. You make a distinction between Jacob and Esau. You will defend Your people. If Esau rejoices over the trials of Your beloved Jacob, it will not go well for Esau. There can be no peace for those who determine to persecute Your church. You will come in power at just the right time. Even when we feel desolate and abandoned, You will rescue us forever. Teach us Your Way. Show us how to trust in You every day.

Ezekiel 36

Glorious Lord, Your Word is perfect. As we wait for the great blessings you have promised, we should hear Your voice with reverence and joy. Grant especially that all of Your ministers would not only hear Your Word, but also that they would rightly preach it and obey it. Grant that Your church will be doers of the Word rather than imitators of the world. Help us to follow in Your ways, and bless Your church in the days to come. We have defiled Your church with our disobedience, and You have disciplined us in love. Will we ever change? In Your concern for Your holy Name, fill us with Your Spirit so that we will turn away from sin. Cause us to believe in Your power and Your love. Grant to us a new heart and a new Spirit. Why should we not do the things that Christ has commanded? We will follow You by the strength of Your Spirit. Bring us growth in holiness and every good and appropriate prosperity by Your grace.

Ezekiel 37

Great Lord and King, You have displayed to us the reality of the resurrection to come in the vision of prophets, in the words of the Scriptures, and especially in the firstfruits of that resurrection in Jesus Christ our Lord. Only You could create the world. Only You could bring spiritual life to souls that were dead in sin. Only You can bring physical resurrection to bodies that have been resting in the graves for centuries. Only You can bring immortal souls together again with resurrection bodies. This You have promised to do, and this You will do. In that day there will be one people of God. This community of redemption will be gathered together in Jesus Christ. We shall rejoice in Him in the new Jerusalem. We thank You for this best of all promises. Your Son will be King over us. We will be imitators of You in that place. We will be participants in an everlasting covenant of peace. You sanctify Your people. Your sanctuary will be in our midst forevermore.

Ezekiel 38

O God of Glory, what will become of this present world in the Day of Your Son's return? There is no hope in the strength of men. When You go out against those who have persecuted Your people, they will not be able to stand. All the evil schemes of powerful people will come to nothing. We will be so perfectly secure in Your Son in that Day! No one will be able to answer You when You bring Your just judgments upon the world. You will vindicate Your holiness before the eyes of all men. Though many presume that Your Son will never come in judgment, You have promised His return, and have spoken clearly about the sword that is coming against the world. In His first coming, Your Son did not come to judge the world, but to save it. One day He will return again to judge both the living and the dead.

Ezekiel 39

Lord of Hosts, what will the strong nations of the world do when You come against them with Your almighty power? No assault against Your holy mountain will ever be successful. Your Name will be exalted there forever. We long for that place and that time when it will be so clear that You are our All in all. The coming judgment of the earth will be a frightening and devastating thing. Who can understand it? Who can really feel it and know it? We are thankful that we know only small tastes of this coming horror. We are grateful that we will never really experience that eternal curse. Though we have dealt treacherously with You and Your people to our shame, Your Son has taken the full weight of Your wrath against us for our sin. You will vindicate Your holiness in bringing great blessing upon us, for on the cross Your Son has already faced the judgment that was against us.

Ezekiel 40

O Lord God, bring us to Your resurrection temple. Grant that we will be able to walk all around its courts. Bring us into the company of angels and holy men. What a great blessing to be in Your house! Let us see the gates of Your wonderful land. Cause us to walk through all the great rooms, and to see the wonder of everything in Your holy place. What must it be like to be in a place of such wonder, that the finest joys of earth would seem like nothing compared to the glory of even the pavement for the feet of men and angels? We long to walk on the steps in that place. We want to see it from every direction, and to explore it all from every vantage point. How we praise You, O Lord! What a joy it will be to be in the place won for us through the blood and righteousness of Christ. We think of the pain of Your Son as He longed to return to such a great place of glory. He faced the faithlessness of men here below everywhere He went. Everything here had the imprint of sin and misery on it. Yet He came and gave His life as the perfect whole burnt offering. There was nothing missing in the fullness of His life. He obeyed You perfectly with such an unusual combination of holiness and modesty. In His death He became the perfect sin offering for us. He is our great High Priest forever. Now He lives forever in the holy place above. We are overcome by the glory of this thought: We will be with Him one day, and we will see Him as He is!

Ezekiel 41

Father God, we want to worship You forever and ever. How can we dwell with You? We will have to be changed in our deepest nature. All sin will be utterly removed from us. We will be in the Holy Place in Your great habitation. Yes, we will be even in the Most Holy Place. We will see the wonderful dimensions of it. All the sins of our old hearts that distract us now in public worship and private devotion will be completely removed from us. All the clamor of human weakness and sin will be far from that place of glory. Let us walk around Your temple above, like Your prophet of old. He had such an experience, walking through the most excellent creation with an angelic guide. There we would see things that we have never seen before. How would we ever describe it? Yet, we want something even more than the prophet experienced during His visit. We want to be there with all the inhabitants of Your temple forever. We want to experience that glory without any concern that our joy will ever be taken away. Grant this, together with the forgiveness of our sins.

Ezekiel 42

O God in Heaven, when we are brought to Your temple above, where will we will live, and how will we serve You there? We know that we will be as priests forever. Even now we are among the priesthood of all who believe. What will it be like for us to be in the secure company of holy men and angels forever? In Your house above there are many mansions. Each chamber in Your temple must be like a mansion in its holiness and glory. We look forward to the provision of holy garments for our life above. Even now we have been clothed with the garments of the perfect righteousness of Jesus Christ. How could there be any better clothing for us? Yet our perfect garments above will be visible. What a glorious thought!

Ezekiel 43

Glorious God, fill Your church with Your glory. Here below we have a taste of Your greatness. We are hungry for more of Your glory. We long to be in that place where You will dwell with Your people forever. No longer will our defiling sin give us trouble. All of our evil will be utterly put away. This is what we long for. We are ashamed of our horrible iniquities. Even before the return of Your Son, when our bodies rest in the grave, even then our sin will be utterly removed from our eternal souls. Grant that our perfected spirits will one day be brought to dwell in our resurrected bodies forever. May we enjoy Your temple forever in that day with purified spirits in resurrection splendor. May we walk all around it, and contemplate the glory of it in all of its greatness. Thank You for the blood of Your Son, by which we have been granted such a glorious expectation. Surely our sin has been atoned for. Send Your Son to us. Fill the temple of Your living church even now, as we wait for the fulfillment of Your most excellent promises. We are acceptable in the Beloved. What a wonderful hope we have!

Ezekiel 44

Great Lord, You are the God of Heaven and Earth. Your Son has entered into the heavenly sanctuary. He has made an entrance into Your temple for us in Him. We repent of all known sin. We want to be numbered among the Israel that is above. We receive You with joy today, and turn away from every foolish desire, thought, saying, action, and inclination. We draw near to You now through Jesus Christ. We want to minister to You one day in Your holy sanctuary. Father, we understand that You are preparing us for that day even now. How are You using the troubles of Your church to prepare us for the life to come? We are assured that our labor in Your Son is not in vain. What glory is coming for Your martyrs, and for those who have given up everything in order to serve You here below? Forgive us when we have made foolish choice after foolish choice. We have missed the opportunity to suffer for You and to serve You. Don't we understand anything about the glory of the life to come? How else could we make such worldly decisions day by day, as if the current age were everything and the life to come was nothing? But with You there is abundant forgiveness.

Ezekiel 45

Lord God, we long for Immanuel's land. You have a place for us there. Your Son went ahead to prepare that place for us. How extensive is Your great land! There is a room there for Your beloved children. The priesthood of all believers is laboring here below by Your grace. Today we face oppression, even from those who should be godly leaders in our midst. Here people lie to us and cheat us. Here we worry about the danger that our money will run out. We spend our resources in foolish ways, with little sense of our purpose in life. We long for Your courts above. We will thank You forever for our perfect atonement in the sacrifice of Jesus Christ. There we will not be plagued by evil people around us or from the remaining sin within and among us. We wait, O Lord, and we love You and one another in the strength of our eternal hope.

Ezekiel 46

God of Grace, we long for the fullness of Sabbath rest that has been won for us through the work of Jesus Christ. His offering of Himself for us will be a testimony in Your Kingdom forever. We thank You for this great Prince, the Captain of our salvation. Will we actually be able to see Him in the temple above? We know that we will, for You have assured us that we will see Him as He is. We will fall before Him with the great joy of heavenly worship. O Father, we do not understand the things of heaven as we ought to. We do know that we are the property of Your Son. We are a part of Your glorious inheritance in the saints. We strain to understand the pictures of heaven presented to us in Your Scriptures. We so easily misinterpret Your Word. We humbly beseech You, take us, one day, to be with You, so that we can see You.

Ezekiel 47

Our God, we want to see the water coming forth from Your heavenly temple. We want to put our hands in it, walk in it, and swim in it. We need the life from this river even now. That water brings fresh new life everywhere it goes. Bring the Word of life everywhere, so that the dead may be brought to life again in Your Son. Lord show us the way of the greatest spiritual health even now, that we may walk in it. Where is our place in Your great land? Surely there is a place for all those who rest in Your Son. Will we want to explore the whole length and breadth of Your land for all eternity, or will we stay as near to You as we can be? We were foreigners to the covenant of grace, but now we have been brought near to You through the blood of the Lamb. Where will we live in glory? We know we will be in Christ, and that our joy will be full.

Ezekiel 48

Father, we are coming to You in just a little while. We are not coming to visit, but to stay. One day Your Son will take us with Him again as He comes back to usher in the new age to come in all of its fullness. Then all those who are His in this world that is fading away will be changed and we will be together with Your Son forever. Teach us to be faithful to You even now. It is appointed for us to live once, and then to face judgment. You will carry us safely through that coming judgment. Christ has died for our sins. We long for the new holy work that You have prepared for us. There will be no evil in that work, but much holy joy. Here we feel so out of place. We are not at home. We long for the revelation of this new land. It is our inheritance. We have a portion in it. O grant that we would enter that city through the gate appointed for us at just the right time. We want to live in the city with that glorious name. The name of that city is "The Lord is there."

Daniel

Daniel 1

Glorious and Sovereign Lord, make Your plans for Your people shine forth in brightest colors in our darkest days. When our prospects appear very bleak, You remain a bountiful Provider of every good gift. You can still care for Your children though they are strangers in a strange land. We are strengthened by Your Word and refreshed by Your Spirit. When it would appear that we would fade away in a time of trouble, You are able to do amazing things. You can give Your servants health, wisdom, learning, grace, diligence, and many other blessings. When we lack everything else, there is no greater gift than Your presence among us. Be with us day by day, and bless Your church in wonderful ways as we live in the midst of this fading world. Glorify Your Name through the provision of help that could only have come from You.

Daniel 2

Father God, You are sovereign over both our waking and sleeping. You are aware of every detail of history and have a full understanding of all that is yet to come. This is not merely a knowledge of the future, for You have decreed all things that will come to pass. You are God, and there is no other. In various times and places You have chosen to reveal a small portion of Your great knowledge to Your servants the prophets. You gave them revelations in visions, events, and in words. You blessed them with a greater knowledge of who You are, and revealed deep and hidden things about the past, present, and future according to Your holy will. You never said more then You intended. You never spoke incorrectly. Your Word is perfect. You can make a slave the most important man in a mighty empire when You choose to reveal mysteries through a humble son of Adam. The truth that You speak through Your servants is various but it is also entirely unified. It tells us that You ordain the rising and falling of kings and kingdoms. Beyond all of the powers of men, and all of their authority, You have brought about the coming of the kingdom of Your Son. This kingdom shall never end. You inaugurated this new kingdom during the time of a very impressive empire among men. That empire is now long gone, but Your kingdom continues to this day. It is on the offensive through numerous struggles, and even the gates of hell shall not prevail against it. You are a Revealer of mysteries, now wonderfully contained in written revelation. Your Scripture is a living Word that daily brings the breath of life to Your people in Your church.

Daniel 3

Great God and King, the rulers of this world are so easily carried away with their grandeur. We do not face their exact temptations, and we pray for them that You will grant them a new humility through recognition of Your greatness and glory. We will not worship the rulers of this world. We will submit to lawful authority, and we will attempt to serve You by living in an orderly way, but we will only worship You. Neither will we serve false gods, though we may face the persecution of powerful men. Surely You will either deliver us from that persecution, or will deliver us through death into Your glorious presence. In all the difficulties that we may face, we trust that the Son of God is with us, according to His solemn promise. The fire of men is nothing compared to the eternal fire that Your enemies will face. Forgive us for our sins against You, O God. There is no other God who is able to rescue us, for Yours is the kingdom, and the power, and the glory forever.

Daniel 4

O Father, You reveal the truth to people according to Your great plan. You have shown amazing signs and wonders, and You have humbled the hearts of the proudest men. Your prophets have spoken to us a Word from You. We have heard things that we never could have known. Many of these things have touched on important matters that have changed our lives. We have learned that You have created the heavens and the earth. We have been told that even a sparrow does not fall to the ground unless You have decreed this. We have heard the message of our abundant redemption through Jesus Christ. We have found the way to every spiritual blessing through Your Son. You have spoken to us sure words about our eternal security. There is a King who is far above all the rulers of this world, and we have heard of Him and have eagerly received Him. There is a way for us to worship You through this great King. We know that our sins are forgiven. We have learned that heaven rules. We have been shown the way of righteousness. All of this is a great help to us in our lives. We are so thankful for Your servants who have brought us the Word of truth. Through this wonderful blessing of a godly message, we have been kept from great foolishness and pride. You have rescued us from all kinds of dangerous thinking and behavior. May we use all that we are and all that we have for Your purposes. May we extol You forever, for You are able to bring low all those who walk in pride, and to lift up all those who walk humbly with You.

Daniel 5

O God, we have a better King than even the best rulers of the earth. Not every ruler on earth is one of the best among men. Some are exceedingly wicked, foolish, and oppressive. They come for a season and then they are gone. The time comes when they discover that their days are numbered. They learn that they have been found wanting, and their authority is taken from them. Father, how are we to submit to wicked kings? We know that we must worship You only. We cannot do those things that would be against Your commandments just to have peace with those who are powerful. We cannot avoid duties to You just to have safety among those who would demand our absolute devotion. Though these leaders may have the power to kill, they cannot cast us into hell. We will not fear them above You. Father, help us to be faithful stewards of any authority we have been granted during our brief lives. May we use what You have given us to honor You, for we know that we may be called to account for our lives even this very day.

Daniel 6

Father God, You place Your servants in all kinds of strategic positions in surprising places. May we be faithful in our time. In every opportunity for obedience, surely we should expect that opposition may arise. Keep us turning to You in prayer. May we be moved by what You want more than anything else in our lives. You are able to deliver us even from the dens of lions. You know our enemies, seen and unseen. You surely can send Your angel to shut the mouths of many lions. Pick us up out of dangerous snares of trial and temptation at just the right time. There is no other God like You. Why would we fear men and ignore You? Your kingdom shall never be destroyed. Your dominion is from everlasting to everlasting. Grant us success and joy in Your service now and forever.

Daniel 7

Lord God, a day is coming that will signal the end of this current age and the beginning of the age to come. On that day Your Son will come on clouds of glory. Until then we will bring the message of Jesus Christ everywhere as You open doors for the gospel and give Your servants both desire and strength for the task ahead. Thank You for the great gift of Your Son. His Kingdom shall never be destroyed. We enjoy many blessings of the age to come even now, but we long for the revealing of the fullness of Your Son's dominion. You have spoken to Your prophets about great things concerning men and nations. You also revealed to them good news about the coming of Your Son. He first came in humble service, but He shall return in judgment and glory. We believe Your Word, and we long for the appearing of Jesus Christ. Save us, O God!

Daniel 8

God of Glory, You have given us hope in the midst of challenging days that so many face in this current evil age. We are often quite perplexed. We do not know how to interpret the events all around us. You surely are the sovereign Lord over all things. One great land reaches the end of its time. In its place comes a mighty empire that will exist for Your purposes. You rule over men and angels. You could lay out for us the future of all things from the current moment until the return of Your Son. Nonetheless it is not Your will that we should know all the details of Your future acts of providence. Such knowledge would be too much for us. Help us to rise up from our beds each morning and to be about the business of our great King Jesus Christ. We will do well to serve Him always, and to wait for His return with joy and expectation.

Daniel 9

Lord God, hear us when we cry out to You. You know the facts about our sin. You are perfectly righteous, but Your church has committed treachery against You. You have mercy and forgiveness which we need so desperately, for we have sinned against both Your Law and Your grace. We have sinned against Your Law because we have ignored Your commandments. We have sinned against Your grace. We have been given so much and have responded as if Your gifts to us were small. Please incline Your ear to us again and see that Your church is in great need. Please hear us and forgive us. Do this for Your own glory, for we are Your people for whom Your Son shed His precious blood. We know that we are greatly loved by You. We have been granted a holy union with Your Son, who is the King and Head of Your church. Grant to us Your salvation now, and sanctify Your church.

Daniel 10

Father God, there are troubling things all around us that we do not understand. Our comfort is that You not only understand all things, but You also have planned all things, and know where all things are heading. We are able to stand only because You are in charge. The earthly days of the Old Testament prophets are long gone. They now live above where Your Son is at Your right hand. They once longed to understand the visions and messages that had come to them. Now they see Your Son and live with Your people who have been perfected in holiness. We thank You for the coming of Jesus Christ, and the pouring out of the Holy Spirit. We have been granted increased clarity about Your eternal plan through these great events. Yet there is so much that we do not know, and so much that we do not comprehend. Your prophets of old trusted You when they spoke of great things little by little and in various ways. Help us to keep our eyes focused upon Your Son who has spoken so wonderfully to us in His life, death, and resurrection. Help us to trust You with our lives even when we do not understand.

Daniel 11

Sovereign Lord, You are the Lord of men and angels. You rule over our families and churches. You send us help from on high to confirm and strengthen us. You also correct us when we wander from Your way. Nations rise and fall according to Your plan, but Your church shall move forward in the strength of our Messiah King. He will have a great victory against all false gods and hypocrisy. You will bring low the pride of men. You will use all of the resources in Your hands in order to accomplish Your purposes. Even with all the strength of men in their arsenals, no armies among men can stand against You. You have sent forth Your gospel to every land near and far, and Your Word is winning a great victory as Your Spirit works powerfully over the centuries. Throughout this age there is much suffering alongside the great victories of faith. Men make their plans for grandeur, but they shall not stand. Armies are swept away, and even the strongest men face the end of their days. For centuries men and nations have set themselves against Your covenant people. They would insult Your Name, and destroy Your people, but You give help to Your beloved children. Though we stumble, You have a plan for the coming age that will certainly be accomplished. You will magnify Your own Name, and You will easily defeat the proudest foes. No enemy that expects to destroy You, Your gospel, or Your people will be able to see the fullness of their evil desires accomplished. They shall all come to their end, and there will be none to help them. You are the everlasting God, and You will be praised forever and ever.

Daniel 12

Lord God Almighty, carry Your people through the great tribulation that will come against the earth. Help us in the day of rebellion and apostasy. Guard us from the wrath of the most powerful adversaries. We do not know the day or the hour of the times that are coming. We do know You. We know Your Son. We know that He will surely have a great victory and vindication when He returns. Every knee shall bow and every tongue will confess that Jesus Christ is Lord, to the glory of Your Holy Name.

Hosea

Hosea 1

Father God, Your Son is far above all other husbands. You have had such mercy upon us. We sinned against You with our horrible immorality and idolatry. What hope would we have if You determined to have no more mercy upon us? Thank You for taking us as Your people. We were once far off, but now we are called the children of the living God in our association with Christ our King.

Hosea 2

Lord God, there is hope now for all of our brothers and sisters in Christ. We should put away our foolish sinning, for we have been redeemed by Your Son. When we look back upon our lives of sin, we hate our rebellion against You. You continued to provide for us day by day, and yet we used Your good gifts for more and more sinning. Our false lovers were no good for us at all. How could we have ever thought that idols would be the answer for us? Turn us back home again moment by moment. Keep us far away from the love of sinning. Open up our hearts to the great hope that is ours in Christ the Lord. Make us lie down in safety again. We receive Your steadfast love for us with amazement. Our glorious God, Your grace is great, and Your mercy is very powerful.

Hosea 3

Our Father, You have given us new hope in Christ. Your faithfulness is great. You found us on the rubbish heap of the rebellious and You redeemed us with an extravagant love. We must never turn away from You. We will seek the glory of Your Son forever.

Hosea 4

Lord Almighty, what will You do with Your church when we go the way of the murderous and faithless? Surely You will not allow us to stand in Your presence when we give ourselves to continual foolishness and sin. We were to be a glorious and royal priesthood. How can we be loved by You when we treat a piece of wood as an object of worship? How can we live if we are full of immorality? Oh the burden of our sin! Surely there is a better end for us. We will not be stubborn forever. Surely there is a remnant that will be ashamed of their sin, and will be kept according to Your abundant mercy.

Hosea 5

Glorious God, there is a day of wrath coming, and a day of division in the church. There will be a separation of the sheep and the goats. Our pride will do us no good. In that day we may seem to seek You, but many will not be acknowledged by You as Your children. Are we all lost? How can we stand Your wrath? We have been determined in our pursuit of filth. Our real hope is not in the power of men and governments. Our hope is in You, and our deliverance comes through Christ alone.

Hosea 6

Father, teach us the difference between mere words and true repentance. We want to return to You and know You. Meet us now with the Bread from heaven. He is our sure and holy Redeemer. Our love to You has been temporary and conditional, and so we have transgressed Your Law. Teach us the way of steadfast love and patient endurance. Show us how to turn away from all sin, and restore the fortunes of Your people.

Hosea 7

Great Savior, what will we do if You remember our evil forever? Surely You have accomplished our redemption through the work of Your Son Jesus. Everything about Him is holy and good. He never wandered from You. He never looked to the world for His hope. He never rebelled against You, or spoke lies to You. He has received Your Word with the fullness of joy and with happy obedience. Your Son's perfect righteousness has been credited to our account. What a gift to the ungodly!

Hosea 8

God of Glory, we have a sure hope in Christ. Though we have often spurned Your good gifts, He has not rejected us. Though we have foolishly turned our hearts to the making of idols, He has taught us the difference between a true Savior and objects that are not gods. We should live in Him always. We should listen to Him fully. The way of the world will not solve our problems. If we follow that path we will only multiply our troubles. You are the only answer for Your people. Please forgive us.

Hosea 9

Lord God, we rejoice in You, and we hate our sin. Why should we return to the way of evil? There was nothing good there for us. That way is a place for those who seek to be defiled. That way is the way of slavery. There is only one road for us. We have one great Prophet, and He leads us in the path of righteousness. We were found by You when we were dead in our trespasses and sins. We do not want to return to our days of sin and disaster again. Please protect us from dangerous choices and unhealthy inclinations. Our wickedness would only lead us into fruitless patterns of death. Please do not reject us. Bring us near to You day by day, and never let us go.

Hosea 10

God of Grace, You have brought us through many challenging times. We have faced trials from enemies, and great troubles from our own false words and filthy actions. We repent, O Lord God. We do not want to go back to the place of our ugly sin. We want to move forward toward the land of Your great promises. You have spared us from the punishment that we deserved. We have plowed iniquity, and would have reaped only sorrow. Yet Your Son has taken upon Himself the trouble that we deserved. He was cut off from the land of the living for us and by His life and death we are fully restored. We thank You for Your abundant mercy. We receive this Word of reconciliation with joy because of our risen Messiah.

Hosea 11

Father God, You rescued Your children out of Egypt. You have been patient with us, though we have often rebelled against You. Thank You for Your gift of Your only-begotten Son. He too was called out of Egypt as a very young child, but He never disobeyed Your commandments. He walked with You in perfect faithfulness. In Him, we have been granted the benefits of covenant love.

Hosea 12

Lord of Hosts, how could Your people have ever have thought that it was wise to treat powerful nations as trusted fathers? How could it have ever seemed wise to forsake You, the only true God and Father of Your people? Yet we have loved sin. The nations care little about our iniquity, but You are holy. You have spoken through the prophets. You have made it clear to Your loved ones that we must live according to Your Word. Rescue us not only from our enemies, but also from our rebellious sin nature and from our disgraceful deeds.

Hosea 13

Great God, we have a new hope in Your Son Jesus Christ. Idols cannot help us, and we will not trust in them. You are the Savior who brought us through the wilderness. Your Son is the Lion of the tribe of Judah. He will save us. He will not devour Your elect. We confess that we have been unwise sons and daughters. Yet through the resurrection of our great Atoning Sacrifice, the sting of death has been removed far from us. We have a Redeemer in Jesus Christ, and He will never forsake us.

Hosea 14

Father God, we return to You with sincere sadness for our sin, but abundant joy because of Your greatness. We think of Your mercy to the orphan, and we love You. You will make Your children beautiful. We will flourish under Your protective love. Your love and greatness are eternal. Your ways are right, and we will walk in them forever. Please pick us up when we stumble, and rescue us when the battle of this age is more than we can bear.

Joel

Joel 1

Lord God, when You sound the alarm to Your people through Your ambassadors will we listen? Will we give attention to Your word of warning? When You call us home for Your fatherly care and discipline, will we humble ourselves and return to You? Thank You for Your Word. We should wail over our sin. We should mourn because of the trouble that we face in our life and mission. We should gather together in a solemn assembly and call upon Your Name. Hear us, O Lord, when we cry out to You.

Joel 2

Father, help us to get the point of personal and societal disaster. Is not the Day of Your Judgment coming upon the whole earth in due time? Will we be ready for that Day? Locusts destroy the produce of the land. Invading armies take Your people captive and destroy life as we know it. Yet even in difficult days of trouble, the call goes out to Your people. We can repent today. We can return to You. We can gather together in solemn assembly. Spare Your people! Hear us, O Lord, and be jealous for Your children, for You love us. You can remove invading armies in a moment. You can give health to the land again, and restore what the locust has consumed. You can bring about a day of blessing that is beyond anything that we ask for or imagine. You are the Lord God. The Day is surely coming when we will all be full of the spirit like the prophets of old. On that same Day there will be frightening signs of Your judgment in the heavens and upon the earth. Yet all who call upon Your name shall be saved. We call upon Your Name now, O Lord, for You have provided Your perfect Son, through whom we have bold access to Your heavenly sanctuary. You have called us to Yourself. You will bless us forever.

Joel 3

Glorious God, a great age is coming. When Your Son returns to judge, He will surely save us from this evil day. You will bring judgment upon men. You will purify Your church, and You will reveal all of the sons of God. You will judge all the nations. We wait for You, O Lord. We turn to You now, trusting You for today, and believing Your Word for tomorrow. You are the Lord, our God. You shall make Your new Jerusalem perfectly holy, and You will bless us forever and ever. We will eat and drink with perfect peace and joy. Even now You are with Your people, and You will dwell with us forever.

Amos

Amos 1

Lord of Hosts, in the midst of this world of trial and woe, You roar through Your prophets. You had a word for the nations of old like Syria and the Philistines. You hated their oppression and anger. Men have always looked for opportunities to have some selfish benefit at the cost of the weak. Ancient peoples like the Edomites and the Ammonites have been soundly condemned for their brutality and greed. Will we be imitators of them, rather than imitators of Your Son? Rescue us from base impulses that would harm us and others, for we are Your people. We have been set apart from the world for a better purpose than the abuse of the helpless.

Amos 2

Lord God, there is a hatred of man against man that goes beyond the customary depravity of the sons of Adam. How long will You allow a nation to stand when it is so wickedly vicious, abusing the living and desecrating the remains of the dead? Surely Your people should be far from such a habit of vigorous evil. Yet we have so often ignored Your Word, and have become imitators of the world. Our lies have led us astray into sinful pattern of life. Will we sell the righteous for silver, engage in gross immorality, and participate in idolatrous worship? You have done so much for us, delivering us out of the slavery of sin, and allowing us to taste of the good things of the age to come. Will we return to the old way of bondage again? May it never be so! We should not presume to fight against You. We will surely lose that battle. Have mercy on us, O God, and call us back home again.

Amos 3

Father, You have a special plan for Your people, therefore You chastise us for our iniquities. You call us Your family. We thank You for Your discipline. Only preserve our lives for Your service, first here, and then above with those who have already gone to be with Your Son. Surely You have reason to correct us. We should listen carefully to You. Though the world would witness our embarrassing correction, You will speak to us as a true Father. Even if only a small remnant survives, not one of Your elect shall be lost. All of our pomp and wealth will perish, but Your people shall live forever.

Amos 4

Glorious Lord, where is the righteous woman who gives herself completely to Your service? Are all given over to base pleasures and lazy living? Thank you for the godly examples that You have given to us. Thank You also for Your correction of us even through suffering. How could we be so insensitive to Your acts of correction? We are very slow to return to You. Will it be necessary for You to remove the lampstand of Your church in many places? You are the Lord of Hosts. You know what is right and good, and You will accomplish Your glorious plan. Save us, O God!

Amos 5

Father God, there is so much sin all around us, and even among us and within us. Why do we seek after idols? Why will we not run to You, O Lord? You put the stars up in the heavens and formed the constellations. You bring water upon the earth, and floods upon the lands according to Your decree. Will we turn aside the needy when they come to us for help? Will we pursue injustice as our fathers did in former days? Do we not recognize that there will be consequences for the iniquity within us? We can only see the Day of the Lord as a day of joy because of what Christ has done for us. Send forth His righteousness among us like a mighty stream, that we might pursue the way of holiness with integrity.

Amos 6

Our Father, we care about Your church. We will not be at ease in the face of so much iniquity in Zion. We look for the pleasures of the life to come, and give up on the pride of our hearts and the passing pleasures of sin among Your people.

Grant to us a due regard for the seriousness of disobedience within Your covenant community. Please forgive us, for we have not loved justice and holiness as we should.

Amos 7

Sovereign Lord, You have displayed to us the serious consequences of the rebellion of men. Even within Your church we could never stand the discipline that we rightly deserve as a consequence of our sin. Set Your Son as a plumb line among Your people. He is the standard of all righteousness. Help us to regard Him in all His holy beauty, and to consider the glory of His work as our Substitute. This one great King has given His life for us, and Yet He lives. He has brought the Word of truth to us. He was a most unexpected prophet. Yet His words were the fullest expression of truth ever known among men. Shall we ignore Him, and die as if we were strangers to the covenant of grace? Have mercy, O Lord.

Amos 8

Glorious God, the world all around us is moving forward toward destruction day by day. There is a Day of Judgment coming. Men treat their companions and neighbors as objects with no real dignity. They will surely face Your discipline and wrath. Will we presume upon Your mercy and do the very same things as Your enemies? Father, look upon our weakness and speak to us with clarity and power. Please do not remove Your Word from among us. Make us a people of love and service. Use us as a testimony to all around us, for You love Your people. Rescue us from every peril.

Amos 9

Lord God, there will finally come a Day of Judgment. Just as the Old Covenant eventually came to an end, the current age will one day be completed. No man shall be able to escape from You. Our only hope in that Day will be the great Son of David, the Lord Jesus Christ. Because He lives, You will not make a full end of Your people. Through the resurrection of Christ You have raised up the booth of David. Even the nations who were far off have now come to You through this Messiah. A great day is yet coming for all the Jews and Gentiles who are called by Your name. Peace and prosperity shall be ours forever in You.

Obadiah

Lord Almighty, King of the Nations, the pride of the most amazing men will not win for them any eternal security. Though we may belong to a wonderful nation in the opinion of our own countrymen, though we may have many wise and mighty men in our number, though other nations may respect or fear us, You are able to bring us down in a moment. You can destroy the descendants of Esau so fully that no sign of life would remain. You can surely destroy us very quickly. If this is the destiny of the people of Jacob's brother, why would we think that we should fare any better? What is the case that we would make before You? Esau gloated over Jerusalem in the day of her misfortune. Have our nations loved You and served You? There can never be a secure hope for us in any of the nations of this world.

There is much trouble and sin in every corner of creation. Your Day of Judgment is near upon all the nations, and there is only one place of safety. That place of deliverance is called the city of God, and in it are all those who belong to You. We are Your possession, and we shall inherit the earth. The Kingdom is Yours, O Lord, and we are Your happy subjects. Our safety is in Christ alone.

Jonah

Jonah 1

Father God, You surely love Your people, and You use us as messengers of that great love. Can we refuse You? Are we free to abandon Your calling upon Your servants? Will we be like Jonah, determining by our own counsel that it is wise to run from You? Such a man brings much trouble upon himself and others. It will do us no good to flee from Your presence in the day of chastisement. Surely if we decide to fight against Your purposes, You will win. We bow before You, for You have appointed a Savior for our rescue in Christ the Lord. Who are we to reject Your call to speak for Your kingdom?

Jonah 2

Blessed Lord, Your Son called out to You from the belly of Sheol, and You heard His cry. He trusted You fully. Though He died for our sins, You brought up His life from the pit, for He had authority to lay down His life, and authority to pick it back up again. He has vowed to give to You the fullness of Your Kingdom of grace. What He has vowed, He will surely pay.

Jonah 3

Lord of Glory, grant us courage to move forward in mission in the most frightening places. Will we have the boldness to cry out, "Yet forty days and Nineveh will be destroyed?" If we will not speak, we will miss the joy of true repentance in the darkest corners of creation. Angels are ready to rejoice. Teach Your church to call all men everywhere to repent. Perhaps You have granted life to many. Perhaps they will repent like the king and his subjects in Nineveh in the days of Jonah. You have commanded. We must follow Your call upon our lives.

Jonah 4

Great God of Israel, You have a plan for the nations of the world. You are a God of grace. Will we hate mercy? We do not do well to be angry about Your kindness. Your Son is our shade and our protection. The scorching heat of Your judgment is coming upon the nations of the world. Make us to pity the people who live in darkness, for there are so many children that are facing judgment with no knowledge of Your Word. Send us forward in Your service, O Lord, that the nations may know that You are God.

Micah

Micah 1

Father God, thank You for Your true Word through Your holy prophets. You are against all wickedness. We will never be able to stand if You come against us for our sins and transgressions. The problem of our unrighteousness was something that we needed to learn. How could we have understood the work of our Savior, if we did not see the reality of our mortal wound? You gave Your people the Law, and through that system we began to see the punishment that we deserved. Bring us the Glory of Israel even today, not in wrath or discipline, but for the gathering of the elect, for Your Son has accomplished our redemption.

Micah 2

Great God and King, we turn away from our private schemes of wickedness. We cannot fool You. The lesson of Your ancient people should be powerfully obvious to us. There is no wisdom in turning away from Your truth. We must not resist Your true Word, as Your people did so long ago. Even their shepherds knew only license. They did not follow in the way of godliness. They destroyed whole families and pursued horrible uncleanness. Come soon, Lord God! Save us from all iniquity!

Micah 3

Lord God, You have granted leaders in Your church to be shepherds over Your people. What shall we do if those servants only serve themselves, and destroy the people they should be helping? Father, we thank You for the provision of the greatest and best Shepherd, the Lord Jesus Christ. His heart is always fully seeking our good, and His strength will accomplish His purposes. Even now He is ascended on high and He grants pastors and teachers as gifts to Your people. Restrain the wickedness of men, O God. Thank You for the provision of godly men who will lead Your people in a day of trouble.

Micah 4

Our Father, bring us up to Your holy mountain. Bring many nations there through the work of Your Son. Speak to us from Your heavenly Zion. Bring us eternal peace. We long for the fulfillment of Your great promises. We will walk in Your Name forever and ever. Bring the weak and the lame into Your house, O God. We cry out to You for help! We long for Your rescue. Though the nations will one day assemble against Your church, Your Son will deliver us from every trouble.

Micah 5

Father, You have sent us a great Savior to be our holy Ruler. Your eternal Son was born in Bethlehem, according to Your Word. He is now the Shepherd over Your people. We are being gathered from many nations. You have helped us in the midst of our adversaries. You have brought us into a safe place, for You have cut off from among us all our idolatries. Your Son will come again to execute vengeance upon the people that will not obey You. Our only refuge is in His perfect righteousness, for He is our Substitute.

Micah 6

Lord God Almighty, You had an indictment against Your people under the Old Covenant. You provided them with many blessings and with great saving acts.

What did You require of Israel? They should have done justice, loved kindness, and walked humbly with You. These are the weightier matters of the Law. How have we fared by the same holy requirements? O how we need Your grace! We who have been saved through the righteousness of Your Son are not required to do less then those who came before us. We have been given much. Much is required of us. Your Son has covered our sins. Please forgive us, and fill us with Your Spirit, so that we will walk in love according to Your commandments.

Micah 7

Glorious Lord, have mercy on Your church. We feel so small in times of trouble. The evil of the world around us seems to enter quickly into the life of Your assembly. Our families face unusual iniquity, and our watchmen become easily corrupted. Grant us wisdom and courage in the day of difficulty. You will be our help. We look to Your holy Son Jesus, and we turn away from the sinful pattern of the world all around us. Gather Your elect, O Lord God. Fill us with joy even in the time of testing. Provide for us what we need for our lives by Your marvelous and mighty hand. There is no other god like You. You delight in steadfast love. You have tread our iniquities underfoot through the cross of Christ. In Him there is hope for all Your chosen people.

Nahum

Nahum 1

Lord God Almighty, the day of Your Judgment will come upon Your enemies. You are slow to anger, but when You come in vengeance, who can stand? When Your wrath is poured out like fire, You will make an end to Your adversaries. You love those who take refuge in You. This is our greatest desire, to rejoice evermore in Your protective love. We do not want to stand before You in our own righteousness, for we could not last for a moment. Bring us good news of the perfect righteousness of Your Son. Publish the news of Your peace to Your people throughout the world. Keep every invading foe far away from us, that Your kingdom may be utterly secure.

Nahum 2

Father God, if men and nations had their way with Your church we would have been overcome long ago. Violent men want to kill and destroy the weak. They would carry away people and possessions as though they were in the right. What will happen to the world in the day of Your justice? You know the desires of every heart and the actions of every life. Powerful men and empires have set up for themselves decades of privilege, but there is a day of reckoning coming for every man. Even the strongest nations that once seemed perfectly secure can be swept aside in a moment. Keep us in Your kingdom, for in You alone we have safety.

Nahum 3

Glorious God, the age of violence will soon be over. We do not know the day or the hour, but we do know that our lives will not last forever. When our mortal bodies fail, we will still rejoice in You. No longer will we fear enemies from without or within. Today we do not know the one who knocks at the door with an evil heart. But we can trust You, even in this present age. Give us a mind for the life to come. Help us to meditate on the reality of heavenly habitations. Did not Jesus have a resurrection body? Did He not ascend in clouds of glory? Can any evil empire hurt Him today? Have not Your beloved children found their safety in Him? The day of wickedness will soon be gone, and we will serve You with rejoicing forever.

Habakkuk

Habakkuk 1
Lord God, we know that You love justice. We are amazed at Your patience, for there is still evil all around us. We see perversions of every kind. Yet we know that Your ways are great. You have a plan involving even powerful and evil nations. You work out Your holy goodness using armies and peoples who are swift to devour. Even evil angels fit into Your glorious plan. You are the everlasting God. You have ordained judgments upon the earth. Will You use a wicked nation to discipline Your church? Surely we are brought to wonder about the unfolding of events even in our time, but it is well beyond us to guess the details of what will come to pass. We do know what You have revealed in Your Word, and we have come to know You, O great and majestic God.

Habakkuk 2
Sovereign Lord, we wait for Your Word. There is much that we do not understand. Your Word will finally come with power. Your people will live by faith. Though the wicked man will gather up what is not his own, he cannot take it with him beyond this life. There will be surprising witnesses that will rise against him in the day of resurrection that he does not expect. There are many things that we do not know now, but we know that the earth shall be covered with the knowledge of Your greatness and Your glory. All idols will be exposed as nothing. You are in Your holy temple. You do what is right now. You will do what is right forever. We worship You with awe and reverence, and trust You in everything.

Habakkuk 3
Father God, we humbly beseech You that You would remember mercy in Your wrath. We plead the blood of Christ Your Son. You sent Him to be a Substitute for sinners. Your justice has already come upon Him centuries ago. There was nothing missing in His atoning sacrifice for Your people. Surely our wickedness has been utterly crushed through His merciful death for Your people. We tremble at the truth of Your holiness and Your costly love. The wicked who hate You will not prosper forever. Though we seem empty now, we are full of the joy of Your glory, and we will worship You in the splendor of Your majesty forever.

Zephaniah

Zephaniah 1

Lord of Hosts, a great Day of Destruction is coming against the world. You have warned us that judgment begins with Your household. You will purify Your church. How will we stand when You bring distress upon mankind? Please forgive us, for we have violated Your commandments. Will we be safe if we worship You and also worship false gods? Our money will not deliver us from Your hand. Your Son is our only hope. Please have mercy upon us.

Zephaniah 2

Sovereign Lord, we are ashamed of our sin. We should seek You and obey Your commandments. We pray that You would grant to us both righteousness and humility. Father, You will make a distinction between Your people and their enemies. You love Your church. Your Son gave His blood for us. You will bring a devastating judgment upon the world. We must be found by You in mercy, and kept by Your steadfast love, or we will be destroyed with the wicked.

Zephaniah 3

Father God, we hear Your Word of correction and fear. Speak to us day by day and grant us a new heart by Your Holy Spirit. Will we be cut off with the world? By Your grace, we will turn from our iniquities. We will wait for You. When You pour out Your indignation, You will keep us as Your people. We will be with You on Your holy mountain. Our sin will be removed far from us, and we will rejoice with all our hearts. You have taken away the judgments that were against us. You will be in our midst. You will save us. You will rejoice over us with singing. This is our glorious hope. You will heal us and restore our fortunes according to the promises that You have made to us in Your Son Jesus Christ who is our Mediator and our Atoning Sacrifice. Teach us to walk in this faith today, for You will surely do these things.

Haggai

Haggai 1

Lord God, we must seek first Your Kingdom. We are busy with our own affairs, but nothing has seemed to work out according to our plans. We have looked for much, but our efforts have not been very fruitful. We recommit ourselves to Your Word and we give ourselves to Your service. Be with us, O Lord. Fill Your servants with holy boldness for the glory of Your Name. Build up Your house, O God! Help us to see the part that You have for us and to give our lives for Your wonderful purposes.

Haggai 2

Father, give us a vision for the glory of Your house. Grant to us strength for the work that You have called us to do. Forgive us when we consider the remnant of Your Kingdom as something too small for our most fervent desires and efforts. Touch us day by day by Your Spirit. Take away the unclean impulse of inner rebellion within us. Make us clean. Bless us from this day forward. Shake the heavens and the earth to accomplish Your perfect purposes. May Your Son be greatly desired by all who call upon His Name.

Zechariah

Zechariah 1

Lord of Hosts, You were angry with our Fathers. We must return to You, and You will surely return to us. Grant us the gift of repentance that we would rejoice in You and obey Your Word. Give us perfect rest in Your Son Jesus Christ. Build up Your Jerusalem through Your great mercy. Bring us prosperity, comfort, and joy, even in this age of suffering. Will we be able to endure the rage of the nations that come against us? Defend Your church, O Lord. Make the ministry of Your Word powerful for the restoration of Your people.

Zechariah 2

Lord God, what is the measure of Your church? Will we be as a nation without walls? Will we be faithful to Your commands? Be the glory in our midst, O Lord. Be with us forever. Gather Your people from every tribe and tongue and nation. Protect us, for we are the apple of Your eye. Come to us, and dwell with us. May we be a glorious inheritance for Your Son. We are Yours, O God.

Zechariah 3

Father God, Jesus is our great High Priest. He has taken away our filthy garments, and has carried our ugliness far away. He has taken away our iniquity. We have been given the clean garments of His perfect righteousness. May we be with You as Your servants forever? Our guilt has been removed in a single day, for our Savior died for us. There is room in Your house for all who rest in Your Son.

Zechariah 4

Lord God, purify Your church. Make it a lampstand of the finest gold. Build up Your people by the power and presence of Your Holy Spirit. Fill us with Your grace. Build up this living temple with the fullness of Jesus Christ. Make us witnesses of Your holiness and Your goodness, for You have blessed us in our glorious King.

Zechariah 5

Sovereign Lord, bring the Word to us in power. Show us how the curse of the covenant has come upon our Redeemer so that the fullness of Your blessing would rest upon Your humble servants. Take away our iniquity now and forever. Remove the ugliness of our sin very far from us. Though we were once enslaved in wickedness, Jesus Christ has made us free.

Zechariah 6

Father God, You are sovereign over all the events that take place in all places and ages. You make Your messengers strong for Your eternal purposes. You will protect Your people, and all of the earth will know Your almighty justice. Your Son, the Branch, will build His church as Your holy temple. Use us, O God, in the building of this living temple. We will diligently obey Your voice, O Lord our God.

Zechariah 7

Lord God, Your people of old pretended to be diligent concerning matters of obedience to Your Law, yet they made up laws that You had not given to them. Though they pretended to serve You, they would not listen to Your Word. Will we go the same way? Take away our hypocrisy. Soften our hearts to hear You. Make us generous to the poor, and use us as ambassadors of Your loving-kindness wherever You send us.

Zechariah 8

Our Father, You have a great jealousy for Your people. You discipline those You love, but You will bring about the fullness of Your wonderful promises and all Your prophetic visions. You will save us, and we will dwell with You safely forever. Help us to be strong, that Your temple might be built. You have given Your Son a holy body. We shall live in the midst of a great and fruitful land, and we will somehow be a blessing to those all around us. We long for the day when You will bring the greatest good to Your church. In response to Your clear commandment, we commit our lives to the sincerity of truth. Help us, O Spirit of Truth! Fill us with joy, love, and peace. Bring us together as those who will seek Your favor with full confidence. May we take hold of our Savior's robe, for He is powerful to bless, and He is bringing us to Your city.

Zechariah 9

Creator God, all the nations will come before You. There is no safety in the might of men. The hopes of many nations shall perish when You come to cut off the pride of the arrogant. You will bring Your loved ones to a place of the greatest security and peace. Your Son will be our great King. He will give to us an age of perfect peace. He will rule to the very ends of the earth. We long for this wonderful day. Stir up Your sons, O Lord, that we might move forward even now in Christian love. Others may seek to kill, but we come as agents of salvation. How great is Your goodness! How wonderful is Your beauty!

Zechariah 10

Lord God, You bring rain and sun, even upon pagan peoples, but You care especially for Your flock. You have sent us the great Cornerstone of our salvation. He has saved us and strengthened us. He will bring us back to a safe and bountiful land, and we shall rejoice and be glad in You forever. We shall live there with our children and with all Your chosen people. You will strike down anyone or anything that could threaten us, and we shall walk in Your Name forever.

Zechariah 11

Great God, we are so prone to wander, for we take glory in things that do not last. Our idolatry has brought so much trouble upon so many people. Please bring Your favor upon Your chosen people now because of Your love for Your Son. Bring about a new union of Your people, for we have been united together with Christ, the Suffering Servant, who was betrayed for silver. He gave His life for us. He is a completely faithful shepherd, for He has served You to the end, and has saved us by the gift of His own blood.

Zechariah 12

Our Father, You have created the world. You have redeemed a people for a coming day of new creation. Though there is much tribulation around us, Your eyes are open, and You will not forget us. Even if we are in the midst of a crowd of strangers, You will know us at once. You will see us and You will rescue us, even if everyone to the right and to the left will be destroyed in their sin. You will give us the grace of the full salvation that You have shown to us in the resurrection of the Son of David. He was pierced for us, and He has become the firstborn among many brethren.

Zechariah 13

Lord of Hosts, there is a fountain of cleansing for us through the blood of the Lamb. Pour out the fresh water of Your Spirit upon Your children even now. Though we may suffer greatly at the hands of the wicked, our situation is still very good. We have a finished Word granted to us in the Old and New Testaments, so we have Your voice with us continually. More than this, the final Shepherd has come, and when He was struck down for us, He won for us the fullest peace with You. We are His people, and He is our God.

Zechariah 14

Sovereign Lord, You are the God of salvation, and You are the God of tribulation. Though we may suffer greatly, though we may have to flee from the hands of those who long to kill us, yet You will save us. Your Son will be king over all the earth. We shall be Your temple and Your Jerusalem. We long for that day. Though it shall be a day of horrible panic and death for Your enemies, for Your servants it will be a day of survival, of celebration, and of joy. You will make everything and everyone holy to You.

Malachi

Malachi 1

Lord of Glory, You have spoken through Your messengers the prophets. You revealed Your love for Israel. Yet Your plans have always been great even beyond the borders of Israel. Father, You sent Your Son to be the Savior of both Jews and Gentiles. He accomplished His work as our High Priest with full integrity. He did everything perfectly. His offering was pure, for He gave Himself as a holy sacrifice. In Him there was no blemish. Now He is our great King, and His Name shall be exalted throughout the earth.

Malachi 2

Great God, we will honor Your Name. We humble ourselves under Your almighty hand. We are to be priests before You. Your priests should be different from the world. We should guard knowledge, give good instruction to one another, and follow in the way that we teach to others. Please forgive us, for we have corrupted Your word. Particularly within our homes we should be good examples of love and sacrificial commitment. We should seek You and serve You as we train up our children in the way they should go. Have we spoken thoughtlessly and acted as if You do not care about justice? Have mercy on us, O Lord.

Malachi 3

Father God, You have sent Your Son as the Mediator of a New Covenant. He has provided a way for those who fear You, but He will come again to judge the wicked. We must return to You. We must be faithful with the wealth that You have given to us. We will generously support the work of Your church. We will give to the poor within our midst. Grant to us true joy in Your service. Bless us with a deeper repentance. We have committed ourselves to the way of righteousness. We will serve You.

Malachi 4

O God, the Day of Judgment is surely coming. Yet, the sun has risen in our hearts through the gift of Jesus Christ. In Him we have the greatest blessing. You have turned our hearts back to You, our Father. He has destroyed the destruction that was coming against us. United to Him we have a most secure peace and hope. Come soon, Lord Jesus!

Matthew

Matthew 1

Lord God, grant that we would see Jesus Christ rightly in Your Word. He is the fulfillment of Your every promise. You have granted many kings to reign over Your people, but Jesus is far above them all. We thank You for the wonder of His two natures, for He is both human and divine. In His one person He has fully saved us from our sins. He is not only the Son of Mary. He is God with us. In Him we have been given a most excellent and secure heritage.

Matthew 2

Father, why have men hated Your Son even before He was known by them? What kind of spirit causes a Herod to pretend to be a worshiper of the one that he seeks to destroy? Yet this Jesus is the hope of even Gentiles who were seeking the coming of the Holy One as they looked to the skies. You have protected Your Son from powerful and evil men who hated His coming. Yet He was born to die according to Your own plan of salvation. Grant us more life in Him even now, for though He died, yet He lives forever.

Matthew 3

Sovereign Lord, there is so much for us to learn from Your Word. It is there plainly for us to hear and receive, but what will the condition of our hearts be when we hear the truth preached to us? Will we be willing to repent of our sin? Your Son had a complete commitment to fulfill all righteousness in the depths of His being. Grant to us this same Spirit, that we might be eager to hear and obey Your Word. Our Savior is fully pleasing to You. In Him we are Your beloved children.

Matthew 4

Glorious Lord, we do not understand the minds of men. How can we fathom the thoughts and actions of angels? Yet men and angels are all perfectly known by You. By Your Word Your Son resisted the temptations of Satan. He would not be distracted from His mission. Thank You for the light that has dawned upon us in the life and work of our King. We have been granted eyes to see Him as our hearts have been made alive by Your Spirit. When He called us to follow Him, we were given the grace to leave the world behind, and to serve our Messiah. Remind us day by day of the greatness of the One we serve, lest we foolishly return to the way that leads to death.

Matthew 5

Lord God, Your Son came to teach us and then to die for us. There is a perfect connection between His instruction and His cross. He has blessed us greatly and we are glad, even though men may hate us. We look to the age to come according to Your promise. Grant that we would have in us a taste of the resurrection and the light of a glory that shall one day be fully revealed. Your Son has obeyed all Your commandments for us. He calls us to follow Him in the way of righteousness. Grant us a heart that loves Your Law, so that we will not grieve Your Spirit. Teach us to be aware of the slavery of sin. We long to live forever in the light of Your great holiness. Show us how to live now in the simplicity of love. This way of life need not be mysterious to us, for Your Son has displayed to us the way.

Matthew 6

Father God, bless us with a deep desire for secret opportunities to do what is good. Teach us to pray as those who love Your smile more than the praise of men. We seek now the glory of Your Name, the progress of Your Kingdom, and the beauty of Your holy will. As we serve You day by day, we humbly ask that You would supply our needs, forgive our sins, and lead us away from every snare of evil. We willingly forgive everyone who has ever sinned against us. We mourn our own sin and weakness, and we seek the power of Your presence among us. Will we be caught again in the clutches of love for money? We claim that we are free from such base impulses, yet we are easily anxious about food and clothing when there is even a slight danger of poverty among us. Teach us to seek first Your Kingdom and Your righteousness. We know that You will take care of us now and forever.

Matthew 7

Sovereign Lord, we feel the weight of our own sin, and we mourn. Teach us how to live as forgiven sinners in a world full of sin. We truly repent and come now to You for help. We ask for You. We seek You. We knock at Your door. Fill us with Your Spirit. You are the Father of Your people, and we know that You will give us good gifts when we approach You through Your Son. Grant us perseverance in the way that leads to life. Bless us with true and lasting fruitfulness. Above all, we ask that we would be known by You on the Day of Judgment that is coming upon the world. We stand in union with Your Son upon the rock of Your holy Word. In Him we not only hear Your Word, we also do what you command. Have mercy on us in our foolish doubts and wanderings.

Matthew 8

Father God, You have made us clean from the leprosy of sin. Though we were not worthy of having You come to dwell with us, You have come to us and have helped us. We are very thankful. Touch us even now. May the sickness of unbelief be driven far from us. We need to be up and serving You. May nothing stand in our way. You are strong to turn away every obstacle from our hearts and minds. You are powerful over the world and over every proud adversary who would try to defy You. Help us, O God! Save us by Your mighty presence and by Your matchless Word.

Matthew 9

O God, give us faith even for those in need all around us. Why should men and women everywhere not rise and walk? Your Son has come, and He is still calling all kinds of people to follow Him. We need You. We are those who are sick, and You are the most powerful doctor. We rejoice in the presence of Your Son, but we long for Your coming again. We have already received much grace, and we taste the blessings of the age to come. Nonetheless, we cannot be satisfied without the full arrival of the age of resurrection. We believe that You are able to do this. Open our eyes even now. Give us the words to speak, that we might rightly live out the gospel of the kingdom. Send forth many laborers into Your harvest field. May many captives of sin and death be freed by Your Word of truth.

Matthew 10

Lord God, You are building Your kingdom on the cornerstone of Your Son and the foundation of apostles and prophets. We rejoice in Jesus Christ and in His glorious Word. Use Your servants as messengers of life in a dangerous and dying world. Grant Your Spirit to Your servants that they might speak the truth with power and love. We need You. Bring to light all that is necessary for the conversion of many. May many people acknowledge You before men, for it is a horrible thing to deny You. We take up our cross and follow Your Son. We gladly receive Your children and care for their needs. This world is passing away, and all of its pride, but Your kingdom is forever.

Matthew 11

Great God, You sent Your Son preaching and teaching. He performed the signs of the Messiah. We will not be offended by Him. John the Baptist prepared the way for Him as a great Prophet. Now we have been brought into Your Kingdom, and we have seen things in Your Word that prophets of old longed to see. We have heard of Your Son's mighty works, and we believe that He is the Anointed One. We are Your children through faith in this Christ. We have come to Him, and in Him we have found rest for our souls.

Matthew 12

Glorious Lord, Your Son understood Your Law perfectly. Even more than this, He obeyed Your Law perfectly. He came as the One who was greater than the temple. He is the Lord of the Sabbath. He is the Messiah King. You have given us a powerful expectation of the fullness of Sabbath life in Him. Help us to believe in the coming resurrection, and to live as those who have already been made alive through Jesus Christ. He is the Son of David. He defeats all the works of Satan. It is a glorious privilege to be a part of His Kingdom, O God. Teach us how to gather people for Your Son. Help us to walk in the goodness and love that comes from above, and to speak as those who know and honor the truth. Thank You for the glorious sign of Your Son's resurrection. In Him we have the greatest gift known to man. Shall we have life again through the Man who rose from the dead? Shall we have the wisdom of the Holy Spirit through the One who is wiser than Solomon? We hear His Word, and we believe. We have been given new life, and we shall follow You.

Matthew 13

Lord of Glory, You have spoken Your Word through Your servants. We pray that we might be good soil, fruitful for Your service. Father, there is an enemy who is ready to take away the Word before we would even hear it. Keep him far from our hearts. There is a world of distraction all around us. Clear away the rocky ground of our minds. Keep out the thorns that would hide the glory of Your Word. Though Your church may contain both weeds and wheat in this present age, You shall surely make a distinction between them at the harvest. Have mercy, O Lord. Forgive our sins. Build up Your kingdom over these centuries for the glory of Your Name. Bring into Your home all of Your elect. We long for the day when the righteous will shine like the sun in Your kingdom. We should prefer Your kingdom to everything that the world would offer to us. Eternal life is so important. Grant us clarity of thought, speech, and action on these matters. Take away from us all the fogginess and confusion of sin. We honor You, O God. Do many works of blessing through the people who long for Your Son's appearing.

Matthew 14

Father God, the fact of an uneasy conscience cannot be wished away. Only through the blood of Your Son can we truly have peace. Have compassion upon us, O Lord. Help us to know true forgiveness and restoration. Feed us with bread from heaven. Speak to our hearts in a way that will satisfy our deepest needs and desires. Send us forth in peace that we may serve You. Teach us to pray with a secure faith, for we know that You control all things. Come to us in our moments of fear. Take hold of us when we doubt and keep us from sinking under the weight of many cares. We long for the day when sickness and disease will be far away from all of Your people. Until the trumpet sounds and the new life of resurrection appears, keep our eyes fixed upon the face of our Redeemer.

Matthew 15

Lord of Glory, help us to distinguish between the traditions of men and the Word that comes from You. Cleanse us from within, that we would no longer be filled with evil thoughts. Have mercy upon us and upon our children. Defeat the forces of evil that oppress us. Grant to us a crumb from the table of the kingdom in the midst of this world of death. Thank You for Your kind compassion upon us in our time of need. Use us day by day as agents of Your abundant mercy.

Matthew 16

Great God, why have we been so slow to love You and to follow You? Why do we approach Your Word with doubt? Please grant to us a fuller measure of faith. The leaven of false teachers and hypocrites too easily finds a ready ear among us. Send us the Christ, Your holy Son. Build Your church. Move us forward with the message of the forgiveness of sins. Help us to boast in the cross. We too easily move in the direction of the ways of men. Set our hearts upon Your ways, and show us Your glory.

Matthew 17

Father, when Your Son ministered in this world of death, You gave us an amazing glimpse of His glory in the Transfiguration. How we long for that vision today! How can we live by the light of resurrection glory when we never see that kind of glorious sight with our eyes? Teach us how to see with the eyes of faith and how to live by faith. Move us ahead in works of faith according to Your commandments. Without faith it is impossible to please You. Thank You for Your Son's great work of faith that was fulfilled through the cross. By that cross we who were so far off have been made sons of the Kingdom. What looked like utter failure in the sight of the world was truly the greatest of victories for Your people.

Matthew 18

Sovereign Lord, make us like children in every appropriate way, that we might know what it is to walk by faith in Your kingdom. We turn away from all sin. We lift up to You the young ones in our midst, and we pray that You would lead them in paths of righteousness for Your Name's sake. Make us wise in dealing with offenses in our midst. Restore those who repent. We need to be a people of extravagant forgiveness, for we have been forgiven a massive debt. Our sin against You was a burden that we could never bear. We have found peace with You only through Your merciful grace. Will we now treat others as if peace could come to us through law? We will truly forgive one another from our hearts even now, for we have been completely forgiven through the grace of Your Son.

Matthew 19

Our Father, You have granted to many in Your church the joy of having lifelong partners in marriage. What a blessing is this one flesh relationship. Why do we engage in entangling sins that are destructive of this great gift? There is so much sadness around us. We mourn our sinful thoughts, words and actions. We regret the seed of hate that has brought about the destruction of many marriages, particularly in Your church. We pray that You would help us to find life again after such significant loss. Father we hear Your call to us, that we should follow You in this and in every way. We offer up to You now all that we are and everything that we possess. Your call to obedience is absolute and complete. We confess that this seems impossible to us. Yet You have the power to do things that men cannot do. You will give us the fullness of Your kingdom. Grant to us even now the wisdom of complete devotion to You.

Matthew 20

Lord God, Your kingdom has come to us by Your sovereign gift. We should always receive it with the greatest joy and gratitude. Yet we find a disturbing tendency in our hearts. We act as if we have been given the kingdom as a wage, when it is clearly the best gift that anyone could ever receive. Remind us again of the meaning of the cross. Let our eyes be opened to the wonder of Your love, that we might believe the gospel and follow Your Son. Change our thinking about Your kingdom, so that we embrace the suffering that You have ordained for us. Your Son came to serve. We offer up our lives in His service.

Matthew 21

Father God, You are in charge of every detail of our salvation. In the most important week of human history, You brought Your Son into Jerusalem in complete fulfillment of all prophecy. Your Son cleansed the temple. The salvation that He brings is wonderful. We ask You to purify our worship and to make us whole in body and soul. We look for fruitfulness in Your church even now. Grant us faith that is able to move mountains of unbelief. Help us to submissively hear the Word of Your Son and to obey. Cast out of us any spirit of arrogance or evil. We want to follow You, O Lord, not only with our words, but especially with our lives. Bring many into Your kingdom even today. Why should we be hypocrites, when You have done a powerful work of redemption in our lives? Make us faithful in Your service. We build our lives upon the Stone that the builders rejected. He is the one source of eternal life.

Matthew 22

Father, the cross is a great story of love, but it is also a horror to us. You sent Your Son to die. He suffered greatly. Through the shedding of His own blood, He provided for us the holy garments of righteousness necessary for us to have peace with You. Yet men of malice tried to trap the One who came to die for our sins. Others thought that they could make Him look like a fool. How wrong they were. He is Your wisdom and Your power. We thank You for this Word of life given to us. He loved You with all His heart, soul, mind, and strength; and He loved His neighbor as Himself. Here is the fulfillment of all the Law and the Prophets. Thank You for this holy Messiah who is both David's Son and David's Lord.

Matthew 23

Lord of Hosts, we reject the Pharisaic way. We must know You and we must be known by You. We must love You, and we must be loved by You. We cannot have peace with You through law. We need Jesus. We have ways of serving ourselves while acting like we are serving You. Come and save us. We are in a battle between the gospel and religious hypocrisy. We will only win if Your Son is with us as One who lives in us. Cast away from us all false pretense of holiness. We know our need. We can only have righteousness and mercy as Your gifts to us through the blood of the Lamb. Please help us now. If we do not have Your presence, we have nothing, and we cannot move forward in Your service.

Matthew 24

Glorious God, You are building a wonderful living temple. Your Son is that temple, and we are a true temple in Him. We want no false prophets or false Messiahs. We need Christ. The love of many has grown cold. There is much trouble all around us. Thank You for warning us that these days would come.

Thank You also for cutting short these days, for You know our weakness. Come, O God! Come, Lord Jesus Christ! Shine upon us in Your glorious return with all Your great host. Let us see the resurrection. Though we do not know the day and hour, we know You. Though we do not yet see the resurrection kingdom in glory, we see Your Son through Your Word. May the gospel be preached everywhere, and may we be found faithful and fruitful, as those who endure to the end.

Matthew 25

God of Glory, when You come in judgment, will we be ready? Will we be waiting with expectation? Please do not exclude us from that marriage feast. You have given us certain gifts and graces according to Your will. We want to use what we have been given for Your glory. Beat back the enemy who desires that we would have no fruit. We will not bury the gifts that we have been given. We long to hear the words that You will speak on that day when You would call us good and faithful servants in Jesus Christ. Lead us by Your presence within us, so that we will serve the least among us with joy. We love You, Lord God, and we love Your church. We long for the day of our bodily entrance into the world of eternal life. We commit to Your care our riches, our friends and loved ones, even our own lives, and we look for the day of Your Son's glorious coming.

Matthew 26

Father God, the entirety of our faith is about Jesus Christ. People plotted to arrest Him and to kill Him, but so few understood what was actually happening. He gave His body. He shed His blood. He did this in faith, assuring us that He will eat and drink with us in His coming kingdom. We could not have saved ourselves. We would have denied Him. We would not have been able to watch and pray even for one hour. Yet His time was at hand according to Your sovereign will. He was betrayed with a kiss. His enemies seized Him. They accused Him falsely. They sentenced Him to death. They abused Him. Yet He was and is the Christ, our Redeemer.

Matthew 27

Lord God, the events of the cross are overwhelming. Who killed our Lord? Was it the Romans? Was it the chief priests and elders? Was it Judas? Was it Pilate? Was it the crowd? Was it the soldiers? Was it not me? It was our sins that brought Him to this atoning death. It was Your will to save us. There was no other way. Be glorified, O Lord. We cannot claim to be innocent of the blood of Jesus. What is left for us to do? We will carry His cross, for He is our King. Father God, remember us. Your Son died for us. We have been delivered from death and hell. He was forsaken that we might live forever. He yielded up His Spirit that we might have the gift of Your Spirit. He is most certainly Your eternal Son. Yet He was buried in a tomb for us. What wondrous love is this!

Matthew 28

Lord of Hosts, Your Son is risen! The stone is rolled away and the tomb is empty. More than this, our Risen Savior has met with His disciples. All authority in heaven and on earth has been given to Him. We must go forth and make disciples of all nations, baptizing them in the Triune Name. We will teach and do what He has commanded. Our confidence is in His presence, for He is with us always, even to the end of the age. Cast far away from us all doubt. Strengthen us by Your Spirit that we might stand firm in the face of every foe, for Jesus is Lord, forever and ever.

Mark

Mark 1

God and Father of our Lord Jesus Christ, we thank You for the gospel of Your Son. You have prepared His way through the prophets of old and the ministry of John the Baptist. We are not worthy to be the lowest servants of Your beloved Son, with whom You are well pleased. We thank You for Your Kingdom, and for Your power in calling Your disciples into Your church. Today we leave our worries and fears behind and follow You. Teach us from Your Word with all authority and power. Your ways are amazing. You have victory over all foes, seen and unseen. You touch the dying woman, and she rises up to serve You. You heal crowds of sick people and cast out demonic hosts. You have prayed faithfully and preached throughout the world through Your servants. Make us clean today, and cause us to give careful attention to Your holy commandments.

Mark 2

Father God, we come to hear Your Son today and to be near Him who has come near to us with His Word and Spirit. Thank You for the forgiveness of sins, and the power to make a man rise and walk. Lord, throw off from us this day the paralysis of hatred and doubt, that we might walk by faith in Your Spirit. Help us to walk away from the love of money and the approval of men as we receive the healing of body and Spirit that comes from our holy Bridegroom. We mourn because of our sin, but we rejoice with the news of the new wine of full salvation through a Substitute. Today we will serve You and rest in Your Son. He is the King. We are His disciples and we will hear His voice this day.

Mark 3

Lord God, You see us in our weakness and shame. Do good to us this day for the glory of Your holy name. Though many sought ways to destroy Your Son, and such were some of us, we now bow before You in reverence, believing fervently in Jesus the Messiah. Thank You for Your apostles, and for the Word to which they gave full testimony. We benefit from their testimony to Your Son, though they were weak. You filled them with Your Holy Spirit and enabled them to proclaim a Word that we have now heard. Now the kingdom of darkness is coming to an end. Bind the strong man and cast Him out of Your house. Let us rejoice in You as those who have been granted the honor of being called Your mothers and brothers and sisters, for we hear Your Word and follow You this day.

Mark 4

O Sovereign Lord, teach us, that we might listen and live. Turn away the devil who would want us to ignore Your word. We will not fear persecution. We will not be distracted by other engagements. We want to be fruitful disciples. Speak to us and we will live. Use Your servants to show us the truth. Encourage us in the day of tribulation. Keep us from the deceitfulness of riches. Bring a harvest among us of righteousness and peace. Bring to light the greatness and glory of Your Son. Enlarge our hearts in the mercy of the gospel. Make the seed of Your Word sprout and grow among us with astounding results in the day of Your glory. Though today we may be few in number, give us confidence that You are well able to build Your kingdom. You can calm the waves and winds when they threaten us. You will not let us perish. Lord, see the tumult within our souls, and calm our hearts again this day.

Mark 5

Lord God, an enemy would take aim at our bodies and souls. An enemy who is stronger than us would attack our children and Your church. Only You can cast him out. We turn to You for Your strong Word. A legion of demons destroys the people of Your possession. God save us! Clothe us in the righteousness of Christ and help us to be in our right minds. We will serve You. Send us out to our friends to tell the truth about the great things that You have done for us. Will our children live? Will our wives have good health? Why should disease and evil seem to win among us? You are the One who can deliver Your church from trouble with a Word. We trust in You. Make us well. Make our families truly live again. We will not fear. We believe. Send away the professional mourners who make their living in celebrating destruction. We want to be up and walking again in Your resurrection power.

Mark 6

Father, why should people reject You? Why do they take offense at the Son of Man? Our great Prophet is worthy of all honor. Look at our remaining unbelief and heal us. We go forth day by day to proclaim Your Name and to perform works of justice, beauty, and order. Glorify the name of Your Son through Your church. Though powerful men may turn against the righteous, You can give us strength in the day of trouble. We do not wish to be moved by foolish lusts or our seeking the approval of men. Give us hope, though people would stand against us. Grant strength and mercy to Your persecuted church. We run the race that You have given us today. We want to see You. We need You to feed us. Do miracles of amazing fruitfulness through Your church. May we see heaven's blessing come down among men that the Name of Jesus would be lifted up. We pray to You, O God. Your Son walked on the sea. There is nothing that is too difficult for You. We will not be afraid. Our hearts are moved in devotion to You. We bring You many who are in great need. If we could touch even the fringe of Your garment on their behalf, we know that they would be made well.

Mark 7

Great Lawgiver of Israel, Your people have twisted together their own traditions and Your holy Law, treating the mixture as somehow divine. Forgive us, for we would reject Your commandments and establish our own traditions as the pathway of righteousness. Help us to see our real duty and the corruption of our wicked hearts. From within, out of the hearts of men, come evil thoughts, words, and actions. Through these habits of sin we have been utterly defiled. Cleanse us, O God! Have mercy also on our sons and daughters. Grant us a crumb from Your holy table, and deliver us from the doctrines and moral directives of demons. Grant to us holy speech, and open our mouths in praise to You. You do all things well.

Mark 8

Father God, have compassion upon us. We have been with You, and we have followed You, but we are hungry. We need daily bread for our bodies, and are often amply supplied, but who will fill our souls with Your truth? Who will fill us with Your Spirit, if You do not give us this great heavenly gift every day? We know that You will give us bread from heaven. May we have eyes to see what is good. May we have ears to hear, understand, and obey. Help us to see more clearly, even when we imagine that we have a perfect understanding of all things. Heal us again, that we might see the glories of Your Son more and more. He is the Christ, who suffered, died, and rose again. Keep us far from the doctrines of the devil, who would turn us away from the cross. Grant that we would embrace the truth and duty of this atoning sacrifice, for Christ has taken away our sin and called us to a new way of love.

Mark 9

Glorious Lord, You will bring us to resurrection life on the day of Your Son's return. We long for the radiance of that glorious hour, for the dead will be raised imperishable, and we shall be changed. We do not see this radiance now, but we see our risen Lord Jesus, the firstborn among many brethren. The Son of Man has suffered many things, as was written of Him in the Scriptures. When He returns, He will not suffer again, but will reign in glory. The healing of that Day will be full and glorious, and the judgment of that Day will be overwhelming. We believe; help our unbelief. Renew our faith in the power and love of Your Son. Make us more knowledgeable of the life to come, that we might speak the truth in comfort to those who are in greatest need. The Son of Man has suffered, died, and risen from the dead. We see with the eyes of faith, and we believe. We will not seek any longer to be the greatest in the view of men, but we will be great by being servants to others. We belong to Christ. Give us His love for the young and helpless. He has had abundant mercy on us when we were in the greatest need. Give us a great expectation concerning the coming of His Kingdom, and may we live at peace with each other.

Mark 10

Father God, we thank You for the beauty and holiness of Your teaching. Help us not to rebel against Your Word. From the beginning of creation, You have made us male and female. You have joined us together in marriage, so that the two are one. Help us to obey You. You have blessed Your church with children. May we never hinder them as they come to You. You are good, O God. We should follow Your Law. We flatter ourselves and overestimate our obedience to Your commandments. Thank You for the perfections of Christ. We come to Him today as Your children. Surely all things are possible for You, even our salvation. Our lives are wonderfully in Your hands. We trust Your promises, and would face even persecutions now, that we might be near You. Your Son was delivered to murderers, and He died for us, yet He rose from the dead. Give us the courage to stay with You, The one who would be close to you will surely suffer. Still, it is better to be near

You. We give our lives in service, for surely You have served us first and best. Have mercy on us. Grant that we might have a depth of godly vision that comes through faith. Draw us near to You today, and make us whole in Jesus Christ, that we might follow You.

Mark 11

Glorious Lord, You came into Jerusalem as a humble and peaceful King. Help us to see You rightly. You are in charge of every detail of life, and have all power and authority, yet You were willing to be low that we might be saved. Is there no fruit in Your church today? May it never be, O Lord. Purify Your temple, and grant us a life of prayer together as those who know that all good things come from You. We ask You for that which we believe to be agreeable to Your will. We trust that we have received these gifts even now, and that all that we rightly request is certainly ours in Your Son, for You have told us to pray with faith. We gladly forgive others, lest our prayers be hindered. Forgive us, O Lord. Your Son came from heaven. We will not ignore His Word.

Mark 12

Great Teacher and Shepherd of Our Souls, show us again the truth of Christ. We want to hear Him and obey. We want to respect Him as Your Son. How could we sin against You? Many religious men have sought only to trap Your Son, and even to kill Him. You have given us earthly rulers. Peaceful government is a good gift from You. Yet Your enemies would want to use this good power against the King of kings. Father, we believe in the resurrection. There we shall see Your Son. We long for that day, O Lord, when even angels and redeemed saints will usher us into Your presence. Lord, grant us grace that we will love You now the way that we will surely love You then, You are One, and when we are near Your Son, we are not far from Your Kingdom. Grant Your servants power in teaching Your Word to Your people. Open up to us the mysteries of the faith that have now been revealed in Your Word. May we also see the way of generous and happy living, in service to You and to others. Out of our poverty, we give to You all that we have. We trust You with our lives.

Mark 13

Eternal Father, we thank You that You have made us to be the temple of Your Holy Spirit. We long for the fulfillment of Your glorious decrees. We know that our redemption is drawing nearer every day. We commit our lives to the preaching of Your gospel to all nations through the church. We ask that You would keep us from every great apostasy and rebellion in Your church before the return of Your Son. We will be held together by You through that frightening day, for Your elect will not be led astray to eternal destruction. Your Son will come. We wait for Him as we hear Your Word. We will pay attention to the tasks ahead of us today with the sure hope of eternal life.

Mark 14

Lord God, the enemies of Your Son were eager to put Him to death. We thank You that You have made us to love our Savior from the heart. We pour out our lives in devotion to Him. Still, the Judas impulse of betrayal troubles Your church in every age, for the false friends of Your Son are not only outside the church. Betrayers are among the ministers and disciples of our King. Despite this treachery, our Lord gave His body and blood for sinners. Forgive us, Father. We think of ourselves more highly than we ought. Like Peter, we imagine that we have the strength to be faithful through any test. Your Son faced the agony of death as our Substitute. There was no other way. Your will was done in the salvation of sinners. Through the sign of a kiss, many would cause trouble in Your church even today. Others believe in the powers of the world, and would attempt to build Your kingdom with the sword of men, rather than the sword of the Spirit. Many would bring false witness against Your Son and His church. How can Your kingdom survive? Through the power that comes from above, You stand against evil and violence. Though brutal men would beat and mock Your Son, He will win His battle without responding to any of the lies of false witnesses. May we not deny You despite the intimidation of those who seem to have power at their disposal. We mourn our unfaithfulness and again commit ourselves to follow in the way of the cross.

Mark 15

Glorious God, how Your Son suffered indignities for our sake! Crowds would choose a Barabbas, rather than have our King released from unjust bondage. The voice of many yelled out the words, "Crucify Him!" How could this be? Men of envy had delivered Him up to the Gentiles. People created in Your image scourged Him and led Him away. They mocked Him and spit on Him. May we be rightly moved at these horrific events. We would follow this true King of the Jews, though we too may face the attacks of brutal men. Many reviled our King and taunted Him, urging Him to abandon the cross and save Himself. Yet our strong Lord was faithful, even facing the divine abandonment that we deserved. Finally, our King breathed His last. Through the powerful death of this one Son of God, a way of access into Your holy presence has been made for us. Our prayer to You this day, offered as it is in Jesus' Name, is possible only because of His death. His body was laid in a tomb, but before long the tomb would be empty as a testimony to the power of His indestructible life.

Mark 16

Father God, the Lord Jesus Christ, Lord of the Sabbath, is risen! The stone was rolled back. The body was gone from the tomb. He was not there. He had risen, as an angel gave perfect testimony. Though His disciples were alarmed and afraid, our hope is not in the courage or wisdom of men, but in Your Son. He has granted to us a new and powerful life of holy Sabbath rest in the incomparable strength of our Redeemer's resurrection.

Luke

Luke 1

Glorious God, we thank You for the good news of Your Son, Jesus Christ. You are a God of order, and You have set out for us the story of Your Son in a way that is clear and wonderful. At just the right time You sent angels and prophets, raised up nations and brought about events, that we might be prepared for the coming of our Redeemer. You sent John the Baptist to Zechariah and Elizabeth. The word of his coming was given through the angel Gabriel. John's father saw a vision, and he was unable to speak until the coming of this forerunner. Even more than the miracle of John's birth, this same angel informed Mary of an event more magnificent than the coming of John. She conceived a Son who would be Your own Son. This Jesus would reign forever and ever, and would be born to a virgin by the power of the Holy Spirit. Thank You for the blessing of the gift of Your Son. Nothing is impossible with You, O Lord. We are Your servants. Let it be to us according to Your holy Word. May we be filled with the Holy Spirit and speak wonderful words of truth throughout our days on earth. We believe Your Word, which shall be fulfilled in due season. Look upon our humble estate and do great things for us according to Your strength and Your promise. You bring the high low, and the low You make high by Your grace. You have fulfilled the promise to Abraham in the gift of Jesus Christ. As John was given that the people might be prepared for a yet more glorious gift, the coming of Your Son means grace upon grace for us and a gift beyond all other gifts. We hear the Word that You have spoken and we wonder about all the marvelous things You have for us. We will be saved from our enemies through Your covenant mercies granted to Your children. May we serve Your Son in holiness and righteousness all our days. Forgive our sins moment by moment, and grant us light, that we might walk in the way of peace.

Luke 2

Father God, in the fullness of time You sent forth Your Son. This best child of Bethlehem is our King. Fully God and fully man, Your Son is Christ the Lord. Born in a lowly manger, He came for Your glory and for our salvation. Thank You for Your mercy to us through Him. We treasure the truth of Jesus Christ in our hearts. Help us to obey Him with our lives. Lord, we are so easily distracted by lesser things. Keep our eyes upon this Jesus. Help us to see the meaning and importance of our days as we see Your salvation in Jesus Christ. Shine forth the light of Christ throughout the earth, that many will come to see the truth of His life, death, and resurrection. We praise You, O God, for You have sent us the One who is our redemption. He is our strong King. Throughout His life He attended to all of Your commandments. He alone has loved You with all of His being. He knew You as Father with perfect wisdom and obedience. He is our Hope.

Luke 3

Sovereign Lord, we need You. We have much sin in our lives. We seek the gift of repentance. Show us Your salvation. Cause us to bear fruit in keeping with repentance. Make us to trust in Christ alone, and not in any lesser association. Teach us to share our food with the hungry. Turn us away from all abuse and oppression. Your Son has come, and He has baptized the church with the Holy Spirit. He will come again in judgment. We must be found in Him on that day. Wicked men will use their power to pursue their own desires, but they will be disappointed. Many would hope to silence the Word that is spoken by Your servants. They will not be able to win the day. Their lives will be swept away, but Your Son lives forever and ever. He is the second Adam, the promised seed of Abraham, and our eternal hope. Have mercy on us, and grant to us great consolations in the glory of the One who is the Your only-begotten Son.

Luke 4

Father, there is great danger all around us. The devil would tempt us, for he is seeking people to devour. We will not worship him. We will not put You to the test. We will not believe Satan's lies. Be with us in power, for we are weak and in need. We can only live by faith in Your great Son. He has had a powerful victory over death. He has proclaimed good news for the weak and the poor. We have been delivered from the clutches of destruction. Though people treated Your Son with disrespect in the days of His earthly service, He lives now, and has demonstrated His great power to us. We were far off from Your promises and from Your people, but we have been brought near through the blood of the Lamb. You have cast out of us the overwhelming weight of wickedness, and we have been made alive by Your grace. Show us the pathway of service. Make us agents of Your new Kingdom. Teach us how to have merciful hearts, words of life, and hands that help and heal.

Luke 5

Lord God, Your Son came to preach and teach, but He had power in everything that He did. He could bring fish into the nets of His disciples. He could heal the leper. He could make the paralytic walk, and even forgive his sins. He has brought millions to trust in Him, and confounded those who would try to stop Him. This great Jesus is our Redeemer and Messiah. Though men resisted Him, we know that He has healed and forgiven us. We have seen extraordinary things through Your Word. Though we were once outside Your assembly, we have been drawn near by Your mercy. We receive the good word of forgiveness, and we celebrate the happy presence of our Savior among His church. This Jesus is the fulfillment of every ancient prophecy, and the giver of every new gift. Blessed be Your name, O God! We give You thanks for the building of Your Kingdom.

Luke 6

Great God and King, we will stay near to You when men come against us. You know how to answer those who bring accusations against Your disciples. Your Son is our holy Rest and the Lord of the Sabbath. We have been restored in our souls through His Word. He has called His disciples, and has made them apostles of the very best news. Though one was a traitor, that treachery could not stop Your plan. Our Savior has power to heal and to teach. He has brought us new hope. There is great blessing for all who put their trust in this great Messiah. Show us the way of life in the day of temptation. Fill our minds with good gifts from Your Son, that we might love even our enemies. Surely You will give us many spiritual blessings. You will bring us out of every trouble. Your plans are perfect. Grant that we would produce something good out of Your gift of a renewed heart. We will build our house on the rock of Christ, for in Him we have kingdom stability.

Luke 7

Father God, You have granted great faith to Your servants. We know that we are unworthy, and that Your Son is perfect. We are well convinced that Your Word is powerful. When You speak, Your command is as good as done. Your Son can even raise the dead. His compassion is warm and generous. Thank You for this great love. You have visited us in Him. He gave sight to the blind. He made the lame walk. He preached good news to the poor. We hear that good news, and find great riches in Him. We love You Lord, and we will follow You by Your grace. Surely You know how to save the weak. We will listen to Your Word with respect, and with a commitment to obey. Bring fruitful deeds forth from our lives as the yield of Christian faith. Help us to love and serve You in a way that is true to the good news that we believe. We have been forgiven an enormous debt. We love You greatly and give our lives to You as Your disciples.

Luke 8

Great God, You sent Your Son preaching and teaching the Kingdom. You provided for His needs every day. He did not worry, but trusted You. As His Word comes to us today, we pray that it would find good soil in our souls, producing a fruitful yield. Keep away any enemy that would seek to destroy the work of Your Word and Spirit in our lives. Help us to have a perfect confidence in You. Grant to us honest and good hearts. Show us Your glory, and move us in the direction of all that is true and lovely. Thank you for the fellowship that we enjoy within Your family as fellow-travelers in the way of righteousness. Together we will keep our eyes upon You, for You can calm the wind and the waves. Your great Son has power in His hands. He knows all the dangers that face us as we work for the progress of Your Kingdom. Grant us close fellowship with Him in our service of You. Teach us amazing and wonderful things. Forgive us when we become filled with everything that this world offers us. We know that there is a much better way. You have done so much for us, O Lord! We appreciate Your many blessings. We thank You for Your healing power and Your sensitivity to us in our pain. We tremble before You with reverence and joy. Thank You for the gift of faith. Give us hope again for eternal life. We cast off the chains of fear and doubt, and walk with You in the way of hope. You make the dead rise. There is nothing too difficult for You.

Luke 9

Lord God, You have full power and authority over all things. You send us forward as representatives of Your goodness and love. Help us to be true ambassadors of Your Kingdom everywhere we go. Thank You for Your kind provision for all who serve You. Your Son is the Bread of heaven. You give us such good gifts. Wonderful things come from Your hand. Open our hearts to the truth of Your Son. Help us to know the truth and to live in it. We now deny ourselves, take up our cross, and follow Jesus Christ. Your Son is coming again in glory. He has given us a glimpse of His heavenly majesty on the Mount of Transfiguration. Give us heaven's view of the life and ministry of Your Son. We will listen to Him. He is the chosen One and we are chosen in Him. The world is full of disorder and unbelief. Help us to care and to act with the strength and love of the One we name as our Savior. We must believe and live. May the cross and the resurrection be shining lights in our daily existence. We will receive even little children in the name of Jesus Christ. We will seek Your wisdom that we might understand who is with us and who is against us, lest we speak harshly against those whom You love. We will follow You wherever You go, O Lord, but do we understand what we are saying when we pledge our lives to Your service? Help us to keep on going, with the glory of Your Son before us moment by moment.

Luke 10

Sovereign Lord, we pray to You as the Lord of the harvest. We ask that You would send forth laborers into Your harvest field. There is much service for Your kingdom that can be done everywhere and at all times. May we honestly call men to repent and believe. May we warn the complacent and encourage all who would trust in Your Son. Your kingdom can defeat every power of the enemy. Whatever setbacks we face here, whatever evil snare we fall into, and whatever foolishness we temporarily embrace, our names are written in heaven. You have revealed great things to Your church, things that even angels long to look into. Take far away from us the impulse to justify ourselves. Will we not give ourselves over to humble Christian service today? Why are we so hard-hearted? Your Son saw us in our need, and He showed us mercy. Grant us peace within Your church as we serve You and others. Help us to choose the best portion of all, Your Son Jesus Christ.

Luke 11

Father God, You have taught us to pray, giving us Your whole Word to move us in this duty. You have also granted one special prayer for us. Thank you for this rich teaching. May we look to You and pray. Teach us to ask You with confidence for good things agreeable to Your will. Fill us with Your Holy Spirit. As we are led by this great Teacher from above, show us the truths of Your Kingdom. Touch us in the depths of our souls and move us in obedience. Take away from us the impurity of all unclean spirits and lying doctrines. May we hear Your pure Word and keep it. Your Son has been a sign to us through His great resurrection. In Him we have the One who is greater than any king or prophet. Your ways are so wonderful. Would we dare to critique Your Son in our hearts? Would we be Your judge? Forgive us, O Lord, and take us through the coming judgment by the righteousness of Christ. Keep us from toxic doctrines that would only lead to death and destruction. Let us point clearly to the beauty of Your Son, entering into His presence ourselves, and leading others to Him as well.

Luke 12

Lord God, we come to You through Your Son together with multitudes throughout the world. We eagerly seek that Kingdom above where we will be with Your Son and all the church. What would it be like to live with You there? Fill us with Your Spirit. We do not want to grieve Your Son or to blaspheme against Him. We need His great work in our lives moment by moment. Father, keep us from being foolishly dedicated to the goods of this world. We want to be rich toward You, O God. Forgive us for our anxious behavior regarding our possessions. Lord, we lift up to You the poor. Please provide everything necessary for our brothers and sisters in need. What might we sell today so that we would have something to give to them? How can we be an answer to prayer for someone else today? Help us to be ready for the return of Your Son. We need You continually. Help us to know Your will, and then to act in accord with Your commandments. Your Son was fully willing to give His life for us. He was eager to pay the full price for our redemption. We thank You for His love. Help us to live in a sensible way in light of such a great love. Help us to see the obvious things that we have been ignoring, and to live with greater faithfulness to You.

Luke 13

Father, we must repent. You know our sins. Your Son atoned for all this evil. We need to produce fruit worthy of the gospel. We are grateful for Your healing power in our lives. We were twisted and maimed through evil. You saw us in our deplorable condition and You gave us life. Show us great things in Your kingdom, so that we might turn away from self and sin, and turn toward You, helping our brothers and sisters more and more. What shall we do Father, when we are angry about the opportunity to help even those in our own families who are in need? We must have true change in our souls by the power of the gospel. It will not do for us to simply be filled with external religion. Please forgive us. Please help us.

Luke 14

Lord God, thank You for the blessing of a day of rest, a day of great kingdom fulfillment and healing. We humbly come into Your presence day by day, and find ourselves lifted up through our association with Jesus Christ. We don't know how to do what is necessary to live rightly in Your kingdom. Lord, do we excuse ourselves from the duties of worship and sacrificial living? How could we be so foolish? Please bring more people into Your great banquet. Bring us to a greater understanding of the cost of our salvation in the life and death of Your Son. We will not hold back our lives any more. We choose you above all that we have, for we would be Your true disciples.

Luke 15

Father God, You love the lost. We love ourselves more than anything to our great shame. Today we repent. We don't want to falsely imagine ourselves to be in some group that needs no repentance. Help us to repent. Take away from us our angry self-righteousness. Bring about a sweet generosity of heart that is so willing to forgive and happy to be merciful. We have sinned against heaven and against You. We are not worthy to be called Your children. Your fatherly love is so large and kind. Thank You for calling us Your sons and daughters through Jesus Christ. Thank You for the celebration that attends our daily rescue by Your grace. Lord, will we run away from heavenly joy because we insist on being angry at Your kindness to the unworthy? Forgive us, O Lord, and bring us home.

Luke 16

Sovereign Lord, You are God over all. We worship You. Your Word is perfect truth. When You speak of the world to come, grant that we would have faith, and act in this age as those who believe in Your promises. Forgive our sinful impulses to live for present riches rather than for You. We need to care for the poor in this age with some sense of joy concerning the opportunities You grant to us for true heavenly investment. There is a life beyond the grave. Help us to understand what that life is like, that we might be wise even now in the affairs of this life. Your Son has risen from the dead in accord with the Scriptures. Bless us, that we might hear Him with the greatest reverence and follow Him with a life of gospel love.

Luke 17

Almighty Lord, protect us. Keep temptation far away from us, and keep us from tempting anyone else to sin. Help us to be good and faithful servants. Every good gift comes to us from Your grace and mercy. Heal us of the disease of sin. Thank You for the gift of faith. Move us forward in Your Kingdom. Show us the greatness of Your Son, and the wonder of the deliverance He has won for us. A Day is coming when the Son of Man will be revealed in judgment. Bring us into the fullness of Your presence. Even now, we are somehow with You in Christ.

Luke 18

Our God and King, we come to You in prayer through Jesus Christ our Lord. You have instructed us to be persistent in our supplications. You bring justice to the oppressed and mercy to those who humble themselves before You. Keep us far away from foolish self-righteousness. Be merciful to us. We are sinners. Bring Your blessings even upon our little ones, for Your kingdom belongs to the children of even one believer. Will we turn away from You? Will our young ones be foolish and love the world more than You? We love Your Law in our minds. Why do we still disobey Your commandments? Could it be that we love wealth more than Your kingdom? Save us, O Lord. Assure us moment by moment of the blessings of Your house, now and forever. Your Son was delivered over to the Gentiles for us. He was killed, and rose again on the third day. Grant that we would see Him rightly. Have mercy on us, O Lord. Give to us the very best spiritual sight. We ask in faith. We will glorify and praise You forever.

Luke 19

Lord God, You know what is in the heart of every man. You see the Zacchaeus hiding in a tree, and even more amazingly, You see the truth of the repentance that You freely grant to a wicked man. You seek and save the lost. Grant to us the patience of true kingdom priorities, that we would be willing to invest our lives for Your glory. Have we known You so little that we would cower in fear and be completely unprofitable for Your purposes? Father, we surrender to You. We will be bold for Your Kingdom. Lead us by Your Spirit in profitable directions. Your Son surely gave everything that He had for Your glory. He rode into Jerusalem as the Messiah King. Even now we cry out to You. Save us, O Lord! Have pity on Your church, our Father. Your enemies would turn Your house of prayer into a den of robbers. They would seek to destroy us. We will take our refuge in You, O God. You will surely deliver us out of every evil.

Luke 20

Father God, Your Son was bold for the truth. Why are we so afraid? Teach us the truth, and grant us both wisdom and courage. We are Your holy vineyard. Make us fruitful in Your service. Send Your Son among Your church day by day. As we hear Your Word, assure us of the truth that He speaks to His humble people through the Scriptures. He is the Stone that the builders rejected. Powerful men tried to trap Him. Some wanted to make Him look like a rebellious insurrectionist. Others thought that they could make a fool of Him, though they only exposed their own ignorance of the Scriptures and of Your power. He put such men to shame. Now He lives forever, and in Him we have found eternal life. He is both David's Son and David's Lord. Though rejected by men, He has become the Cornerstone of a new kingdom.

Luke 21

Our Father, we give You all that we have today, even out of our poverty. Surely we are a part of a new temple through faith in Your Son. There is much trouble all around us, but You will surely protect Your children as we move forward in the tasks that You have given us. Provide for Your servants who are seeking only to do what You have commanded. One day there will be signs in the heavens, and Your Son will come. All Your good plans will be fulfilled. May we be those who wait faithfully, and who serve You diligently, as we long for Your Son's appearing.

Luke 22

Lord God, Your Son is our Passover. His death as the Lamb of God was by the hands of wicked men, but also by Your express purpose and plan. He instituted the sacrament of the Supper for our good. Help us to earnestly desire the celebration of this meal, as Your Son longed to institute this meal in remembrance of Him. He has brought about a new covenant in his death and resurrection. He performed the greatest service to Your church that could ever be accomplished, for He gave His life for us. We are so thankful for His love. We know that Jesus has prayed for us, and that You will keep us forever. Forgive our weakness and our sin. Surely our salvation is dependent on Your strength and not on our own power. He was numbered with the transgressors, and He atoned for our sins. When Your Son offered up loud supplications and tears to You, He was heard. You will not abandon the church that He bought with His blood. We will not betray You. Help us, O God! We must listen to Your Son and follow Him. Preserve us during our hour of darkness, that we might walk in these days by the light of Your Son. We acknowledge You before men, O God. We do know You, and we know Your Son. We love You, and are kept by Your covenant faithfulness. We will not utterly fall, for You will keep us in the day of trial. Your Son suffered greatly for us. Surely You love Your children. Even now we are called to be Your sons and daughters through Him who loved us and gave Himself for us.

Luke 23

Lord God, liars came against Your Son with false accusations, but there was no guilt in Him. Others desired only to see Him do some sign, but they had no heart to hear Your Word. They treated the Lord Jesus Christ with disrespect. Your Son did nothing deserving death, but the crowds strangely preferred the release of another man and demanded the crucifixion of Jesus. He carried a cross that only He could have borne. Through Him, You have delivered us from eternal destruction. Have mercy on us, O Lord, for we have not followed Your great Son in the way that we should. He was willing to save us, though it meant the cross. Now He has been publicly declared to be the King of Your people. Remember us, O Lord, and bless us with a true life of Christian obedience. We have been granted access into Your presence through Your Son's death. He was most certainly innocent, but He took upon Himself our great guilt. His body rested in the grave until the day of His resurrection. O Lord, what a great atonement has been achieved for us!

Luke 24

Sovereign Lord, the stone, the guards, and the seal could not keep Your Son in the grave. He is risen! Thank You for the faithful testimony that we have to the truth of this wonderful event. What marvelous things took place in Jerusalem at that time. Your Son was condemned to death and crucified. On the third day He rose again. This was all according to the Word of the Prophets. Christ suffered and entered into His glory. Now we see and confess that all of the Scriptures teach us about the great things of Jesus. May Your Son be known to us by Word and sacrament. Grant that we too will partake of the promised resurrection. Cast far away from us all doubt concerning the events recorded in Your holy Word. Everything written in all of the books of the Bible must be fulfilled. Now Your Son has ascended into heaven, and we are blessed with the great gift of Your Holy Spirit poured out upon Your church. Strengthen us by faith as we seek Your help day by day.

John

John 1

Eternal God, You and Your Son were in the beginning, together with the Holy Spirit. We rejoice in You, the Triune God of Creation. We thank You for Your Word of truth through the prophets, now recorded for us in the Scriptures. We receive Your Son this day. We believe in the name of the One who is full of grace and truth, who became flesh and dwelt among men for our salvation. Your Son is now at Your right hand in glory. We thank You for this great Messiah. Announced by the prophets, Jesus the Christ is our Savior and Lord. Teach us to follow the Lamb of God who has taken away the sins of people near and far. He is full of the Spirit, and He has sent forth the Spirit. We seek You, Lord Jesus Christ. O Father, grant to us a holy regard for Your great Son. Cause us to stand on this Cornerstone of Your church. He is good and kind. He is wise and full of truth, for He is the God at Your right hand. He has made the way to heaven for us.

John 2

Merciful Father, Your Son is a great husband for the church. We will enjoy the greatest wedding feast when He returns. That day will arrive by Your power and love, and we will rejoice with the fullest happiness, for we long for His appearing. We thank You for the signs that Your Son gave of His glory. He will come with justice as well as salvation. Grant that we would mourn for the state of Your church, yet that we would have confidence that You make all things new. Your Son has built a new Temple, for He raised up His body in divine power, and we are now united in that great Temple of the Holy Spirit.

John 3

Glorious Lord, we must be born from above. We must have life that can only come from You. Help us to embrace the wonderful miracle of regeneration by the effectual calling of Your Holy Spirit. Send Your Spirit to Your people in greater fullness. We will not resist You, O Lord. Please forgive us and help us. We look to Your Son, O God, and we are alive in Him. We do believe in Jesus Christ, and now we live, for You have promised that we have eternal life through Him. We hate our wickedness. Please expose our sinful deeds, and forgive us. We turn toward You again that we might pursue the righteousness that can only come as a gift from You. Cleanse us in that water that comes from above. We rejoice at the voice of the Son of God. Speak to us through Your Word. Our Savior has come from heaven. We receive His testimony, for He is the Truth. We believe in Your Son and will follow Him. Be merciful to us, for we trust in Your holy Name.

John 4

God of Truth and Mercy, Your Son manifested a wonderful fullness of all Your divine attributes even during the days of His humiliation. He knew what was in every heart. He had great mercy upon the weak. He pronounced the truth of new life boldly and with great compassion. We want the living water that can only come from You. You know the truth of both our sin and Your eternal plan. We must worship in Your Son, for He is the new Temple. We must worship in Him, for we are called to worship in Spirit and in Truth. He is the only Messiah. Will You save the unworthy? We know that You will. There is hope for us. The harvest is plentiful. Send forth workers for the preaching of the gospel. Help us each to do the part that You have for us, that Your body might testify to the truth and live in love. Your Son had great mercy upon the weak. By His Word we shall live forever. There is power in His voice. One day He will call forth the dead from their graves, and there will be a glorious resurrection.

John 5

Father God, we thank You for the healing power of Jesus Christ. Here we have a great help for us today, and a great hope for the future. We need You now. We trust You forever. Thank you for the forgiveness of sins. Your Son has perfectly fulfilled the Law. He is our Sabbath rest. In Him we have the rest that is to come. We honor Your Son just as we honor You, for You sent Your Son. We long to hear His voice and to see the coming resurrection of the dead. Your judgment is just. You have demonstrated with great clarity that salvation is in Your Son. We have never seen You, but we gladly receive Your Word. Your love is in us, and we rejoice in Your Son. We believe the Scriptures. They confirm to us that Jesus is the Christ.

John 6

Sovereign Lord, You have provided for us in our great need. You sent Your Son, the Bread from heaven, that we might be fully satisfied in our souls. Thank you for using us as Your disciples as You continue to testify to Your Kingdom and Your glory throughout the world. Why should we live in darkness, when Your Son is a bright and shining light? He has demonstrated His authority over creation. Who could He be if not the expected Son of God? You have set Your seal of approval on Him. We need to believe in the One You have sent. He is the Bread of Life. We come to Him. All that You give to Your Son shall surely come to You, and You will keep us and will raise us up on the last day. This is our confident expectation. You have drawn us to Him, and so we come. We need this Living Bread from heaven. He has given us His flesh and blood that we might have eternal life. He will raise us up on the last day. We abide in Your Son, and He abides in us. What can it mean that we abide in Him and He in us? Your Son speaks words of life. Help us to understand these great spiritual truths. He has the words of life. Though others may turn away, we want to stay with You forever. Have mercy on us even when we doubt. We are so weak in our understanding and our courage, but You will never abandon Your children.

John 7

Lord God, even the brothers of Jesus did not believe in Him. Our own faith is far from perfect at present. Surely You will bring us to a perfect trust in Your Son when we see Him. Now we know in part, and we still struggle with sin. Please forgive us. Your Son will grant us a full obedience when we go to be with Him. How foolish we are when we act as the judge of the Son of God. We need to receive Your Word as the truth. We know You and we love You. Thank you that the news of Your Son has reached our land. We hear and believe. According to Your Word, out of our hearts will flow rivers of living Water, even the Holy Spirit. Your Son is the Son of David, born in Bethlehem, but He surely is more than a human deliverer. He is the Son of God, eternally from heaven. Help us to rest in Him today and forever.

John 8

Our Father, Your Son faced such controversy as He moved toward the cross. Why do men not acknowledge the Light of the world? Our sin nature is so powerful in evil. Only You can move us toward the hope and joy that is ours in Christ. Your Son suffered for us. He came from above in order to face many trials for us here below. He was lifted up on the cross after bringing the Word of truth to His disciples. The truth that He has spoken still sets men free today. Grant that we will abide in that Word forever. If Jesus sets us free, we will be free indeed. We do not want to return to the way of the devil. We desire to know You day by day as our Father, and to follow You. Protect us from the dangers that come from the Father of lies. Your promise is so wonderful. We shall not see the second death, though our mortal bodies may rest in the grave. Your Son is the great "I AM" forever.

John 9

Father God, we need to see the truth about You day by day. We cry out to You for spiritual sight. We do not want to pretend that we understand all that we should understand by this time. Grant us more sight from Your Word. Your Son gave sight to a man who was born blind. What a wonderful day of Kingdom wholeness it was when such a miracle was performed! Yet those who sat on Moses' seat had distorted Your Law into a system of angry self-justification. Is it a violation of Your Law to open the eyes of a blind man on the Sabbath? How could we get so far off track and yet be so sure of our rightness? One day we shall see Jesus. We long for that greatest of all Sabbaths. Keep us from the undue influence of those who promote destructive and man-centered religious philosophies, lest we abandon the clarity of sight that Christ has already granted to us.

John 10

Lord God, You have granted to us the Good Shepherd. He knows us, and we know Him. We hear His voice, and we love Him. He is the Door to heaven. We enter into Your Kingdom through Him. He has given us the fullness of life. Protect us from vicious wolves, and from under-shepherds who would abandon us in times of danger. Unite Your church together as one flock under our one true Shepherd. Your Son laid down His life for us, and He picked it up again in His resurrection. He has revealed Himself as the Christ, but many who saw and heard Him did not believe. We believe. Keep us in Your hand forever. You and Your Son are One. He is fully God and fully man, and He is our Redeemer. You consecrated Him and sent Him into the world. He performed many great works which clearly fulfilled all true expectations of the coming Messiah. We thank You for the wonderful gift of Your Son, the great Shepherd of the Sheep.

John 11

Sovereign Lord, we struggle with our mortality in this dark world. The ones we love live and die. Grant us faith to believe in the resurrection. Your Son is the Resurrection. On the last day He will awaken those who sleep in Him. Their souls are alive and awake with You even now. Whatever Your Son asks of You, You will surely give Him. He is our life. Grant us more and more life in Him day by day. Comfort us in our grief and loss. Console us in a day of distress. Remind us of the truth, that though we weep, Your Son is the Resurrection. He loves us. We do not want to grieve Your Holy Spirit today with our unbelief. Grant us a fuller assurance. We do believe, but we seem to ignore the power of the resurrection. You sent Your Son to save us. He will come again to call our resting bodies from the grave. He will not be stopped. It was most necessary for this one Man to die, so that we might live as Your people. We are Your children who were scattered abroad, but now we are being gathered together into Your church. Grant us all a great delight in worship as we anticipate together the glory of the coming Day.

John 12

Great God, thank You for the hope that we have in Christ, a hope of resurrection life. Help us to testify to this great hope by giving ourselves to the work of the Kingdom even now. We know of the death of Christ for sinners, and we believe in His resurrection. Your Son has come in Your Name as the King of Israel. What kind of King is Your Son? Gentiles find their place in this great King of the Jews. This could not happen without His death. He gave His life for us, and we now have life. You have glorified Your Name in Your Son. He was lifted up on the cross, defeating the power of evil and drawing many people from all the nations to Himself. Today we walk in His light, for He has made us to be sons of light through faith in Him. We have believed the report that has been revealed to us by Your Word and Spirit. Help us to be courageous in our testimony to Your Son. Let us love the glory that will come from you more than the glory that men give.

John 13

Holy Father in Heaven, what is love? Your Son demonstrated to us the way of love. He was willing to take the place of the lowest servant in order to work our redemption. He did more than wash the feet of His disciples. He became the lowest sinner on the cross and won for us the kingdom of heaven. In this He has also set an example for us. He is our Lord and Master. Shall we run away from the cross that we are to bear? Strengthen us in faith, so that we will never betray Your Son and His people. What we do against Your church, we do against Your Son. Forgive us

Father, and help us to resist the devil. We seek the Lord Jesus Christ. It is our pledge and intention to love Your disciples, but will we really do it? Lord, have mercy upon us. Keep us from arrogant presumption, and glorify Your Name among us.

John 14

Lord God, You have given us a great assurance of eternal life. Your Son is the Way, and the Truth, and the Life. When we Know Him, then we know You. You are in Your Son and Your Son is in You. His works testify to His own divine nature. What an amazing thing that Your Son has called us to do an even broader work in bringing the message of life to the whole world! Because He lives, we also shall live. Teach us to love His commandments and to keep them. Make Your home with us, O Lord. Fill us with Your Spirit. Help us to learn the truth through His great ministry. Your Son is with You, and in Him we are with You. He faced the most devastating loss for us. Help us to walk faithfully in His ways.

John 15

O God, we do not want to ever walk away from Jesus. We do not want to resist Your Spirit because of the pain of Your pruning work. We need to abide in the vine. Apart from You we can do nothing. We ask You now for the blessing of much fruit. Enable us to abide in Your love and to keep Your commandments. May our joy be full. Your Son has laid down His life for us, and we are His friends. He has chosen us. He has a plan for godly fruit that will come from our lives. We are not of the world. We have been chosen out of the world. Help us to have courage to do the work that You have for us in the world, though the world may hate us. Grant us a fuller measure of the Spirit of truth, that we may bear witness to Your greatness and Your love.

John 16

Lord God, grant to us the strength that we need in order to face the persecution that will come against Your church. Help us to embrace the sorrows of the present age, that we might have the fullness of joy even now, a joy that comes from the assurance of the age of joy that is yet to come. We ask that the Holy Spirit would lead us into all truth. May Your Word be boldly declared to us, and may we have ears to hear the greatness of Your message. Your Son's days on this earth were brief. He was here for a little while, and then He was gone, yet His disciples did not have sorrow. No one could take away their joy. Help us to believe in resurrection life in the way that they did. Help us to ask and receive from You. You desire that we should not only seek, but find. Help us to stay firm in the faith through every tribulation, for Your Son has overcome the world.

John 17

Father, surely You heard the entreaties of Your Son when He prayed on earth. You have glorified Jesus. Through Him we have eternal life. Grant that we will keep Your Word day by day. Protect us from the lies of our adversary. Help us to hold fast to the truth by Your grace. Your Son has prayed for us. What a tremendous source of confidence to Your people in times of trouble! Even now He intercedes for us. Thank You for this great gift. Sanctify us in the truth. Bring others to us who will hear of Jesus Christ through our words. Grant that we will be one in Your Son forever. May the love with which You love Your Son be in us, and may He Himself be in us.

John 18

Great God, we seek You. In former days we used the Name of Your Son in vain attempts to tear Him down. Forgive us, O Lord. Now we approach You with fear and joy through Him who loved us with an everlasting love. He has forgiven our sins. Even now, though we want to serve You, we speak rash words and do things that are not in accord with Your holy will. Would we even deny You under some awful temptation? Father, we do not want to overestimate our strength. We turn away from all sin. Your son died for us. We ask for Your help immediately, lest we bring some disgrace upon Your Name. We are so easily moved by those who observe us and by our own foolish thinking. Help us to see You only, to love You entirely, and then to love our neighbors as ourselves. Grant that we will be faithful through many attacks and trials. Fill us with the power and love of Christ, who endured the assaults of men for our sake. He is our King. There was no guilt in Him at all. Grant us ears to hear His voice through the Scriptures, that we might believe the truth, and bear witness to Him, now and forever.

John 19

Father God, give us strength for the work of prayer and service that You have appointed for us this day. We don't want to give up, but we are so weak. Your Son faced such brutal attacks for us, yet without sin. Let His heart and mind be in us now so that we will serve You with integrity and zeal. He is the man above men, yet He took the lowest place in history when He died for our sins. He is the King of kings, but His crown was a crown of thorns, and His royal robe the gift of those who mocked Him. He is the Son of God, but the people of His creation demanded that He be crucified. Father, we know that You govern all things, and that the day of the death of Your Son came by Your express plan and foreknowledge. Will we still resist You in some area of our lives? Your Son is the fulfillment of every hope and expectation of Your Word. Thank You for the gift of Your church. In Your household we find a family that will live forever. The death of Your Son has won for us eternal life. Through the events of His burial we know of the certainty of His death. Though our bodies may one day rest in the grave, we shall be alive forever in Christ.

John 20

Lord God, we marvel at the empty tomb. We consider the placement of the linen cloths lying there, cloths that once covered the dead body of Your Son. We think of the other cloth that once covered a lifeless face, now folded in a place by itself. We believe. Then we consider the familiar voice of Jesus calling His friend by her own name, the voice of a risen Man who walks in the presence of angels. Yes, we believe. He is risen. He is the firstborn of many brethren. As He is, so shall we be. Though we die, there is no point in anyone clinging to our flesh, for our spirits shall ascend on high, and when the Son of Man calls us out from the grave, we shall rise again, not with mortal flesh, but with immortal bodies. We long for Your coming, O Lord! Your Father is our Father. Your God is our God, and we have peace. Father God, fill Your church with Your Holy Spirit. As You sent Your Son, not to be served, but to serve, send us forward in Your love. Use Your church to declare the forgiveness of sins. Grant us a very secure faith in the resurrection of Jesus Christ and in our coming resurrection. Though we have not yet seen, we do sincerely believe.

John 21

Father God, Your Son has revealed Himself to us through His Word and Spirit, and also in the breaking of bread together as Your church worships You through our Redeemer. Your Son is full of blessing for us. He continues to serve Your church with unexpected joys according to Your great plan. We feast together at Your table with confidence in Him. You use us as fishers of men according to Your Word. You know our defiling sin, and You restore us again with forgiveness and a call to serve. We do love You. We will feed Your sheep. You know all things, and our lives are in Your hands. If we live, we live for You. If we die, we go to be with You, and our lives are still in Your hands. Teach us to trust You with our own lives and with the lives of everyone around us near and far. We thank You for the testimony of Your apostles regarding our great Savior. We hear the truth recorded for us in the Scriptures, and we rest in Your love.

Acts

Acts 1

Sovereign Lord, Your plans are full and wonderful. You have promised us the great gift of Your Holy Spirit. By this same Spirit we are Your witnesses to the end of the earth. You direct this great work of mission from Your seat on high. Continue to supply us with all things necessary for the life that You have given to us. We thank You for the apostolic witness granted to us in the New Testament. Through this good Word we have the perfect interpretation of the Old Testament. Please direct us into a true understanding of the Scriptures, and lead us in the preaching and teaching of Your Word. Build Your glorious kingdom by Your mighty power even in our day.

Acts 2

Great God, You have granted to Your church the promised blessing of the Holy Spirit. You have enabled us to hear the message of Your mighty works. Glory to Your Name, O God! You will pour out Your Spirit on all flesh in the age to come. That age has broken in now through Your great work of salvation. All who call upon the Name of the Lord as worshipers in the covenant assembly shall be brought from death to life. That Name above all names is Jesus, who is the Lord of Glory. He is yet alive, and so we call upon Him even now, for He is both Man and God. He is David's Son and David's Lord. He is our King and our Messiah. Our sins sent Him to the cross. We now repent of all known sin. We thank You for the covenant sign and seal of baptism, testifying of the life to come by the cleansing work of the Spirit and the forgiveness of sins through the blood of Christ. We give ourselves to You and to one another, as we devote ourselves to the way of worship as the community of salvation in this present age.

Acts 3

Our Father, we are so very grateful for Your mercy to the weak. Lord, You provide for our every need. You grant us food, shelter, health, friendship, and families; and these are just the beginning of the blessings that You have for us. Though we have denied Your Son, You have given us faith in His Name. Through Him we have a taste of the life to come. Bring us times of refreshing day by day so that we will remember Your promises and be strengthened for Your service. We have heard Your Word. You will bring about the fulfillment of all that You have promised to Your people of old. Turn us from our wickedness and grant us great joy in the contemplation of Your eternal love.

Acts 4

Lord God Almighty, we know that there are some who do not want to hear the Word. They may be enraged by any signs of life that seem to flow from the Name of Jesus Christ. Grant to us the courage to speak boldly for that Name above all names. There is no other name under heaven given among men by which we must be saved. Keep us near Your resurrected and ascended Son, so that it may be evident to all through our humility and holy boldness that we have been with Jesus. You have done great things for us. You are powerful in all Your works of creation and providence. Why does the world hate You? Why were even the rulers of Your people determined to kill the Son of God? Move our hearts and minds with the presence of Your Spirit, filling us with Your love and power. Make us witnesses of Your grace throughout the church and the world. Teach us to give all that we have and all that we are to You in the face of such obvious and overwhelming goodness.

Acts 5

Our Father, we are so easily tempted by sinful desires. We want to be seen as great among men, even within Your church. Forgive us for this deadly sin. Not only do we bring great trouble upon ourselves, but we also bring trials upon our families and Your church. Despite our foolishness, we know that You will work all things for Your purposes. Please bring great fear upon Your people so that we may remember the seriousness of our commitments. Send Your holy angels to protect us from evil that would be too strong for us. Amaze Your enemies as You accomplish Your heavenly purposes in the midst of this passing age. Teach us not to follow rulers when they command us to violate Your way. We must follow You, even if men would seek to kill us for challenging their authority. Make our witness real. Imposters come and go, and their followers amount to nothing. But the Word and kingdom of Jesus cannot be stopped, for this assembly is the very kingdom of God on earth in this present age. Your Son Jesus is surely the Messiah. To oppose Him is to oppose You.

Acts 6

Lord God, thank You for the way that You solve problems with such wisdom and love. Help us to remember that those who have been set apart for the Word should devote themselves to the duties of leading Your church in prayer, teaching, and preaching. These men should not be distracted by other concerns, however important and legitimate. Raise up men that are full of the Holy Spirit and wisdom to lead all of the believers in service, so that issues of justice, mercy, and order are attended to with diligence and holiness. Fill our hearts with wisdom and with Your Spirit. Grant us godly composure and Christ-like love for You and for others.

Acts 7

Our Father, grant that we would rightly appreciate the privilege of suffering for the name of Jesus Christ. Without this true assessment of our trials, we will always shrink away from a forthright statement of Your Word in situations of danger. You have sent one Man who would truly keep Your perfect Law. Through His death and resurrection He became the cornerstone of a new spiritual temple, Your church throughout the world. All of the patriarchs and heroes of the faith in earlier days longed for this day of the Messiah. Now He has actually visited us. This Jesus did all things well. He has poured out Your Holy Spirit upon Your church. We love the Law of Christ. We rejoice in the Temple of the Holy Spirit. We long for the fulfillment of Your promise in the age to come, in the land of Resurrection. We love the Word of the Prophets which has now come in person in the great beauty of our Messiah. He is the perfect Son of David, and He has built a new house for His people in His own world-wide body. We will not resist the Holy Spirit. We will love and serve the Righteous One. Teach us the truth about our sin, that we might more fully and earnestly repent of it and be forgiven. Though men might work together to kill us, Your truth can never be stopped. Grant us such a beauty of holiness and love that we would be willing to forgive those who seek our destruction.

Acts 8

Sovereign Lord, You have promised that Your truth would not be stopped in Jerusalem, but that it would be heard in all Judea, Samaria, and to the very ends of the earth. As that Word moved forward through Your apostles, many believed, even among those who had formerly been committed to pagan practices. So many in every age are dedicated to the worship of money, or think that they can buy Your gifts. You will bring Your Word even to men such as this. You will open the minds of distant tribes and people groups through Your great power. The faith that comes to one man can eventually touch many more who were once securely bound in the slavery of idolatry. Grant to all Your people the joy of new life, as Your servants are baptized into a community of living hope.

Acts 9

Glorious Lord, You can take a man who is breathing threats against You and Your people and make him into a great servant of the Word. Blessed be Your Name. You help such a man to see the truth that he once condemned. The power of Your gospel changes men, softening proud hearts, and making them willing to suffer for the Name that they hated. Remove from our eyes any remaining spiritual blindness. Help us to see even more clearly that Jesus is Your Son. He is the only Messiah, and this is clearly shown through even the Old Testament Scriptures. Grant that our ministers would preach boldly among men who may be seeking to kill us. Grant us peace and joy in the comfort that comes from Your Truth and from the Holy Spirit. Make us know Your love for us so fully that we cannot help but be overflowing with good works. Remove far from us all ungodly hatred, self-centered distractions, and laziness. Take away all false excuses that we used in earlier days to reject so many great opportunities to serve You.

Acts 10

God of the Nations, we rejoice in the obvious truth that salvation has been granted not only to Jews, but also to the Gentiles. How many a Cornelius have come to know the truth of this great Jewish Messiah! In this Christ we have been declared clean. How often do we treat others as unclean when You have cleansed them for the hearing of Your Word? Thank You for Your providence among men and angels whereby the truth of Jesus has been brought to the ends of the earth. Could it be that Your church would be strangely unmoved by this great expansion of Your kingdom? Are we really so captivated by our private concerns that we only see our own homes and families and the continual needs of our lives? Help us to fear You again and to do what is right. Help us to love the preaching of Jesus Christ here and in distant lands. Will we not be moved by the resurrection of Jesus Christ? Could it be that a man would claim to be alive to the resurrection of Jesus, and yet still be dead to the progress of Your Son's kingdom throughout the world? Open our eyes, O Lord! Some unseen enemy must yet be against us or within us. Open our eyes so that we would love You and serve You! Grant us a more powerful cleansing by Your Spirit and a more wonderful knowledge of the truth so that we would be eager to serve You forever.

Acts 11

Father God, thank You for the great wonder of the message of Christ, which is now coming to all the nations. Thank You that the Messiah of the Jews is the Messiah for the whole world. You have made men in Your image, and we have learned that we should not treat any man as common or unclean. We thank You for the great blessing of the gift of Your Holy Spirit. You have granted even the Gentiles the gift of repentance that leads to life. The task yet ahead of us is large, for the gospel must be preached to all nations. Please bless us with energy, clarity, and diligence that we might rightly serve Jesus Christ. Use all of Your great acts of providence to bring glory to Your Name, as the Word of Your Son is brought to every land.

Acts 12

Lord of Glory, in this age there are many who would lay violent hands upon Your church. We mourn this sin, yet we know that You are working wonderful miracles of grace even through the suffering that we face. We offer up to You earnest prayers for our brothers and sisters in prison. Send Your angels to rescue many who are in great need because of one tribulation or another. Restore all of Your people to the assembly of those who gather in Your presence for worship. Give us a clear and balanced mind so that we can continue to serve You for as many days as You see fit. This age will one day come to an end, and much that is confusing to us today will be brought to light through the radiance of Your Son's appearing. We long for His return and for the dawning of a very new day in the fullness of Your great glory.

Acts 13

Father God, we thank You for the preachers and teachers that You have given to Your church. We pray that You will lead them to the precise places that You have for them to go, that they might serve You in fruitful work according to Your plan. Help these men to be forthright in their speech, for men-pleasers will not be helpful to the progress of the truth. Help these servants to see this life in a right way, so that they will not fall into the many temptations that so easily ensnare those who are called to be servants of the Word. Grant that these preachers and teachers would have an accurate understanding of the Old and New Testaments. May they be in the Word day by day in ways that are helpful for their own souls, and for the understanding of those who will hear them. Help them to see Christ, His atoning work, and His glorious resurrection as the very center of Your living Word. What a joy it is to see Your Son as the surprising fulfillment of the Word given to Your people even under the period of the Law! We have been freed from sin by the message and power of Christ. We pray that the true and bold ministry of Your Word would be powerful in our day. How can this happen if the men that You call as Your servants are trapped by worldliness and idolatry? Sanctify Your church, including her ministers, and grant all of Your assemblies a strong hope of eternal life and the fullness of joy even now through the Holy Spirit.

Acts 14

Our Father, Your missionaries are serving in all kinds of places throughout the world. As the apostle went not only to established places of worship, but also spoke in public places where people had very little knowledge of Your Word, Your servants even today serve in a variety of settings. We pray that You would provide them with every resource necessary for their effective proclamation of Your great works of creation, providence, and redemption. We pray that You would grant all these brothers clarity, energy, health, and especially spiritual strength in the midst of much weakness. We commend them to Your grace. Use their ministry in a powerful way, and grant an open door in many places where the Word has never before been heard.

Acts 15

Great God, there was much dissension in the early church, and there are important disagreements in the church today. Help us to distinguish between those matters where love must cover a multitude of sins, and those matters that must be more fully discussed for Your good purposes. Give us the courage and discipline to call together eminent and godly servants of the truth in order to gain greater clarity by Your Word and Spirit. Make their deliberations a productive and worthwhile use of Your resources. Thank You for the wonderful truth that was displayed so powerfully in Your church in days of old when the age changed from the time of the Law to the new day of the gospel. Thank you for the way of life by grace through the faith that remained the same in both ages. Yet thank You once again for the clarity that the ceremonies of the Law have been fulfilled in Christ. It is now clear that we do not need to be Jewish before we can be Christians. The way of life for us in not through circumcision, Passover, and the regulations of clean and unclean. Nonetheless, we thank You for the record of these matters in the Law, for they show us the wonders of Christ. He has become our circumcision through His death on the cross. Through Him alone we have been rescued from sure destruction, for He is our Passover. By His blood sprinkled upon our hearts we have been cleansed by the Holy Spirit from the guilt and stain of sin.

Acts 16

Our Father, we thank You for the progress of Your church throughout the centuries. You have been pleased to bring spiritual growth through challenging providences. Thank You for Your wisdom and Your mercy. Strengthen us by faith. Help us to hear the call of those who have been granted a true thirst for the Word. Open the hearts of Your elect to not only believe but also to willingly suffer for the Name of Christ. Release many from distraction and oppression so that Your people can serve You with the freedom that comes through faith in Your Son. Thank You for the way that You work through Your suffering church to give a true testimony to the hope that we have in Christ. We believe in You and we believe in Your glorious Son. We have been saved by the blood of the Lamb, and we rejoice in the blessings that have come to us by grace. Teach us to make good use of our sufferings, knowing that even these are a gift from Your powerful hand.

Acts 17

Lord God, Your message came first to the Jews and then to the Gentiles, yet Your truth is the same for all the people groups of the world, that Jesus is the Christ. Thank You for the grace of Your presence in trying times. Grant Your servants encouragement in all kinds of ministry situations. Teach them to do Your work with love and perseverance, trusting You in all times and places. The message of the truth may seem to be a foreign religious system to those who have never heard it. How are our ministers to know how to speak and what they are to say? Lead them in their teaching so that they can present the wonder of Your being and the grandeur and glory of Your works. Show them engaging truths all around them that will help in explaining the beauty of the gospel to those who are being saved.

Acts 18

O Sovereign Lord, You gave us the facts of redemption and have granted men reasoning capability so that they might hear and believe. Why do we resist Your good news? Why is there so much hatred expressed against the loveliest truths known among men? Grant to Your church in many places a season of peace, that many will be taught in an orderly way. You know the right moments for various trials. Teach us the blessings of those seasons as well. Even when we are unable to understand Your providence, help us to keep on going in the tasks that You have for us. Help us to rejoice in the way that You raise up many servants who have a variety of wonderful gifts that can be used for Your glory.

Acts 19

Great God, the story of Your Son's work through Your church is exciting and inspiring. We ask that You would fill Your assembly with Your Spirit, that the work of the ministry may move forward according to Your holy will. You have ordained great works of speech and service for the progress of the truth. May Your Son's Name be greatly extolled and may the lives of many people be aided in wonderful ways according to Your merciful plan. Father, we know that in every culture there will be those who gain their wealth through idolatrous enterprises. Those who continue to cling to old ways of sin will not be friends of the message of Your Son. Teach us how to live well for You in such situations. You are able to accomplish wonderful ends through the use of amazing means. We desire to live at peace with all men, but some may not be willing to be at peace with us. Through even these times of unwelcome animosity, be pleased to accomplish the purposes of Your grace.

Acts 20

Father God, thank You for the encouragement that we receive through the good news that You have granted to us by the preaching of Your Word. Thank You also for the communion that we enjoy as we remember Your Son's death for us. We are comforted as we see Your kind provision for us in our every need. Lord, we are grateful for the faithful ministry of the Word. Grant to us open hearts so that we will receive Your entire counsel. Protect Your church from enemies who would try to destroy us, even from within our own number. Grant to us diligence and love in serving Your Son and all His people. We trust You with our lives, for You have redeemed us through the blood of Your Son.

Acts 21

Lord God, You call us to a life of suffering love in this age. Make us willing to face the challenges that come our way with joy, knowing that You are very powerful and full of compassion. We are ready not only to face trials, but even to die in order to serve You. We thank You for the great things that You have accomplished through the ministry of the Word over many centuries. We rejoice in the truth that the message of salvation through Christ has gone beyond the borders of Israel. The age of the Old Testament has been fulfilled. The New Testament age has come. Your Son is ruling Your church from on high. Even when civil authorities are greatly confused and take hostile action against Your church, You are still working out Your holy will. You do all things well.

Acts 22

Father God, You have prepared us from our birth for a particular path of service. Nonetheless, we were once dead to Your love and to Your plans for our good, but You came to us and helped us. You have led us by the hand to the One who has given us sight. We thank You for this Righteous One, Jesus Christ. Our sins have been washed away through the blood of the Lamb and the cleansing water of the Holy Spirit. We rejoice in Your Son, and we celebrate our baptism in the Triune Name. Though men may be impressed by our citizenship in one nation or another, we rejoice that we are citizens in heaven, knowing that You have a good purpose for us even here and now.

Acts 23

Lord of Hosts, we believe in the resurrection of the dead. We know that if our bodies soon rest in the grave, our spirits will yet live in the presence of Your Son, our Lord Jesus Christ. When He returns in glory, there will be a resurrection of both the righteous and the wicked. As we wait for that great day it is our aim to serve You faithfully. Thank You that You have granted to some of Your servants the privilege of giving their lives for the truth of Christ. Even if only a few will be martyrs who would die at the hands of the enemies of the gospel, we all commit our lives to You. We entrust our bodies and souls to Your great care, for You know what is best for Your servants.

Acts 24

Almighty God, though Your children may be detained unreasonably by evil men, we know that You are working all things for our good and for Your own glory. Help us to cheerfully submit to all lawful authority. Our hope is in You. There will be a resurrection of the just and the unjust. This confident expectation is at the center of our faith, for Christ, our Resurrected Lord, is our eternal King. We thank You that one Man has already attained to the resurrection life. He is the firstborn among many brethren. In Him we have the assurance of new life both in body and soul, though we may suffer many indignities in the present age.

Acts 25

Lord God, though our plans seem to be frustrated and we face strange delays for unexpected reasons, help us to patient, for we know that You are sovereign over all the affairs of men. Lead us to speak and to act in accord with Your secret providence. When it is Your will for Your servant to go to Rome, put in His mouth the words, "I appeal to Caesar." May all who hear us know that we believe that Jesus is alive. May we count our lives and our comforts as nothing if we have the privilege of testifying before many of our hope in Christ.

Acts 26

God of our Fathers, when we have an opportunity to speak, give us the boldness to tell of Your Son and the hope that is ours in Him. Your promises are secure. Why is it thought incredible by men that You would raise the dead? You created all things out of nothing. To grant us resurrection life is not too difficult for You. Teach us to suffer for Your Son according to Your good plan. We do not wish to grieve Your Spirit by distracting Your church from her mission with our own agendas. We testify to the truth of Your Word. Your Son is the first to rise from the dead. Through Him we proclaim the coming of the hope of the prophets. Use us to persuade many of the truth of Jesus Christ. Though it may seem that no one is responding to Your message, we trust You to use our words and lives for Your own glory.

Acts 27

Lord God, You rule over land and sea. If Your calling upon our lives requires us to make long or dangerous voyages, we can trust You even in the most frightening providences. We cannot keep ourselves alive for one moment even in the absence of any obvious distress. It is wise for us to listen to You in times of difficulty and times of safety. Bring us through every danger, for we live or die at Your command. Help us in the suspense of a dangerous life to know that You are not weak, for You love Your children, and You will not abandon them to the wind and the waves.

Acts 28

Father, we seem to move from danger to danger in this world of suffering and opportunity. We are neither gods nor demons. We are men created in Your image. We have been redeemed through the blood of our Mediator. As men loved by You, we can be used for Your good purposes, since the gospel moves forward through the ministry of men. Make Your Word powerful in the hearts of those who are appointed for eternal life. Heal Jews and Gentiles through the glory of the Word proclaimed.

Romans

Romans 1

Father God, we thank You for the calling that You have put upon our lives through the gift of Jesus Christ. We have received Your grace through Him and He has granted to us meaningful opportunities of love and service. We thank You for Your church. We pray that You would bless Your people everywhere with the truth of the gospel. We pray that this good news would be powerful for salvation through the gift of faith. Everyone knows of You by Your works of creation, yet we have been fools, for we would not worship and serve You. Our lives have been examples of outrageous sin, even in ways that are contrary to nature and reason. In every way we have turned against You, and have encouraged others in pathways of evil. Our situation was desperate, but You have provided an answer for us in the righteousness and mercy of Your Son.

Romans 2

Righteous Lord, would we dare to judge others when we would do the same things that we critique in them? You have been so kind to us, but we have not repented as we should. We are to be patient and careful in doing good, but we have sought out the evil way continually. Even when we have had much exposure to Your commandments, we still have not kept Your Law. Your Son will judge the secrets of men's hearts when He returns. How will we stand? We cannot stand by Law. Even if we boast in our knowledge of the Law, still we violate Your precepts. Are we counting on some sacrament or family association to bring us peace with You? You require a true life of obedience, even love for You and for others from the depths of our hearts. We need Your appointed way of mercy, O God. Thank You for Jesus Christ.

Romans 3

Lord God, we thank You for the privilege of being associated with Your worshiping assembly. Grant to us an appreciation of the reason for our acceptance in Your sight. Surely our confidence is only in Christ. The problem of unrighteousness is universal, but now You have shown us the way of life through the Substitute that You have appointed for us. By the works of the Law no one could ever be justified in Your sight. We have been saved by grace through faith in the great work of Your Son alone. He is our Propitiation. We boast in Christ, for we have been saved by Him apart from any good thing that we claim to accomplish. Thank You for Your abundant mercy.

Romans 4

Lord of Hosts, we could never have been justified by our works. Even Abraham was given righteousness by believing You. His works that proceeded from faith were the proof of Your gift of life to Him. With all who live in Your presence from every age we rejoice in You and in the blessing that has come to us by faith, for our sins have not been counted against us and our great debt has been forgiven. We also rejoice in the extent of Your mercy, for You have provided a way of righteousness for people from every land. What a glorious promise You made to Abraham so long ago! To think that such a great promise has now touched our lives! Surely we could never have received peace with You through the Law, but You have been pleased to give us the best of all gifts. Grant us growth in grace and faith day by day. We know that You will hear us when we cry out to You, for Your Son died for our sins, and He was raised for our justification.

Romans 5

Glorious Lord, do we now have access to You through Jesus Christ? We rejoice in Him. We rejoice even in our sufferings, for we know You are doing good things through whatever trials are appointed for us. We have peace with You in Him. He is our holy representative. He was the great Law-Keeper, and He did this for us. Now His obedience is credited to us. We give You glory for this great gift. We are so very thankful. We were dead in Adam's transgression, but now we have found life through the righteousness of Jesus Christ, our Lord. Reign in our hearts day by day. What a joy is ours, for our Representative has won for us the most abundant blessings.

Romans 6

Our Father, help us moment by moment in our fight against sin. Thank You for our baptism. Help us to remember our union with Your Son. We have been united with Him in His life, in His death, and in His resurrection. He lives, and so shall we live. Let the fact of His resurrection remind us of our own resurrection which is surely coming. To continue in sin makes no sense for us. Why would we willingly present ourselves to sin as servants again? We have been saved from that horrible master. We do not want to serve him any more. We know that sin just leads to death. This is not the way for us. Our way is the way of life. Help us, O God, for we are still sinning.

Romans 7

Father God, we have been released from the system of the Law, for we have died to the Law through the death of Christ. Fill us now with Your Spirit, that we might pursue obedience in a new and powerful way. We hate our sin. Will we ever have victory over such a powerful enemy? We thank You that we have seen our sin more clearly through the Law, but we need stronger help that we might stop sinning. Though in our minds we have had a desire to follow the good things in Your Law, our flesh has been too strong for us. We need Christ. We need the gift of the Holy Spirit. Thank You for Your bountiful provision. Now we humbly and earnestly beseech that You would defeat sin in us day by day through Your presence and power at work within us.

Romans 8

Lord God, what a great and solid hope is ours through Christ! Help us by Your Spirit to live by that same Spirit rather than by the flesh. We have Your Spirit in us, and we belong to You. Even if our body should die because of sin, we shall be alive because of Jesus. Thanks be to You, O God, for this blessed assurance! You have given us hope for even the weakest saint. You will give life again to our mortal bodies. Teach us how to live. Teach us how to put to death the deeds of the flesh that we might live for You now in the way that we should. Thank You that You have granted to us the Spirit of Adoption, by which we cry out to You, our merciful Heavenly Father. Your Spirit bears witness with our spirits that we are Your children. Make us willing to suffer for You today, knowing the truth of the age of glory that is surely coming. We are longing for that day. We long for the redemption of our bodies. This is our hope. Help us now by Your Spirit, that we might know how to seek You in prayer. We know that You are for us. You loved us so long ago, and You have planned everything that is necessary for our joyful participation in the age of resurrection. Even now You will help us. One day we will see that You have given us all things. Father, may Your Son take our prayers and intercede for us in ways that are right and good. Please do not let anyone or anything separate us from Your love for us in Christ Jesus, our Lord.

Romans 9

Sovereign God, we rejoice in Your plan for the salvation of Jews and Gentiles. Your promises to Your people of old have not failed, for not all of the children of Abraham, Isaac, and Jacob according to the flesh were Your children according to the promise. Thank You for the grace of election in the lives of Your loved ones. You will have mercy on whom You will have mercy. We will not speak against You concerning Your judgments. We do not demand that we know or understand everything that You have done or everything that You will do. You will make known the riches of Your glory in all of Your great works according to Your own will and in Your own appointed time. We rejoice that some who were not viewed as Your people in former days have now been granted righteousness by faith in Your Son. Father, may we never stumble over Christ, for He is the Rock of our salvation.

Romans 10

O God, we submit now to Your plan for righteousness by faith. Christ, the fullness of all righteousness, has come from heaven to save us. He has now returned on high to send forth Your Holy Spirit upon Your chosen people. He has given to us the Word of truth which is being preached all over the world. That Word is near us, in our hearts and in our mouths. We believe in Him. We profess this faith within the assembly of those who call upon Your Name. Send forth many true ambassadors of the truth, so that the good news of this Word can go forward everywhere with great power. Grant us joy as we gather together in Your presence to call upon Your Name. Help us to remember that we are a part of a body that transcends our time and place. Help us to consider that we worship together with those who are alive with Christ in the heavens.

Romans 11

Our Father, do great and marvelous works of grace everywhere according to Your sovereign will. In every generation You have chosen a remnant by grace who will not bow the knee to Baal. We marvel that we have had such a spirit of stupor for so long, refusing to hear and love the truth. We grieve sincerely concerning the condition of those all around us who will not yet come to You. Father, have mercy on a great host of Jews and Gentiles. Bring them in, O God. Your gifts and Your calling will never be taken away. All have been disobedient. We seek Your mercy upon all. You are God. You know the beginning from the end. Everything is from You. Everything comes through You. Everything is going to You. To You be glory forever.

Romans 12

Merciful Lord, we think of the great story of grace that You have revealed to us in Christ, and we give ourselves again to You. Teach us how to be Your people, not as imitators of the world, but as members of one another within the glorious body of Christ. Grant us genuine love for one another and true goodness and affection. Teach us to serve You with energy and gladness in accord with the calling that You have given to each of us. Teach us how to live in this world by the power of Your Son as those who are committed to goodness and love.

Romans 13

Father God, thank You for the gift of civil authority structures that You have appointed in this world. Use them for Your good purposes in the restraint of evil and for the encouragement of good. May we rightly honor them, and joyfully follow them. We would cooperate with them as conscience permits, but may we not be distracted from seeking first Your kingdom and Your righteousness. Teach us to love our neighbors as ourselves. Salvation is nearer to us now than when we first believed. Grant us the incomparable blessing of the Spirit of Christ in us, that we would make no provision for the flesh to gratify its desires. In all these ways may we relate honorably with all those around us.

Romans 14

Lord God, teach us to be patient and appropriately tolerant within Your church. May we live unto You in all situations, for we belong to You. Teach us not to despise one another, but show us the way of love. Grant us the spiritual strength to serve You in peace within the body of Christ. We want to see our brothers and sisters built up in faith and godliness. We want to walk in faith ourselves. We need to turn away from all arrogance. Teach us the wisdom that comes from following Your Son.

Romans 15

Glorious God, there are those around us everywhere who are in great need. We lift them up to You now. We long for Your blessing upon all of our brothers and sisters from every land. Your plan of redemption is so vast and so marvelous. Use the gifts that You have granted to us for the fulfillment of this great plan as we bring the gospel of Christ to all who have never heard of His glorious Name. We lift up to You the missionaries and pastors that we have had the blessing of knowing and supporting personally. We pray for Your financial provision for them. May they also be granted every spiritual gift, excellent health in body and mind, and true peace that can only come from You. Grant them fruitfulness in their labors for the glory of Your Name.

Romans 16

Father God, thank You for Your servants throughout the church who are performing a great variety of good works in the Name of Your Son. We thank You for these men and women and ask that You would grant them great success in their important deeds of love and service. We thank You for the friends that You grant us as we labor together in Your body. May we never bring foolish obstacles in Your church, distracting others from the simple duty of faith working itself out through love. May we be wise in what is good and innocent concerning evil. Defeat Satan through Your church according to the power of the gospel and the will of Christ. Glorify Your Name forever, even using us for Your eternal purposes.

1 Corinthians

1 Corinthians 1

Glorious Lord, may Your Name be blessed forever. We thank You for the calling that You have granted to us by Your great grace. We rejoice in the testimony of Christ that has been preached among us. In Him and in the message of the gospel all of Your people have the most extraordinary oneness which will be ours forever. We thank You for the word of the cross which has so powerfully changed our lives. He who saved us through His blood is the greatest wisdom and the greatest power. We pray that through this one gospel that You would be pleased to cause Your church to grow in sanctification.

1 Corinthians 2

Our Father, we thank You for Jesus Christ and Him crucified. Our faith rests in Your power and in Your eternal wisdom. We long for the age to come which has been revealed to us through Your Word. Your Spirit has taught us these things. We accept Your truth gladly. Forgive us when we become captivated by something other than the mind of Christ. Please deliver us from all evil.

1 Corinthians 3

Lord God, will we behave according to the flesh even within Your church? Make us something more than ordinary men. Help us to move by the power of the Holy Spirit. Take away from us all foolish divisions. Christ alone is our foundation. He is the Cornerstone. Bless our ministers in their gospel labors, that Your temple might be built up in truth and love. We adore You in Your perfect wisdom and mercy. We will not boast in men, but we will glorify You forever.

1 Corinthians 4

Father God, make us to be trustworthy servants of Jesus Christ. Take away from us all filth and pompous arrogance that would demand the worship of men. Anything good in us is surely from You. Why would we expect to reign like kings now, when our true King was crucified by men? Teach us to live as those who might be treated as the refuse of the world, as long as we may continue to have the privilege of worshiping You. Make us to be faithful imitators of our glorious Lord, who willingly suffered for our sake.

1 Corinthians 5

Holy God, will immorality be tolerated within Your church? Will there be no correction of those who do what even pagans know to be evil? Protect Your body from the destructive leaven of sin. Help us to walk in the unleavened way of sincerity and truth. Purify Your people and sanctify Your church.

1 Corinthians 6

Great God and King, teach us how to rightly discern matters within Your church. Raise up those who are spiritually wise who can rightly receive Your holy Word and rightly apply it in all situations. Make Your servants wise in considering the world and speaking Your Word. Keep us from prostitution and every kind of adultery. How can we remain spiritually pure when we have become so unclean in sin? We need You now. Help us to walk with humility and love.

1 Corinthians 7

Lord of Hosts, protect us from the temptations of this world. Help us not to consider ourselves as stronger than we really are. Thank You for the gift of marriage. Help us to stay close to each other as husbands and wives. Keep us from hatred and divorce. Bless our young children with fruitful peace within loving and stable families. We need to concern ourselves with You, as those who are called to be worshipers of You. Free us from the slavery of sin, and help us to live as those who know what true freedom is. Build up Your church in wisdom and order. Let us live as those who are well aware of the seriousness of this day and the wonder of the age to come. Show us the way to walk as those who love You with undivided hearts. Grant those who are single the contentment and self-control of a holy chastity. Grant those who are called to be married both faithfulness and blessedness in their special care for one another. Bless us all with unity in Christ as we worship and serve You together as Your church.

1 Corinthians 8

O Lord God, we know that there is only one God and one Lord. We seek You this day that we who belong to You might continue to turn away from idolatry. Grant us a powerful love that builds up, and help us to reject the kind of knowledge that we would use only to puff ourselves up. We were made by You and we exist for You. Help us to love the weak and to learn from those who are strong in grace and faith.

1 Corinthians 9

O Lord of our liberty, we thank You for the freedom that You have granted to us in Christ. We thank You for our families and for every gift of food and shelter that You have given to Your servants. We are grateful for the ministers of the Word that You have bestowed upon Your church over the centuries. Help us to take joy in supporting the earthly needs of those who have been sent by You for the preaching of the gospel. We especially thank you for this precious good news of Jesus Christ, and for the power of this truth to save all kinds of people. May we be willing to humble ourselves for the sake of the progress of this message of hope. Help us to run today as those who would win the prize by the power that You supply to Your children.

1 Corinthians 10

Lord God, thank You for Your holy providence during the days of our fathers in the faith, and for the record that we have of their struggles. Help us to be people of faith, lest we be destroyed by the destroyer. The end of the ages has come upon us. May we stand in the evil day. Provide the way of escape from idolatry that we might live according to the dictates of true godliness. Thank you for the spiritual communion that we have together with the church in the body and blood of the Lord Jesus Christ. Help us to daily choose those things that are good for our spiritual growth and that build up Your church. We are grateful for every good gift that comes from Your generous hand. Whatever we do, let us do all to Your glory. We seek the salvation of many, and wish to live for the praise of Your glorious grace throughout the earth.

1 Corinthians 11

Great God and Father of our Lord Jesus Christ, You have called us to be imitators of Your holy Son. We happily devote ourselves to this wonderful duty. He is the Head of the church, His bride. We should submit to Him in all things. You have made us in Your image and given to us the blessing of family relationships which display wonderful truths of Your covenant with Your people. Help us to live honorably in our family lives. When we come together in Your house, we pray that You would assist us in living out the fellowship of peace that Your Son has won for His people. Particularly when we come to Your table we ask that You would grant to us a fuller appreciation of the love of Your Son for His bride. May our enjoyment of Word and sacrament embrace all who are in Christ as brothers and sisters in this common faith. Help us to remember that Christ gave His body and blood for us. May we not partake in an unworthy way, but instead let us proclaim the Lord's death together as fellow-heirs of the salvation that comes from His abounding grace to unworthy sinners.

1 Corinthians 12

Great Giver of every good gift, Your Son Jesus is Lord. You have given us many spiritual blessings. Help us to walk in Your Spirit, and to use Your gifts for Your glory. We thank You for Your one body. We thank You for our baptism and the union that we enjoy with our Lord Jesus Christ. We lift up to You Your body throughout the world, and the particular part of the body where we worship You. Have mercy especially on those who are the weakest. Provide for them in their time of need. Help us to see our oneness in Jesus. We are the body of Christ, and individually members of it. We do not all have the same spiritual gifts, but we earnestly desire the highest gift, as imitators of the love of Christ.

1 Corinthians 13

O God of Love and Glory, we thank You for Your merciful love toward us. No matter what gifts and abilities we may possess, we are nothing without Your love. Help us to rejoice in the truth and to move ahead in endurance. What we seem to have in the flesh will surely pass away. Help us to grow in spiritual maturity, and grant to us a great hope for the fulfillment of Your promises.

1 Corinthians 14

Father God, thank You for the gift of the forthright proclamation of the truth. Over the course of the history of Your church You have provided preachers of the Word. We thank You for this gift. Fill our preachers and teachers with Your Spirit, that they may boldly speak to us the gospel of Jesus Christ from the Scriptures. Build up Your church with messages that can be understood with the mind, and loved with the spirit. Make us infants in evil, but mature in the truth of Your Word. Gather and perfect Your people with the clarity of Your message. May we know that You are really among us as we gather together in worship. May we have decency and order, but with the greatest spiritual fervor and obedience. Grant to us peace, and cast out all distracting confusion. Help us to have the kind of order in Your church that is clearly commanded in Your Word.

1 Corinthians 15

Lord God, we have heard the truth of the gospel, and we hold fast to this message. We thank you for the death and resurrection of our Savior. We have been given many evidences of the truth of these events recorded in Your Word. By Your grace, help us to work hard for the furtherance of this good news. Our faith is not in vain, for Christ surely has been raised from the dead, the firstfruits among many brethren. Those who have fallen asleep in Him are not lost, but are safe and alive in Him. We look forward to the return of Your Son, when He will destroy death and bring the fullness of life for Your people. We thank You for the great assurance that we have in the fact of Your Son's resurrection. You are our all in all. We turn away from the stupor of sin, and wake up again to the beauty of resurrection hope. You will give to each of us an amazing gift on the last day. We long for our resurrection bodies, surpassing in glory above the perishable bodies with which we praise you today. Christ is our life-giving Spirit. Though our fleshly bodies will return to dust, we shall bear the image of the Man of heaven. We will inherit the kingdom of God. We shall all be changed at the last trumpet. We devote ourselves now, not to the ministry of death, but to the proclamation of life, for Christ has given us the victory. May we abound in Your work, knowing that our labor in Him is not in vain.

1 Corinthians 16

O Generous Lord, thank You for the privilege of our participation in the giving of Your church. Thank you also for the joy of personal contact with brothers and sisters in Christ. We are greatly aided by those who work alongside us in this common ministry. Together we are devoted to the service of the saints, the believers in Christ here and throughout the world. Thank You for those who lead us in these labors of love. May Your grace be with us day by day.

2 Corinthians

2 Corinthians 1

God of Glory, You sent Your Son to be our Redeemer. Jesus Christ is the fullest expression of both Your Wisdom and Your Power. You are the Father of Mercies. You have given us abundant spiritual comfort. All who share in Your Son's sufferings know the comfort that You bring to Your children. Help us in the burdens of ministry and service as we live for Your Son today. Grant us perseverance in family life, and in our duties throughout the church and the world. We need Christ for a full life of love. He is Your Yes and Amen for every promise that You have made to Your people.

2 Corinthians 2

Lord of Love, we know that the Word that You speak to us sometimes brings pain, for we are convicted of our sin. Yet You bring us the comfort of the gospel, for there is much joy for Your children. We are not ignorant of the design of Satan. He would try to steal away our joy, but Christ will lead us in glorious triumph. Make Your church a pleasant aroma of life unto life for all who will receive Your Word and follow Your Son.

2 Corinthians 3

Father God, You have made the church a living letter in Christ. May we be a letter full of true spiritual life. We thank You for the blessing of the New Covenant, and for the gospel ministry. Because of the surpassing glory and righteousness of Christ, we have a great hope, and are very bold. A veil of ignorance has been removed from our hearts. Fill us with Your Spirit, and enable us more and more to behold Your Son's beauty, and to grow from glory to glory.

2 Corinthians 4

God of Glory, we want to be committed to an open statement of truth. We have no interest in trickery in our proclamation of the gospel of Your Son. The power of change is in You, and not in us. May we who know the meaning of the death of Jesus be faithful agents of His life. Raise us up in heavenly knowledge and service. We look for an eternal weight of glory beyond this present day of comparatively light and momentary affliction.

2 Corinthians 5

Heavenly Father, we long for our eternal dwelling. Swallow up our mortality with resurrection life. Make us courageous as we walk by faith and not by sight. We know that our lives here are significant. Make us faithful in Your service. May we live for You, for Christ has died for us. Thank You for the new creation that You have given us in Christ. We commit ourselves to the ministry of reconciliation. You made Your Son to be sin for us, and we have become Your righteousness in Him.

2 Corinthians 6

Lord God of grace, help us. Now is the time for true progress in faith and obedience. Will we shrink back from suffering when opportunities for gospel service are so near at hand? Will we reject the gift that comes from Your hand? May we be partners together in the church for the glory of Your Name. Do not abandon us, but welcome us and lead us in the way of true holiness.

2 Corinthians 7

Holy God, we thank You for Your servants who have helped us on the pathway to life in Your Son. We are deeply appreciative of their sacrificial ministry of prayer and service. May we not be a grief to those who lead us in our heavenly calling. May we instead have the gift of a godly grief that turns away from sin, and leads to new gospel joys in Christ. We rejoice with all the church in the power and love of Your Son, for He is our hope.

2 Corinthians 8

Gracious Lord, You have given to us great things from Your extraordinary riches. We thank You for the gift of Your Son. May we excel in all acts of grace. We count it a great blessing to be able to contribute to Your church. We are ready to give out of that which we have been given. Bless us with a great sense of the unity that we have in Your church throughout the world. As one region has need, and one region has plenty, it is our glory to be able to supply good things to one another. Everything that we have is a gift from You. Thank you also for the messengers of the glory of Christ who come to us from every corner of the world, and grant that each true servant of Your Son be well supplied in every need.

2 Corinthians 9

Glorious God, where is our cheerfulness and zeal in good works? Why are we selfish and self-absorbed? Make us willing people that we might sow bountifully in every act of service. You have distributed very many blessings so freely to us through Your Son. As we consider this kindness, we are thankful to You. May many others glorify and worship You as we serve them in love. We magnify Your Name on account of Your inexpressible gift.

2 Corinthians 10

Merciful Lord, we bless Your Name for the spiritual ministry that You have established. Use true teachers to take every thought captive in Your Son's church. Use also the written works of Your servants over the centuries for the growth in godliness of many congregations. All this is from You, O God. The gospel of Jesus Christ is Your precious gift to all who will believe. We boast in You, O Lord.

2 Corinthians 11

Our Father, You have given us to be a pure bride for Christ. Keep us from false teachers that would come and preach a new Jesus or a new gospel. Teach us to reject super-apostles who teach error, and to cling to the one Christ and the one gospel that has patiently been taught to us by servants of the truth. Protect us from the Father of Lies who would pretend to be an angel of light. Thank you for ministers who have been willing to suffer for the glorious message of the atoning sacrifice of Christ for sinners. Give us the discernment to receive the faithful ministry of those who have rightly spent their lives for Your glory. Most of all, we thank You for the One Good Shepherd of the sheep who gave His life for us on the cross.

2 Corinthians 12

Great Master and King, You gave to Your servants of old amazing experiences in Your presence. Despite those times of great revelation, our full assurance of the truth of their teaching comes to us through the ministry of the Holy Spirit as we read the settled deposit of Your Word in the Scriptures. You are able to use a man with even humble gifts of communication for the profit of many others. Help us to expound the Word of Your love for the weak communicated to us throughout the Bible. We are thankful for Your power in our lives. Keep us from sins of the tongue that bring such disaster upon the church, and help us to build one another up in love, that we might all praise You together with one voice.

2 Corinthians 13

God of Glory, bring purity and peace to Your church. Speak to us through the ministry of the Word, that we might live by Your power. May Christ live in us, for He is our hope. Help us to pursue that which is true and good. Build us up in our holy faith. May we live in peace with one another, as we together receive Your grace day by day.

Galatians

Galatians 1

God of Glory, You have sent us apostles to speak to us the truth of Christ. Help us to hold fast to the gospel that we have received, that message of the good news of our redemption through Jesus. We want to please You and serve You in this one gospel. We would not want to use our gifts as instruments of wickedness as in former days. Help us to look to You as our Master and our Father, and to glorify You with lives of obedient love and joy.

Galatians 2

Father God, You lead us in paths of gospel service, for You have redeemed us for Your purposes. We do not want to yield even for a moment to false doctrines that deny the good news of Christ. We lift up to You those who are in need, and pray that we might be of some use to others today. Make our conduct to be in accord with the gospel that we believe. We know that we are not justified by our service or by any other works of the Law. We have died to the Law in Christ that we might live to You. Help us to live and serve others by faith, for by faith in Your great Son we have been justified.

Galatians 3

Great Protector of Your Children, keep us in the faith that has been proclaimed to us. Fill us with Your Spirit as we hear Your Word. We follow in the faith of Abraham of old, the man of faith. He believed and it was credited to Him as righteousness. Your Son died for us, so that in Him we would obtain the blessing of Abraham. Your promises to Your Son have been secured by His blood. Your Word is sure and eternal. The great Seed of the woman has come and has accomplished our redemption. Righteousness is by faith in Him. Keep us captive to this gospel, that we might have the true liberty of Your children. We remember our baptism this day, for we are one in Christ, and have been cleansed and forgiven as heirs according to Your promise.

Galatians 4

Lord God, what a wonderful truth it is that we have been adopted into Your family. Thank you for the gift of Your Son. We have now received even the Spirit of Your Son, and we cry out to You as our heavenly Father. Help us to resist the temptation to return to foolish and dead works that can save no one. Give us again hearts of true charity based on the excellent message of the gospel. Together with Your church throughout the world, help us to live by faith in Christ. We are partakers of a better covenant. We are citizens of the Jerusalem that is above and children of the promise. Help us in the day of persecution to be faithful to Your Son and to the message of truth that we have received.

Galatians 5

Almighty Father, thank You for the freedom that we have through Christ. Thank You that we have been freed from bondage to the Law. Grant us now a true faith that works through love. Help us to hold to the truth of the freedom that we have through the victory of the cross of Christ. Protect Your church from false teaching, and help us to love one another. Teach us to walk by the Spirit, and keep us from being led by the flesh. We turn away from godlessness. Grant us the fruit of the Spirit in increasing measure. We belong to Jesus Christ, and we are thankful for Your everlasting love.

Galatians 6

Merciful Lord, keep us from the pathway of temptation, and help us to rescue those who wander from the truth. Lord, if we sow to our own flesh, what kind of good will we reap? We want to do what is right, and to resist evil. We turn away from false displays of religious superiority. Our boast is not in our own works, but in the cross of Christ. Grant to us a kind of resurrection life that is the evidence of a new creation that could only have come from You.

Ephesians

Ephesians 1

Sovereign Lord, our lives have been saved through Your powerful and merciful love. You chose us, O Lord, before the foundation of the world. We are blessed through the blood of Jesus Christ. Your plan is wonderful, and with great expectation, we long for it to be fully accomplished. You will surely bring about all of Your perfect and holy will. Thank You for the seal of Your Holy Spirit. Give us confidence in Your Son, and grant to us the Spirit of wisdom and revelation that we might know Your love and power, and have an even greater hope. We believe Your promises and submit to Your Son.

Ephesians 2

Lord God, could there ever be a greater love than Yours? We were dead in our sins. You loved us and saved us. You gave us life in Christ. In Him we are with You in heaven even now. Thank You, Lord. We rejoice in Christ and in His wonderful cross. We will take up the life of love, following Him, for He has prepared good works for us to walk in. He is our peace. We are together as Jews and Gentiles in one church, fellow citizens with our brothers and sisters in an apostolic faith. We boast in the Cornerstone of this temple, the Lord Jesus Christ, who has risen from the dead.

Ephesians 3

Father God, we thank You for the witness of Your apostles in the Scriptures. We especially thank You for Your great works of revelation, through which we have Your sure Word of truth. Through Your church the unsearchable riches of Jesus Christ are now proclaimed. You are bringing about the fulfillment of Your eternal purpose even now. Grant us power though Your Spirit, that Christ might dwell in our hearts by faith, and that we might know the love of Your Son. You are able, O Lord. We believe, and we will follow.

Ephesians 4

Lord God, we thank You for the blessing of Your church. We are together in Christ, and united in our enjoyment of all that Christ has for the church. Though we have a variety of gifts, we rejoice in You, our one Lord. Help us to grow together in Christ through the ministry of pastors and teachers who bring us the Word day by day. Grant us willingness to use the gifts that You have given us, not for the service of our own foolish pride, but to serve You and one another. We put on the new man in Christ by the power of the Holy Spirit. We hate the works of the devil and the filth of corruption that battles for ascendancy within us. Bring relief to those who are in pain and trouble today, for we care for one another and forgive each other, as members together of one body.

Ephesians 5

Great God and Father, teach us to walk as we should, in a way that is proper for those who are to be holy in Christ. We turn away from all immorality and idolatry. Please help us to live as children of light. Teach us not to hide in the darkness just to win the approval of the world. Show us how to live as the light of Your Son, that the darkness would be exposed. Fill us with the Spirit, that we might worship You always with great thanksgiving and submission. Teach us how to live in our marriages as followers of Your Son. Help the wives in Your church to respect their husbands. Show our men how to love their wives as Christ loves the church. Grant to all of us a solid awareness of the pattern of life given to us in the cross of Your Son.

Ephesians 6

Almighty Father, we need help in our homes. Forgive us for our many family sins. We have not done what Your Word has clearly commanded. Bring the hearts of fathers back to their children, and the hearts of children back to their parents. Bring about a fruitfulness through the church that will overflow into the world with a yield of much love and righteousness. We commit ourselves to prayer, seeking Your power for Your purposes. We long to see Your churches moving forward in health. Grant boldness to Your servants who bring Your Word in truth to Your people. We love You with an undying love.

Philippians

Philippians 1

Almighty Father, we thank You for Your Son and for His church in every place throughout the world. May our love for one another grow more and more in accord with the truth of Your Word. We seek the progress of the gospel here and everywhere, and the comfort of the gospel in our lives by faith, though we may face suffering now. Help Your servants in their afflictions, for we know that even our troubles will work toward the progress of Your good plan. Thank You for the great gain that will come to us when we depart from this world in order to be with Christ. Thank You also for Your grace during the time of our life here in this age. It is Your plan that we would remain here at least until this present moment, and perhaps even beyond this day. May we serve You and love one another as we do the work that You have called us to do.

Philippians 2

Glorious Lord, we thank You for the wonderful work of Your Son. He humbled Himself and was born as a man, and even died on a cross. He is now exalted high above every name. Make us like Him. May we be willing to give up our ugly pride and our foolish contentiousness, so that we will be like Him in His willingness to be lowly. At just the right time, make us like Your Son even in His exaltation, so that we will become partakers of the glory of resurrection. Send forth ministers of truth everywhere to proclaim the message of Christ. Protect them in the physical and spiritual challenges that they face, and grant to them all things necessary for life and godliness.

Philippians 3

Lord God, we rejoice in You. Thank You for the gift of Your Spirit. We have no confidence in our own flesh. We have no boast in our own obedience. Our gain is not in these things, but in Christ, our Lord! Our righteousness is through faith in Him. We long to know Jesus more and more, and we long for the resurrection from the dead. We belong to You, O God. Move us forward toward the goal of the glory that is before us. Help us to hold to the truth that we profess. The danger of sin is everywhere around us, and even within us. Keep us living in the resurrection way by the power of Jesus Christ.

Philippians 4

Our God and King, take away from our hearts unproductive and vicious thoughts that are out of accord with godliness. Take away our foolish anxieties, and help us to rejoice in You always. Keep our minds on You and on Your great works of creation, providence, and redemption. Fill us with peace as we fill our minds with the glorious wonders of Your greatness and beauty. Thank You for those You have given to us as companions and partners in the way of faith and life. We have confidence in You, for You will not abandon us. You will supply our every need, according to the abundance of Your grace for all of Your children.

Colossians

Colossians 1

Great God and King, You have sent forth apostles in former days proclaiming the glory and suffering of the life of faith in Christ. Thank You for this good Word, and help us to walk in a manner worthy of Your Son. Grant to us spiritual power that we might give thanks to You for the forgiveness of sins. We glorify Your Name, O Lord, for the greatness of Your Son. He is before all things, and in Him all things hold together. All Your fullness dwells in Him. We have a full reconciliation in Him as we continue in the faith. Thank You for the opportunity to testify to Your glory day by day. Through lives of gospel love we rejoice in the truth that Your Son is alive in us.

Colossians 2

Lord God, in Your Son is hidden all the treasures of wisdom and knowledge. Help us to reject false philosophies and deceitful traditions that would take us away from the greatness of the person and work of Your Son. We were dead in sin, but through our great Savior we have been made alive through His cross and resurrection. Teach us not to settle for shadows when we have been given the glory of Christ both within us and among us in Your church. We have died in Christ. Let us not return to worldly religious practices that may appear holy and disciplined, but are of no value in our fight against sin.

Colossians 3

Father, we are with Christ in heavenly realms. Therefore we earnestly seek those things which are above. Help us to turn away from all ugly thoughts, words, and actions. These will do us no good. Help us to put on compassion, forgiveness, and love. May the peace of Your Son and the dignity of His Word dwell in our hearts richly as we sing to You with joy. Help us to live appropriately in all relationships, particularly within our families. We want to serve You, O God, for Your Son died for us, and we are alive in Him.

Colossians 4

Great King and Master, we want to be kind to all. Help us, O Lord. Grant us graciousness and true wisdom, that we might conduct ourselves well in this passing world. Help us to love the brothers and sisters throughout Your church. We are thankful for the love for You and for Your entire household that You have granted to us. Fill us with Your grace moment by moment, that we might live as followers of our great Redeemer.

1 Thessalonians

1 Thessalonians 1

Lord God, we give thanks to You for the blessing of Your church. You have chosen us for Your glorious purposes. Move us forward in word and work in accord with the hope that is ours in Christ. Fill us with Your Spirit that we might truly serve You through whatever afflictions we may face in this life. We turn away from all idolatry with a confident expectation that Your Son has delivered us from the wrath to come.

1 Thessalonians 2

Our Father, we love our brothers and sisters in faith. Together we believe the glorious gospel of Jesus Christ. With Your scattered children throughout the world we know the blessings of Your Holy Spirit. With warm affection we constantly lift them up to You in prayer. We love Your Son and we thank You sincerely for His people. You have called us into Your own kingdom and glory. Your Word is at work within Your church. We receive it with joy. Others may persecute Your children and blaspheme Your Name, but You will grant them help in the day of trouble. When we hear good news of Your church, our hearts rejoice out of sincere love for Your people. Surely this love comes from You. Please help all those who wait for Your deliverance even now.

1 Thessalonians 3

Sovereign Lord, we need to be established in the faith through the preaching of Your Word. Your people face afflictions everywhere. The lives and comforts of many are threatened even now. We long to be together with our suffering brothers and sisters, face to face, so that all of our hearts may be established in the truth. Lord, help us to live out our lives, not according to the evil devices of the tempter, but according to the grace of our Lord Jesus Christ. We thank You, O God, for the blessings that You have granted to Your people, especially the faithful love and eternal hope that could only have come from You.

1 Thessalonians 4

O Lord, we hear of the way of the true Christian life, the way of sanctification. We know that this is Your will for Your people. Keep us away from all sexual immorality. Help husbands and wives to enjoy a warm affection for each other, and to be careful not to cause trouble in the marriages of others. Move us in a holy love for all the church more and more. Help us to live quiet lives of reverent obedience. Grant that we would think rightly about our loved ones who sleep in the Lord even now. Bless us with true faith that we will be with them forever in Your holy presence, according to Your Word. We are encouraged again with the promise of the resurrection to come. We embrace this hope with the full assurance of Your Holy Spirit.

1 Thessalonians 5

Father, we know that the Day of Your Son's return is coming, as it has been for these many years since His ascension into heaven. We do not know the exact hour, but we know that we need to wait for that day with the testimony of a holy life. How can we work fruitfully and wait patiently without strong help from You today? Your Son died for us so that we might live for Him. Thank You for those pastors and elders who feed us Your Word and watch over our souls. Help us to hear Your Word eagerly and to obey it diligently by Your powerful grace. We pray that You would give us great help from on high, that we might live in the fullness of joy before You, praying to You and thanking You continually for Your many blessings. May Your grace fill our hearts as we contemplate the truth of our coming deliverance from this evil age, and as we work in Your church and throughout the world for the furtherance of all that is holy and good. Have mercy on us, and make us gentle and merciful to others, even in the midst of persecution.

2 Thessalonians

2 Thessalonians 1

Father God, We thank You for Your church everywhere. We are especially grateful for Your grace to our brothers and sisters who are being afflicted throughout the world. We know that their pain is not the end of the story. Your Son is coming again. He will have vengeance against the enemies of His church, and will powerfully deliver those who are suffering for the glory of His Name. Grant us steadfastness, faith, and love in every difficulty. Make us worthy of the wonderful calling that we have received.

2 Thessalonians 2

Lord of the Nations, You will surely gather all Your people to Yourself through the preaching of the gospel. Before Your Son returns, we understand that a man of lawlessness will appear and that there will be a great apostasy in the church. Many will be deceived who refuse to love the truth and are willing to worship an abomination. You have chosen us for sanctification by the Spirit and belief in the truth of Christ. Help us to hold fast to Your Word, and to love Your Son, who has redeemed us from a life of sin, rebellion, and lawlessness.

2 Thessalonians 3

Holy God, deliver Your servants from wicked men as the Word moves forward with power. Establish our hearts in Your love. Make us wise in our relationships within the body of Christ. Protect us from the sinful example of many. Some are lazy and fruitless. Others disrupt whole households with dangerous talk. We ask that You would make us imitators of the most faithful Christians of our generation. As they follow Christ, help us to follow them in holiness. Forgive our sins. Grant us grace to live by the power of Your Holy Spirit, and hold us together in Your love forever.

1 Timothy

1 Timothy 1

Lord God, Your church is plagued by false teachers. Have we ourselves been a part of the problem? So many do not seem to know the truth and are not living out their faith in love. Will we be no better than the Pharisees, considering ourselves experts in the Law, but ignoring the weightiest matters of Your commandments? We thank You for the good news of Christ. Your Son came into the world to save sinners, and we are the recipients of His great grace. We worship You and give You all glory and honor. We humbly request Your protection, that we might avoid dangerous heresies and ugly arrogance. Make us more like Christ as we seek You in Word and prayer. Help us to remember Your Son's death until He comes.

1 Timothy 2

Father, we find the work of prayer to be very difficult. Is there opposition all around us? Protect us, O Lord. Thank You for our great Mediator, Jesus Christ. Through Him we lift up to You our prayers with modesty and simplicity, but also with earnestness and boldness. Help us to learn the truth and to serve You and others with joy and self-control.

1 Timothy 3

Father, we thank You for the elders that You have provided for Your church. Lead the right men into these positions of responsibility and service. May the ones that You provide be filled with the Holy Spirit, with grace, and all obedience. Thank You also for the deacons that You have kindly supplied. These men and their wives are so helpful for the work of Your kingdom. Your Son is worthy of all our works of worship and mercy. He has served us in lowliness, and is now exalted on high, where we shall be with Him in glory.

1 Timothy 4

Merciful God, keep us in the faith. We have no interest in deceitful spirits and ceremonial actions with only the appearance of humility. We need real faith and true humble service. Grant to us the self-discipline of holiness. May we toil and strive in hope, for our Savior has provided us with the most perfect example. Grant that we will always follow Him. Provide us with those preachers and teachers who will persist in teaching us Your Word day by day, and who will live in accord with the way of true godliness.

1 Timothy 5

Glorious God, we thank You for the family that we enjoy within Your church. Help us to understand our right obligation to our households and to the community of worshipers. Help us to have an eye for the weak. Grant that our deacons will be wise in their care for the poor among us, that we might rightly encourage everyone in the direction of diligence, responsibility, and service. Supply everything necessary for those who would devote their lives to preaching and teaching. Protect us from foolish haste in ordaining men as leaders in Your church. Guide us all in the way of Christ.

1 Timothy 6

Sovereign Lord, we bow before You. We would willingly serve You as Your children. Keep us from counterproductive controversies. Cause us to understand what true godliness is. Show us the way of Christian contentment, that we might not be enslaved by greed and the ugly love of money. Help Your ministers to be faithful to the high calling that they have. You are the one immortal and wise God. We worship and serve You. May we be rich in good works, setting our hearts on things that are above. Keep us from unfruitful knowledge that would only lead us away from the true righteousness of Christ.

2 Timothy

2 Timothy 1

Our Father, we thank You that we have been brought into Your family as beloved children. We also thank You for the blessing of those who have gone before who have led us in the way of love and self-control. Continue this great work of Your Holy Spirit among us. You have displayed to us Your wonderful grace. We know something of the new life even now. One day we shall see the fullness of the resurrection. We long for the glorious coming of Your Son. We commit ourselves to the sure foundation of Your holy Word. We will guard that good deposit. Keep us in the faith, and move us forward in love.

2 Timothy 2

Lord God, help us to be faithful to Your Word. Grant that we would entrust Your truth to the next generation. Help us to see the battle and to commit ourselves to the work that You have granted to us. Christ is surely with us. May we never abandon Him. Thank You, O God, that He remains faithful, even in our moments of weakness and unbelief. Your Son will not deny Himself. You know those who are Yours. We depart from iniquity again by Your power. We are to be Your holy people. We want to pursue Your truth and righteousness with stable hearts. Grant us persistence and victory as we serve You day by day.

2 Timothy 3

Sovereign Lord, there is much sin in the world, and there is even much wickedness in the church. Bless us with spiritual wisdom, courage, and perseverance. We do not want to follow in the way of the proud. Grant us Your power so that we will resist foolish passions and hypocrisy. We thank You for the Scriptures. Keep us in Your Word, that we might live a godly life in Christ Jesus, lest we be deceived. Provide us constant faith and repentance. Thank You for the ministers of the Word You have granted to us. May they be equipped for every good work by Your wonderful Word.

2 Timothy 4

Almighty Father, help Your ministers to preach the Word faithfully. Why should Your people wander off into myths and the philosophies of men? Help us to keep the faith. We long for the appearing of Your Son. Keep us from an inordinate love of this world that would lead us in directions that would not be profitable for Your Kingdom. Despite whatever persecution we may face, help us to continue boldly in the gospel of Christ by Your grace.

Titus

Titus 1

Lord God, we thank You for Your Son and Your Word. We ask that You would raise up faithful pastors and elders throughout Your church. Please provide us with those who will be gracious and capable in the faithful discharge of their important spiritual duties. May this good provision bring about a wonderful growth in holiness and faithfulness among Your people, to the glory of Your Name.

Titus 2

Great God, help our elders as they work with the various groups within your congregations. We pray that You would also provide other godly men and women in the churches who are willingly submitting to Your Word. Such believers will be so helpful to us as friends and mentors. Teach us through their good example how we may live more godly lives as those who love Your Son and are truly zealous for good works.

Titus 3

Faithful Lord, we thank You for the grace that You are giving to Your church day by day. We consider our lives of sin in former days, and we thank You for the measure of sanctification that we have come to know at present. We still feel the troubles that continue to come to us through the foolishness of our remaining sin. Help us to take the spiritual battle in front of us more seriously. Our days on this earth are few, and we desire to use them in a more godly way.

Philemon

Great God and King, we have come to You as servants, but You have received us as Your sons and daughters. Help us to live in a way that is more consistent with the love and freedom that have come to us through Your Son. Why should we deny freedom to others, when we have been so fully delivered from hell by Jesus Christ? Help us to serve You together as partners in the gospel. How can we ever pay You back for the generosity that You have shown to us? We look forward to our heavenly reunion with Your Son and with all those who are in Christ Jesus.

Hebrews

Hebrews 1

Lord God, Your Son is the Word of creation, providence, and redemption. He has spoken to us through His life, through His teaching, and through the apostolic gospel. He is greater than the angels, those glorious creatures You made to be ministering spirits for the sake of men. Though Your Son is far above men, in His lowliness He became a man in order to redeem us.

Hebrews 2

Our Father, help us to pay close attention to Your Word. From the sanctions of the Old Covenant it was clear that obedience to Your Law was a serious duty. How much more serious is the gospel, as the very Word of Your Son! You have put everything in subjection under the feet of Jesus Christ. He was made lower than the angels for a little while in order to face the suffering of death. Now He has been highly exalted forever. We are the children of the age to come who have been redeemed by the blood of Christ. He is our merciful and faithful High Priest. He made propitiation for our sins, and is able to help us through every temptation.

Hebrews 3

Our God in heaven, Jesus the Messiah is the builder of Your holy temple. He is superior to Moses, for He is faithful over Your house as a Son. We will not harden our hearts against Him. We will hear His voice in the Scriptures, and enter into His rest. Keep far from us the deceitfulness of sin. We do not want to fall because of unbelief. Fill us with faith and joy by the power of Christ at work within us.

Hebrews 4

Glorious Father, we have received the good news of Christ in the depths of our hearts, and we have entered into Your rest. While there remains yet a coming Sabbath rest for Your people, even today we rejoice in the rest that has come to us through Jesus. If we will be filled with faith as a gift from You, surely we will follow in the way of faith with godly obedience. We thank You that our great High Priest is able to sympathize with us in our weakness. Through Him we draw near to You with the full assurance of Your love and care for Your children.

Hebrews 5

Merciful Lord, the priests of the Old Covenant had to offer sacrifices for their own sins. Our High Priest Jesus Christ has no sin. His sacrifice was for us. He is a new kind of priest. He lives forever. Through Him we receive the Word of truth. Grant that we will now move on to greater Christian maturity through the message that we have eagerly received.

Hebrews 6

Father, we are often stuck in the most elementary truths of the faith, as if unwilling to grow in knowledge, grace, and assurance. How could we thus turn away from Christ who calls us forward to a more godly maturity? We do not want to be lazy anymore in the matter of true Christian growth. Help us to have a steadfast earnestness about our life of faith and patience. You have given us the most secure promise, since You have sworn by Yourself. It is impossible for You to lie. Your promise to Your children is sure. We have a firm hope as an anchor for our souls in Your sanctuary above. How can we doubt Your Word or abandon Your instruction? Empower us in Your service, we pray.

Hebrews 7

Great King of Righteousness, in Jesus Christ we have perfect holiness and peace. He is Your Son forever, and our great Mediator. He is superior to every hero of the Bible. No one else could have attained the blessings of perfection for Your people. He has become our Priest not by legal descent from Aaron, but through Your special provision and by Your solemn oath. He is a Priest forever. Your eternal Son is completely unstained. He gave Himself on the cross as a sacrifice once for all time. There is nothing lacking in His life, and there is nothing missing from His death and resurrection.

Hebrews 8

Our Father, thank You for our great High Priest. He is at Your right Hand in the heavenly sanctuary. What a wonderful gift to have a Friend in the seat of highest power! He is the Mediator of a New Covenant. He established this covenant with His own obedience. We thank You that You have put Your laws into our hearts and minds. We thank You that You have sent to us the Heavenly Teacher, the Holy Spirit. Fill us with this same Teacher even now, that we would delight in the truth of Your Word and follow You.

Hebrews 9

Lord God, You have given us a new way of worship that is different from the ceremonies of the Old Covenant. This is Your good pleasure. No longer do we have the ark of the covenant or the old festivals and sacrifices. Our High Priest has entered into the Holy Place in the heavens. You have sent forth the great gift of Your Holy Spirit, purifying our consciences from the dead works of false religion and sin, that we might serve You in resurrection life. We have a great eternal inheritance. Our position in the life to come is secure through the blood of Jesus Christ. No longer do we have only a picture of heaven in our worship. We have a participation in worship above even now in Christ, our Lord. We are in Him. What can this mean, O Lord God? We live here now and then we die. What is the life that we have beyond death? What will our future state be like when Your Son returns? Come Lord Jesus, and save those who are eager for Your appearing. Though we do not understand heavenly things very well, our hearts are longing for You.

Hebrews 10

Father God, we have a better way to You than the Law could ever have provided. The blood of Christ has actually taken away the stain of our sin. He came to do Your will. He provided the perfect righteousness necessary for us to be in Your presence forever. We have been sanctified by the one final sacrifice of the Lamb of God. He is now exalted forever. He reigns at Your right hand. Nothing can stop You, O Lord. You are God. You have promised that You will remember our lawless deeds no more. We have confidence to enter into the heavenly sanctuary through Christ even now. We have boldness in our confession of faith and in our petitions before you day by day. We will not forsake Your church. We will not spurn the Son of God. We will not outrage the Holy Spirit. We will worship You forever, O God. We will love Your people. We will not throw away our confidence. Please forgive us when we stumble. Grant us a perfect endurance, so that we will live by faith.

Hebrews 11

Sovereign Lord, what does it mean for us to live by faith? How can we live based on those things that are unseen? Convince our hearts about the reality of Your existence and the certainty of all Your great promises. Thank You for the people of faith that You have given to us in the history of salvation. We look forward to the city that You have promised. We live our lives here as those who are yet away from home. We will not be satisfied with any country here below. We want our homeland, for we are Your people. Help us to speak words of blessing to others based on the faith that we have in the truth that You have announced in Your Word. Make us willing to even suffer now, for we look for the reward that will be revealed at just the right time. Our lives ahead of us here below are largely unknown to us. We trust You through it all. We look to the day of certainty beyond this age of questioning. You will reveal the sons of God at just the right time as You have promised. Until that new day dawns, we will live by faith.

Hebrews 12

Lord God, if we follow in the way of faith, we must set aside the entanglements of sin by Your grace and look to Jesus Christ moment by moment. We are Your children. We are disciplined by You because we are loved by You. We trust that You are working out good things in us, that we might somehow share in Your holiness. We will not be discouraged today, because Your promises and love are secure in Christ. We turn away from all bitterness and immorality. We will be accepted in the Beloved One who is at Your right hand in the Zion that is above. We look to You, O God. We long to be in the company of men and angels in the presence of Jesus Christ. We absolutely will not refuse You. We are afraid to make such a bold pledge, but we are convinced that we must, and that Your strength is enough to help us in our obvious weakness. You are speaking to us clearly by Your Word. We will not refuse You. Give us more grace to keep our pledge. Forgive us again and again through Christ and restore us to Your fellowship when we foolishly wander away.

Hebrews 13

Merciful Lord, we thank You for the grace that You give us. Help us to be merciful to others. Move us far from every immoral impulse and action. Be our Helper always and grant us courage in every struggle. Your Son is with us, and He is the same forever. Help us to go where He goes – to suffer outside the camp, and to bear the reproach that He endured. We will not run away from His church. We will profess together His glorious Name and live in generous love. Help our leaders in the church that they might be faithful in serving You in the midst of special troubles and temptations. Equip us with everything that we need that we might be holy, even in the day of the greatest strife and persecution. Grant us the grace that can only come from You.

James

James 1

Father God, We are Your servants. Help us to remember that You are working out our perfection through the suffering that we face day by day. Grant us wisdom. We are persuaded of Your goodness, and of our need for Your gifts. Our lives come and go. Make us to be steadfast under trial. We look for the crown of life that only You can give. Turn us away from every evil desire. These things only lead to death. Grant us instead a love for You and for every blessing that You send to us. We turn away from sinful anger. We devote ourselves now to doing the Word that we have heard. Help us in our fight against sin, that we might use our tongues for good and our hands to care for those in need.

James 2

Lord God, how could we be so worldly? Our desires instinctively rush to the rich, and we treat the poor as creatures of another god. We have dishonored You. You give to so many suffering people the precious gift of faith in Christ. How can we violate Your Law so obviously when You have shown such mercy to us in Christ? Grant that we who have faith in Your Son might move forward in works of true love and righteousness. May our lives show forth the true faith that You have granted to us. May our faith be completed by our works. Father, we want to live as Your friends. Give us courage to do what You are calling us to do, for we know that mere assent to the doctrines of our faith apart from works is dead.

James 3

Sovereign God, thank You for the teachers of faith that You have sent to us. We know that they need to be examples to us of Christian living. Help them to guard their tongues carefully, for they face many temptations. Be our strong Deliverer, that we might all use our speech in holiness, as people of blessing. Grant us the fresh and cleansing water of Your Holy Spirit. Cast out of us demonic impulses that only cause fruitless quarrels. Fill us with true wisdom that comes from above. Make us love what is pure, and help us to pursue godliness with hearts that long for true peace.

James 4

Great King, restrain our sin and foolishness, and fill us with new and holy passions. Teach us to ask You for what we need, that we might serve You in accordance with Your purposes. We submit to You even now, and we resist the devil. Thank you for the promise that he will flee from us. We pledge to speak kindly of each other. Help us, O Lord. Grant that we would give up on old habits of arrogant thinking and proud boasting. We live according to Your pleasure. You may bring us home at any moment. We are Your children.

James 5

Glorious Lord, we will not trust in our prosperity. We will be fair and generous to everyone around us. Father, though we pledge to obey You over and over, we cannot bear the perfect standard of Your Law. We have surely sinned against You in horrifying ways. Will we stop sinning now? Grant us more grace day by day, and move us forward in perfect obedience. Fill us with hearts of delight in You, that we might be patient and worship You. Shower us with Your Spirit and help us to offer up to You earnest and faithful prayers. Grant us mercy for the weak, and help us to save those who wander into pathways of evil.

1 Peter

1 Peter 1

Glorious Lord, we thank You that You have sent out apostles to bring to us a message of Your Son, and to proclaim the hope in which we now rejoice. Grant to us a faith that is more precious than gold. Fill us with inexpressible joy in the salvation that is coming at the full revelation of Christ. Your Son has suffered for us. He has also been glorified. We look to the coming of the fullness of Your grace.

Help us to pursue holiness day by day, for we have been ransomed from our futile ways by the precious blood of Christ. Our faith and hope are in You. We have been born again from above through the living and abiding Word that shall remain forever.

1 Peter 2

Almighty God, We long for the pure spiritual milk of Your Word. Build us up as living stones in Your temple. Your Son is the Cornerstone in a new Zion. Rejected by the leading men in Old Testament Israel, He has called us out of darkness into His marvelous light. Keep us from the foolish passions of the flesh. Help us to live respectfully within the societies of this world. Help us to move forward in holiness as free men who do not use our freedom as a cloak for evil. Thank You for the path that Your Son has traveled for us. It is a way of life, even though it leads through suffering. By His wounds we have been healed. We return again to Him, the Shepherd and Overseer of our souls.

1 Peter 3

Lord God, show us the way of following Your Son in our families. We no longer want to run our lives by our own understanding. We dedicate ourselves to a new way of love and submission. We need to have humility and tenderness that can only come from You. Show us how to love the truth, and to pursue peace and goodness. You will bless us, even if we have to face some suffering for a time. Teach us to sanctify Christ in our hearts, and to be ready to give a reason for the hope that we possess by faith. Put our enemies to shame, and convict their hearts, so that they too may find life. Bring us safely through this world, as those who have been baptized and are kept within the ark of safety which is Your church.

1 Peter 4

Sovereign Lord, Your Son suffered in the flesh for us. May we see the benefits of trials in our own lives, that we might make true progress in turning away from sin. Father, we can not simply join in with the debauchery of the world. May we live in the Spirit, as those who know communion with You. Grant us hearts that are willing to serve You and others through the use of every gift from Your hand. Why should we be surprised when we share in the sufferings of Jesus? May Your Spirit rest upon us. Grant us a godly response to persecution, for we know that You are working out Your good purposes.

1 Peter 5

Great God and King, be with those among us who have the special responsibility of shepherding Your flock. Clothe them with Your gracious humility. Help us all to humble ourselves under Your almighty hand day by day. We turn from sin, and rest in Your Son. To Him be all dominion forever. Grant that we will stand firm in the grace that is ours in Christ Jesus.

2 Peter

2 Peter 1

Our Father, help us to remember that You are with us even now. You have granted to us all things for life and godliness. May we take responsibility for our growth in faith, knowing that it is only by Your grace that we will be fruitful in the knowledge of Your Son. Help us to see the blessing that comes from earnestly striving toward the goodness that You have for Your church. Thank You for the message of Your Son through those who were eyewitnesses of the glory of His transfiguration and the amazing fact of His resurrection. We thank You for the written Word of apostles and prophets recorded for us in the Scriptures of the Old and New Testaments.

2 Peter 2

Great Master, protect Your church from false teachers. They bring destructive heresies and immoral sensuality upon Your beloved bride. Surely evildoers will be judged for the trouble that they bring upon Your loved ones. You know how to preserve us and how to stop the evil works of ungodly men. As You rescued Lot and his daughters from Sodom, rescue Your church in our weakness day by day. Teach us not to speak proudly about things that we do not really understand. Keep us in Your word and protect us from greed and adulterous lust. Restrain the madness of those who are bent on the destruction of Your church. Despite the troubles that we may face now, grant that we would be joyful servants of Jesus Christ and not slaves of sin. Teach us to move forward in holiness, and not to look back longingly on our former lives as something to be desired.

2 Peter 3

Lord God, teach us to remember what the Scriptures say about the new age that is coming. There have been prior ages that are now completely gone. What was life like before the flood? Those days are gone forever. One day this gospel age of gathering through the Word will be entirely over. When Your Son returns He will bring the fullness of a new day, a day that has already begun in His resurrection and in the spiritual life that we have been granted from on high even now. He will judge the world. He will also bring with Him the new heavens and earth, that great place where righteousness dwells. Grant that we would be nourished in Your Word day by day, that we might grow in the grace and knowledge of our Lord Jesus Christ.

1 John

1 John 1

Glorious God, You sent Your Son. He is the Word of Life made manifest to us. We have heard the truth of Christ and we now proclaim this truth everywhere. Grant that we would walk in the light as He is in the light. Forgive us our sins and cleanse us from all unrighteousness.

1 John 2

Father God, teach us the right way to go. We don't want to sin anymore. Thank you that Your Son is our Advocate. We will follow Your commandments, for we will walk in the way of love. Help us to love You and to love our brothers and sisters in Christ. Teach us to walk in the light as those who know the One who is from the beginning. Teach the young ones to love You more than they love the world. We need all the good gifts that come from You. Grant us the simplicity of godly discernment, so that we will not wander from the truth. We know Your Son, and He is the Truth. Keep us from the antichrists who would lead us away from Jesus our Messiah. Grant us the blessing of an anointing that comes from You. May we abide in You today, O God? We ask for this because we love You.

1 John 3

Lord God, what a blessing it is that we are truly Your children! We are blessed already, and we shall be blessed much more when we go to be with You. Even more still, we will be greatly blessed in the Day of resurrection. Father, why should we keep on sinning? We don't want to walk in evil anymore. We don't want to act like children of the devil. We should love one another. We don't want to be murderers like Cain. We love our brothers and sisters in Christ. We ought to lay down our lives for one another. Teach us not to close our hearts when we see Your people in need. Lord, You know everything. We don't want our hearts to condemn us. We believe in Your Son. We will keep Your commandments, for You have given us Your Spirit.

1 John 4

Sovereign Lord, teach us to test the spirits. We know that Jesus the Messiah has come from You. We should be able to discern who is from You. The people who are from You listen to Your Word and follow Your Word. The people that are from You love You and love Your people. You loved us first, and You sent Your son to be the propitiation for our sins. Cause Your love to be perfected in us. You have given us Your Spirit. You love us and abide in us. We will abide in love, for we want to abide in You always. Cast out all fear from our hearts, for You are perfecting us in love. We don't want to be liars. We will love You and we will also love Your church.

1 John 5

Almighty God, we have been born of You. We love You. We keep Your commandments. We love Your people. You have granted to us the victory of faith in Jesus Christ. The Spirit and the water and the blood testify to the truth. The Spirit has opened up our hearts to the Word. Through the water of new life we know that we belong to You. The blood of Christ speaks a good word of Your love for us. You love Your children, and we are Your children. Keep us from sin that leads to death. Help us to pray for one another, and to know true forgiveness from You. We do not want to be in the power of the evil one. Your Son is the true God and eternal life. Keep us from idols.

2 John

Great God and Father of our Lord Jesus Christ, we thank You for Your church. Your truth, love, and grace will be with us forever. Help us to walk in obedience to that way of faith and life that we have heard from the beginning. Grant us discernment. There are those who would teach in Your church who do not abide in the truth of Christ. Bless us with the courage to humbly and graciously oppose their entry into the office or exercise of a teaching ministry, for they would only dismantle what others have lovingly labored to build.

3 John

Father God, we pray that there would be good health in the body of Christ, and that Your people would always walk in truth. We ask that You would give us love for those missionaries who have been sent out by Your church. Help us to be dedicated to a life of goodness and truth. Bless us with the courage to turn away from evil paths even now. Fill Your house with gracious servants and leaders who truly follow Your Son. Help us to rejoice at the encouragement that can be ours when we learn of the progress of Your Word in far-off lands, and supply us with ample resources for the furtherance of the gospel throughout the world.

Jude

Blessed Lord, we have been called by You and we are loved by You. Keep us in the faith, and give us the courage to contend for the truth. There have always been those who serve the wicked one more than they serve Your Son. We do not want to be led by such men. Protect us, O God, for we are weak, and we need more discernment. We turn away from all sexual immorality. We pray that You would keep our ministers from boasting about spiritual complexities that they do not understand. Rid from Your teachers the impulse to impress many with complexity of instruction that will not be helpful to those who have gathered to hear the truth of Christ. We have been warned that not every man who would call himself a Christian teacher or preacher is a true minister of the Word. Look on us in our weakness and help us from on high. Father, many among our number are confused and vulnerable. You surely will have mercy on those who doubt, for You have instructed us to do the same. Keep us true to the holy faith that is the same yesterday, today, and forever. To Your Name be glory for all eternity.

Revelation

Revelation 1

Glorious King, You have revealed to us wonderful things that we might hear and obey what is written in Your Word. We believe in Your victorious Son. He has freed us from our sins by His blood. He is coming again in clouds of glory. Grant us patient endurance in any trial that we may face now. Fill us with a true vision from Your Word of the greatness of Your Son. Take from our minds every false image of Jesus and fill us with the truth. He is Lord, and He is powerful and alive. He is more than able to save us. He watches over Your church throughout the world and provides us with everything that we need for progress in holiness. Thank You for the wonder of Your household even now in this present age. Thank You especially for the greatness of Your Son who rules and reigns from His throne in glory.

Revelation 2

Father God, there is much trouble in Your church. We need patient endurance even now. There are those who come to us as if they were apostles, but they are workers of iniquity. Help us to remember our first love. Teach us the truth of our riches in Christ. Though we may be very poor and sorely persecuted in this life, You have given us victory over eternal judgment through the cross of Christ. Help us to hold fast to Your Name even in the place where Satan seems to dwell. Teach Your church to turn away from all false doctrine in places that love wickedness. Thank You for the truth of Your Son. Help us to move forward in wonderful works consistent with Your Word. There is so much immorality and idolatry all around us, and even within us. We turn away from wickedness by Your power. We will conquer falsehood and evil in Your Son's Name. Grant us the Morning-Star, for we eagerly long for His appearing.

Revelation 3

Lord God, we need the fullness of Your Spirit, lest we wander far from the truth. Wake us up even now, for Your Son is coming at a time that we do not know. Grant us the garments of Christ's righteousness, for our names are written in the Book of Life. You are God. You open the door that no man can shut. Teach us to hold fast to Your Word in this hour of great trial. Make us to be pillars in Your temple, for we are not strangers to Your grace. Glorious Lord, we hear that there is a new Jerusalem coming! What a day of glory! Will we be lukewarm about the return of Your Son? This makes no sense for those who believe the truth of Your Word. How have we become so easily distracted and deceived? We hear You knocking even now at the door of this assembly. We rush to You and open that door of grace and faith with some holy fear, but also with abundant joy and expectation. Come Lord God into Your holy temple, for we are Your people! Never cast us away! You know our weakness and our sinful doubting. Fill us with Your forgiveness and Your love.

Revelation 4

God of Glory, there is a door to heaven open for us in Jesus Christ our Lord. We see Your apostles there together with the sons of Jacob. We see the angels around Your glorious throne. We are overcome with the wonder of Your incomparable holiness. We give glory to You even now with apostles, patriarchs, and angels. We extol You as the great God of creation. You made everything for Your glory, and we worship You.

Revelation 5

Father God, where would we be without the gift of Your Son, Jesus Christ? There was no man among men who was worthy to open the scroll of the future. This current age that we live in must move forward and eventually come to an end. Would we have been trapped in this world of sin and misery forever if the heavenly scroll had not been opened? But the seals of that scroll were opened, because Your perfectly wise and wonderful Son was worthy. He ransomed us from death and hell through His blood. Because of His great worthiness we will join those who have gone before us into the company of myriads of angels. We will worship and serve You forever.

Revelation 6

O Great and Glorious God, there is no one like Your Son. He is worthy and has opened the seven seals of Your judgment and salvation. We live now in the midst of a world of danger and difficulty. There is much trouble everywhere. Throughout this age we see and feel hunger, illness, persecution, and even death. Yet You will judge wickedness and will bring deliverance to all who fear Your Name. This age will come to a conclusion, and there will be a better age for all who believe in the Lamb.

Revelation 7

Father God, who is the one who is the commander of Your host on high? Surely Your Son rules over men and angels. We look to see the fullness of Your people in the age to come. There we will stand before Your glorious throne. Salvation belongs to You and to the Lamb. You are worthy of all blessing and glory and wisdom and power and might. You know every suffering servant who faces trials now for the glory of Your Name. You love Your people, and have sent Your Son as Your greatest Servant, that we might be in the number of Jews and Gentiles who would love You and enjoy Your presence forever.

Revelation 8

Father, who can stand before You when You come in judgment? We offer up our prayers through our Mediator who perfects our humble offering. You use our prayers to bring about wonderful things, but we do not understand very much about the way that You do this, or even why You do such important things in this way. We do trust You, for You are great, and You love us. There is an amazing devastation coming upon the earth from Your glorious throne. Our only hope now and forever is to be found in Christ. Whether we live or die, we ask that You would keep us through Your abiding love.

Revelation 9

Glorious Lord, there is an adversary who stands against You and hates us. It is comforting to know that You are sovereign over everything. This age will come to an end. Until that day there will be much trouble. We thank You that Satan is not equal to You, but must follow Your decrees. Through whatever sin or curse we travel, we pray that You will move us forward toward the coming age. Grant us perseverance and true repentance. We want to live and die well. We want to walk in faith through even the darkest night. Have mercy on us. Keep us from utterly falling, and give us a peace that passes understanding.

Revelation 10

Merciful Lord, Your Son is coming, and He will be over all of creation in an obvious way. He is glorious in beauty and terrible in His wrath. His Word is powerful, and His decrees will stand. When He determines that there will be no more delay, then the trumpet will sound. All that You have promised through the prophets will surely be accomplished. You have spoken words that bring both comfort and horror, words that touch on many nations and rulers. Your Son is above them all, and His will shall be accomplished.

Revelation 11

Great God, You will fulfill Your every Word concerning the glory of the age to come. At the return of Your Son, You will bring Your judgment upon the false church and the world. You have warned us that this current age is a period of tribulation, yet You have promised us that You know how to rescue Your servants and to bring them to Your side even now. How we thank You, Father, that even when Your servants die today, they do not have to wait for millennia to see You. Today they are with You and Your Son in paradise. Nonetheless, we long for the day when we will hear the announcement that You reign in glory over all the earth. Father, if Your temple in heaven were open to our eyes at this moment, what would we see? Grant us faith to believe all of Your promises. Something very good is surely coming, for You do not lie.

Revelation 12

Father God, Your Son has come as a Child of the Old Covenant community. This Son of Mary is also Your only-begotten Son. Blessed be Your Name! He faced the greatest tribulation for our sake. Bring us through this current period of birth pains as we wait for the fullness of the New Covenant community. There is a warfare going on that we do not fully see. You must carry us through the evil day. The devil and his angels have been cast down upon the earth, and there is much hatred against Your church. Protect us, O Lord! Reign over this accuser of our brothers. His time is measured and will swiftly come to an end. Give us wings to fly to safety through all kinds of trouble, and give us strength and courage as we fight the battle that You have ordained for us in this life. It does help us to know that our trials are not accidental, and that You, who gave Your Son for us, can never be defeated.

Revelation 13

Lord God, the world is so impressive to our carnal minds. Teach us to reject its blasphemies and deceptions. There is a better way for us. Grant us endurance and faith. Bless us with a love of heaven and a delight in our great Savior who dwells at Your right hand. How will we live through the kind of tribulations that come to us in this age? Show us the way of wisdom, that we might resist the devil and submit to You.

Revelation 14

Almighty Father, we rejoice in the Lamb, and we thank You for the full temple that He is gathering from every tribe, tongue, and nation. We have been redeemed from mankind by Your powerful Spirit. Thank You for the eternal good news that we now proclaim throughout the earth. Our hope has never been in the Babylon of this world. Give us courage to make righteous choices while we have the opportunity to obey You and to endure in the midst of trouble. If we lose our lives because of our faithfulness to the Son of Man, we will yet be blessed by You. The day of the final harvest of the earth will surely come. Our hope in that day will be in

Christ alone. Send forth Your holy angels at just the right time. Glorify Your Name and the Name of Your Son Jesus Christ, and rescue Your children whom You have called out of darkness to serve You forever.

Revelation 15

Heavenly Father, can it be that one day Your wrath will be finished? Great and amazing are Your deeds. Just and true are Your ways. All nations should worship and serve You. You live forever and ever, and You fill Your temple with the glory of Your presence.

Revelation 16

Almighty God, it is not safe for us to follow the ways of the world. You are just and holy, and we cannot support those who shed the blood of Your people. We cannot be in league with those who curse Your Name and hate Your discipline. We repent of our evil deeds. You will deliver us from all wickedness. We know that Your Son is coming. We thank You for Your sure promise to us. The powers of the world as we know them will come to an end, but Your kingdom will endure forever.

Revelation 17

Lord of Hosts, a Day of Judgment is coming. The adultery of Your church cannot go on forever. Has Your church loved the mysteries of idolatrous worship? Forgive us, O Lord, and turn us back to the purity of Your love. We turn away from all the murderous hatred that has filled the hearts of false brothers over many centuries. Your electing love is more precious to us than any enticing lie of the world. The word and the devil promise us many pleasures with all their deception and power. We will not follow the one who denies the truth of Your Son. Our Lamb will subdue every enemy. We would too easily be deceived by spectacular lies. Help us, O God! Keep us in Your Word.

Revelation 18

Merciful God, there is a day coming when all the filthy deceptions of this current age will be gone. We will not be lost in the ugliness of rebellion on that day. We want none of this world's immorality. We separate ourselves from the love of the world even now, for we do not want to die in our sins. We reject that wicked queen, that Jezebel who entices millions. All her luxury will be turned to dust and ashes. All her many comforts and wonders will be taken away from her. She captured people with her lies and enslaved them. She hated Your wisdom and love. We cast away all her jewels and spices. We cling to our Savior Jesus. We would rather have Him than all of the wonders of the city of this world. You will rescue us and will judge the world. Grant us the wisdom of knowing the difference between eternal life and everlasting destruction. We want none of the strange sorceries of this age. We want You, and we hold fast to Your excellent promises.

Revelation 19

We praise You, O Lord! Your judgments are true and just. The heavens have always declared Your glory. We long to join the great multitude on high who rejoice in Your glorious eternal reign. We have been clothed with the righteousness of Christ, and even with the fine linen of the good works that You have prepared for us, that we should walk in them. We thank You for Your grace. Our salvation is in Your Son alone. He is our Redeemer. He will rule forever, He is King of kings and Lord of lords. The day of destruction is coming upon the earth, but we will be with You forever and ever. O the great clarity of that glorious day of our rescue! Grant us true insight even now, according to the perfection of Your holy Word.

Revelation 20

Father God, You have been victorious over Satan through the cross of Christ. This enemy is restrained even now, that the Word might be proclaimed to all the nations. Thank You for this day of gospel opportunity. Thank You also for the privilege of dying for the truth of Your Son. Though Satan is restrained, yet His fury is known and felt by Your church. Before Your Son returns, we understand that a day of the most intense trouble will come. Yet then Your Son will return and put away the devil and his allies. Father, our names are written in the book of life. Our unrighteousness has been defeated through the glorious life and death of Your Son.

Revelation 21

Great God and King, we long for the new age that is coming. What a joy it is to contemplate what we will soon see: the new heavens, the new earth, the holy city, the glorious bride, the perfect Husband, no more mourning, no more crying, no more pain. We are so thoroughly blessed by Your wonderful love. You will dwell with us forever. Can it be – death shall be no more? Yes, You are making all things new. You will bring all Your gracious plans to the most perfect fulfillment. There will be a complete separation of the righteous and the wicked. O God in heaven, embrace us forever in Your perfect grace. Keep us in Your holy new Jerusalem. Knit us together in love even now. This new city is surely coming with all of its beauty and wonderful glory. What gates! What walls! What streets of gold! What light is there forever! What a temple is ours in Christ the Lord! We thank You, O Lord, forever and ever.

Revelation 22

Our Father in Heaven, we long for You and for the place of Your glory. We rejoice in Your promises. Your Word is trustworthy and true. The Lord Jesus Christ is coming soon. We wait in hope for the age of resurrection. Teach us to worship You day by day, for the time is near. Your Son is the Alpha and the Omega. Bring us into Your holy city through Him. He is the One Gate, the Son of David, the Bright Morningstar. Please do not cast us off forever! We are Your children! Come, Lord Jesus! Amen.

Made in the USA
Lexington, KY
09 March 2015